WITHDRAWN
UTSA LIBRARIES

Veiled Employment

Contemporary Issues in the Middle East

OTHER TITLES FROM CONTEMPORARY ISSUES IN THE MIDDLE EAST

Citizenship and the State in the Middle East: Approaches and Applications
  NILS A. BUTENSCHON, URI DAVIS, and MANUEL HASSASSIAN, eds.

Gender and Citizenship in the Middle East
  SUAD JOSEPH, ed.

In the Eye of the Storm: Women in Post-Revolutionary Iran
  MAHNAZ AFKHAMI AND ERIKA FRIEDL, eds.

Iranian Cities: Formation and Development
  MASOUD KHEIRABADI

Islam, Arabs, and the Intelligent World of the Jinn
  AMIRA EL-ZEIN

Labor Unions and Autocracy in Iran
  HABIB LADJEVARDI

The Second Message of Islam
  MAHMOUD MOHAMED TAHA; ABDULLAHI AHMED AN-NA'IM, trans.

Twenty Years of Islamic Revolution: Political and Social Transition in Iran since 1979
  ERIC HOOGLUND, ed.

Women in Muslim Family Law, 2nd ed.
  JOHN L. ESPOSITO, with NATANA J. DELONG-BAS

Women, the Family, and Divorce Laws in Islamic History
  AMIRA EL AZHARY SONBOL, ed.

Veiled Employment

ISLAMISM AND THE POLITICAL ECONOMY
OF WOMEN'S EMPLOYMENT IN IRAN

Edited by
ROKSANA BAHRAMITASH & HADI SALEHI ESFAHANI

SYRACUSE UNIVERSITY PRESS

Copyright © 2011 by Syracuse University Press
Syracuse, New York 13244-5290

All Rights Reserved

First Edition 2011

11 12 13 14 15 16   6 5 4 3 2 1

∞ The paper used in this publication meets the minimum requirements of the American National Standard for Information Sciences—Permanence of Paper for Printed Library Materials, ANSI Z39.48-1992.

For a listing of books published and distributed by Syracuse University Press, visit our Web site at SyracuseUniversityPress.syr.edu.

ISBN: 978-0-8156-3213-9

Library of Congress Cataloging-in-Publication Data

Veiled employment : Islamism and the political economy of women's employment in Iran / edited by Roksana Bahramitash and Hadi Salehi Esfahani. — 1st ed.
    p. cm. — (Contemporary issues in the Middle East)
  Includes bibliographical references and index.
  ISBN 978-0-8156-3213-9 (cloth : alk. paper)
  1. Women—Employment—Iran—History. 2. Women—Employment—Iran—Political aspects. 3. Sexual division of labor—Iran. I. Bahramitash, Roksana, 1956– II. Esfahani, Hadi Salehi.
  HD6182.56.V45 2011
  331.40955—dc22   2010051215

Manufactured in the United States of America

Contents

List of Figures | vii
List of Tables | ix
Acknowledgments | xiii
Contributors | xvii
Acronyms and Abbreviations | xxi

Introduction
ROKSANA BAHRAMITASH *and* HADI SALEHI ESFAHANI | *1*

1. Gender and Globalization
   The Iranian Experience
   JENNIFER C. OLMSTED | *25*

2. Modernization, Revolution, and Islamism
   Political Economy of Women's Employment
   ROKSANA BAHRAMITASH *and* HADI SALEHI ESFAHANI | *53*

3. From Postrevolution to the Reform
   Gender Politics and Employment
   ROKSANA BAHRAMITASH *and* HADI SALEHI ESFAHANI | *83*

4. The Transformation of the Female Labor Market
   ROKSANA BAHRAMITASH *and* HADI SALEHI ESFAHANI | *123*

5. The Effects of International Trade on Gender Inequality in Iran
   The Case of Women Carpet Weavers
   ZAHRA KARIMI | *166*

6. Female-Headed Households in Iran
   Microcredit versus Charity
   ROKSANA BAHRAMITASH | 191

7. Veiled Economy
   Gender and the Informal Sector
   ROKSANA BAHRAMITASH *and* SHAHLA KAZEMIPOUR | 226

8. Iran's Missing Working Women
   FATEMEH ETEMAD MOGHADAM | 256

9. Iranian Immigrant Women's Labor Market Strategies
   A Complex and Entangled Process
   ZOHREH MIRZADEGAN NIKNIA | 273

References | 307
Index | 329

Figures

2.1. Income Distribution in Iran | 66
3.1. Iran's Economic Growth in Comparative Perspective | 94
3.2. Sectoral Shares in Iran's Non-Oil Value-Added Production | 95
3.3. Age Pyramid of Iran's Population, 2006 | 106
4.1. Share of Women in Labor Force | 126
4.2. Share of Women in Employment | 128
4.3. Value of Iran's Carpet Exports in Constant 1983 US Dollars | 129
4.4. Employment Shares of Main Economic Sectors in Urban Areas | 133
4.5. Employment Shares of Main Economic Sectors in Rural Areas | 134
4.6. Share of Women Age 10–19 in Female Employment and Population | 137
4.7. Share of Women Age 10–19 in Economy-Wide and Manufacturing Female Employment | 138
4.8. Age Pattern of Female Labor Force Participation in Urban Areas During Census Years 1956–2006 | 139
4.9. Age Pattern of Female Labor Force Participation in Rural Areas During Census Years 1956–2006 | 140
4.10. Age Pattern of Female Employment and Labor Force Participation Rate in Urban Areas, 1976–1986 | 142
4.11. Age Pattern of Female Employment and Labor Force Participation Rate in Rural Areas, 1976–1986 | 143
4.12. Share of Students in Female Population, Ten Years and Older | 148

Tables

1.1. Female Labor Force Participation, Female Literacy, and Total Fertility Rate for MENA Countries | *40*
1.2. Distribution of Female Employment by Sector for MENA Countries | *44*
3.1. Urbanization and the Share of Women in Rural and Urban Areas | *97*
3.2. Literacy Rate | *101*
3.3. Enrollment Rates | *102*
3.4. Average Age at First Marriage | *105*
3.5. Percentage of Single Women Age 15–24 | *106*
3.6. Life Expectancy at Birth | *107*
3.7. Fertility Rate | *108*
4.1. Female Labor Force, 1956–2006 | *126*
4.2. Sectoral Composition of Female Employment | *136*
4.3. Literacy Rate | *144*
4.4. Iranian Women's Educational Attainment and Employment | *145*
4.5. Education and Labor Force Participation, 1976 and 2006 | *146*
4.6. Share of Public Sector in Total Female Employment | *151*
4.7. Education and Share of Women in Private and Public Employment, 1996 and 2006 | *152*
4.8. Distribution of Female Employment Across Private Sector Positions | *153*
4.9. Education and Share of Women in Private Sector Positions, 2006 | *154*
4.10. Distribution of Female Employment by Occupational Categories | *155*

4.11. Education and Occupational Structure of Female Employment, 1976 and 2006 | *156*
4.12. Unemployment Rates in Urban and Rural Areas, 1956–2006 | *158*
4.13. Education and Unemployment, 1976 and 2006 | *159*
4.14. Age and Female Unemployment Rate, 1976 and 2006 | *161*
4.15. Field of Study and Unemployment among Population with Higher Education, 2006 | *162*
5.1. Persian Carpet Exports | *170*
5.2. Production, Employment, and Exports in Handwoven Carpet Industry in Major Exporting Countries, 2000–2005 | *171*
5.3. Employment in Iran's Textile Industry | *174*
5.4. Employment in Iran's Textile Industry by Working Position | *175*
5.5. Distribution of Carpet Weavers by Location and Nationality | *177*
5.6. Distribution of Sample Carpet Weavers by Sex and Nationality | *179*
5.7. Distribution of Sample Carpet Weavers by Age, Sex, and Nationality | *180*
5.8. Distribution of Sample Carpet Weavers by Education Level | *181*
5.9. Number of Carpet Weavers in Households by Nationality | *183*
5.10. Distribution of Sample Carpet Weavers by Kind of Production | *186*
5.11. Share of Carpet Weaving in Household Income | *187*
6.1. Share of Women among Heads of Households by Activity Status | *198*
6.2. Composition of Women Heads of Households | *199*
7.1. Household Income and Employment Status | *233*
7.2. Housing and Employment Status | *233*
7.3. Work Satisfaction and Income Background among Those in Informal Sector | *235*
7.4. Education and Employment Status | *236*
7.5. Reasons for Entering the Informal Economy | *237*
7.6. Women's Marital and Employment Status | *240*

7.7.	Informal Jobs and Sources of Initial Necessary Capital	241
7.8.	Women's Employment Status and Decision-Making Powers over Basic Household Expenditures	242
7.9.	Income Expenditure and Informal Employment	243
8.1.	Composition of Economically Active Population (Ten Years and Older)	259
8.2.	Labor Market Participation and Education of Female Population (Ten Years and Older)	261
8.3.	Marital Status of Women in Survey Sample	265
8.4.	Education Attainments of Women in Survey Sample	265
8.5.	Time Spent on Work by Women in Survey Sample	265
8.6.	Public versus Private Employment of Women in Survey Sample	266
8.7.	Reasons for Working of Women in Survey Sample	266
8.8.	Responses in Official Surveys versus Informal Survey	267
8.9.	Reasons for Not Declaring Employment in Official Surveys	267
8.10.	Income Levels of Employed Women in Survey Sample	269
8.11.	Share of Women Who Work from Home	270
8.12.	Marketing Methods of Women Who Work from Home	270
8.13.	Obstacles to Advancement of Career/Business	271
9.1.	Labor Market Status of Participants, January 2001	287
9.2.	Occupation of Participants, by Type	287
9.3.	Occupation of Spouses, by Type	287
9.4.	Dollar Income of Participants and Spouses	288

Acknowledgments

THIS PROJECT STARTED in 2004, when I (Bahramitash) went back to Iran after thirteen years. The trip was a shocking experience as I found myself extremely uninformed about changes that had occurred during my absence. I had lived in Iran all my life, as a student in the early 1980s and then as a teacher at university in the late 1980s until my departure to Canada in 1991. Iran had undergone a great deal of transformation and appeared as an extremely dynamic country. As someone whose research area has been poverty in general and women in particular, I had been engaged in fieldwork in Southeast Asia. Comparing the literature on Southeast Asia with that on the Middle East in general and on Iran in particular, I realized that a great deal of what happens in Iran has remained unnoticed. This lack of attention may be partly because many scholars who write are either unable to travel to Iran or do not stay an extended period of time, and not many Iran-based scholars publish their work in English. I became convinced that it was extremely important to carry out fieldwork in order to reflect some of the changes that had occurred in the postrevolutionary era, particularly changes of the reform era.

I first attempted to approach Iranian scholars and read their work. Next, I went through library archives, conducted interviews, attended conferences (and there were many conferences being held throughout the country), and traveled extensively. I found a major gap between the literature in English and what has happened in Iran, particularly with regard to women's work.

While working on this project I delivered a lecture at the University of Illinois at Urbana-Champaign, where I met Hadi Salehi

Esfahani. We exchanged notes, shared our research, and decided to work together. We approached other academics who have worked in Iran, and Fatemeh Moghadam and Zahra Karimi joined us. For a comparative study, we asked Jennifer Olmsted. Here we should mention that Zohreh Niknia was from the start of the project very supportive and involved, for which we are very thankful.

Another person very important to this project is Eric Hooglund. Hooglund has been an extremely influential scholar. He from time to time read drafts of several of these chapters and has been one of the strongest critics of the work but, at the same time, he has been one of my greatest sources of information and inspiration.

Other scholars helped this project in various capacities, and we wish to thank specific Iranian scholars such as Azam Ravad Rad, Maryam Afshary, Fazileh Khani, Nahid Motiei, Susan Bastani, Mohseni Tabrizi, Sam Aram, Nahid Farast, Hossien Nouri, and Maryam Norouzi. They shared their research with us, and we would have liked to have been able to include their work in this book, but we were unable to incorporate them in this particular volume. I (Bahramitash) wish to thank them all and hope to incorporate their work in a different anthology.

Here in Canada and the United States, the book has benefited from the support of a number of scholars. Lillian Robinson, the principal of the Simone de Beauvoir Institute, Concordia University Women's Study Program's intellectual and institutional support, was pivotal during the early stages of the book. She was a true scholar as well as a dear friend who was a great resource person.

The book has benefited from the support of Dr. Patrice Brodeur, the chair of Islam, Pluralism, and Globalization at the University of Montreal, whose expertise has been vital and highly critical. Dr. Haleh Esfandiari, director of the Middle East Program at Woodrow Wilson Center for International Scholars, has provided essential scholarly reinforcement for this book. Also many thanks to Nadereh Chamlou and the Persinate Gender Network for bringing together academics who work on issues related to gender and work in Iran.

There have been other scholars whose help has been crucial. We wish to thank Parvin Alizadeh and Fatemeh Moghadam, who read and commented on our work. We wish to thank Jennifer Olmsted for writing a chapter at such short notice as well as for reading and providing excellent comments. Other academics have supported this project by reading parts of the work and providing constructive criticism, among them Elaheh Rostami Povey, Minoo Moallem, and Valentine Moghadam. Others have been important for the exchange of ideas, and here we want to thank in particular Nayereh Tohidi, Lynda Clark, Fred Reed, Anthony Synnott, and Greta Naumeroff, along with other scholars from the Simone de Beauvoir Institute, the McGill Center for Developing Area Studies, and the University of Montreal.

Thanks to the UN Development Program in Tehran and Dr. Ali Farzin, Mr. Hamidi, and Dr. Parvine Marofi. There have been other organizations such as Hamyaran, where Bahramitash received help from Dr. Reza Sheikh and Sorrayah Bahmanpour, who provided links and information. Tehran University Department of Sociology, from which Bahramitash graduated several years ago was important to some of the data gathering and here we wish to thank Dr. Mirzai, who was my professor back in the late 1980s. Thanks also to Dr. Azkia and Dr. Tavasoli. Last but not least, Shahla Kazemipour has been extremely supportive and has provided the project with her expertise most generously.

On a different note, we would like to extend special thanks to our friends in Iran. For Bahramitash, these are Roshanak Malik, Mitra Pourtorab, Fatima Shobeyri, and Farkhondeh Aghani, supportive women and high school friends who have made her stay in Tehran joyful and exhilarating. Esfahani is indebted to his former colleagues at Tehran University, especially Ali Farsi, Mohammad Ghafourian, and Fariba Riazi. In North America we want to thank all our friends who have made the solitary work of writing less burdensome. Among them Bahramitash is specially grateful to Mahshi Payro, Yasmin Noori, Farzaneh Khadir, Parvin Saghafi, Amir and Arezo Khadir, Rachad Antonious, and Pari Esfandiari. Esfahani's special thanks go to Sima Alikani, Firouz Gahvari, Esmail Meisami, and Hassan Vafai.

Our family members have been great sources of inspiration and support. Esfahani would like to express appreciation to his father, Hossein Salehi-Esfahani, and to his mother, Aghdas Hakim-Elahi, who introduced him at an early age to women's predicament in Iran and set brave examples of what could be done by her own dedicated social activism. He is also thankful to his wife, Niloofar Shambayati, and children, Kumars and Katayun, who are always witty and insightful. Furthermore, he is grateful to his siblings, especially Djavad and Haideh for sharing ideas, data, and research results. Bahramitash wishes to thank her mother, Fatimeh Samadi Haghighi, her uncle Behzad Farrahi, and other family members, Zohreh Baharmast and her wonderful children, Marzieh, Reza, and Hanieh. She also wishes to express her gratitude toward her wonderful children, Mahsana, Arash, Iman, and Atena Sadegh, who remain the single most important social capital of her life. With them around, Bahramitash feels herself connected to the real world where millions of women do what she does: raise their children while working, often with little access to economic resources. Having to deal with the job of raising four children as an immigrant mother, she is not just a researcher on women and work but a participant observer.

Contributors

ROKSANA BAHRAMITASH is a graduate of the McGill University Sociology Department and has received two postdoctoral awards from the Social Sciences and Humanities Council of Canada (SSHRC). She is the winner of the Eileen D. Ross award (2003–4) for her work on female poverty, globalization, Islamization, and women's employment. In 2006 she won a three-year research grant from the SSHRC and in 2008 she was given a grant by the Council for the Arts to write her memoir. Dr. Bahramitash has taught many courses at McGill University and Concordia University and has worked with international development agencies including the Canadian Development Agency (CIDA), the International Development Research Centre (IDRC), the United Nations Development Program (UNDP), and the World Bank–funded project through the Center for Teaching and Research on Arab Women (CAWTAR). Bahramitash is the author of several articles and book chapters. Her first book is *Liberation from Liberalization: Gender and Globalization in Southeast Asia* (2005, reprinted 2008). This book has been translated into Persian by Mr. Hossien Nouri and published by Samt in Tehran. A forthcoming book is entitled *Gendering in Contemporary Iran: Pushing the Boundaries* (coedited with Eric Hooglund). Bahramitash is research director at the Chair of Islam, Pluralism, and Globalization at the University of Montreal.

HADI SALEHI ESFAHANI is professor of economics and director of the Center for South Asian and Middle Eastern Studies at the University of Illinois at Urbana-Champaign. In addition, he currently serves as the editor in chief of the *Quarterly Review of Economics and Finance*. He has also served as president of the Middle East Economic Association during 2007–9 and has worked for the World Bank as a visiting staff economist and a consultant. He received his BSc in engineering from Tehran University and a PhD in economics from the University of California at Berkeley. His theoretical and empirical research is in the field of the political economy of development, focusing in particular on the Middle East and North Africa region. Dr. Esfahani has published numerous articles on the role of politics and governance in fiscal, trade, and regulatory policy formation. His articles have appeared in *The Economic Journal, Review of Economics and Statistics, Journal of Development Economics, International Economic Review, Oxford Economic Review, World Development, International Journal of Middle Eastern Studies*, and *Iranian Studies*, among others.

SHAHLA KAZEMIPOUR is associate professor of demography and deputy director of the Population Studies and Research Centre in Asia and the Pacific. She has done extensive research on development and population. She has worked with a number of professional associations, for example as supervisor of the Demographical Research Section at the Institute of Social Studies and Research, and as head of the advisory board for student affairs at the faculty of social sciences at Tehran University. Dr. Kazemipour is the author of many books and articles in refereed international journals in both English and Persian, including *Primary Methods in Population Analysis* (1991), *A Sociological Study of the City of Tehran* (2001), "Myth and Realities of the Impact of Islam on Women: Women's Changing Marital Status in Iran" (with Roksana Bahramitash, 2006), and "Economy, Informal Economy" in *Today: An Encyclopedia of Life in the Islamic Republic* (with Roksana Bahramitash, 2008).

FATEMEH ETEMAD MOGHADAM is a professor of economics at Hofstra University. She received her D.Phil. in economics from Oxford University, and her MA and BA from Columbia University

(Barnard College). She has published extensively on agricultural economy, economic history, and women and development in Iran. She is the author of *From Land Reform to The Revolution: The Political Economy of Agricultural Development in Iran (1960–1979)*. Her publications on gender and development in Iran include: "Iran's New Islamic Home Economics: An Exploratory Attempt to Conceptualize Women's Work in the Islamic Republic" (2001); "Women and the Labor in the Islamic Republic of Iran," in *Women in Iran from 1800 to the Islamic Republic* (2004); and "Undercounting Women's Work in Iran" (2008). Dr. Moghadam served as executive secretary and president of the Middle East Economic Association. She has also served as board member of a number of scholarly organizations, as well as on editorial boards of scholarly journals. She has worked as a consultant for UNDP and the World Bank.

ZAHRA KARIMI received her PhD in economics from an Iranian state university and is currently an academic staff member and member of the Women's Studies Center at the University of Mazandaran. Her field of research is the labor market in Iran, focusing in recent years on the employment of Iranian women. Dr. Moughari's other fields of interest include heterodox economics and institutional economics.

ZOHREH MIRZADEGAN NIKNIA is a visiting professor at the Department of Economics, Mills College. Her research interests are gender and migration, economic development, and political economy of oil. She has been a visiting scholar at the Department of Gender and Women Studies, University of California, Berkeley (2003–6) and the Women's Leadership Institute at Mills College (2004–5). Dr. Niknia has taught at the University of California, Berkeley, Extension Program; California State University, Sacramento; and the University of Missouri, Kansas City. She is the recipient of the Outstanding Dissertation Award, University of Missouri–Kansas City; the Association of Collegiate Business Schools and Programs Teaching Excellence Award; the National Institute for Staff and Organizational

Development Excellence Award; a Fulbright-Hays Fellowship, East-Central Europe Summer Research Project; and a Faculty Exchange Program Award, Russia.

JENNIFER C. OLMSTED, who grew up in Lebanon and spent a number of years in the Palestinian Territories, has long been interested in globalization, Middle East economies, and the ways conflict shapes economic outcomes. A graduate of Georgetown University and the University of California, Davis, much of her research focuses on socioeconomic conditions facing women in the Middle East. Her current work examines the way conflict and economic isolation affect economic conditions and gender norms, often in contradictory ways, using Iran, Iraq, and Palestine as case studies. Her publications have appeared in various journals, including *World Development, Industrial Relations, The Journal of Development Studies, Feminist Economics,* and *The Journal of Middle East Women's Studies,* as well as numerous book volumes. Dr. Olmsted is currently associate professor and chair in the Department of Economics at Drew University, Madison, New Jersey. She has also worked for various other universities as well as the US Department of Agriculture, and consulted for numerous research organizations, including the Social Science Research Council (SSRC), RAND, the World Bank, the UNDP, and the International Food Policy Research Institute (IFPRI).

Acronyms and Abbreviations

BWA	Bureau of Women's Affairs
CAWTAR	Center for Teaching and Research on Arab Women
CEDAW	Convention on the Elimination of Discrimination Against Women
CIDA	Canadian Development Agency
CPS	*Current Population Survey*
CWP	Center for Women's Participation
ESCAPPRM	Economic and Social Commission for Asia/Pacific Poverty Reduction Method
FPA	Family Planning Association
GDP	gross domestic product
GNP	gross national product
HDI	human development index
HEIS	Household Expenditure and Income Survey
ID	index of dissimilarity
IDC	International Development Committee
IDRC	International Development Research Centre
IFPRI	International Food Policy Research Institute
IGA	income-generating activity
IKRF	Imam Khomeini's Relief Foundation
ILO	International Labor Organization
IMF	International Monetary Fund
IPPF	International Planned Parenthood Federation
IRR	Iranian rial [International Organization for Standardization]
ISI	import substitution industrialization
KILM	Key Indicators of the Labor Market
LFP	labor force participation

MENA	Middle East and North Africa
MP	Member of Parliament
NGO	nongovernmental organization
NIC	newly industrialized countries
NIE	New Institutional Economics
OECD	Organisation for Economic Co-operation and Development
PUMS	Public Use Micro Sample
SAP	Structural Adjustment Program
SAPAP	South Asian Poverty Alleviation Program
SCI	Statistical Center of Iran
SECH	Socio-economic Characteristics of Households
SEWA	Self-Employed Women's Association
SSHRC	Social Sciences and Humanities Council of Canada
SSRC	Social Science Research Council
UNDP	United Nations Development Program
USD	US dollars [International Organization for Standardization]
WIEGO	Women in Informal Employment Globalizing and Organizing
WO	Welfare Organization
WOI	Women's Organization of Iran

Veiled Employment

Introduction

ROKSANA BAHRAMITASH *and* HADI SALEHI ESFAHANI

IN THE WINTER OF 2004 Roksana Bahramitash attended a nationwide conference in Tehran where workers, employers and entrepreneurs, and government officials came together to address issues such as wages and unemployment. The conference was heavily influenced by the International Labor Organization's (ILO's) commitment to the concept of Decent Work. Following the conference an ILO representative gave a lecture at the Ministry of Work and Social Welfare. After the lecture, Bahramitash and a former colleague who was then working with the ILO drove to another seminar. On the way, a discussion about the issue of female employment in Iran started during which Bahramitash and the ILO representative (a native Iranian) shared their frustration over Western conceptions of Iranian women's international image. The discussion revolved around the difference between outsiders' images of Iran and the reality of the country, a point of sympathy between her and the ILO representative who, like her, traveled to Iran on a regular basis and was up-to-date about the changes taking place over the past few decades. Like so many visitors, he admitted that the Western media's portrayal of Iran paints a dark picture of women in the country. For many Westerners the differences between Iran and Iraq or even Saudi Arabia are minor details, irrelevant to how they view the country in question. For the most part Iran is portrayed as a hotbed of radical Islam, a place of misogyny and retrograde views that belong to the Middle Ages. While it is true that the position of women—particularly middle-class women—has suffered as a result of the Islamization process that occurred after the Iranian revolution, the situation of Iranian women is far more nuanced and complex than is often assumed outside of the region.

Development/Modernization

Development studies emerged as a distinct area of research in the aftermath of World War II. The sociological basis of this new field was modernization theory, inspired by structural functionalism and the work of the prominent sociologist of the postwar era Talcott Parsons. Development/modernization prescribed social transformation of previously colonized and semicolonized countries (which were now called the Third World) from traditional to modern. This transformation has been viewed primarily as unidirectional and evolutionary, operating through a market economy. In the case of the mainstream academia in Western countries generally and the United States in particular, and during the Cold War, development studies and modernization theory were preoccupied with the growing popularity of Socialist ideas.

During the same time, in the Soviet Union and the Eastern Bloc, modernization had already been fully embraced, and the only difference was that this policy was carried out by the ruling Communist Party and through heavy-handed government programs. These programs, in some cases harsh, did accelerate industrialization and economic growth in the Soviet Union for a while, especially during the 1930s when the Western world was suffering from the Great Depression. The initial economic success of the Soviet programs added to the political appeal of socialism in the Third World and became a threat to the hegemony of Western powers. This threat strengthened the view in the West that more economic growth was needed in the Third World to counter the proliferation of Socialist tendencies in those countries.

Although the belief in economic development through private markets remained strong in the West, the experience of the Great

Depression and the growth in the Soviet Union gave rise to the view that markets left to themselves might not have been ideal and that extensive government interventions were needed to foster growth, especially in low-income countries. John Maynard Keynes's macroeconomic theory and the perspectives on economic growth developed after World War II—such as Paul Narcyz Rosentein-Rodan's idea of "Big Push" (1943), Arthur Lewis's "dual economy" (1955), and W. W. Rostow's "stages of economic growth" (1956)—all suggested crucial roles for the government in inducing growth through rapid industrialization. In particular, the import substitution industrialization (ISI) strategy, which was often combined with extensive government controls and state ownership of enterprises, became quite popular in Third World countries. Emphasis on rapid industrialization also entailed commercialization of agriculture and the transfer of its labor and other resources to industrial production.

The ISI strategy was successful in generating growth for a while in many developing countries, especially the ones with larger internal markets. However, those growth spurts came to a halt sooner or later, often because the governments did not have the wherewithal necessary to go beyond the ISI strategy once the easy opportunities of the internal markets were exhausted. ISI policies restricted the economy's access to global resources, especially new technologies and organizational assets, and weakened the incentives to invest in productivity. By the 1970s these weaknesses were visible in all countries pursuing ISI. With the oil price shocks of 1973–74 and 1979–80 and the sharp rise in interest rates during 1980–83, many developing countries faced major economic difficulties and crises. In particular, the oil-importing countries that had maintained their old strategies in the face of higher oil prices had to borrow heavily and found themselves in full-fledged debt crises in the early 1980s.

Within the mainstream development literature in Western academic traditions, two strands existed from the beginning. One has heavily emphasized economic growth and has been used by organizations such as the World Bank and USAID. The other has emphasized human development and income equality and has been used by organizations such as the United Nations. While the positions of organizations and individuals over these two strands have not been pure, their preferences over the two alternatives have been rather clear. Over time, the UN moved away from purely economic growth toward adopting models with more emphasis on human development; this motion has gone through different stages, such as the basic needs approach and sustainable development and participatory (people-led) development. However, both strands in the field of development/modernization, especially the view focusing on growth, came under serious criticism during the 1960s and 1970s, largely because they were perceived as supporting the US leadership of the Western world and its foreign policy. These criticisms were posed by sociologists and political economists such as Andre Gunder Frank (1967), the founder of dependency theory, and Immanuel Wallerstein, the founder of the world systems theory (1974).

Development initiatives in many parts of the world have been far from successful. By the early 1970s it was evident that development initiatives had failed miserably in many parts of the world with the notable example of Sub-Saharan Africa. The premises of development had not been delivered, poverty and income disparity had increased, and massive migration to cities had increased urban population where increasingly many people live in shantytowns.

Development/modernization has not only failed in many parts of the world as an economic model but, because it has been part of the Pax Americana, it has been coupled with the US support for rootless dictators such as General Pinochet in Chili, Marcos in the Philippines, and Suharto in Indonesia. While it was true that economically there was an increase in per capita income in the cases just mentioned, much of that increase failed to filter through, creating disappointment and dissatisfaction with dictatorships supported by the United States, most of the European countries, and Japan. In the context of the Muslim world, the United States supported two coups, one in Indonesia and one in Iran. A CIA-backed coup in the mid-1960s in Indonesia led to the massacre of close to one million civilians. While the Western prescriptive for achieving development was not always successful, its alternative, the Soviet model, became equally discredited with the gradual decline of the Soviet Union during the late 1970s. It is in this context and in search of an alternative ideology that support for political Islam started to gather momentum.

The demise of the ISI strategy and the crises of the 1970s and early 1980s led to the resurgence of market-fundamentalist (or neoliberal) views in development economics. The economists espousing this view argued that the maladies of developing countries were caused by extensive government interventions that distorted markets and undermined investment incentives. They maintained that governments were inefficient and that the consequences of their interventions were much worse than market outcomes. Besides, extensive intervention had given rise to corruption and had made matters much worse. They suggested that the role of the state should be rolled back to maintaining law and order and property rights so that markets would be unleashed and free trade would bring about prosperity. Some interpreted the economic "miracles" in East Asia based on export promotion as confirmation of their views and advocated the model (Bhagwati and Desai 1970; Lal 1983; Little 1982, 1988). The World Bank and the International Monetary Fund (IMF) embraced this neoliberal approach and strongly advocated it as part of the structural adjustment programs (SAPs) in many countries of the south. SAPs tried to focus policies on economic growth and led to cutbacks in social welfare programs. As a result, income distribution worsened and in some cases poverty even increased, but long-term growth proved elusive (Easterly 2001, 2006). These policies particularly put major burdens on women from low-income households. For this reason, the neoliberal approach to development has been criticized by many economists and sociologists such as A. Amsden (1985), T. Skocpol (1985), and R. Wade (1992). In the field of feminist economics, many academics documented the negative impact of SAPs on women (Moser 1989; Palmer 1991; Çagatay, Elson, and Grown 1995).

Within the economics discipline, the unsatisfactory outcome of neoliberal policies in many countries led to the rise of a new approach called New Institutional Economics (NIE). The idea was that if institutions (or rules that structure human interactions) did not function well, markets could not work efficiently. (For classic references, see North 1990; Williamson 1985; and Dani Rodrik's and Daron Acemoglu's numerous publications on the subject, e.g., Rodrik 1997 and 2008; Acemoglu, Simon, and James 2001; Acemoglu and Robinson 2005; Acemoglu, Golosov, and Tsyvinski 2008.) As a result, the policy agenda shifted toward building institutions that could enable people to create incentives for investment and increased productivity. In the 1990s, this view gained increasing popularity and was adopted by the World Bank under the rubric of good governance. This approach has also had a mixed record. Many countries that tried to improve their governance found out that it is a long, drawn-out process, and that marginal steps in the process do not necessarily bring about commensurate boosts to economic growth. In fact, the process was riddled with difficulties and setbacks. Meanwhile, a number of countries managed to embark on rapid long-term growth by using innovative medium-term shortcuts that facilitate growth. For example, Korea and Taiwan intervened in favor of production for exports and achieved rapid economic growth (Amsden 1985; Wade 1992). In these cases state interventionist policies enabled them to mobilize their resources and to build more prosperous economies. Quite contrary to the claims of neoliberal economists, neither country liberalized its trade until decades after it had started growing fast. They were pragmatic and responsive to their internal and external conditions. Both countries also used coercion to implement their policies. However, they were also careful to ensure that ultimately the benefits of growth were widely distributed to ensure the legitimacy and sustainability of their policies. These economic success stories and the weak results of the standard governance or neoliberal policies have led to new strands of thought about newly industrialized countries (NICs) (Rodrik 2009; Esfahani, McMahon, and Squire, forthcoming).

Alongside theories about economic development, drawing upon Max Weber (2001), some sociologists have argued that certain aspects of Western culture are congenial and prerequisites to economic development (Bellah 1957; McClelland 1964; Inkeles 1964). These characteristics were identified as individualism, specialization, organizational interdependency, rationality, universalism, and functional specificity. Based on these characteristics, development could only be achieved if cultural transformation took place that would replace collectivity, relative self-sufficiency, social relations based on tradition, particularism, and functional diffuseness, all of which were closely related to the local/traditional culture and the dominant religion. Therefore, local religion—for example, Islam in the case of Middle Eastern countries—has been viewed as an impediment to development.

Such a stand against local cultural values has provoked criticisms, particularly by many sociologists and anthropologists. They contend that development as a field is an extension of what used to be "the white man's burden" and its civilizing mission during the colonial era. Within a postcolonial context, the critics argue, development and economic growth have come to replace the old civilizing mission of the colonialists.

In fact, development as a package that ties economic growth to cultural modernization/Westernization has created a backlash. This reaction has been embodied in the renewed popularity of Islam in the late 1970s throughout the Muslim world. This popularity was not a new phenomenon; it had its roots in the colonial era. In Egypt, for instance, the Muslim Brotherhood was formed as an effort to resist British colonial rule in the early twentieth century. In the case of Indonesia, Islamic ideology united diverse groups of resistance parties throughout the vast archipelago on a nationalist stand, which finally led to the defeat of the Dutch colonial rule after World War II. Similar examples can be drawn from the Algerian struggle against the French. In the case of Iran, an anticolonial pan-Islamist movement was supported by clerics and Muslim intellectuals such as Sayyid Jamal al-Din Asadabadi (al-Afghani) during the late nineteenth to the early twentieth century against the British and the Russians. (It is worth noting that Iran was not a formal colony of either of those two countries, but it was a battleground between the two rivals and, as a result, it was under a semicolonial rule.) In the aftermath of World War II, with the decline of colonial powers and decolonization, resistance toward colonialism in the form of political Islam declined, to the extent that in many Muslim countries secularists came to rule. For example, in Egypt and Indonesia, respectively, Nasser and Sukarno, both secularists with Socialist tendencies, came to power. In Iran, the Pahlavi dynasty, a secularist pro-Western regime (supported first by the British and then by the Americans) established its rule.

However, by the late 1970s development/modernization had disappointed many who were not impressed by either the Western model or the Soviet one. There was a search for an alternative in many parts of the world. In Latin America, first in Peru and then in Brazil, the Left mobilized peasants through the Catholic Church, and liberation theology became an important force. In the Muslim world and within the postcolonial context, Islamic ideology became an anti-Western force and therefore gained popularity again. In Iran, anti-Western sentiment manifested itself in the form of Islamism.

Within academia, development/modernization/Westernization has come under attack by some of the most highly respected sociologists and anthropologists, such as Arturo Escobar, who argued that the mainstream literature on development is ethnocentric and is based on the Western experience (1995). Escobar asserts that development as a linear, universal model of economic and social development that can be objectively applied to diverse local cultures, grouped together and named as the Third World, is ethnocentric. In addition, Escobar argues that when considering the Middle East and North Africa region, it is important to draw upon the work of Edward Said (*Orientalism*, 1979). In Said's view, Orientalism in academia is a tendency toward viewing the West and the Orient as a binary, where the West is modern and the Orient is traditional. The modern West is in such literature the "Self" while the Orient is the "Other." Said argues that such a dichotomy views the Occident as civilized, progressive, rational, honest, trustworthy, and wealthy in contrast to the Muslim/Arab Orient that is perceived as backward, irrational, menacing, untrustworthy, dishonest, superstitious, and economically poor. This view is implicit in writings about the Arab/Muslim "Orient" and takes place within an academic "objectivity" and "fairness" afforded by presumed value-free approaches to history and sociology. Orientalism and development/modernization theory come together at the point where the Orient is economically backward and in need of development to move away from tradition and to enter the stage of modernity. The assumption about the backwardness of the Muslim/Arab (this view includes Iranians even though they are not Arabs) means that the passage from traditional to modern and from poor to rich/developed is only possible if certain cultural transformations take place; namely, backward Muslims must free themselves of their religion in order to enter into a modern progressive world.

The Orientalist discourse continues to dominate a great deal of academic writing on the topic. Michel Foucault's work on the relationship between power and knowledge is most relevant where the Western discourse and its economic and intellectual power over the Orient have found expression in academic production. Foucault's analysis can be extended to the "truth" about Muslims and Islam, which reflects the social structure of power relations and helps to explain how development literature has been shaped in the postcolonial world. This analysis resonates with the work of other critics of development/modernization, such as Samir Amin (1989), who have challenged that perspective on the basis of its ethnocentrism/Eurocentrism. In his pioneer work *Encountering Development* (1995), Arturo Escobar endorsed Said and drew upon Foucault to extend the critique of development/modernization to academic writing on the field of development in what he calls the depiction of "traditional society" under the "gaze of experts" who write and articulate their thoughts within a framework set by Western countries that have power over the "undeveloped" world. In other words, mainstream development writings in an apparently objective fashion rely on the world power structure that is dominated by the "developed world" guiding the "underdeveloped"/poor world. This perspective, in the context of the Muslim/Arab (Iranian) world, translates into how the backward Orient must follow the path of the Occident in order to achieve development.

There are also many feminist economists who criticize the Western academic tradition from a similar angle. In particular, E. Zein-Elabdin and S. Charusheela argue in their book *Post Colonialism Meets Economics* that "[a]s a discipline, [economics] has upheld the narrative of 'development' as the centerpiece of its theoretical construction of formerly colonized regions, presuming the ontological precedence of modern European societies as a basis for its theory of history. As Feyerabend (1987:4) puts it, the discourse on development in effect renders patterns of life outside the (Western) industrial world as a 'mistake'" (Zein-Elabdin and Charusheela 2004, 2).

Orientalism and development/modernization theory have been embraced by some members of the economic and political elite in the Orient, as was the case with the Shah, who sought to hold the hands of his citizens to walk them toward the gates of the "Great Civilization." This was a process through which Iranians had to move away from their own culture and Islam and to embrace Western secularism. In this light it may not be too hard to understand why the broad opposition to the Shah was inspired by an ideology with local roots and Islamist in nature.

Theoretical Framework

Because this book is about employment of women in Iran, it is critical to review the major academic theoretical and conceptual literature on two key topics: "gender and development" and "postcolonial feminist theory." In this section, we will first highlight the major themes on gender and development and then discuss the most recent critique of the literature on women in the Muslim world in the context of postcolonial feminist theory.

Gender and Development

The mainstream development theory has not only been criticized by academics from the Left, it has also come under attack more generally by academics sympathetic toward the rights of women, based on the consequences of development initiatives and policy prescriptions. This critique is because development efforts in many parts of the world have had an adverse impact on women. The critique started with Ester Boserup, who documented how development had deprived women of their access to economic resources (1970). It is now widely acknowledged even within the mainstream development literature that there have been serious problems with the way lopsided economic growth has affected many women. In many cases, development has not only failed to bring improvement for the masses of women in the Third World countries, but it has actually led to the impoverishment of millions. The gender and development literature points to the fact that during the 1950s and 1960s mainstream development was gender blind and in line with colonial-era thinking. It assumed that as developing countries modernized, the inequality of access to resources that systematically discriminated against women would diminish (Tinker 1997, 33–42; Moser 1993; Sen 1987; Kabeer 1994).

More recently and since the late 1970s, the literature on gender and development has focused on neoliberal economic policy and its implications for women's status. In particular, this literature has documented the impact of globalization on women (Çagatay, Elson, and Grown 1995; Kabeer and Mahmud 2003; Elson 1995, 1993; Palmer 1992; Benería 2003). The literature is vast and sheds light on the way women's work has been used as flexible cheap labor serving global markets (Benería 1999a; Standing 1989; Elson 1995; Amy 1997; Benería, Floro, Grown, and MacDonald 2000; Kabeer and Mahmud 2003; Benería 2003). For example, Bahramitash's book on gender and globalization in Southeast Asia drew upon this literature to argue that contrary to neoliberal claims, economic growth in Southeast Asia was achieved (a) because the state was heavily involved in the economy (incidentally, this involvement explains Chinese economic success as well) and (b) because the so-called free trade in Southeast Asia brought benefits to Southeast Asian economies because it was able to exploit women's work as flexible cheap labor (Bahramitash 2005).

However, some scholars argue that because such employment is a source of income outside of the family, it allows women to break away from traditional sources of power. Valentine Moghadam, for instance, has argued in favor of Tunisia's economic policy because it has set up export-processing zones to employ women as cheap labor (and continues to crack down on Islamism) (V. Moghadam 1995b). While it is true that waged employment does bring some benefits to women, generally the data on female poverty present a major challenge. Working as cheap labor for world manufacturing markets in many cases tends to be exploitative rather than emancipating. The type of employment typical of manufacturing for export is low-pay because it is regarded as "unskilled" or "low-skill" work, and increased employment in such positions has not brought prosperity to women broadly. As a form of inexpensive labor, women in these types of work have been subject to flexible employment arrangements. This means they can be hired when there is a demand for their work and fired as soon as there is a decline in consumption demand, as we have witnessed in the recent global economic crisis. When women are made redundant, they often join the ranks of "discouraged workers" and there is often little or no unemployment compensation. For many women in the developing countries, jobs in manufacturing for the global market and in export-processing zones are the only employment option. Yet it is not clear that such working conditions necessarily lead to economic empowerment or translate into increased power for women if they have to rely on their families as a source of unemployment insurance.

It is estimated that one-third of the labor force in manufacturing in low-income countries, both formal and informal, consists of women. While the number of women in the labor force has increased, the wage gap between men and women remains significant. Although there are no reliable and broad data, the ILO estimates that women's earnings are, on average, significantly lower than men's.[1] By the late 1980s (which was after the end of the UN decade for the advancement of women, 1975–85), a published survey indicated that there was no evidence that the situation of women had improved in any major way over that decade, and in some cases it had worsened (Benería 2003, 10).

The literature on gender and development is vast and growing. Some have argued that similar to the case of the West, the process of industrialization initially does lead to worsening conditions for women, but as the economy reaches higher levels of income, women's economic as well as social and political status enhances. This is known as the U-shaped transformation argument (Goldin 1994). This enhancement has certainly been the case in Europe and North America and in some other countries such as the Asian newly industrialized economies. But this is hardly the case with many other parts of the world such as some Latin American countries, the Caribbean, some parts of North Africa, and certainly Sub-Saharan Africa. It may still be possible that we will see more countries achieving a high growth rate as has been the case in China and India and perhaps Brazil, but the extent to which such growth will change the status of women in those countries remains to be seen. Some women may have benefited from growth in parts of Latin America, the Caribbean, and Africa as well as in the Middle East and North Africa (hereafter MENA), namely women of high- and middle-income households. However, it is not entirely clear that the vast majority of women who come from low-income households have in fact reaped benefits from economic growth. Moreover, the U-shaped transformation

---

1. In the Report of the UN Commission on the Status of Women, Kurt Waldheim pointed out at the end of the International Decade for the Advancement of Women, "While women represent half the global population and one-third of the labor force, they receive only one-tenth of the world income and own less than one percent of world property" (R. Morgan 1984, 1).

argument needs more detailed data, careful research, and individual case study, especially in the face of the massive literature on gender and development that generally does not indicate that women's lot has improved massively. Former UN Secretary General Kofi Annan stated at the 2000 World Conference on Women that rural poverty among women had increased by 17 percent over the previous decades (Bahramitash 2005).

This book builds upon the gender and globalization literature and aims to apply some of those approaches to the case of Iran. The original title of this book was "Gender and Globalization in Iran." However, after our initial research on the topic, we realized that there was a dearth of literature on women's employment in Iran and that this lack presented a challenge for writing on the original topic. For this reason, the book's focus shifted toward issues of employment studied by academics in Iran and North America. Moreover, the work on this book took shape while Iran was being subjected to increased economic sanctions. As a result, the mainstream gender and globalization literature was becoming less applicable to Iran. Indeed, it made sense to shift attention toward the impact of economic sanctions on women, a subject that has not been studied much. The situation placed Iran in a rare place not too dissimilar to that in Iraq under Saddam Hussein and to that in the West Bank and Gaza, where in effect deglobalization had taken place, a process that Jennifer Olmsted has illustrated in her work on Iraqi and Palestinian women (2007).

Postcolonial Feminist Theory

Reading the literature on Iran, one cannot fail to notice that there is a major tendency to emphasize the role of culture and modernity versus tradition. In addition to that tendency, commonly held stereotypes about Islam and Muslims view Islamism as backward, and it is often believed that Islamism has turned the clock back on Iranian women. While Iranian women have in fact experienced many setbacks in the aftermath of the revolution, the situation is far more complex than is often assumed. In fact, in the past few decades, a new critique of the field of women in the Muslim world has been articulated by postcolonial feminist theorists. Some scholars have argued that colonial powers in the Muslim world have pointed to the status of Muslim women as an illustration of the backwardness of Muslim countries and thereby legitimized their presence as an effort to civilize Muslims. In the words of Gayatri Spivak, white men colonized the Muslim world in order "to save brown [Muslim] women from brown [Muslim] men" (Spivak 1999, 284). It is worth reminding ourselves of the colonial historical context of places such as Algeria during the French colonial presence. The Arabs were not granted the right to vote because of the issue of the status of Algerian women; the French argued that because Algerian men treat their women unfairly, they are not civilized and should not have the right to decide for their country. Both the French in Algeria and the British in Egypt claimed that they had to be in power because of "the backwardness" the Muslims exhibited through their treatment of women—European men had to civilize the Muslims. These European men, who ruled both in Egypt and Algeria, ironically were the same who repressed European women's rights advocates in their own countries.

In the case of Iran, Minoo Moallem has documented how the position of women was viewed by Europeans as evidence of Iranian barbarism. Moallem quotes from a popular book published in England in 1890: "Persia is an almost barbarous country . . . I have heard that in the case of ladies being wrecked, the young and pretty are sold to great chiefs . . . and the old and Ugly? . . . They are made into slaves or killed outright" (*Alice, the Adventure of an English Girl in Persia,* 1890, 10). In the postcolonial context, the rights of women in the Muslim world have once again attracted attention as evidence of the backwardness of the Muslims and Muslim culture (Moallem 2005).

Treatment of women in Muslim countries as an indication of Muslim backwardness has been questioned by scholars critical of the Orientalist discourse. They question the assumptions implicit in the mainstream development literature and practice: that the process of modernization and development coupled with secularization will automatically improve women's status. Therefore, some academics have become supporters of modernization/Westernization as a means to improve women's status in the Muslim world. While this improvement may in fact be true in some cases, the reality is far more complex than a simple correlation between increased level of modernization/development and improvement in women's lot.

Interestingly, the bulk of the gender and development literature argues that the impact of development (modernization) on women has been negative. But, because such literature tends to typically focus on the non-Muslim world, documentation of the impact of development on women in the Muslim world remains thin. As a result, the assumption that the Muslim world may be an exception to the general findings of research on gender and development has survived in the literature. There is a presumption that the process of development, which has had negative effects in many parts of the world, may be different in MENA, and that its consequences may even have been positive given that development is an antidote to religion. However, in the absence of extensive research, it is difficult to comment on the topic without unwarranted generalization. In this context, the work of Naila Kabeer (1994), who has compared Bangladeshi women working on garment production in Dhaka and in London, is notable. She points out that Bangladeshi women in both cities are equally economically marginalized. In the case of these women, religion and the idea of sexual segregation seem to be completely reversed; in Bangladesh women worked outside and in factories, which is contrary to Islamic gender segregation. In London, Islamic values are not dominant, but women are secluded from the society and stay home and work as home-workers. Kabeer illustrates how the assumption about Muslim women and the impact of Islam can be misleading and how more complex socioeconomic realities determine the fate of women. This irony is why her book is entitled *Reversed Realities*. It is misleading to perceive Islamic culture as the main and in some cases the only determinant of women's fate in the area of employment. Clearly, ideology and Islamic values in the case of Bangladeshi women in

Bangladesh have not played much of a role compared to the forces brought about by the global market. In Bangladesh, women's work as cheap labor for the global market takes place in factories; in London they are forced to work at home. Kabeer is not alone in making such an argument; there are many others taking a similar stand. In their views, emphasizing economic factors no less than the cultural factors (and in interaction with them) as determinants of women's employment is important (German 1996).

It is indeed unfortunate that the literature on women in the Muslim world continues to focus primarily on cultural aspects of women's experience. This focus is particularly problematic because there is high poverty and income disparity throughout the world, including the MENA region, with its negative impact on women (Human Development Report 2005). It is, therefore, pivotal to tackle the issue of female employment/unemployment and poverty in the context of MENA. Overemphasis on the role of culture over and above socioeconomic issues can lead to cultural reductionisms that observers have identified as typical of Orientalist writing.

Within postcolonial feminist theory, a critique of the literature on gender and development and women in the Muslim world has been formulated in the work of scholars such as Chandra Mohanty. They argue that the mainstream of that literature remains in a framework set by development/modernization and Western feminist discourse. Chandra Mohanty writes, "like most other scholarship [the women and development literature] does not comprise merely 'objective' knowledge (similar to mainstream development literature) and scholarly practices take place within power relations which exist between the Western world and that of the 'underdeveloped' world" (Mohanty 2003, 50). Several academics have been critical of the depiction of "Third World women" and "Muslim women" as a homogeneous category, as a powerless group who are victims of patriarchy and as people with no control over their lives (Minh-Ha 1989; Yegenoglu 1998; Lewis and Mills 2003).

The issue of the choice of women to work outside the home has surfaced in recent years in a hot debate within sociology, triggered by the work of Catharine Hakim, who argues that some European women freely choose not to work outside the home and prefer to stay home and be housewives. Hakim asserts that some of the reasons for the gap between male and female employment is because some women have chosen to be housewives. She documents the way many women prefer their families to their careers, describing them as "home-centered" women. She argues that not all women in the West are career women, and for many, their families and children have priority over their careers (see Hakim 2000, 2003, 2006). Her work has received a great deal of attention and has been the subject of criticisms, some extremely relevant and valid. However, some of Hakim's argument may apply to the Muslim world because of the importance of the family within the Muslim cultural context. It is not hard to imagine that given strong family values in the MENA, some women in the Muslim world may prefer not to be engaged in paid employment, especially where childcare services are not easily available. As the fieldwork of Bahramitash and Kazemipour reported in this volume shows, many women prefer the informal sector because it allows them to stay with their family. In Zohreh Niknia's chapter on Iranian women in the United States, we also observe that women give high priority to the well-being of their families. In short, given the fact that the family is very important and women may well prefer to invest their time in their families rather than in their careers, it is entirely possible that the overall low employment figures in the MENA region cannot only be explained by the labor market constraints and the limitations of patriarchy; these figures suggest that women often exercise agency rather than being victims. This agency, of course, may be related to their access to economic resources, so that those with more access are able to have greater agency than those with less.

We wish to end this section by mentioning P. Paidar's work on Iranian women (1995). Paidar is critical of the mainstream views on Iranian women as victims with no agency. She argues that such views are based on the assumption that the West is progressive and is the best place for women while, in contrast to the West, the Muslim world (Iran) is backward and uncivilized, where the conditions are the worst for women. Frances Hasso adds to that opinion by stating that the type of literature that implicitly endorses modernization has a tendency to fall into the binary of East/West, secular/Islamist, and traditional/modern (2005, 653–79)—and ultimately enslaved/liberated.

Western/Modern/Secular/Liberated Women versus Oriental/Traditional/Islamic/Enslaved Women

As mentioned, the mainstream development literature tends to view Iranian women as backward because of the imposition of Islamic values after the 1979 Revolution in Iran. It is believed that before the revolution the situation of women was modern and they were liberated, while afterward they became enslaved. However, as we have seen by the women's leading role in the recent protests, Iranian women participate in public life fully. This reality is in line with some of the feminist postcolonial thoughts that have been discussed in this introduction. It is misleading if not false to assert that women in the West are homogenous and that all are equally empowered. In fact, not all "Western women" have reaped the benefits from liberation in equal measure. The notion that all "Western women" are empowered has been criticized by black feminists as well as by women of color, who point out that white middle-class women have enjoyed greater equality with men than has been the case for black women and women of color. In this book chapter 9 by Zohreh Niknia touches upon this notion by illustrating how those who leave Iran do not necessarily lead a liberated life in the United States and in some cases have been subjected to racism in the workplace. The issue of racism in the workplace against Muslims in Western countries has been documented by academics such as Haddad, Moore, and Smith (2006).

The issue of liberated/Western/secular/modern/progressive women versus enslaved/Eastern (Muslim)/religious/traditional/backward has been a subject of many writings. Judith Tucker, for example, argues that the assumption about women in "traditional societies" as categorically worse off is simplistic, if not erroneous. Historically, evidence from Egypt shows that the process of colonization (modernization) has hurt women's work. Through the process of colonization Europe developed a demand for raw materials that in turn led to a decline of the cotton and silk industry in Egypt. Moreover, modernization has led to the decline of the subsistence economy and an increase in cash cropping and has undermined women's access to means of production at least in the case of Egypt (Tucker 1994). "The idea that economic 'modernization' gradually brought women out of the 'traditional' confines of a harem or a peasant family into a 'modern' labor force can no longer be an accepted generalization: new research suggests far greater complexity in the process. Stereotypes of the traditional sheltered woman who contributed little to economic life outside the home fit poorly with what we now know about women, at least in Arab urban history" (Tucker 1994, xi). Tucker provides evidence that women were engaged in a range of urban occupations such as peddling, cosmetics, midwifery, entertainment, and domestic service. For upper-class women, there is evidence from court cases that women have owned many properties (at the time, British women had no ownership rights). Egyptian women of the late nineteenth and early twentieth centuries had a great deal of *waqf* (property endowed for religious and charitable use); Shari'a court archives of these *waqf*s show that women played a critical role in property and real estate of upper Egypt (Cuno 1999). Margaret Meriwether's research on Aleppo women during the nineteenth century indicates that women were highly involved in the textile industry, an industry that suffered from colonial rule and European competition, resulting in losses of jobs for women. In the case of Aleppo (in Syria), women played a key role in the real estate market and were in charge of most of *waqf* administration (Meriwether 1994). Generally, women's historic economic role has transformed from a unit of production in cottage industries into one in which family members become wage laborers (Gran 1977).

But even in the contemporary world, the issue of traditional oppressed and modern liberated women is contested. Evelyn Early writes about traditional Egyptian women, the Baladi women, as women involved in national and international economic and bureaucratic networks. She argues that these women, through their networks in their communities, are engaged in activities ranging from finding a job for themselves as a taxi driver to arranging a job at a Saudi construction firm for their male relatives. They may finance a trip to a country in the Persian Gulf for a family member or buy and sell goods and act as middle merchants for those returning from foreign shopping trips. Clearly, drawing distinctions along the lines of economic activity between traditional and modern women, both historically and contemporaneously, is simplistic.

The binary between Western/secular/modern versus Oriental/Iranian/traditional/Islamic/enslaved can further be explored in view of more recent ideas raised by scholars such as Laura Deeb. Drawing upon the work of Lila Abu-Lughod, she argues that Islamism can be viewed as "a cultural resistance to a Western modernity and a process which is selectively modern" (Deeb 2006, 15). Deeb argues that Islamism can be viewed as alternative modernity (2006, 4). These are some of the most recent reflections by feminist academics on the nature of Islamism and its impact on women that need to be taken into account in a book on the topic. In the case of Iran, a vast body of literature has documented complexities and nuances of the impact of Islamism on women (F. Moghadam 1985; Paidar 1995; Najmabadi 1998; Mehran 2003b; Hoodfar 1999; Poya 1999; Mir-Hosseini 1999; Rostami-Povey 2001; Adelkhah 2004; Alizadeh 2000; Alizadeh and Harper 2003; Halper 2005; Bahramitash 2007a; V. Moghadam 2002; Tohidi 2007; Kian-Thiebaut 2008; Afshar 1996b). The bulk of this writing has been primarily on the general status of women and helps us explain and explore the issue of female employment/unemployment and poverty in Iran.

The chapters in this book address a series of questions concerning women and work in Iran: What has been the impact of development on Iranian women's employment? Does evidence from Iranian women's employment present different results than what is generally found in the gender and globalization literature? Is it true that modernization with secularization liberated Iranian women and increased their employment while Islamism undermined their access to paid work? Are women victims of religious fundamentalism or is there evidence to suggest that women have in fact managed to exercise agency in the area of employment?

The book starts with a chapter by Jennifer Olmsted on gender and globalization focusing on Iranian women's experience. In placing Iran in the literature she emphasizes an interesting angle of globalization (as well as deglobalization), namely the impact of sanctions and the embargo. Drawing from other chapters of the book, she discusses the impact of economic sanctions on female employment. The embargo, similar to the case of Iraq and Gaza, has a direct negative impact on the lives of women from the lowest paid segment of Iranian society. Olmsted analyzes Iran from a comparative perspective and draws several conclusions when comparing Iran with other MENA countries. Olmsted discusses some of the challenges that working with quantitative data presents, some of which have been raised by others (Alizadeh and Harper 2003).

The second chapter is primarily focused on the period leading up to the revolution and the first two decades of the revolution. It first examines the impact of the Shah's modernization agenda. While it is true that women of the urban middle and upper classes benefited from some of the changes that took place in the legal, social, economic, and political sphere, women of peasant background, traditional classes, and those living in the rural areas had experiences similar to those of women in many other parts of the Third World where the process of modernization and development alienated them from their traditional access to social and economic power. This alienation may well explain why a huge number of women, particularly from low-income urban and rural backgrounds, joined the revolution en masse and continued to remain the backbone of postrevolutionary popular support. This support continued during the first decade of the revolution and the Iran-Iraq war. The third chapter discusses the last dozen years following the election of President Khatami in 1997, which may be called the "reform period."

The fourth chapter documents the transformation of the female labor market in the past five decades using decennial census data from 1956 to 2006. It questions many commonly held stereotypical views about the impact of Islamization on women's employment in Iran. The data analysis shows that employment for women declined sharply in the aftermath of the revolution, but that much of this decline took place in rural areas among the very young women who used to work in handicraft, especially carpet weaving. Most of them were unpaid family workers. While it is true that in the aftermath of the revolution some women of middle- and high-income classes lost their jobs because of Islamization, the bulk of the decline occurred in the rural areas, where there was no need for Islamization because they had not been "modernized" to begin with. The decline in labor force participation and employment was related to an increase in education for girls in rural areas and, more important, to the US economic sanctions and the war with Iraq, which impeded domestic and foreign trade, especially carpet exports. Therefore, contrary to what is often assumed, most of those women who "lost" their jobs were in fact girls who went to school or lost their (often unpaid) jobs in the carpet industry. Chapter 4 also examines the role of demographic change, sector shifts, and educational attainments in the pattern of women's labor force participation, employment positions, and occupations as well as unemployment. It shows that women's employment has shifted toward the service sector, especially professional, technical, and clerical positions that require more education. These happen to be the expanding parts of the economy and, interestingly, women have found positions in them much faster than men, largely because of their significant investment in education. Increased education and reduced fertility rates seem to have enabled women to overcome social and cultural biases against them and to outcompete men in the markets for many high-quality jobs. The irony is that while there has been progress in these respects, female unemployment remains high and many obstacles and challenges continue to confront women.

Chapter 5 provides a more detailed picture of the decline in the carpet industry owing to globalization. Zahra Karimi argues that because of the declining world market for Iranian carpets and the increased education of girls, carpet weaving has been transferred from Iranian girls and women as unpaid family workers to Afghan girls and women.

Given that the issue of female poverty and feminization of poverty (with particular emphasis on female-headed households) has been an important part of the gender and development literature, chapter 6 focuses on female-headed households. The chapter looks at poverty of female-headed households and the microcredit versus the charity model. The next two chapters (chapters 7 and 8) focus on the informal sector. In chapter 7 Bahramitash and Kazemipour present research on the role of women in the informal sector from low-income neighborhoods. The chapter ends with data from street vendors in Tehran and Mashhad. Fatemeh Moghadam (chapter 8) discusses her research on the informal sector among high- and middle-income households. Her work sheds light on the way women from middle- and high-income households have created employment for themselves in the informal sector. In the last chapter (chapter 9), Zohreh Niknia follows similar types of women who have left Iran, some of whom continue to work in the informal sector in the United States. Some of her data enlighten our readers on the issue of traditional oppressed versus liberated modern women, incorporating the general literature on immigrant women's labor market position in the United States and their opportunities and challenges.

We wish to argue that it may be false to view the Iranian revolution as an event that has turned the clock back. Rather, it seems that the process of modernization/development has in fact continued in spite of, and sometimes through, the process of Islamization. The modernization process has brought improvements in some areas, such as education, but it has also led to a great deal of disappointment and frustration, manifested for example in high unemployment rates, particularly among educated women.

1

Gender and Globalization

The Iranian Experience

JENNIFER C. OLMSTED

THE WAYS GLOBALIZATION has reshaped employment patterns and its implications for gender relations have been the subject of a number of studies. Few studies, though, have looked explicitly at this question for Iran. In this chapter I examine women's employment in Iran within the context of globalization. Iran provides an interesting example of how both internal and external economic policies can shape socioeconomic outcomes and the ways such policies can gender employment outcomes. Insights can be gained not only about the situation in Iran, but also more generally about the process of globalization and how diverse that experience has been.

In the case of Iran, one obvious question concerns how Iran has experienced globalization since the establishment of the Islamic Republic. What has that meant both in terms of the economic decisions that individuals and the government have made since the 1979 Revolution, and in terms of how other nations have responded to Iran? Certainly, in recent years fierce debates have taken place within Iran about what level of openness is appropriate for the economy. In addition, Iran has experienced various population shifts, with members of the educated elite leaving the country, while at the same time the country has had to absorb a fairly large Afghan refugee population. And last but certainly not least, since the 1979 Revolution the United States has punished Iran through a policy of economic isolation. All of these factors are part of Iran's globalization experience and suggest ways that both external and internal policy decisions have played a role in shaping employment outcomes in Iran. These policies may not only have a differential impact by sex, but also by class. It is also important to ask in what ways the Iranian experience is unique and/or typical, by comparing it to that of other countries in the region.

(Economic) Globalization

The term *globalization* is generally used to describe various technological and policy changes that have caused the world to "shrink."[1] The economic factors that are generally stressed in discussions of globalization are increases in the exchange of goods (and more recently shifts in the location of service production), greater capital mobility and increased human mobility.[2] Much of the globalization literature has focused on countries that went through a debt crisis and on the ways that the World Bank and the International Monetary Fund (IMF) became involved in pushing those countries to open up to international trade and foreign capital investments, a process that is generally referred to as structural adjustment. (See for example Stiglitz 2003 and Buckman 2004.) In discussing the concept of globalization, though, it is important to emphasize the diversity of globalization experiences, and the fact that just as the international community has pushed some countries to open up, in other cases external powers, particularly the United States, have pushed to economically isolate countries. The case of Iran is particularly complex,

---

1. A growing literature that examines various cultural and political changes that have occurred as a result of intensified globalization has also emerged, but the focus in this chapter will be on the link between economics, gender, and globalization in the context of Iran.
2. For a more general discussion of economic globalization in the context of Iran, see Esfahani and Pesaran (2009).

because within Iran fierce debates have taken place concerning the level of economic openness (Bahramitash 2004; Marossi 2006), but at the same time, it is also among those countries upon which the United States has imposed sanctions. As such, the Iranian case provides an example of how complex the relationship between a nation and the global economy can be, and the reasons why the term *globalization* needs to be carefully defined.

In addition to the general literature on globalization, a growing body of work also exists that examines how men's and women's economic experiences have differed during this era of increased globalization. Given that structural adjustment policies often involved reduced government spending and trade barriers, the two literatures are often intertwined. In the case of MENA, the World Bank and the IMF have long been advocating for reductions in the size of government. Feminists have expressed concerns about what impact this reduction might have. For example, in Egypt, Mervat Hatem speculated early in Egypt's structural adjustment period that the public sector would shrink, and that this shrinkage would in turn reduce women's access to paid employment (Hatem 1994). Ragui Assaad instead found that the Egyptian government did not reduce the size of government, but instead froze wages, which led to inflation-adjusted wages in government employment falling over time (Assaad 2005). While men fled the public sector, women remained. So the result was not a reduction in women's jobs, but instead an increased feminization of the public sector and an increasing wage gap. Although a number of scholars have examined how Iranian employment patterns have changed over time, to my knowledge none of them has focused in depth on how structural adjustment policies in Iran have affected women's access to employment, because the major focus has been on the impact of the revolution.

While reducing the size of government has often meant fewer jobs for women, trade openness has been seen as a way of increasing women's access to paid employment, which in turn is seen as a sign of increased women's empowerment. Some feminists, though, have argued that more caution is needed in reaching this conclusion, because there is also evidence that the work conditions facing women are often poor and that women have become increasingly vulnerable to the double burden and to poverty with increased globalization. Another issue that has been raised is whether the early trends in terms of women's increased participation are part of a long-term trend or a temporary phenomenon (Berik 1999). Particularly in the case of MENA, the question of whether increased openness does lead to rising women's participation is worth exploring, given that much of the existing literature focuses on East Asia and Latin America.

Valentine Moghadam is one scholar who has examined openness and its impact on women's employment in MENA. She argues that countries such as Morocco and Tunisia, which had more open policies, also saw higher female participation rates (see V. Moghadam 1995b; Karshenas and V. Moghadam 2001). Assaad, on the other hand, points out that in the case of Egypt, increased openness did not lead to a higher rate of participation in manufacturing for women, thus suggesting that the link between trade openness and women being drawn into export-oriented manufacturing is not universal (2005). So one question this paper will address is where Iran fits within this discussion of the link between manufactured exports and women's employment.

With the rise to power of Rafsanjani, in 1989, Iran began implementing various economic reforms, similar to the types of structural adjustment policies being put in place elsewhere (Bahramitash 2004; Marossi 2006). But the Iranian case is complicated by the fact that it has also been subject to economic sanctions imposed by the United States, which has meant that even as Iranian interest in participating in the global economy increased, the country was restricted from full participation owing to the decision of an outside government. While a considerable literature focuses on the role outside pressure has played in pushing countries to open up (which is less the case in Iran, where a debt crisis did not precipitate increased openness), far less discussion has been devoted to the question of the opposite phenomenon: countries forcibly isolated from the global economy through sanctions or other tools of economic isolation.

Some form of economic boycott against Iran has been in place since 1979, when President Carter initiated the policy.[3] Sanctions have been renewed and in some cases strengthened by subsequent presidents, particularly by President Clinton, who imposed a broader ban on trade and investment on Iran in 1995. In 2000 these restrictions were eased somewhat, but more recently, the United States has again been pushing for a more comprehensive set of sanctions, operating through the UN.

How effective has the boycott been? According to Akbar Torbat, the sanctions have imposed a cost on Iran, by raising the cost of capital and reducing export markets, particularly in the non-oil sector (2005). He estimates that GDP (gross domestic product) has been reduced by on average 1.1 percent annually owing to the sanctions. More important for the purposes of this chapter is the fact that Torbat argues that sanctions impacted the carpet industry in a particularly negative manner, with that sector declining in 1966 to "almost one-third of its pre-sanctions year" (2005, 416). This fact suggests that not only does the imposition of sanctions have implications for macroeconomic outcomes, it may also reshape domestic employment patterns, which in turn could have implications in terms of women's employment options.

Iran has also, not unlike other parts of the region, experienced globalization through the process of migration. Not only has the country experienced a rather large out-migration of citizens, particularly the more educated ones, in the form of a brain drain, but

---

3. See the US Treasury Department website for various documents that explain the nature and duration of sanctions against Iran. http://www.treas.gov/offices/enforcement/ofac/programs/iran/iran.shtml.

Iran has also had to absorb large numbers of low-skilled refugees, particularly from neighboring Afghanistan.

Data on Female Employment

Before discussing the Iranian case in more detail, it is worthwhile to point out that obtaining consistent data on women's economic activities is generally a challenge (Anker 1998). Iran is no exception to this problem. Measuring female labor force participation is fraught with difficulties, because often women's labor is hidden. For example Richard and Martha Anker estimate that female employment levels in Egypt vary from 6.2 to 41.3 percent, depending on the way work is defined (Anker and Anker 1995). The World Bank more recently discussed some of the problems with measuring female labor force participation in Iran, Egypt, Jordan, Lebanon, and Tunisia, suggesting that although scholars, statisticians, and policy makers have become more aware that this is an issue in recent years, these problems are far from being resolved (World Bank 2004, 87).

In the case of Iran, official statistics reported by the Census Bureau suggest that women's labor force participation remains quite low. There also appears to be considerable variation in the numbers reported, depending on whether census or labor force survey data are used. In 1976 Iranian census data suggested that the labor force participation rate for women was 12.9 percent. Following the revolution there appeared to be a drop in women's participation, which in 1986 was measured to be 8.2 percent. In 2006 the rate was similar to the prerevolution rate, at 12.5 percent. But data from labor force surveys suggest a considerably higher level of participation. For example, the 2005 labor force survey provides an estimate of female labor force participation of 19.2 percent. Thus if one were to take the 1996, 2005, and 2006 data at their face value, in 1996 about two million Iranian women were working, and over a ten-year period the number more than doubled, to 4.5 million, but then in just one year participation dropped by over one million, an unlikely pattern. Comparing across data sets is generally not advised, and in the literature labor force surveys are often recognized as being better instruments for capturing female employment than census data.[4]

When one looks at the data provided by the ILO, particularly the numbers estimated as part of the Key Indicators of the Labor Market (KILM) data, a third picture of female employment patterns in Iran emerges. The KILM data, which unfortunately are not available for the prerevolution period, report labor force participation rates for Iranian women that are considerably higher, and rising far more rapidly in recent years. In 1986 the ILO estimated that women over the age of fifteen had a labor force participation rate of 20.6 percent, which was slightly below the average for the region, at 23 percent. By 2005, though, the ILO was estimating that 38.6 percent of women were working, suggesting that labor force participation had almost doubled. The data that are being reported by the ILO for Iran suggest that the ILO feels that government statistics severely underestimate women's employment for a number of reasons. Iranian estimates of labor force participation, for example, use a different age cutoff in their estimates of labor force participation and so are not directly comparable (although they can easily be adjusted to be comparable). The ILO uses fifteen as their cutoff age, while Iran used ten for the 1976 census and used six for the 1986 census. Also, Iran does not follow the ILO convention of including "persons engaged in the production of goods or services for own final use" in its labor force statistics, many of whom are unpaid agricultural workers, and thus underestimates female labor force participation in particular.[5] Given that ILO KILM data have been adjusted to make them more comparable across countries, it is preferable to use these data in making cross-country comparisons, cognizant of the fact that because they

---

4. Despite its shortcomings in terms of estimating female employment levels, researchers continue to use census data, which may provide other advantages.

5. Between July 11, 2008, and July 14, 2008, I exchanged a number of e-mails with ILO staff members Steve Kapsos, Sara Elder, and Valentina Stoevska, who were very helpful in explaining to me how KILM and Iranian census estimates differ.

are econometric estimates rather than actual figures, they may not precisely reflect Iranian women's participation rates.

It is worth noting that most of the studies of Iranian women's employment in the postrevolution period have relied heavily on census statistics, which are the most conservative in terms of their estimates of women's employment and clearly underestimate women's participation in a number of ways. A couple of questions thus arise. One concerns whether the previous analyses would have come to different conclusions had they used other data sets. Another concerns the question of whether any changes were made to the way census data were measured over time. As was noted above, one change that has been documented is that the age cutoff changed between 1976 and 1986. If the statistics office made this change, one wonders what other changes they might have made. Certainly under normal circumstances it makes sense to assume that census data, although they may underestimate female employment, would be subject to the same error biases decade after decade, but in the case of Iran it is worth speculating about whether this was the case, given the change of regime that took place and the differences in ideology between the two governments, with the first putting itself forth as a Westernizing, modernizing force, eager to show that it was incorporating women into the public sphere (F. Moghadam 1994) and the second bent, particularly in the immediate postrevolution period, on portraying itself as having veered from the path down which the Shah had been pushing the country. It is possible that the Shah's regime had an interest in inflating female labor force participation figures, while the Islamist regime was trying to downplay this phenomenon, particularly initially.

Overall Female Labor Force Trends in Iran

A number of authors have looked at women's employment in Iran, comparing patterns in the prerevolution and postrevolution periods. These studies rely on census data and only analyze data through 1996 (F. Moghadam 1994; Alizadeh 2001; V. Moghadam 2003;

Nomani and Behdad 2006). The data suggest that between 1976 and 1986 women's labor force participation dropped considerably, from 12.9 to 8.2 percent, and previous studies link this decline to the rise to power of Islamists.

While there is no doubt that the introduction of a conservative government in Iran played some role in reshaping female employment, either directly or indirectly, I think it is worthwhile to delve in more detail into the question of how both internal and external forces may have played a role in shaping women's employment options in the prerevolutionary and postrevolutionary periods, as well as to revisit the question of data accuracy in light of political changes. I suggest that in addition to a more conservative regime's impacting female employment, a number of other factors could have contributed to the trend observed in the census data. The first, and I would argue most important, concerns the role that the US-imposed boycott may have played in reducing female participation in the carpet-weaving industry (and possibly other fields as well). The second concerns the role that both in-migration and out-migration may have played. Finally, although Farhad Nomani and Sohrab Behdad raise and dismiss the suggestion that the method for collecting the census data may have changed in the aftermath of the revolution (Nomani and Behdad 2006), I think it may be worth revisiting this question, in particular in light of certain trends that appear in the data over time.

Concerning the first issue, as Bahramitash and Esfahani (forthcoming and this volume) point out, the manufacturing sector in Iran declined in the postrevolution period. US sanctions, Torbat argues (2005), had a particularly devastating impact on the carpet industry, which also happened to be one of the primary sectors that employed less educated women. Data provided by Zahra Karimi (chapter 5) suggest that the number of women employed in textiles (most of whom are carpet weavers) declined from 606,646 to 337,436 between 1976 and 1986, while the overall number of workers in the sector declined from 1,010,246 to 830,286.

This decline raises a number of questions concerning the impact that US sanctions have had not only on women in the carpet industry, but also on overall female labor force participation. While it is difficult to provide a precise number without more elaborate data analysis, if one assumes that at least 30 percent of the decline in women's job opportunities in manufacturing can be attributed to the sanctions, which is somewhat on the low side given how much and how rapidly carpet exports declined, and given that more than 50 percent of female employment was in the manufacturing sector in 1976, this suggests that of the overall decline in labor force participation (from 12.9 to 8.2), 2 percentage points of that decline could have been explained by US policies.[6]

Although Nomani and Behdad mention briefly the impact of US sanctions (2006), they do not examine the impact this policy change may have had on overall female participation. Instead they focus on the ideological shift of the Iranian government. In doing so, they argue that a decline such as the one observed in Iran is unprecedented. But as I have argued elsewhere, two other communities in the Middle East have experienced either stagnating or declining female labor force participation rates, owing to isolation policies imposed by outsiders. These two communities are Iraq, which suffered through years of sanctions, and Palestine, which has been increasingly economically isolated by Israel in recent years (see Olmsted 2007 and 2008 for more details).[7] The Iranian case, I would argue, is far less

---

6. Author's calculations. I am assuming that women in this sector would have few other employment possibilities and so are likely to have dropped out of the labor market when these jobs disappeared. The number would of course be smaller if the women stayed in the labor market and either entered the ranks of the unemployed or found other work. The number would also be smaller if other factors contributed to the decline of the carpet industry. Thanks to Hadi Esfahani for pointing this out to me. On the other hand, given that Torbat argues that the carpet industry was reduced to one-third of its former size owing to sanctions (2005), the number could also be larger.

7. A third country, Turkey, has also experienced declining female labor force participation rates in recent years. Turkey, though, looks very different from Iran, Palestine, and Iraq, because it has historically had some of the highest labor force participation rates in the region. A fairly in-depth analysis by Tansil (2002) suggests

extreme, in the sense that the negative economic impact this change has had on the *overall macroeconomy* has not been that great,[8] but one common thread that emerges in all three cases is that forced economic isolation has contributed to a decline in women's employment opportunities. And given that a considerable literature points to how economic liberalization often is followed by an increase in female labor force participation, it is not surprising that the imposition of some form of economic sanctions would have the opposite effect.

Other factors linked to globalization could have contributed to the decline in women's employment as well. William Carrington and Enrica Detragiache, for example, argue that Iran has one of the highest brain drains globally, yet to my knowledge there appears to be very little research analyzing the impact of the brain drain on the Iranian economy and on women's employment (1998). An article by M. Malek (1991) does focus on part of this question by looking at the impact the brain drain has had on one sector of the Iranian economy: health care. He argues that about 20 percent of doctors, 14 percent of dentists, and as many as 45 percent of pharmacists left in the aftermath of the revolution. His focus is on the impact this exodus had on the ability of Iran to deliver health care to its people,[9] and he is concerned about the quality of instruction that occurred in the aftermath of the exodus, but an interesting corollary to his questions is how this out-migration of professionals might have affected Ira-

---

that the primary reason for the decline in Turkey is the transition away from a primarily agricultural economy, because the rate at which women are being absorbed into the manufacturing and service sectors of the economy is slower than the rate at which they are leaving agriculture.

8. While Torbat estimates a rather moderate decline of 1 percent per annum owing to the sanctions in Iran (2005), Iraq and Palestine, in contrast, have experienced much more drastic declines in GDP (Olmsted 2007).

9. He does not, though, look at health care outcomes, and the postrevolution data from Iran do suggest that health care outcomes did not suffer a setback, but instead have continued to improve. Thanks to Roksana Bahramitash for pointing this out to me.

nian labor markets. It is not clear whether more educated men were more likely to migrate than women, or vice versa, but two issues are worth speculating about. The first concerns the initial impact of this brain drain on female labor force participation. Given that highly educated women in general have higher labor force participation, the exodus of a large segment of the elite is likely another factor that led to the decline in female labor force participation that was observed after the revolution. This factor would suggest that a number of elite women did not simply drop out of the labor force, but many of them also left the country. My "back of the napkin" estimates suggest that if about 20 percent of educated, employed women left, labor force participation could have declined by 0.4 percent (from 12.9 to 12.5) owing to the brain drain.[10]

Although substantially less than the impact of sanctions on working-class women's employment, these two factors together could explain at least 2.4 points (just over half) of the total 4.7-point decline. This explanation does not preclude arguing that the rise of an Islamic government led to a decline in the female labor force, given that both the sanctions and the brain drain occurred in response to the change in government, but it does provide a somewhat more nuanced picture of the mechanism whereby this decline happened. It also raises the interesting question of what changes in class structure occurred as a result of the exodus of a large portion of the educated elite, which would have opened up various opportunities for previously lower-class men and women.

At the same time that Iran experienced a considerable brain drain, it also had to absorb a large group of poor, low-skilled Afghans. In fact, according to the UN Refugee Agency (UNHCR 2007), Iran and Pakistan were the largest recipients of refugees in

---

10. Professional women made up about 14 percent of all working women in 1976. If 20 percent of these women not only left the labor market, but also left Iran altogether, then this would lead to a drop in both the number of women working and the total number of women available for work from 12.9 to 12.5 percent.

the world, with each hosting about one million, resulting in about 1.5 percent of the people in Iran being refugees. This situation raises more difficult data questions. Are Afghani refugees included in labor force estimates and if so, how might an influx of these refugees have impacted overall female labor force participation and labor markets more generally? One of the issues that Karimi points out in chapter 5 is that the influx of these refugees had an effect on unskilled labor markets, driving down wages and thus making paid employment less desirable for working-class Iranian women. So the influx of refugees could both directly affect labor force participation estimates (if these individuals are included in the statistics) and could also reshape labor markets, leading to Iranian women's reevaluating their decision about whether to work. In the absence of more detailed data, it is difficult to determine how much these various global factors, such as trade relations and migration patterns, contributed to declining women's labor force participation, but it is certainly safe to conclude that the ideological shift of the government alone probably does not explain the entire pattern.

The issue of data collection also remains unresolved. Nomani and Behdad dismiss the idea that the census data might not be comparable between 1976 and 1986 (Nomani and Behdad 2006), but some of the data trends are difficult to explain empirically, suggesting the need to explore this question further. For example, why does the number of women in the textiles industry appear to drop considerably between 1976 and 1986 and then rise considerably between 1986 and 1996? These data suggest that this industry went from being fairly feminized (with 60 percent of workers being women) to being somewhat defeminized (41 percent in 1986) and then refeminized again in 1996 (59 percent), a rather unlikely pattern. Are these data to be believed, or is it possible that the agency collecting the data was less careful about documenting women's contributions to the economy in the first census following the revolution, perhaps because their conservative ideology made it difficult for them to "see" all those working women? Or perhaps households became more hesitant to report female participation in the postrevolution period, because they wanted to be seen as being in line with the gender ideology being espoused by the state. For whatever reason, the data for 1986 appear to be outliers in a number of ways, raising questions about how easy it is to simply compare the immediate postrevolution data with the prerevolution statistics on female employment.

Comparing Iran to Other Countries in MENA

If comparing data across time in Iran is fraught with difficulties, so too is comparing data from Iran with data from other countries. Still, I venture to point out some interesting patterns observed in comparing Iranian socioeconomic statistics with those of other countries within the region. Table 1.1 provides KILM estimates of female labor force participation, as well as life expectancy, fertility, and female literacy indicators that are often of interest to policy makers concerned about women's socioeconomic situation. The KILM data suggest a very different picture from the census data. According to the KILM data, while the entire MENA region experienced a rather striking rise in female participation in recent years (averaging about 9 percentage points in the past ten years), Iran stands out as being one of the countries that has experienced the largest increase. The same (in reverse) is true of fertility patterns. Whereas in 1970/75 Iran's total fertility rate was estimated to be about 6.4 children per woman, which was about average for the region, by 2001 that number had dropped to 2.1, the second lowest fertility rate in the region, behind Tunisia. Iran also has a contraceptive prevalence rate that is well above the global mean of 59 percent and is the highest in the region, which no doubt in part explains the shift from high to low fertility (World Bank 2004, 48). In fact a number of scholars have discussed the rather abrupt change in Iran's population policy and how closely policy and changes in fertility outcomes are linked (Roudi-Fahimi 1999; Salehi-Isfahani 2001; Roudi-Fahimi 2002; Hakimian 2006), but less work has been done to explore why Iranian women's labor force trajectory may differ from that of other countries in the region. It seems pretty clear that the changes in both of these statistics are connected, given that with falling fertility rates women's home responsibilities are often reduced, making entry into the labor market easier.[11] Few, if any, authors, though, have remarked on the relative shift in Iran's position, which, according to the KILM labor force participation data, has led to Iran's rising from twelfth to fourth, just behind Israel, Kuwait, and the UAE, in terms of female employment, and from tenth to second in terms of fertility. These data suggest that fertility in Iran has dropped very fast and that the ILO at least estimates that particularly in the past ten years Iranian women have been entering the labor force in large numbers.

As argued by Bahramitash and Esfahani (forthcoming and this volume), education has played an important role in changing how many women work and where they find employment. Similar patterns have been found in other parts of MENA (Shakhatreh 1995; Olmsted 1996 and 2001; Assaad and El-Hamidi 2001; Tansil 2002), but if looked at from a comparative perspective, it does not appear that the change in Iran's relative position is owing to a more dramatic shift in literacy than has occurred in other parts of MENA. Certainly Iran's female literacy rate has risen considerably, from 55 percent in 1995 to 76.8 by 2005, but Iran's relative position in this case has shifted relatively little, with Iran going from being slightly below the mean to slightly above the mean during this period. As a result, Iran, which ranked tenth in terms of female literacy in the 1970s, still holds the same relative position today. Part of the reason Iran does not stand out in terms of literacy is that the entire region has made rapid gains in terms of literacy, with the youngest cohorts in the majority of countries having over a 90 percent literacy rate.

---

11. Economists have long postulated that declining fertility and rising female employment are linked, although the causal relationship is not entirely clear (Browning 1992), nor is the relationship between these two variables always negative. In Europe for instance the relationship is now positive (S. P. Morgan 2003). See Olmsted 2003 for a more in-depth discussion of the relationship between fertility and women's employment in the context of MENA.

Table 1.1 Female Labor Force Participation, Female Literacy, and Total Fertility Rate for MENA Countries, Various Years*

| | Labor Force Participation | | | | |
| | 1995 | | 2005 | | 2005–1995 |
Country	Rate	Rank	Rate	Rank	Change
Algeria	8.0	19	35.7	7	27.7
Bahrain	17.0	12	29.3	11	12.3
Egypt	9.0	16	20.1	18	11.1
Iran	19.0	10	38.6	3	19.6
Iraq	23.0	7	13.0	20	-10.0
Israel	45.6	1	50.1	1	4.5
Jordan	10.0	15	27.5	14	17.5
Kuwait	27.0	3	49.0	2	22.0
Lebanon	25.0	6	32.4	8	7.4
Libya			32.1	9	
Morocco	21.0	9	26.8	15	5.8
Oman	9.0	16	22.7	17	13.7
Palestinian Territories	14.0	14	10.3	21	-3.7
Qatar	19.0	10	36.3	6	17.3
Saudi Arabia	9.0	16	17.6	19	8.6
Sudan	26.0	4	23.7	16	-2.3
Syria	16.0	13	38.6	3	22.6
Tunisia	26.0	4	28.6	12	2.6
Turkey	45.0	2	27.7	13	-17.3
UAE	23.0	7	38.2	5	15.2
Yemen			29.7	10	
Average	20.6		29.9		9.2
Literacy Correlation	0.23		0.37		
Fertility Correlation	-0.56		-0.57		2.6

Sources: International Labor Office (ILO) LABORSTA data available through KILM database, www.ilo.org/public/english/employment/strat/kilm/index.htm.
Literacy and Fertility Data, United Nations, http://data.un.org/Data.aspx?q=null&d=GenderStat&f=in ID%3a14.

* The LFP and literacy data are ranked from 1 to 21, with 1 being the highest rate and 21 being the lowest. The fertility data are ranked from 1 to 21, with 1 being the lowest and 20 being the highest.

	Female Literacy			Total Fertility			
1995		2005		1990–1995		2000–2005	
Rate	Rank	Rate	Rank	Rate	Rank	Rate	Rank
44.1	14	60.1	17	4.1	10	2.5	6
76.7	4	83.6	8	3.4	6	2.5	6
36.1	16	59.4	18	3.9	8	3.2	13
55.0	10	76.8	10	4.3	13	2.1	2
40.9	15	64.2	16	5.7	17	4.9	19
		97.7	1	2.9	1	2.9	10
75.4	5	84.7	7	5.1	15	3.5	14
72.9	6	91.0	3	3.2	5	2.3	4
89.0	1	93.6	2	3.0	3	2.3	4
57.4	9	74.8	11	4.1	11	3.0	12
27.7	18	39.6	20	3.7	7	2.5	6
		73.5	13	6.3	19	3.7	16
62.0	8	88.0	5	6.5	20	5.6	20
77.4	2	88.6	4	4.1	12	2.9	10
46.3	13	69.3	14	5.4	16	3.8	17
30.6	17	51.8	19	5.8	18	4.8	18
51.6	11	73.6	12	4.9	14	3.5	14
50.2	12	65.3	15	3.1	4	2.0	1
70.1	7	79.6	9	2.9	2	2.2	3
77.3	3	87.8	6	3.9	9	2.5	6
		34.7	21	7.7	21	6.0	21
57.8		73.2		4.5		3.3	
				-0.37		-0.38	
50.2	15	65.3	15	3.1	4	2.0	1

These data trends suggest that in looking at Iran in comparison with the rest of the region, the decline in fertility may have played more of a role in changing Iran's relative position in the overall rankings than did the rise in education. This is not to say that education did not play an extremely important role in driving changes in overall employment patterns. And in fact, it is difficult to separate these two effects, which often move together.[12]

Sectoral Analysis

While a look at women's overall employment rates in conjunction with literacy and fertility outcomes can provide some insight into the question of what factors may have altered labor supply, it is also worth exploring how the structure of the economy has changed, causing a change in the demand for women's labor over time. Industry-level data can show which sectors have been absorbing increasing numbers of female workers and, again, how Iran compares to other countries in the region. Industry-disaggregated data can also be used to look at the level of occupational segregation in a country.

The ILO LABORSTA data presented in table 1.2 provide employment broken down by industry for most MENA countries.[13] Two patterns that stand out in looking at these data are that throughout the region a large proportion of working women are professionals,

---

12. Measuring the interaction between fertility, education, and female labor force participation is difficult, because causality can go in multiple directions and there may be a direct as well as an indirect impact of each of these variables on each other. While a number of analyses have looked at the impact of fertility and education on employment within individual countries, a cross-country analysis that looks at the relative importance of each of these factors has to my knowledge not been carried out for MENA.

13. Here again the question of data accuracy arises. As these data are taken from the censuses and do not include persons engaged in the production of goods or services for own final use, they may not accurately reflect the relative distribution of women across various sectors. In particular, women's participation in the agricultural sector may be undercounted.

primarily in the educational and health care sectors, and that a relatively small number of women are in sales and manufacturing. All four of these sectors have been to various degrees defined as stereotypical female fields (Anker 1998), but interestingly, in the MENA region, neither manufacturing nor sales has become feminized to date. The case of Iran thus is of particular interest for a number of reasons. First, although still relatively small in comparison to other sectors, the percentage of women categorized as working in sales has risen faster in Iran than in other parts of MENA. Also, although declining in relative size, Iran's manufacturing sector continues to be the largest in terms of employment of women. Iranian women in fact have high levels of representation in manufacturing (as a percentage of total female employment) compared both to Iranian men and to women in the rest of the region. (In terms of counts, more men tend to be employed in manufacturing in most countries, because men have higher labor force participation rates.)

Countries where more than 20 percent of all working women are employed in manufacturing are relatively rare in the region. The list includes only Algeria, Iran, and Morocco. Compared to other countries in the region, Iran thus stands out quite starkly, given that in 1996 33 percent of all employed females were employed in the manufacturing sector and in 2006 23 percent were, compared to an average for the region of 10 percent. Iran in fact ranks above Morocco, one of the countries that Valentine Moghadam identified as being particularly open and as encouraging manufacturing exports, which she argued also explained the relatively high levels of labor force participation among Moroccan women. Moghadam, though, does not identify Iran as one of the countries in the region where manufacturing has been an important sector for absorbing women's labor, primarily because her focus is on what she calls the modern manufacturing sector, and she no doubt would categorize carpet weaving as a traditional form of manufacturing labor. With the exception of the 1986 data, Iran stands out as being one of the few MENA countries where a large portion of employed women have been located in the manufacturing sector in recent years, even when the country

Table 1.2 Distribution of Female Employment by Sector for MENA Countries with Available Data, Various Years* (Percentage of Total Female Employment)

Country	Year	Agriculture	Manufacturing	Sales
Algeria	2003	10.9	22.5	2.9
Bahrain	1991	0.0	5.9	3.8
Bahrain	2001	0.1	12.1	5.6
Egypt	1997	40.4	6.9	6.5
Egypt	2003	39.0	4.8	6.3
Iran	1996	16.7	33.0	2.2
Iran	2006	14.5	23.4	5.3
Iraq	2004	32.6	6.5	5.1
Jordan	2003	2.0	10.6	5.5
Morocco	2002	57.1	18.5	3.7
Morocco	2005	61.4	15.5	5.1
Oman	1996	4.7	5.2	6.9
Oman	2000	5.3	11.6	6.2
Palestinian Territories	1996	29.0	15.2	8.8
Palestinian Territories	2004	33.7	8.0	7.1
Qatar	1997	0.0	0.4	1.5
Qatar	2004	0.1	0.6	3.3
Saudi Arabia	1999	1.0	1.2	0.5
Saudi Arabia	2002	0.6	1.1	0.7
Syria	1994	29.4	14.5	2.8
Syria	2003	49.1	6.8	3.5
United Arab Emirates	1995	0.1	12.1	6.5
Yemen	1994	86.8	2.6	1.1

Sources: International Labor Office (ILO) LABORSTA data available through KILM database, www.ilo.org/public/english/employment/strat/kilm/index.htm.
Literacy and Fertility Data, United Nations, http://data.un.org/Data.aspx?q=null&d=GenderStat&f=inID%3a14.

* While for most MENA countries these six sectors made up over 80% of all female employment, in some Gulf countries, the category "Private Households with Employed Persons" accounted for a large percentage of female employment. Hence the large "other" category for these countries.

Public Admin. & Defense	Education	Health & Social Work	Other
12.1	24.4	10.9	16.3
10.0	16.3	8.2	55.8
7.1	13.1	7.3	54.7
11.4	22.4	6.0	6.4
12.8	22.5	7.3	7.3
5.6	26.0	6.7	9.8
2.7	24.0	8.9	21.2
16.3	29.8	4.5	5.2
5.1	40.6	13.8	22.4
3.7	13.1	—	3.9
14.9	—	—	3.1
26.0	32.8	9.3	15.1
8.7	41.4	14.1	12.7
5.2	27.4	7.6	6.8
5.8	28.0	8.2	9.2
5.9	21.8	7.6	62.8
9.5	19.3	9.6	57.6
2.5	40.0	8.5	46.3
2.2	41.7	6.4	47.3
14.5	29.8	2.3	6.7
12.4	21.6	2.5	4.1
4.4	16.4	7.2	53.3
2.5	3.5	1.0	2.5

remained relatively closed and was subject to US sanctions. This fact suggests that in the absence of US sanctions, women's participation in manufacturing would have been even higher.

While the US sanctions doubtless had an impact, the resilience of this sector and the fact that it was still absorbing almost one-quarter of all Iranian women workers in 2006 despite the impact of the sanctions are noteworthy. Of course another globalization-linked phenomenon that can help explain why Iran remained competitive in this sector, despite the sanctions, is the influx of Afghan refugees, who may have kept wages cheap in the sector, but who also may have driven down economic returns. It is possible that it was only because of the availability of cheap refugee labor that Iranian carpets have remained competitive internationally.

It is also worth noting that the long-term impact of sanctions on the carpet industry in Iran is probably understated, because by boycotting Iranian carpets the United States has set in motion a shift in production loci. Zahra Karimi points out that India and China began producing "Persian" carpets in response to US demand and the inability of buyers to access Iranian carpets. While it is of course possible that globalization would have led to this shift anyway, given that the speed with which markets adjust to lower costs has increased, it is also no doubt the case that the US boycott sped the decline in the dominance of Iran's carpet sector globally, by providing competitors with easier access to markets. This situation would suggest that even once sanctions were eased, as they were in 2000, it would be difficult for Iran to regain its earlier market position because its competitors had been able to establish themselves more firmly in the market.

If the manufacturing sector is shrinking but women's rates of employment are rising, where are Iranian women increasingly working and how does this situation compare with the rest of the region? As Bahramitash and Esfahani (forthcoming and this volume) illustrate, much of the growth in women's employment in Iran is in the service sector. In this regard, Iran looks quite similar to the rest of the region. In particular, large numbers of women in MENA work in education. On average in the region about 25 percent of women workers are in the education sector, and this is also the case for Iran. The percentage of women employed in health and social work is also about the same as in the entire region, with the average in these sectors being 8.6 percent for the region and with these sectors in Iran absorbing 9 percent of women in 2006.

Interestingly, though, women in Iran rely less on the public sector than women in other countries in the region. According to recent data reported by the World Bank (2004, 80), in 2000 women in Iran were among those least likely, within the region, to rely on the public sector for employment, with a percentage of around 20. The only countries with smaller percentages were Morocco and Lebanon.

In Iran, in fact, men are more dependent on public sector employment than women, with a rate closer to 30 percent. This male dependence is in sharp contrast to countries such as Egypt and Jordan, where the increasing feminization of the public sector is quite marked (see for example Assaad and Arntz [2005] for the case of Egypt and a more general discussion in World Bank 2004). Nomani and Behdad (2006, 151), who are looking more at changes rather than absolute levels, argue that the "state sector prefers male employees at the upper-level work groups," because the state has "a firm ideological requirement for its employees and many professional and highly skilled women refuse to conform to the code of Islamic conduct." Although this preference may be true in terms of looking at changes that occurred between 1976 and 1986, data provided by the World Bank suggest that it is precisely educated women, not unlike in other parts of MENA, who have access to these public sector jobs, whereas for their less educated counterparts, public sector employment is not an option. The World Bank reports that in Iran more than 32 percent of men in the public sector had primary schooling or less, but among less educated women that rate was only 6 percent. Similar patterns, and in some cases even more of a bias in favor of educated women (and men), can be seen in other MENA communities. In Jordan, for instance, fewer than 4 percent of public sector female employees have a primary school education or less, while among men the number was 22 percent. Among Palestinians, similarly, 4 percent of working women with a primary education or less work in the public sector, but men also are more educated, with only 13 percent of men working for the government having primary education or less.

The World Bank data suggest that Iranian women's employment in the public sector, as a percentage of their total employment, has declined considerably in recent years. This decline also suggests that in comparison to other countries in the region, Iran has been one of the most effective in implementing reforms that involve reducing the size of the public sector. So is the low rate of dependency on the public sector among Iranian women to be viewed in a positive or a negative light? The World Bank has certainly expressed concern, not only about large public sectors, but also about the high rates of public sector employment among women in particular, and so should view recent changes in Iran in a positive light (2004). On the other hand, there are many reasons why women prefer public sector employment, not only in Iran but in other parts of the world, because of the excellent benefits the government often offers, as well as because there is some evidence that wage differences between male and female workers are less among government sector workers (Tansel 1999). It is thus worth raising the question of what the effect this drop in public sector jobs has had on women. Has the wage gap increased in Iran, for instance, in recent years? Is the declining public sector related to the rise in female unemployment that has been observed in recent years?

Unlike in Egypt, in Iran women do appear to be being absorbed into the private sector, but primarily in informal work. But female unemployment is also rising. Educated women, whose eligibility for and expectations concerning government employment are greater, have likely suffered the most from changes in the size of Iran's public sector. How much the shrinking of the public sector is linked to rising unemployment among women is one question that has been raised in the general structural adjustment literature, as well as by Valentine Moghadam (2005), but needs to be addressed in more detail in the case of Iran. Are the ranks of the informal sector being filled mostly with less educated women, or are more educated women, who would have previously had access to government sector jobs, also relying more on informal sector work?

Certainly women's representation in the informal sector is high throughout the region (World Bank 2004, 85). Iran is no exception to this finding. Only Tunisia, the Palestinian territories, and Yemen had higher rates of informal participation among women than Iran (World Bank 2004, 82). So it is not clear that a reduction in women's employment in the public sector is such a positive accomplishment, given that the alternative employment options offer more tenuous employment conditions that are well known to the informal sector.

And even as these various research questions remain unanswered, the reliability of the data when it comes to unemployment rates is also of some concern. The World Bank, for example, reports that female unemployment in Iran was 11.3 percent for 2000, and slightly lower than male unemployment (2004). But the ILO data suggest that female unemployment has been consistently higher than men's in recent years. And, although it appears that overall rates of female unemployment may have declined a bit in recent years, the number the ILO reports is considerably higher than the World Bank figure,[14] with a rate of 17.1 percent being reported for 2005.

The data presented in table 1.2 suggest that men and women have differing employment opportunities, but even more detailed analysis is needed to address the question of how pervasive occupational segregation is in Iran. Richard Anker, Helina Melkas, and Ailsa Korten calculate an index of dissimilarity (ID) for Iran that is above 0.6 (0 is no segregation; 1 is perfect segregation). This ID is considerably higher than in other countries for which they calculated the index, both in and outside MENA (Anker, Melkas, and Korten 2003). Earlier work by Parvin Alizadeh suggests not only that occupational segregation in Iran is high, but that the labor market

---

14. The World Bank used Iran's 2000 Household Expenditure and Income Survey (HEIS) for their unemployment estimates, while acknowledging that the survey was not ideal for measuring unemployment.

has become more segregated in recent years (Alizadeh and Harper 2003). Studies in other countries have found that occupational segregation is often linked to wage discrimination against women (Burnell 1999), and it is likely that this wage discrimination is also the case in Iran. Certainly the imposition of more gender segregation in the aftermath of the revolution contributed to this trend. But as Fatemeh Moghadam points out (1994), the imposition of greater sex segregation may have increased employment opportunities for women in certain fields. Not only might particular positions have opened up that were only available to women, but more conservative women and/or their families might have felt more comfortable with employment arrangements that were sex-segregated. Both the questions of how occupational segregation may have negatively affected women's wages and whether it is linked to more or fewer employment opportunities deserve further investigation in the case of Iran.

Conclusions

Iran is an interesting case for a number of reasons. The impact that the rise to power of the Islamist government has had is a question that a number of researchers have addressed, with most arguing that this rise led to a sharp decline in women's participation in the labor force. I argue, though, that this result needs to be examined in a more nuanced way, within the context of globalization, given that Iran also experienced a number of other economic shocks when this political transition took place, thus complicating the question of causality. In their book, Nomani and Behdad raise the question: What was the impact of the Iranian revolution on class relations in general and labor markets in particular (2006)? In an era of increasing globalization, it is worthwhile to add another dimension to that question, by asking whether class relations and employment patterns were also substantially impacted by the intervention of an outside power. US sanctions, for example, had the perhaps unintended consequence of depriving less skilled, rural women of economic opportunities in postrevolutionary Iran. Also worth exploring further is the question of how the exodus of a large segment of the elite, which may have driven down female labor force participation rates in the short run, reshaped class lines, because the departure of the more educated middle class would have opened up opportunities for others to enter this class. A later shift, which also has class implications, occurred when the government sector began downsizing, thus reducing employment opportunities for more educated women.

One of the most interesting findings is that despite experiencing economic isolation and public sector downsizing in recent years, Iranian women's overall participation in the labor force has been rising. This rise suggests that despite a lack of export markets and even in the absence of more desirable public sector jobs, women in Iran are being drawn into the labor market either out of a desire or a need to earn their own income. Most of these women are being pulled into informal sector employment, an area about which researchers know very little. The motivations behind women's entry into these jobs, even in the face of declines in two of the most important historical sectors for women, is worth exploring further, particularly given the economic vulnerability that is often associated with the informal sector.

It is also worthwhile to reflect on Iran in comparison with other countries in MENA. One noteworthy point is that Iran has a long history of incorporating women's labor into its manufacturing sector. In some ways Iran thus looks more similar to developing countries outside MENA, where women's incorporation into the manufacturing sector was more widespread, a phenomenon that occurred only in a few countries within MENA and was particularly rare in the case of countries with oil.

At the same time, there is evidence more generally that occupations in Iran are particularly segregated, and that the introduction of an Islamist government exacerbated this trend. Two questions that this finding raises are whether high levels of occupational segregation actually contributed to encouraging more women to work, and what the impact on women's wages was. Also worth investigating further is the intriguing finding that despite the implementation of ostensibly stricter sex segregation, Iran has seen one of the fastest rises in the percentage of women working in sales positions, which, one assumes, require considerable contact with the public, compared to other countries in MENA. Are these positions in which women serve women, or instead a sign that in Iran sales positions, which involve considerable contact with the public, are more acceptable as women's work?

Finally, the Iranian case also exemplifies one of the most serious problems with doing research on women's employment in the region, which is that different agencies report wildly different female labor force participation rates for Iran, making it difficult to come to any very firm conclusions about what is happening in the country in terms of women's employment. According to data collected by the Iranian Census Bureau, Iranian women's labor force participation remains very low, at 12.5 percent in 2005. But the ILO data suggest a much higher participation rate of 38.6 percent. These wildly different estimates of women's labor force participation suggest the need for far more research to uncover what is actually happening in Iran in terms of women's employment.

2

Modernization, Revolution, and Islamism
Political Economy of Women's Employment

ROKSANA BAHRAMITASH *and* HADI SALEHI ESFAHANI

Background to the Modernization Era

Iran is a country of geographical and cultural diversity. More than a third of the country is covered by deserts and mountains that separate regions characterized by a variety of climatic and agricultural conditions. The people who settled in these regions have unique dialects and traditions that add to the variety of socioeconomic conditions in the country. This diversity resulted in a variety of production processes and different ways in which women were incorporated into the production process. Women played an important role at different stages of production throughout the country. In agriculture, they were always present in planting, weeding, picking, harvesting (tea leaves and cotton), and working in rice paddies. Other types of production activities in which women's roles were prominent included raising livestock and poultry, bee-keeping, and silkworm cultivation. In industry, they were involved in handicraft and in carpet weaving. In fact, it is still a woman's job to spin, dye, and weave yarn. Cloth and carpets were and still are handed over mainly to male members of the family for trade (Beck and Keddi 1978, 358–60). Historically, some 70 percent of all cloth weaving was done by women in Iran. In rural areas, where more than 70 percent of carpet weaving was done, about 90 percent of the tasks were carried out by women (Halliday

1979, 191–93). There is evidence that Iran's textile industry was dominated by home-based production, and wool and spinning and cotton were produced in cottage industries by women who were at the heart of cotton and silk production in many parts of Iran such as Gilan, Mazandran, Kashan, Yazd, and Isfahan (Seyf 2001). Moreover, nomadic and pastoralist societies relied on the work of women in significant ways; activities such as milk processing, preparation of animal derivatives, caring for animals, fuel gathering, baking bread, weaving, spinning, and dyeing yarn have traditionally been women's jobs (Poya 1999, 45–47).

Traditional production processes typically did not separate work from the home. This meant that women's engagement in the economy was part of community life, similar to other subsistence economies where the household is the basic unit both of production and of consumption. Parvin Paidar argues that in the late nineteenth and early twentieth centuries, Iran experienced a shift away from family subsistence production to cash crops for export. This shift led to a transition from small private landownership and state-owned lands to large-scale private holdings whose landlords lived in cities. The transition had a major impact on the family as a unit of production, as part of the trend toward commercialization of agriculture. Such a transition is typically associated with a deterioration in women's economic position as it cuts them off from the means of production. Along with the shift toward commercialized agriculture, there was a shift from cottage production of carpet weaving to more commercial workshops. As the demand for export of Persian carpets increased, cottage industry shifted to factory production with notorious conditions for women (Foran 1989, 40; Paidar 1995, 49).

As discussed in the introduction, transition from a nonindustrial to an industrial (modern) economy is not necessarily positive for all women. In fact, contrary to the commonly held view that modernization liberates women, the great bulk of gender and development literature indicates an inverse relationship between development process and women's economic status, at least in the early stage of the transition process. This relationship was first documented in the work of Ester Boserup in 1970 (here we use modernization, industrialization, and development interchangeably, a point discussed in the introductory chapter). Beginning with Boserup, there has been a vast and growing literature on how early stages of development deprived women of means and resources of production (Bennholdt-Thomsen and Mies 1988; Shiva 1991; Kabeer 1991; Benería 2003).

One of the ways that women's economic status is undermined in the early development stages lies in a declining level of access to resources when compared to the situations in preindustrial and subsistence economies. With the process of modernization/industrialization, access to means of production is consolidated in the hands of men, thereby alienating women from both the production process and the allocation of economic resources. Furthermore, according to the argument of Lourdes Benería and Gita Sen, with modernization "the intensive penetration of capital into the agricultural sector, and the redefinition of men's and women's work responsibilities both within and outside of the household have generally resulted in a displacement of women from productive activities, with a consequent diminishment of their social status and power" (Benería and Sen 1981). From this displacement one may conclude that, in the context of developing countries, the process of transition from a nonindustrial, agrarian economy to an industrial economy not only undermines women's economic status but could also weaken their social power.

In the case of Iran, an example can be drawn from an anthropological study on Boyr Ahmad pastoralists from central Iran. G. Reza Fazel's research shows that women play a key role in the domestic economy and have "almost complete control over the production and allocation of economic resources" (Fazel 1977, 87). For instance, important decisions, such as the timing of spring migration, that are made by men rely heavily on women, who are the sources of knowledge. Because of the proximity of women to nature, their information and knowledge have been vital. "Irrespective of the formal rules of decision-making or the external political constraints it is ultimately the women who must support a decision." This access to economic resources, Fazel argues, is a source of power and authority in the private domain. Moreover, because of the centrality of women in the production process, they are stakeholders of shared and contractual labor relations "among the households in the nomadic camp." This type of power works through networks of kinship ties. Fazel points out that because of what he calls a "conversion" between the private and the public sphere, women enjoy a certain degree of power. This observation concurs with the body of literature that documents women's role in a subsistence economy. Moreover, the element of class is also important. Women who are close to the ruling elite wield more power over others. Among Boyr Ahmad pastoralists, traditional sources of power exercised through their role in the extended family and community can provide access to political decision-making through male members of the tribe (Fazel 1977, 78). Some of the results may be extended to other pastoralists such as the Lurs and the Bakhtiaris.

Women's role in the production process was transformed as pastoralists and nomads were forced to settle with the beginnings of the process of modernization and nation building of the Iranian state. The process started in the early part of the twentieth century and continued during the reign of Reza Shah. With the settlement of these nomadic tribes, women's traditional role in production and power and authority has declined. Erika Friedl has made the same observation about the Boyr Ahmad pastoralists: a similar decline in women's economic and social status where transition from a traditional and subsistence economy to an industrial and commercialized agriculture occurs.

Until World War I, Iran was primarily an agrarian society. Alongside the agrarian economy Iran always had an urban population that included many landowners. In the context of the urban economy, both gender segregation and class affiliation played a role in women's access to employment. Many women worked in jobs where the clientele was exclusively women, such as working in women's public baths, selling goods in houses, playing music, performing dancing and singing for all-female occasions, hairdressing, working as midwives, and performing community healing and preaching. Apart from all-female business environments, there have been jobs open to lower-class women such as working as seamstresses, spinners, weavers, maids, laundry women, and nannies (Ravandi 1978, 403).

Alongside women of the lower classes, women who belonged to higher social classes, the elite, and women from the royal family also participated in the economy. However, women of higher income classes were far more restricted in their activities than women of lower economic classes, which did not necessarily mean that their access to economic resources was nonexistent. Documentation of women's property ownership remains underresearched. However, a recent UN publication, UN-HABITAT (2005), documents women's property ownership from Ottoman court records, which show that the Ottoman period, commonly assumed to be rigidly patriarchal, has records of women holding property. Through studies of Ottoman records of court disputes, it becomes evident that women's property ownership and property rights were upheld by the judges. UN-HABITAT documents women's control over the family trust/endowment *(waqf)*, the earliest records dating back as early as sixteenth-century Istanbul. The report indicates that one-third of all founders of trusts *(awqaf)* were women who also managed the funds generated. F. Zarinebaf-Shahr has written about the role of women's contribution to *waqf* during the Safavid era in the city of Ardabil in the northwestern part of Iran (Zarinebaf-Shahr 1998). Finally, the UN report then points out that as a result of colonization, elite and middle-class Muslim women lost access to property ownership.

Starting in the nineteenth and the early twentieth centuries, Iran gradually entered into a semicolonial state. Following two major defeats in the early nineteenth century by the Russians, Iran came under the control of the British from the south and the Russians from the north. While European influence in the country threw the country into a semicolonial status, the same Europeans introduced their science and technology. The failure of Iran to secure its national sovereignty, having been defeated by European powers, and its failure to advance scientifically and technologically became a point of contention for the urban middle and upper classes. The two treaties that conceded a huge part of Iran to the Russians along with a host of concessions given to the British brought shame to the country and created a great deal of resentment throughout different segments of Iranian society.

Concurrently, many young Iranians, disturbed by the state of their country, were sent to be educated in Europe. Many of those educated in Europe became proponents of the ideas of the European Enlightenment, and when they came back to Iran called themselves *roshanfekr,* the exact translation of the word *enlightened.* Several members of the Iranian elite (some of them belonging to *roshanfekran* [plural of "the enlightened"]) celebrated liberal ideals such as secularism. Orientalist discourse was adopted by some members of the educated elite and *roshanfekran* as part of the embracing of Western thought. Certain types of self-Orientalization can be traced in the works of some members of the Iranian elite. For example, Mirza Fath Ali Akhundzadeh viewed European society as the apogee of civilization, progress, and rationality, a place of liberal values and liberation of women while looking at Iran as a place of backwardness, irrationality, religious dogmatism and despotism, and women's enslavement. Other members of the elite looked at ways their indigenous culture could use European science and technology without denouncing all that is Iranian and Muslim. The most influential of these was Jamal din Asadabadi (al-Afghani Asadabadi)(1834–1897). Afghani was critical of traditionalist Islam and supported European science and technology. At the same time, he was against imperialism and believed in the emancipation of women. Next to the urban political elite, the mainstream religious community was categorically opposed to the Europeanization of Iranian society, especially with regard to the question of women. These debates about Iran's encounter with European modernity made little impact on women's access to employment prior to 1914, but they determined the context for the post–World War I era.

Political Economy of Prerevolutionary Iran

Reza Shah and the Shah, 1914–1979

An accelerated modernization started with Reza Shah and in the aftermath of the First World War, when he came into power with a coup d'état in 1921. He was a military man and in many ways his vision of Iran resonated with that of Kemal Ataturk (Amine 2002). Reza Shah embarked on massive infrastructure projects and public utilities. Reza Shah was initially supported by the British but increasingly he built his power through creating an army and a process of state-building. Initially, Reza Shah did not oppose religious power, but as his power was consolidated he began to challenge religious authorities. Reza Shah's vision of a modernized Iran was that of a secular state. His conflict with religious authorities reached its apex when upon his return from Turkey in 1936 he imposed de-veiling on women. This was an attempt to bring women into the public domain to participate in a new Iran.

The new policy of de-veiling was successful among the elite and the upper and middle classes, especially in major Iranian cities such as Tehran (the percentage of unveiled women in the rest of the country remained low and was limited to those closely associated with the regime). The de-veiling policy was particularly important in bringing women into modern, secular education. Traditionally, women of different classes had access to two types of education: Quranic education and an informal type of education.[1] The latter was vital to training women to pursue professions such midwifery. Women played a major role in the traditional economy, and many of the skills and knowledge required to succeed within this economy were transferred through the family and via informal education.

---

1. Bahramitash's great-grandmother refused to de-veil herself by choosing not to leave the house and pursue Quranic education. Hers was not a particularly religious family, but rather one of the déclassé aristocracies who both admired Reza Shah for his nationalism and also detested him for having no respect for traditional values.

With the introduction of the modern, secular education system, many women of middle- and high-income groups in urban areas sent their daughters, for the first time, to these schools to learn to read and write, in ways that they had never done before. The urban elite, the upper and middle classes, started to flourish slowly, and women of these classes attended schools where they were trained to become teachers and health professionals. As in other parts of the world, women's entry into the public workforce took place in domains that had strong affinities with their roles as mothers and wives.

With the outbreak of the Second World War, Reza Shah declared Iran a neutral country. Iran was subsequently invaded by the Allied forces and Reza Shah's army was dismantled. He abdicated and went to exile in Mauritius, leaving the throne to his eldest son, Mohammad-Reza Pahlavi, with the consent of the British and American governments. The post–Second World War era is characterized by relative political freedom and the formation of a multitude of political parties, most notably the fast-growing and disciplined Tudeh Party, the Communist Party of Iran, which was backed by the Soviet Union. Alongside the Communists and other groups of the Left, there were many nationalist political figures who enjoyed broad support in the population. These politicians had formed groups or parties around themselves, but none of them was as well organized as the Tudeh Party. Nevertheless, a charismatic leader, Mohammad Mossadegh, and some crucial nationalist causes with widespread support at the time enabled them to form a grand coalition—the National Front—and come to power through elections in 1951, with Mossadegh as the prime minister. Soon after taking office, Mossadegh nationalized Iran's oil resources, but faced an effective boycott by the major oil companies, backed by the British and American governments. The consequent economic hardship in the country prepared the ground for a CIA-engineered coup in 1953, which overthrew Mossadegh and installed the Shah as a heavy-handed dictator. The coup once again reminded Iranians that they were not in charge of their own destiny and that their ruler was picked by the British and then by the Americans.

After the coup, until the time of the revolution in 1979, the Shah's main economic strategy was accelerated industrialization. In the 1960s and the early 1970s, this policy became part of his Great Civilization plan for the nation. As the father of the nation, the Shah had a vision of taking Iranians from the dark ages into the age of modern civilization. The Shah celebrated the 2,500-year-old history of Iranian monarchy, promising to bring back the glory of the Persian Empire, which had fallen because of the Arab invasion and the rise of Islam in Iran. To recapture the glory of the past, the country had to make great strides to enter into the twentieth century and set off on the path of turning into a secular liberal democracy. The process of secularization had already started under Reza Shah, but the ideals of turning into a liberal democracy were more difficult to achieve. The Shah was heavily supported, both militarily and financially, by the United States and, particularly after the 1953 coup, he was regarded as the puppet of the Americans. In an effort to gain some support among economically and socially disadvantaged members of Iranian society, particularly those in rural areas, he embarked on a major land reform in the early 1960s as part of what he called a "White Revolution." The objectives of the land reform were twofold. On the one hand, it aimed to raise support among the low-income rural population. On the other hand, it sought to undermine the political elite (many of whom were from the landowning class). The Shah's search for political legitimacy in the aftermath of the coup was also partially responsible for his support for women. Similar to the strategy of Habib Bourguiba in Tunisia, the Shah sought to improve the status of women in order to mobilize political support among urban women.

The Shah after the 1953 Coup: Development/Modernization

Because the bulk of the population at the time was rural, state policy toward rural development was particularly important. In order to avoid a peasant uprising, the Shah, following the counsel of his

American advisors, embarked on a land reform. Although his land reform did not fully satisfy those calling for a major land reform inside Iran, it still represented a major step in the right direction. It was part of a major economic and social policy initiative, the White Revolution, or "Shah and People's Revolution."[2] The revolution was meant to facilitate modernization both economically and socially. While land redistribution is generally viewed as positive, there were several problems with the land reform of the White Revolution. First, it granted land to men as heads of households, a step that deprived women of land ownership and consolidated the male breadwinner/female homemaker model. Second, it overlooked landless peasants, many of whom were women. Third, it provided little financial support for sharecroppers while leaving them vulnerable. Also, the state policy for the mechanization and commercialization of agriculture made it difficult for small landholders to make a profit. This difficulty, in turn, led to the failure of small landholders to survive, many of them leaving their land and migrating to cities to find jobs in the booming construction industry, leaving their women to pick up the slack. The declining agricultural sector became a source of employment for women, many of them peasants. These women were paid half the salary of men (Najmabadi 1987, 220). From the 1950s until the 1970s, the agricultural sector continued to decline but women's share of employment increased consistently. What happened in Iran is very similar to what happened in other parts of the developing world. The process of development did not empower women economically, because women's share of employment increased in a declining sector of the economy. It must be noted, however, that data on female employment in the rural sector are always problematic and

---

2. The United States supported the White Revolution on the basis of its previous experience with peasant uprisings during the 1950s and 1960s where communism had grown, notably in Asia and in Korea and Vietnam, where the United States fought two wars to prevent the spread of communism. The White Revolution of the 1960s was not limited to economic issues but aimed to provide social programs as well.

tend to overlook the role of women in the production process. This is because what women produce often does not directly enter into the market and, at times, is consumed within the household. When activities do not take place in a market context, their values may not be captured by official economic data or may not be attributed properly to those actually carrying them out.

The pastoralist part of the rural economy was hit particularly hard by the White Revolution and the forced settlement of tribes. During the White Revolution, both forests and pastoral lands became nationalized. Limited access to lands coupled with forced settlements turned pastoralist tribal peasants into landless peasants who lived in villages. As Erika Friedl has demonstrated (1997), the forced settlement of the Boyr Ahmad tribes devastated the economic and political structures of the tribe. Although many men from the tribes could migrate and take advantage of the expanding labor markets in industrial and construction sectors of the economy, women's opportunities were far more limited. They lost access to the means of production and were forced to become wage laborers, either seasonal or permanent, in the sluggish rural sector.

In contrast to the negative trend representative of the agricultural sector, female employment within the manufacturing sector experienced an increase and continued to stay elevated during the prerevolutionary era. Some of the increase in employment was owing to rising world demand for Persian carpets. In addition, with the process of industrialization, women entered into employment in the textile and food processing sectors.

Women's deteriorating conditions in the rural areas became so alarming that, as part of the White Revolution, a literacy and health corps was created to improve women's quality of life in the agricultural sector. This corps mainly consisted of young men who were fulfilling part of their compulsory military service, but some young unmarried women had to join through a lottery system. The young women who joined these corps were all unveiled. Many of the female members of the corps were sent to remote parts of the country, where they often faced harassment.

As far as the urban economy was concerned, those women who migrated to the cities with their men made up part of the evolving urban low-income class, which, in fact, became the majority of the urban population. Some of these women joined the ranks of urban low-income employees. They worked as maids or had other low-paying jobs in both the formal and informal economies. Some women whose husbands earned a sufficient living stayed at home.

Moreover, as part of his mission to bring Iran into the age of the "Great Civilization," the Shah aimed to change women's role in society and to bring Iran in line with liberal ideas. The Shah believed that Iranian women should participate in public life the same way as European and American women do. His views about women, however, were not very different from many of his male counterparts in the West who opposed feminism. In a famous interview with Oriana Fallaci in 1976, he expressed his views by indicating that he "respected women as long as they were beautiful, feminine, and moderately clever" (Fallaci 1976, 271–72). His view was that women should have the opportunity to play a role in society although their primary roles were being a wife and a mother, roles determined by their biology. During the reign of the Shah, the Women's Organization of Iran (WOI) was founded and headed by Princess Ashraf (the Shah's sister) and the queen mother. Its mandate was to set up various committees that were to address women's issues in health care, literacy, education, law, and social welfare. The WOI's mandate was to promote women's interests within the state and concurrently to garner political support for the state (recruiting for political activities such as joining Iran's only official political party of the time, the Rastakhis party (Sanasarian 1982, 83). The WOI participated in the 1975 International Women's Conference, at which an eleven-point resolution called for the complete elimination of discrimination against women and an equal opportunity and welfare for women from all walks of life (Paidar 1995, 159). None of those resolutions was adopted by the WOI. Nonetheless, women were incorporated into the development process both at the rural and the urban level. This inclusion, however, did not lead to an improvement in all conditions for women.

The most significant changes vis-à-vis women working in the urban sector that had a positive outcome on the life of women only affected upper- and middle-class urban women—the real beneficiaries of modernization. The official and ideal role for women of modern Iran was to enter into public life by removing their veil. Women were encouraged to join secular public life. Many women entered the teaching and health professions but they also held clerical, administrative, and professional jobs. In chapter 3 we will further discuss the employment trends in the service sector.

The mid-1960s saw a decline in female employment in the urban sector (Paidar 1995, 164), a result of a state ideology that supported women's primary role as homemakers. In addition, some men, whose income from oil-related revenues was sufficient, were not inclined to allow their wives to work. The number of women in professional jobs remained low. Statistics gathered by the Women's Organization of Iran in 1975 indicated that only one in seven to ten doctors were female.

The Shah's modernization program, as in many other parts of the developing world, failed to bring wealth to the population as a whole. The trickle-down effect was limited and the revenue generated by the export of oil was largely concentrated in the hands of the upper social strata. (The upward trends in the income inequality measures in the 1970s can be seen in figure 2.1). While the elite, the middle class, and the close circle associated with the royal family benefited, many Iranians, particularly those living in the rural sector, remained marginalized. In spite of the promises of its advocates, Westernization/modernization built around land reform and industrialization ultimately did not give rise to a prosperous society for all. The majority of people in low-income groups were rural peasants and agricultural workers, who, according to the statistical data, enjoyed relatively little improvement in their standard of living during the two decades prior to the 1979 Revolution.

Iran's case may be viewed against the backdrop of a world disenchanted with more than two decades of Western-style "development." By the late 1970s, there was growing skepticism in the Third World regarding development efforts and modernization theory.

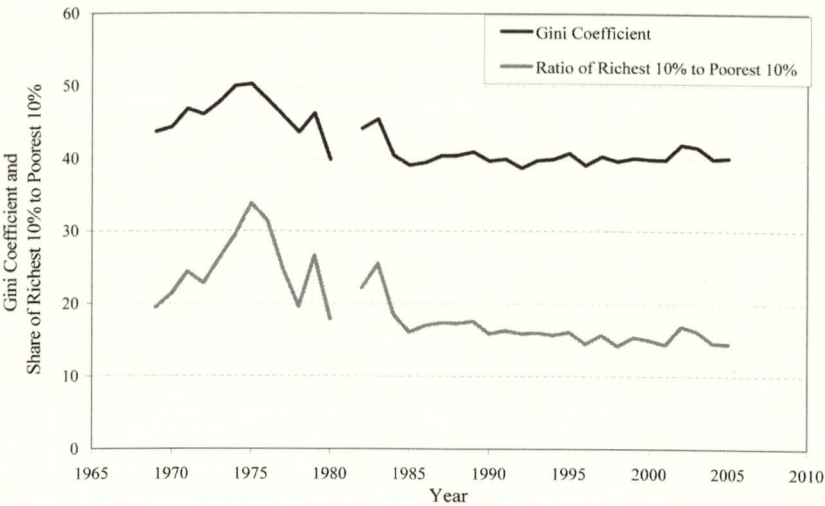

2.1. Income Distribution in Iran. *Source:* Central Bank of Iran, http://tsd.cbi.ir/IntTSD/EnDisplay/Display/aspx.

The same period experienced the decline of Soviet-inspired Communist models. The search for alternative models took diverse forms in different parts of the world. In Latin America, liberation theology became popular and inspired social movements on a massive scale. In the Middle East, there was a slow but sure decline in support for both Western-style modernization and Soviet-style socialism, particularly after the failure of Nasser in Egypt and the disappointing performance of the Ba'ath party in Iraq. In Iran the coup had dismantled the Tudeh party and the Left had been crushed completely, leaving the Islamists as the only potential organizing force.

The general impulse throughout the Middle East was to search for an alternative that was more compatible with local and indigenous economic and cultural norms. In Iran, the writings of Ali Shariati, inspired by the Algerian postcolonial writer Frantz Fanon, enjoyed wide popularity, especially among the younger generation. Shariati preached a revolutionary interpretation of Islam that emphasized Islam's role as a religion of social justice (Z. Sullivan 2000, 239). Here it is worth noting that the original ideas of the revolution and Islamism in Iran were anything but traditional. Shariati, for instance, in his famous book *Fatima Is Fatima* called upon Iranian women to look into their own history and religion for role models. He did not encourage women to stay at home but rather to stand up against social injustice, like the prophet's daughter, and to revolutionize their lives and transform their society (Shariati n.d.). Nationalism also gained ground, signaled by the ephemeral rise to power of nationalists such as Bazargan, an engineer who became the head of the postrevolutionary interim government. Bazargan was also a practicing Muslim and believed in redistribution of income and power. The number of groups who came together around ideas that emphasized Islam as an alternative continued to grow. This new interpretation of Islam accommodated political ideas that mobilized large numbers of people, particularly the young and the educated, against the repression and social injustices of the Shah's regime.

It was under such conditions that many Iranian women joined the Islamist movement. To them, many of the measures that the Shah had taken to facilitate the emancipation of women—such as granting them the right to vote—seemed quite meaningless given that there were no democratic elections in the Shah's absolutist monarchy. Many female activists were imprisoned and tortured during the Shah's era. Traditionalist women from low-income families were marginalized within a political climate that strongly discouraged veiled women from entering certain public places frequented by middle- and upper-class women.

In the late 1970s, many women from educated, middle-class backgrounds joined the Islamist movement, some of them in response to the message of Shariati and others who propagated an Islamic model based on the concept of social justice (Abrahamian 1982, 464–73; Z. Sullivan 2000, 239). Two pillars of Shi'a Muslims that set them aside from the rest of the Muslims are justice and Imamat (believing in the prophet's descendents). Therefore the issue of justice, particularly social justice, has been a strong driving force within the Shi'a tradition.

At the same time, the SAVAK (secret police) continued to torture feminist activists and suppressed feminist organizations not associated with the state (Bahar 1983). Ayatollah Ruhollah Khomeini, tempering his earlier reactionary position regarding the role of women, began to address men as well as women. He stressed the importance of female mobilization, which supported the ayatollah.

The Revolution: 1979

The economic inequality that characterized the reign of the Shah and his political repression led to a massive uprising. Although the middle class was mobilized early on, soon the lower classes joined in, and a call for establishing social justice became the rallying cry of the 1979 Revolution, a revolution that brought an end to more than two thousand years of monarchy. The revolution brought together the Left, nationalists, and Islamists. In the period following the revolution, Iran's political scene became extremely vibrant and animated. But it was soon apparent that Ayatollah Khomeini was not going to remain just a religious leader and that he sought to remain a powerful figure in postrevolutionary Iran. Parties other than those closely associated with the ayatollah were banned and most political organizations were dismantled. Yet social and economic justice continued to remain an important part of the legacy of the revolution. The ayatollah was successful in responding to the revolutionaries' demand for economic justice and focused on the issue of poverty and the empowerment of economically and politically disenfranchised Iranians. Khomeini, in an attempt to accommodate revolutionary ideas and appeal to those who found Socialist ideas attractive, adopted Shariati's religious vocabulary, calling *mostazafin* those who had been exploited and marginalized and *mostakberin* those who exploited the masses. These terms represented Shariati's appropriation of the direct translation of Fanon's "wretched of the earth," that is, the poor, deprived masses exploited by the mostakberin, that is, colonialists and their local surrogates.

In Shariati's analysis, the mostazafin and the mostakberin were the two fundamental classes of people in Iranian society. He supported his analysis with Quranic verses, saying that it was God's will to empower the mostazafin. These two terms were applied to global politics and became key symbols of the battle against imperialism and dictatorship. Khomeini appropriated these popular terms and advocated an international people's movement inspired by social justice and embedded in Islamic culture, in opposition to a Western global hegemony led by the United States. Some observers have argued that this was merely a populist political stance to attract support and that in reality the new regime's intention was to change lives for the masses. However, given the paucity of articulated views about economic policies among the revolutionary elite and their heterogeneity of interests and perspectives, it seems difficult to ascribe many widely accepted policy intents to the new regime.

As part of his economic justice agenda, Khomeini partly suspended the real estate market in cities. This was a different position from his original stand during the White Revolution when the ayatollah stood against land reform. However, suppressing real estate transactions came short of supporting a full-fledged land reform in rural areas. This was particularly reflected in the revolutionary regime's response in early 1979 when peasants across the country took over properties of large landowners, accusing them of violating the rules inscribed in the 1960s land reform laws. The state never officially endorsed these spontaneous expropriations, reversing many of them, especially in the Baluchi, Kurdish, and Turkmen areas, where the state intervened for national security reasons. Some of these takeovers enjoyed the support of Socialist groups. In places where the state did not actively intervene, local courts let some of the expropriations stand while rescinding others. In Guyom (a village close to Shiraz), for instance, the landlord, who lived in Tehran and suddenly became a pious Muslim in February 1979, won the backing of the courts in the capital for reclaiming his lands, only to see the courts in Shiraz refuse to implement the court order. The dispute remained unresolved until 2002.[3]

---

3. Interview with Dr. Eric Hooglund, senior scholar of Iranian Studies and the editor of *Critique: Critical Middle Eastern Studies*, Washington, 2006.

Khomeini's initial apparent support of the social justice agenda and land reform led to his popularity among part of the Iranian Left, especially the Tudeh Party and its close ally the Fadaiayn-e Khalgh-Aksariyyat (People's Fadaian–Majority Faction, a Marxist party that had started before the revolution as a guerilla organization). In the aftermath of the revolution and with the establishment of the Islamic Republic, most political organizations were gradually banned, a process that culminated in the ban of the above leftist parties. The process was far from being smooth and it came at a huge price.[4] Some have argued that in postrevolutionary Iran political repression continued and that there was very little difference between the Shah and the regime that came to replace it, except that this time the repression was imposed by a religious clerical elite. However, the process entailed substantial political and institutional change. Although a relatively small elite came to dominate the new regime, they were

---

4. Many top officials of the previous regime were executed along with those who resisted the Islamic Republic. Although there has been vast criticism of the brutality that followed the revolution, the cycle of violence dates back to the time of the coup in 1953. Many members of the opposition to the Shah were executed after the coup. The cycle of violence continued with the overthrow of the Shah's regime. Among those who suffered the most were members of the Mujahedin-e-Khalgh (People's Mujahedin); members of a left-wing Islamist group were imprisoned and killed. These reprisals took place in retaliation for several events: the bombings of Iranian Parliament and the headquarters of the Islamic Republic Party that killed more than seventy top officials; and the assassinations of the Iranian president, prime minister, and more than twenty members of Parliament within the course of two months in 1981. These events shook the very foundations of the regime, and ultimately changed its character, giving power to the revolutionary militia army, Sepah Pasdaran (Revolutionary Guards). Not only active members of the opposition but those who merely sympathized became subject to execution. Mujahedin-e-Khalgh later joined Saddam Hussein and took part in the war against Iran, remaining loyal to Saddam Hussein until the downfall of his regime. Revolutionary groups such as Fadaiayn and Mujahedin recruited women into their ranks, while Sepah Pasdaran and the regime in general recruited women who stayed in the background but came out during demonstrations. This factor may have been important in Mujahedin's success in recruiting quite a few educated women into their ranks.

factionalized and, to various degrees, represented a host of different economic and political interests in Iranian society (Moslem 2002).

What must be kept in mind is that a major force behind Ayatollah Khomeini was the bazaar (the urban traditional merchant class). This force put Ayatollah Khomeini in a delicate balancing act. On the one hand he needed the support of people who wanted economic redistribution, but, on the other hand, he could not afford to upset his major source of support: the bazaar. The bazaar was and has been culturally traditionalist and economically conservative. They opposed the Shah's modernization policies, an opposition that led to their economic and cultural alienation. Khomeini skillfully kept the two opposing forces together. When the Islamic Republic Party was formed in mid-1979, there were clear divisions within it between the "Left" that stressed economic justice issues and the "Right" that reflected the interests of the bazaar and a large part of the clerical establishment. These divisions had crystallized into actual factions by the time the party was dissolved in 1987. Following the dissolution of the party, the left-leaning factions began to emerge around a reformist agenda while the right-leaning groups became known as the conservatives, each side still rather heterogeneous in interests and perspectives.[5]

In the aftermath of the 1979 Revolution, the Mossavi government pursued economic redistribution and economic nationalism in

---

5. Khomeini pacified the traditional merchant class who believed in profit-making and did not support economic redistribution. Their faction was exemplified by an alliance called the Hey'at-e Mo'talefeh (the Alliance Society), a pressure group that lobbied for the implementation of policies that catered to their particular economic interests. Mo'talefeh was a player in the political life of the 1950s and early 1960s, but it gained a stronger voice in the aftermath of the revolution. Although Khomeini also supported social justice programs that had a huge constituency among the Iranian masses, he could not afford to alienate those opposed to economic redistribution—particularly the *bazaaris*. Their support was vital to hold the country together against the interference of foreign powers. As a result, the *bazaaris* benefited from protectionist economic policies, and they may have benefited from the arrangement of import quotas.

the form of agricultural self-sufficiency and import substitution. The postrevolutionary era was marked by the rise in popularity of ideologues who advocated anticonsumerism and anticapitalism. They were partly influenced by the legacy of Shariati and other Islamic intellectuals of the 1960s and 1970s who made socialism more palatable to the Islamic political activists. These new ideologues advocated and preached modesty of lifestyle and economic self-sufficiency, which emanated from the ethos of the revolution. A version of a welfare state was established in accordance with the ideal of building a strong Islamic nation *(ummat e islami)*. The new state's social programs, largely financed through oil revenues, aimed at providing the masses with basic services such as food subsidies, health care, and free education. However, many of the policies were incoherent and inefficient. This inefficiency was partly owing to lack of expertise among the new elite, which was made up of families and individuals closely connected with the clergy and the bazaar. They came to control the top policymaking and administrative positions based on connections and loyalty and were distrustful of experts outside their own circles. In fact, after the revolution, most capable and experienced government personnel were purged. Many of the professionals inside and outside the government who could have helped with policymaking either retired altogether or left the country. Another reason for the incoherence of policies was the factionalized nature of the elite. Despite their common interest in maintaining the new regime, each small faction tried to pull policies in the direction of its interests, loading the policymaking process with contradictory forces and, ultimately, fragmenting it.

The war with Iraq made it imperative for the regime to present a united front. Those in favor of economic justice programs passed laws in the Majlis (the Parliament) in support of public social services. Those who opposed the redistribution of wealth were able to exert their influence and weaken or defuse the impact of the redistribution agenda, a move that had obvious ramifications on low-income women's lives. With Khomeini's death these factions entered into open political conflict.

Postrevolutionary Iran and Women's Work

Khomeini's views on women, similar to his views on private property, changed during the course of the revolution. Initially and during the 1960s, Khomeini's view of the public role of women was extremely conservative and against the Shah's modernizing of women's role. However, during the revolution he came to rely heavily on women's support. In return, he moved away from his earlier interpretations that saw the exclusive role of women as wives and mothers. His need for women's contributions to strengthen his political power base (and later his economic agenda) required a transformed definition of the role of women in society, one that required women to be present in the public domain.

While some middle-class and professional women became alienated by the new veiling laws and were forced to leave their jobs, low-income urban and rural peasants were drawn into the public domain. This trend was exacerbated by the war with Iraq. The combination of the US–led economic sanctions against Iran and the war with Iraq created a need for women to be actively involved in the political and economic life of the country. Thus, very much like the situation during World War II in Europe and North America, the Iran-Iraq war brought many Iranian women into public life. However, this development was countered by policies of segregation and restrictive rules on women's participation in public life, a process that had particularly adverse effects on educated, secular women. At the same time, the economic disruptions caused by the radical policies of the government and the war created a significant need for skilled labor. Indeed, labor market data indicate a drop in recorded employment for women. But, as we shall see in chapter 4, the drop in recorded employment was largely because of the decline in jobs in rural areas rather than in urban areas. Moreover, there were other ways in which women's role expanded, though not captured in official statistics. In particular, there was a major increase in women's participation as volunteers in support of the war effort, in literacy campaigns, and so forth.

Iran experienced a major economic recession during the postrevolutionary years and during the war (see chapter 4). The government embarked on a policy of establishing economic self-sufficiency and on a program to strengthen the agricultural sector. As a result, this sector made a recovery during the decade following the revolution. Women's share of employment in the agricultural sector continued to increase, although their percentage within the total economy declined as did their labor force participation rate (see chapter 4). This increase in agricultural sector employment is in line with general trends in the global south where women's employment is growing in sectors in decline. But there were other reasons; for example a nationwide campaign on basic literacy and expansion of the education system have been responsible for a decrease in labor supply of females in the rural sector (as illustrated in chapter 4). Moreover, state policies offering early retirement to government employees and pensions to private-sector employees induced many women to leave the labor force (Fatemeh Moghadam 2004). A policy that echoed as revolutionary—namely, retirement benefits for rural workers—backfired on women. During this period, the manufacturing sector suffered a major blow because of the cumulative effect of the mismanagement of nationalized factories, an economic embargo, and inward-looking economic policies. Women's share of employment within the sector suffered immensely, rural areas being hit the hardest (see chapter 4). As far as the service sector was concerned, while women increased their share of employment in health care and education, their share declined in other areas. This decline was partly because with forced veiling many women either chose or were forced to leave their jobs.

Khomeini's social justice programs relied on the role of volunteers, including many women. Khomeini's nationwide initiatives, such as basic literacy programs, could not have been realized without the participation of women. In fact, Khomeini's policies mobilized a large number of women, especially from traditional families, bringing them into the public sphere. These rural women were often alienated during the Shah's regime because of enforced Westernization and modernization. Women who embraced Westernization were encouraged to enter the public sphere during the Shah's reign, but only those women who were not veiled could be hired in professional offices. In fact, veiled women were banned from entering certain public places. Under the Islamic Republic, this situation was reversed, and when Khomeini asked women to join the Islamist cause, many women, now all veiled, entered the public domain en masse (Paidar 1995).

Many women who volunteered for the literacy campaign were not necessarily Islamists. Many feminists and women from the Left joined Khomeini's effort to eradicate female illiteracy. These middle-class women worked side by side with the Islamists for a common cause, and the program was a major success. Khomeini's literacy campaign provided feminist and leftist women with an opportunity to participate in programs that empowered women. Illiterate women, once prevented from attending schools because of their husband's objections, could now receive an education because the literacy campaigns were held in mosques and their teachers were ostensibly "religious" women volunteers. The reception of Khomeini's volunteers was in sharp contrast to that of the Shah's health and literacy corps, made up of unveiled women whose presence in certain rural areas caused a community uproar. In postrevolutionary Iran, veiled female volunteers received much wider acceptance than the unveiled corps of the Shah. Education and popular mobilization consolidated women's public presence and greatly facilitated their entry into the paid workforce.

Postrevolutionary Iran saw the enforcement of sexual segregation policies that created the need for female labor in certain sectors of the economy, such as in education and in health care. Over time, segregation-generated female employment extended to other sectors, which included retail sales and services aimed at female clients. In many instances, women actually had privileged access to jobs, in the sense that they could enter into certain professions free from male competition. Moreover, there were jobs that could not be filled by men because of forbidden contact with female clients, such as security and customs at airports, or jobs where male presence was not permitted, such as caretakers of all-female institutions (student dormitories, sport centers, etc.)

The ongoing war with Iraq coupled with Iran's resistance to get involved in international trade had devastating effects on the nation's economy. Internally, Khomeini had alienated the rich and the entrepreneurial classes of the Shah's period, who, closely allied with professionals and skilled labor, refused to lend any support to the regime. The continuing economic crisis, a chronic shortage of skilled labor, and widespread, often severe political repression created a great deal of popular discontent.

There is extensive literature on women in Iran that blames women's limited access to employment on Islamization. The reality is more complicated. Women's employment did decline, but much of that was because of an ailing economy and a decline in rural employment. Although women's employment in urban areas experienced a marginal decline, this decline was in many respects the result of a downward trend that had began prior to the revolution (see chapter 4). Moreover, the impact of Islamization in rural areas was very limited as secularization and modernization had never reached many parts of the rural sector.

Postwar Iran's Economy, Discourse on Women's Public Role (and Employment)

Khomeini died in 1989, a year after bringing an inconclusive and unsatisfying end to the war with Iraq. While his role as Supreme Leader was formally taken over by his successor, Ali Khamene'i, a great deal of power fell into the hands of the new Iranian president, Ali Akbar Hashemi Rafsanjani, a former student of Khomeini who was wealthy and influential. Rafsanjani, a man of refined political skills, managed to keep different factions together to the advantage of those who wanted economic prosperity over economic justice. For Rafsanjani, creating jobs and higher income opportunities required a strong entrepreneurial class, a class that had to be established and nurtured in postrevolutionary Iran. The conflict between the factions, however, did not disappear, and it came to an open and hostile confrontation during the Khatami era (1997–2005). Rafsanjani believed it was time for Iran to recover from the revolution and war and concentrated his efforts on the economic reconstruction of the country. In his endeavors he had to face two problems. First, he lacked the expert personnel needed to design effective new policies. Second, the late 1980s saw a dramatic plunge in the price of oil. This latter was a major obstacle to rebuilding the country's war-torn economy. And third, the impact of the sanctions was hurting the masses.

Rafsanjani realized the need for Iran to transform itself. He initiated programs to create a new generation of revolutionaries who could lead the country economically and politically while remaining true to the idea of an Islamic Republic. During Rafsanjani's term in office, many students were sent abroad to receive their higher education, replacing the class of exiles who would never consider coming back to an Islamist Iran. Rafsanjani strengthened groups of the religious elite who then became an important part of the reform movement in the next decade. In spite of Rafsanjani's effort to bring unity, fragmentation of the political elite continued and the country often suffered from the consequences of contradictory approaches to political and economic reform.

Rafsanjani's main focus was on the country's postwar economic recovery, and he believed this recovery could be best achieved by encouraging the entrepreneurial class. He initiated a series of reforms to open up markets and encourage private-sector development. By the early 1990s, the revolutionary ideals of social justice had largely receded to the background, and the concepts of the mostazafin and the mostakberin almost disappeared from Iran's political vocabulary.[6] Rafsanjani also sought to build closer ties with other countries,

---

6. Support for liberalization was not unanimous, as reflected in the fact that Ayatollah Khamene'i, while supporting economic liberalization, also emphasized his vision of an Islamic society in which poverty would be eradicated. Some argue that Iran's government has followed a populist agenda and that Ayatollah Khamene'i does not support a real transformation of the situation for the poor.

both in the East and in the West. He tried to break many taboos of the Islamist state and gave indications that he was not against the idea of reopening relations with the United States.

Rafsanjani's policies led to major economic growth and a rise in the level of income across the population, but this trend lasted only for a few years. Poorly designed policies undermined the recovery of the early 1990s, which came to an abrupt end with a major economic crisis in 1994–95. The economic crisis resulted in further impoverishment of the poor and ultimately led to the virtual stagnation of the economy until the late 1990s. It was a limited knowledge of economics, unwarranted acceptance of neoliberal policies, and the poor design and poor execution of policies that led to the eventual economic decline. In particular, when foreign capital accounts were opened following trade liberalization in the early 1990s, many firms, especially enterprises belonging to state institutions and *bonyads* (foundations run under the auspices of the Supreme Leader's office), opted to borrow heavily and imported goods on favorable terms. Many of these loans were in the form of short-term credits from European and Japanese banks (Pesaran 2001). The banks provided these loans based on a belief that the capital accounts would remain operative and that there would be sufficient short-term revenues to repay the loans. However, as the amount of loans increased, firms started to anticipate a reversal of the government policies and decided to take advantage of the openness while it lasted, so that they could have sufficient stocks of foreign inputs and resources in case there was a closedown of the economy. The result was that foreign borrowing soared and put the economy in a very risky situation. In 1994, when the price of oil began to drop, the government realized that the volume of loans that had to be fulfilled was far larger than available revenues. The consequent devaluation of the domestic currency (rial) did not solve the lack of solvency because that policy

---

Iran's elite politics is extremely complicated and there are major divisions within the conservative camp (Rubin and Clawson 2005).

only made it difficult for the borrowing company to obtain foreign currency and repay their loans. The government ended up closing down the economy again, rationing foreign currency and providing substantial subsidies to borrowers in order to enable them to repay the loans. Government intervention translated into high inflation, shortages in imported products, and rising prices for basic goods, all these having a disastrous impact on low-income families. Ultimately, low-income groups, who were the original political base of the revolution, became increasingly alienated from it.

Economic dissatisfaction, along with a general sense of disappointment with the achievements of the revolution, caused some members of the religious intellectual elite to search for sources of change. These intellectuals drew upon the legacy of earlier movements that sought to reconfigure how Islamic law was understood and that led to the growing popular support for a "dynamic jurisprudence" *(fegheh-e poya)*. This approach had its roots in Iran's encounter with European Enlightenment in the late nineteenth and the early twentieth centuries, in Iran's semicolonial status, and within the economic development process. The grounds for receptivity for dynamic jurisprudence had already formed in the religious thinking of progressive Muslims of the time, who were anti-imperialist and were seeking to implement economic development policies within Iran's cultural integrity and Islamic culture. With the rise of conservative religious forces, tensions between traditionalist interpretations of Islam, dynamic jurisprudence, and a secularist agenda came to a head. The religious elite remained divided between those who pursued a social justice program and those who embraced free-market Islamization without economic redistribution. To an already divided picture one has to add a group of religious conservatives who did not tolerate any compromise and who remained adamant in their position that Islam should not be subject to multiple interpretations, rejecting dynamic jurisprudence altogether. While those for and against a free-market economy have been more open to women's public role, the religious conservatives continued to hold onto a more traditional interpretation. Some members of the opposition argue that all these factions are the same and that disagreement within the ruling elite is an instrument of manipulation of public opinion.

Under Rafsanjani's administration, women's employment rates started to pick up following the upward trends that characterized the general economic recovery of the country. This trend in female employment continued into the late 1990s and on into the next decade. The increase in overall female employment was mainly owing to increases in health care and education, as well as in other categories of the service sectors (see chapter 4). The general increase in female employment was owing to a set of factors both on the supply side and on the demand side. On the supply side, there were more women seeking employment for pay. These were the large cohorts of women born just before and just after the revolution who were finishing their schooling and were entering the labor market. There were also women who had worked as volunteers during the previous decade and were not seeking employment for pay. The revolutionary ideal of creating a just society persisted—an idealistic model of pure altruism pursued on the basis of Islamic principles by devoted Muslim women and, followed for secular reasons, by leftist feminists—and many women had happily continued to provide the regime with their free labor. Once these women gained visibility in the public domain, seeking employment and paid work for women was much more acceptable. Moreover, with general improvement of the economy there were more jobs for the total population. This point has been elaborated by Elaheh Rostami-Povey, who has documented women's volunteer work in the aftermath of the revolution (Rostami-Povey 2005).

Women's employment in the public sector was an important component of the state policy. This policy was partly the result of the jump in the demand for female labor following the implementation of segregation policies. At the same time, many revolutionaries supporting the government were keen to see the expansion of social programs, especially for women, in health, education, and welfare services. Finally, the nationalization of many private firms automatically shifted employment from the private sector to the public sector. These themes will be elaborated in chapter 4.

During the war, economic hardship hit low-income households and women the hardest. In the late 1980s and the early 1990s, there was an increasing need to address poverty. This need became even more pressing when postrevolutionary charitable foundations, such as bonyads, failed to deliver services to the poor and eventually morphed into independent, profit-oriented organizations that were often plagued by corruption and fraud. These foundations, ostensibly designed to assist poor families, alienated them instead and ended up losing their base support, many of whom were women.

While bonyads have failed to meet the needs of the poor, the Emdad (Relief) Committee, founded shortly after the revolution by Mo'talefeh (a political group from the traditional merchant class of the bazaar) under the auspices of Ayatollah Khomeini, provided some aid to families in financial need (Esfahani 2006). Emdad Committee is now one of the most prominent nationwide charitable foundations that has allocated funds to women. It manages a variety of funds. Some of the funds are earmarked for aiding girls and women, and they are used for bursaries for basic literacy education for women and for girls' primary and secondary education. (It also hands out bursaries to support young women who live in dormitories.) The actual amount of funds distributed to women is not significant, yet it bears a symbolic importance. The committee has extensive fundraising programs. It gives microcredits to low-income families and female-headed households, and establishes training programs for low-income women. A sizable part of the committee's activities is focused on rural areas, with a concentration on traditional female professions such as carpet weaving, sewing, agricultural production, and handicrafts. The committee provides credit and training and, in some cases, buys the finished products and markets them (http://www.emdad.ir). Today, its emphasis lies in economic empowerment, integrating people in financial need into local development projects and increasing income-generating activities.

In general, the economic policies in the 1990s continued to remain nonconducive to increasing employment, and in fact many of the policy initiatives, such as supporting a capital-intensive automotive industry, were continuations of policies originally begun under the Shah. While such industries are often not beneficial to female employment, employment also declined in the kind of labor-intensive industries that typically employ women, including textile manufacturing, food processing, and leather and shoe making, these latter suffering from official negligence and policies of privatization.

3

From Postrevolution to the Reform

Gender Politics and Employment

ROKSANA BAHRAMITASH *and* HADI SALEHI ESFAHANI

Gender Rights and the Reform Movement

The previous chapter concluded with a brief discussion of dynamic jurisprudence. In the current chapter we will further examine how this hermeneutical turn became an important part of the reform movement. The concept of dynamic jurisprudence was not a novel one, but it was in the aftermath of the revolution that debates over it became animated. Once in power, religious authorities faced short-term and long-term economic and social problems. To tackle the complexities involved in the economic and social planning for a huge country like Iran, a certain flexibility of religious interpretation was required. From the very beginning, the religion-based state had to operate on a pragmatic level to maintain the operations of a state and national economy in an increasingly globalized world. For instance, immediately after the revolution with the onslaught of the Islamization process, a debate erupted over the question of charging interest, putting in jeopardy the whole banking system. According to Shari'a law, any interest charged is considered usury and is therefore forbidden. However, it became immediately clear that it was not possible to envision a country such as Iran closing all its banks. Iran's ruling clerics wanted the Islamic banking system to be an example, one that would inspire the rest of the Muslim world. The founding elite of the Islamic republic were not the Taliban; there was a pressing need to solve matters in such a way that would reconcile religion with the everyday reality of the country. Ironically, the debate over usury and banking took place while the banks continued to operate. Until a solution was found, banks did not pay interest; instead, they paid their clients a share of their profits. Debates similar to the one just mentioned were subject to heated discussion while Iran's new constitution was written. One of these subjects became increasingly central, eliciting a debate that was long-lasting and in some eyes the most significant debate of postrevolutionary Iran, namely the question of women and their public role.

The revolution relied heavily on the massive support of women, many of whom came from low-income backgrounds. After the revolution, the Islamic government and the ruling elite needed the support of women to carry out social and economic programs. As discussed in the previous chapter, a large number of women worked as volunteers, and without their effort the Islamic Republic could not have survived (see Rostami-Povey 2001). During the war with Iraq, millions of women, many of them from small cities and villages, supported the war effort by preparing food and clothing and donating money.[1] Ironically, while the state needed their support, the same state changed women's legal status in such a way that it undermined women's significance in Iranian society. What few rights women had gained under the Shah's family law reform were suddenly lost.

Millions of women who supported their husbands, sons, and brothers as they went into battle for their country and for the revolution found themselves, when their husband or son-in-law died on the front, losing custody of their children, or grandchildren, to their father-in-law. There was a huge contradiction between the state's need for women's support for its legitimization, coupled with public celebration of female roles as mothers and wives, and the state's withdrawal of support for the same mothers and wives when it came

---

1. Interview by Bahramitash with Professor Sam Aram in Tehran, 2005.

to gender laws such as the custody of their children. The loss of custody rights in particular sent shock waves throughout Iranian society and outraged women, especially those who had fought hard to bring the Islamic Republic into power. For many of these pious women who had worked hard in the service of revolutionary goals, violation of their rights was unacceptable. The unjust changes in women's rights fueled a movement of gender advocacy among both religious and secular women. This process slowly gathered momentum, particularly among the Islamist women. Islamist women, inspired by the revolutionary rhetoric of social justice and equality, demanded an extension of the concept of justice to women's issues in order to address gender inequalities. They were mobilized around the issue of gender equality using Islamic texts and exegetical techniques to interpret Islam. To their mind, Ayatollah Khomeini could and should change his interpretations.

This change had already happened. During the 1960s the ayatollah had taken a very conservative stand toward women's public role. His stand had changed dramatically when he called on women during the late 1970s to support the revolution and to take to the streets for demonstrations and then later to help social services to materialize. The basis of their argument was that if Islam is a religion of justice and equality—and here they relied on the popularized distinction between mostazafin and mostakberin, oppressed and oppressors—then religious texts can be interpreted as important sources for gender rights advocacy (see Afshar 1996a; Mir-Hosseini 1999; Halper 2005).

In response to the growing movement, Rafsanjani himself set up an Islamic Human Rights Committee during his term of office, composed of well-educated women, to address the issue of gender inequality. He also encouraged open debate about gender rights within an Islamic context. Rafsanjani's daughter established a pioneering publication in the Islamist women's press called *Hajar,* which was one of the first women's newspapers devoted to women's rights. This was followed by the launching of another women's magazine, *Zanan,* where articles about women's rights from a religious perspective became subjects of much criticism. A male cleric published articles under a female pseudonym and wrote one of the most critical articles of the time, mostly because of his close familiarity with the vocabulary of Islamic texts and *Kalam* (science of word of the Quran and *hadith*). This series of articles as well as other writings were the origins of a new interpretation of Islamic text and jurisprudence from a woman's rights perspective, a major breakaway from more than a millennium of male dominance over religious interpretations *(tafsir)*. This shift from a male narrative and male-centered tafsir to that of a female one has been a historical and profound shift with major ramifications not just on gender and religion but on the entire social and political debates of Iran.

Reinterpretation of Islamic text and hadith from women's point of view has played a vital role in the making of dynamic jurisprudence. This reinterpretation, as we will soon see, energized and fed a new movement in postrevolutionary Iran: the reform movement. Although it would be misleading to claim that women were the only driving force behind the reform movement, we will argue that gender debates were one of the major driving forces behind new debates regarding dynamic jurisprudence, and women were a major political force behind the victory of reform. The reform movement was heavily supported by women, but unlike during the revolution and the war with Iraq, women no longer relied on the goodwill of the leaders; they joined the political process and demanded their rights. This point will be elaborated in the next section, where the election results of 1997 and the coming into power of the reformist president Khatami are discussed.

Political Economy and Female Employment in the Reform Era

A host of economic and political factors contributed to the birth of the reform movement. During the first decade after the revolution, as the new state consolidated its power, income redistribution and the war with Iraq were the two dominant public debates. Once the war was over and after Ayatollah Khomeini's death, there was a political opening that brought to the surface some of the tensions suppressed during the years of war. Mehdi Moslem points out that while Russia and China were ruled by a strong, centralized power, the Iranian ruling elite, particularly after Khomeini's death, became fragmented into factions, each vying for power (2002).

One set of elite groups, which was largely in control of the executive and the legislature during the war, was similar to Christian Democratic parties in Europe that favored income redistribution. According to Moslem, this faction "for lack of a better word is called the 'left' or the 'radical' in Iran" (Moslem 2002, 5). Another faction was largely defined by Rafsanjani, who was in favor of building a business community, focusing on economic reconstructing of the country after the war. This faction came to occupy executive offices after Rafsanjani was elected president in 1989. A third faction was a collection of conservative groups, representing a large part of the clergy and the old merchant class, the bazaaris, who had a powerful lobby. The conservatives were most powerful in the judiciary and a host of institutions built around the office of the Supreme Leader. They were also present in the legislature, along with the other factions. These divisions were managed skillfully during Rafsanjani's term of office. He moved the leftist politicians from their government high offices to peripheral positions and provided opportunities for them to study for higher degrees or engage in teaching and research. The conservatives remained in their positions, but were initially kept at bay. However, the divisions and tensions between various factions within the ruling elite remained alive and at times intensified, making Iran's political scene quite dynamic.

From the outside, the political nuances of Iran's ruling elite are primarily overlooked, and the ruling elite is viewed as traditionalist. Moreover, it has been argued, particularly by the opposition outside Iran, that tensions between factions are either nonexistent or are part of populist politics designed to mislead the public. Nonetheless, on the one hand, when analyzing Iran's postrevolutionary political economy, it is difficult to argue that postrevolutionary Iran was antiscience and antitechnology or sought to return to ways of life that characterized preindustrial societies. Moreover, there have been major shifts in public policies under different presidents, with substantial consequences for Iran's social, economic, and political conditions, both domestically and internationally; these shifts must be reviewed. On the other hand, it should be noted that the ruling elite has been in agreement about maintaining the Islamic Republic and clearly is in major conflict with the type of opposition that wants to bring it down and supports a regime change in Iran.

At this juncture, it is important to lay out the basic structure of Iran's political configuration. While the president and Parliament are elected, they have to share power with other, unelected political institutions, which include the Supreme Leader, the head of the judiciary, the Expediency Council, and the Council of Guardians of the Constitution (Guardian Council) appointed by the Supreme Leader. The Guardian Council, a nonelected body with a great deal of political power and normally counting among its members the most conservative members of the elite, exerts a great deal of pressure on elected bodies. A constant battle is fought between the Guardian Council, on the one hand, and the elected members of the legislature and sometimes of the judiciary, on the other hand. The Guardian Council reviews all the laws passed by Parliament with a right to veto. It also has the prerogative to reject anyone's candidacy to run for Parliament seats or for president. Moreover, there is endless strife between civil society representatives and the Guardian Council.

One of the fiercest struggles was waged by women over the interpretation of the word *rajol-e siasy* (politically learned hu/man). Women, including Islamist women such as the daughter of Ayatollah Taleghani, Azam Talgani, and Rafat Bayat (member of Parliament during the last Parliament) have tried to run as candidates for the presidency. There have been protests against the interpretation of the constitution that the president must be a man. Muslim women have quietly been resisting by nominating themselves and running for president, despite the fact that it was common knowledge that the Guardian Council would automatically strike down their candidacy.

They have been arguing that rajol-e siasi means any person, either male or female, with sufficient knowledge of public affairs and refined political skills. The issue unified women of different backgrounds, Islamist and secular women alike. On June 12, 2005, just before Iran's presidential election, approximately two thousand women of diverse backgrounds participated in a sit-in demonstration in front of Tehran University. They campaigned for a revision of Iran's constitution that would allow women to run for the presidency. Over ninety women's groups signed a declaration that had been prepared in advance of the sit-in. Similar protests took place in major cities such as Esfahan, Tabriz, and Kermanshah, as well as in smaller cities in the provinces of Kurdistan, Lorestan, Sistan and Baluchistan, and Khorasan (Shekarloo 2005).

In spite of the pressure by civil organizations, the Guardian Council has retained its powerful influence over Iranian political life. In the late 1990s, following Rafsanjani's term in office, the challenge against the bulwark of clerical authority gained momentum by means of the reform movement. The roots of this movement date back to the early days of the revolution. The leaders of the "Left" faction, who were preparing in the wings to return to power, brought together the educated and nationalist members of the elite who were searching for an alternative from *within* existing power structures. This new coalition sought changes through reform, not revolution. The movement was strongly nationalistic, sharing the ideals of the incipient Iranian nationalism of the nineteenth century, which envisioned a society that defined itself by a dynamic understanding of its Islamic culture. The influence of nationalism has been elaborated in the work of many scholars who documented women's involvement in politics throughout the postrevolutionary period (Kian 1995; Poya 1999; Rostami-Povey 2001; Halper 2005; Bahramitash 2007a).

The reform movement became a major political force during the 1997 presidential election when Khatami, supported by the coalition of the "Left" faction, went head to head against a conservative candidate, Nategh Nori. Khatami, an eloquent speaker, appealed to the public and to all who wanted a more democratic government to unite for reform. Some have argued that the 1997 election, known as *Dovom-e Khordad* (May 23), was in itself a revolution, while others refer to it as a major deception of the Iranian public. The election brought the "Left" faction, now known as the Dovom-e Khordad Front or simply the Reformists, back to power. However, at this time it is considered by some a turning point in the social transformation of postrevolutionary Iran. It was certainly unlike the events of 1979 as far as women were concerned. In 1997, two decades after the revolution, Iranians seemed to aspire more purposefully to greater freedom, a more equitable rule of law, commitment to human rights, and building of a civil society. More important, the issue of women's rights was brought on the agenda for public debate.

Khatami and the Reformists' main political constituents were women and youths, who were enthusiastic about a new president who promised to address their concerns. While in 1979 women had been mobilized by Ayatollah Khomeini, who urged them to dedicate themselves to the revolution, two decades later women began demanding their proper rights. Having learned from the mistakes of the revolution era, a new generation of women realized that if they were not vigilant about the preservation of their rights they might be excluded again from the political life of their country.

Khatami's major domestic political platform was to strengthen civil society while his foreign policy revolved around the concept of a dialogue among civilizations. Spending less time than his predecessors on economic policies, Khatami focused on social issues, expansion of funding for civil society organizations such as nongovernmental organizations (NGOs). Although a substantial part of the funds and government support went to individuals and groups closely connected with the Reformists, the opportunities became more widely available for others to assume active roles in the civil society. Indeed, the number of NGOs skyrocketed during the eight years of Khatami's government, providing a window of opportunity for collective and organized social action toward advancement of women's causes.

The extent of the dependence of the civil society activities under the Khatami administration on government support and political ties can only be understood when considering how NGOs suffered after the departure of the Reformists from the legislature and the executive during 2004–5. Today, after nearly three years of Ahmadinejad's presidency, funding has almost completely dried up and most NGOs are left to fend for themselves. Many leaders of women's NGOs who relied on the state for funds and other resources are now working hard to maintain their function. They do not relinquish, yet challenges are immense.[2] The fact that Khatami's government provided funding for NGOs has become a point of criticism for those who argue that state funding undermines women's independent agendas and makes them dependent on and complacent about state policies. Women's organizations that did rely on state funding had to remain within certain boundaries, and they might well have been in danger of being co-opted. Yet it could equally be possible that while the state sought to co-opt women's organizations, these organizations might have also engaged in co-opting the state to their own ends, some for public causes and others perhaps for more specific purposes.

The Reformists' control over Iran's political agenda started waning after the reelection of President Khatami in 2001, when the conservatives managed to block their efforts through legal battles. The Reformists' effort to work through the constitution was severely undermined by the Conservatives, entrenched in the nonelected institutions of the political apparatus. The public frustration with the inability of the Reformists to push forward their agenda prompted the Khatami administration to quietly shift its attention from political reform to economic reform. While in his first term Khatami did not have a clear economic strategy, he pursued a gradual market liberalization, privatization, and regulatory reform. This process coincided with an increase in Iran's oil revenues and produced respectable

---

2. Fieldwork, winter 2008.

rates of economic growth after 2001. However, economic issues had become a major challenge to the postrevolutionary political elite.

During the late 1980s and in the early 1990s the country experienced a quick economic recovery from the war, which led to improvements in some of the basic economic indicators. The economy suffered a major setback in the wake of the 1994–95 balance of payments crises. The crises, combined with an intensification of external economic sanctions imposed by the United States, slowed down the economy considerably in the mid-1990s. However, growth resumed in the late 1990s and accelerated during 2001–5. It should be noted that while economic problems have been a major source of dissatisfaction, particularly among those who live in urban areas, some of the basic indicators have been improving. For instance, despite sanctions and the eight years of war, a United Nations report in 2003 indicated that "Iran's 65 million inhabitants enjoy an average quality of life, which when quantified by the Human Development Index (HDI), is near the top of the middle-level human development category. With a value of around 0.72 in 2002, Iran appears to be within reach of the level of medium human development index (starting at 1)" (United Nations 2003, 14). The improvement in general and overall human development took place in spite of the fact that Iran absorbed the largest refugee population in the world (mainly Afghan refugees who now constitute 4 percent of the total population), receiving "little international assistance to help refugees" (United Nations 2003, 20). Apparently the spirit of the revolution has won some of the battles Iranians had sought to fight in the long run. At the same time, as some of the critics point out, some of these improvements could have been brought about through more cost-effective means.

The broad trends in economic performance since the revolution can be seen in historical perspective in figures 3.1 and 3.2. Exploring these trends is important for understanding the economic conditions for women's employment in Iran. As figure 3.1 shows, GDP per capita had grown quite fast between the mid-1950s and the mid-1970s and declined sharply after the revolution until the end of the Iran-Iraq War in 1988. After a quick recovery between 1989 and 1993, per capita growth became sluggish until about 2001, when it reached a more or less stable rate, averaging about 3.8 percent per year. In 2006 Iran's annual per capita income had returned to its historical peak in 1976, which was about $8,000 in constant international dollars for year 2000. If since 1979 Iran had grown every year at the same rate as the average for all the developing countries (on average 2.78 percent per year during 1979–2006), its per capita income in 2006 would have been about $14,800, or 85 percent higher than where it stood, not a trivial amount at all. Given Iran's population of 70.5 million in 2006, the difference would have meant $480 billion additional GDP in that year. For the entire period 1979–2006, the difference would have added up to more than $6.4 trillion.

Contrary to what is often assumed, Iran's economy has been undergoing substantial transformations. The share of the agricultural sector in the non-oil economy, which was on a steep decline between 1953 and 1978, recovered somewhat during the first decade after the revolution. It then experienced consistent decline again in the reconstruction and reform period, reaching its lowest prerevolution level by 2005. The share of non-oil industrial and manufacturing sectors followed the opposite path until 1990, after which it fluctuated around a stationary path. Like industry, the share of the services sector had also risen steadily before the revolution, but it stagnated during the 1980s and resumed its expansion afterward. Overall, the service sector has had the highest rate of growth in Iran's economy since the revolution. These trends seem to be driven largely by the availability and use of oil rents in the Iranian economy. As oil revenues increase and induce greater government expenditure, demands for all products rise. In the past, the government has generally tried to meet the excess demand for agricultural products by increasing imports to keep their prices low. But importing services has been far more difficult and, as a result, that part of the economy has expanded faster at the expense of agriculture. Only during the 1980s, when oil revenues had declined and were largely committed to the war effort, did these trends reverse. In the case of manufacturing, the government has had the option to import, as in agriculture.

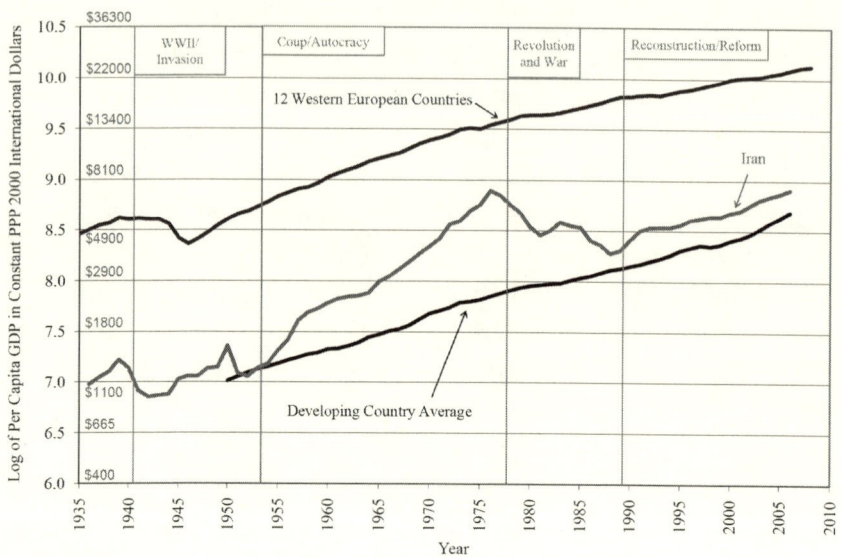

3.1. Iran's Economic Growth in Comparative Perspective. *Source:* Esfahani and Pesaran 2009.

However, it has opted to protect manufacturing and to subsidize its investments to various degrees. As a result, that sector grew for most of the prerevolutionary period and did not decline as agriculture did after 1989. These patterns are important particularly because they have implications for women's employment in Iran. Specifically, the rise of the service sector seems to be congruent with the skills and job preferences of the new entrants into the female labor market in Iran.

The statistical data on women's role in the Iranian economy will be explored in detail in the next chapter. Here we provide an overview of the main trends in women's employment since the revolution. The most eye-catching and most debated aspect of the women's labor market experience in the past three decades in Iran is the sharp decline in their participation and employment rates in the 1980s. Many observers initially viewed this decline as a definite consequence of Islamization that sharply intensified ideological and cultural biases against women's participation in the county's social and economic life. However, our analysis of the data shows that

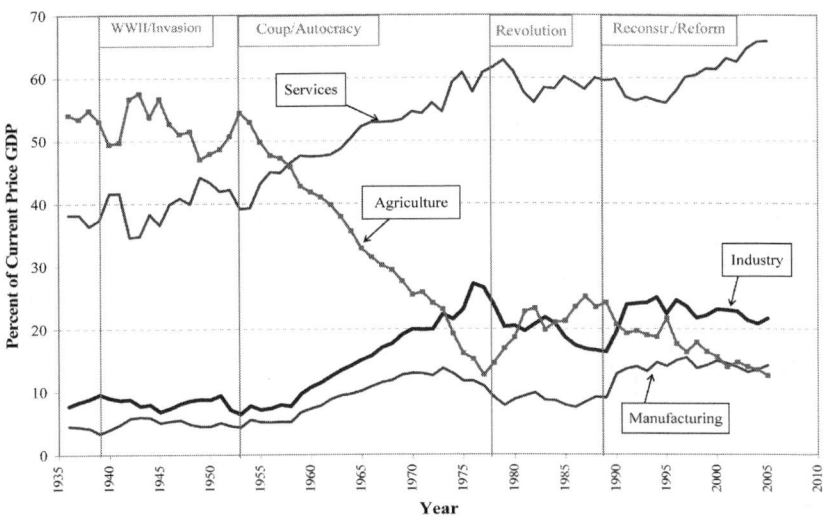

3.2. Sectoral Shares in Iran's Non-Oil Value-Added Production. *Source:* Esfahani and Pesaran 2009.

while that factor had indeed affected many women in the modern sectors of the economy, the bulk of the decline in female employment had a different origin.[3] To gain insight into the process, one should first note that most of the increase in female employment prior to the revolution was owing to the expansion of carpet and handicraft industries that relied largely on very young uneducated women, mostly age ten to twenty years old and living in rural areas. In most of the 1960s and 1970s, almost two-thirds of manufacturing workers in rural areas were women, almost 60 percent of them below twenty years of age, largely working as unpaid family labor. Those industries faced major difficulties in the 1980s because of disruption of trade and shortage of raw materials, hence the sharp decline in their demand for labor, especially female workers. While

---

3. Valentine Moghadam in her earlier work does recognize that the decline of female labor may have been more the result of disruption of production than of discrimination (V. Moghadam 1988).

the share of women in the labor force age twenty years and above declined from 10 to 8.9 percent in urban areas, the corresponding drop for the rural areas was from 11.7 to 7.1 percent, largely owing to the decline in women's rural manufacturing jobs. It is possible that in the absence of the ideological biases against women, more of them would have kept their jobs and the government might have tried harder to support those industries. But a sizable decline seems to have been unavoidable given the ongoing war and the serious fiscal conditions facing the government.

As in manufacturing, the share of women in service activities declined in the 1980s. But this decline had a relatively small impact on overall female employment because of the fact that the percentage of women in this sector was relatively low. Interestingly, the share of women in agriculture seems to have increased in the 1980s. However, the agricultural figures must be treated with caution because of data irregularities. This sector of the economy has suffered from inaccurate data collection during the census that took place in the 1970s and 1980s. This inaccuracy is because these censuses did not treat the seasonally unemployed workers as employed.

Since the mid-1980s, the share of women in the labor force and employment has increased tangibly, especially since the mid-1990s. There has also been a significant shift in the structure of the female labor force from teenage, uneducated workers in rural manufacturing toward twenty- to fifty-year-old educated professionals in the urban service sector. This shift has been driven by a number of factors. First, education has expanded tremendously in both urban and rural areas, providing women with the ability and aspiration to work in a variety of positions beyond manual manufacturing work, which was their main mode of employment until the 1980s (F. Moghadam 2004). Second, rising incomes fueled by oil rents have increased the reservation wages of most women, making it costly to employ them as cheap manual labor (Karshenas and Moghadam 2001; V. Moghadam 2005). Third, urbanization has proceeded at a fast pace (see table 3.1). As a result, far fewer women now live in rural areas where cottage industries used to employ them. These days almost

Table 3.1 Urbanization and the Share of Women in Rural and Urban Areas

Year	Urban Population as Percentage of Total Population	Share of Women in Urban Population (%)	Share of Women in Rural Population (%)
1956	31.4	48.1	49.2
1966	37.3	47.6	48.7
1976	47.3	47.3	50.1
1986	53.3	48.5	49.1
1996	60.8	48.9	49.9
2006	68.5	49.1	49.3

Source: Statistical Center of Iran, www.sci.org.ir.

70 percent of women live in urban areas, where they have chances of finding service sector jobs that pay more and better match their skills and preferences. Finally, as pointed out earlier, the inflow of oil revenues and economic growth have raised the demand for services, especially modern professional services, creating new employment opportunities for educated women.

Another notable trend in the female labor market is the steady rise in women's share in agricultural employment. This trend may partly be a consequence of the glitches in data collection mentioned earlier, particularly increasing recognition of the roles that women have always had in agricultural production (V. Moghadam 1995b). However, it may also reflect many other factors, especially economic ones such as the replacement of higher-cost male workers with lower-cost female workers in a sector that faces strong competition from imports. Alternatively, shifts in cropping and productions patterns, particularly toward lines of activity facing less competition such as production of fruits, vegetables, and animal husbandry, where women have always played greater roles, may have increased the demand for female labor. It should be noted that the rising presence of women in rural agriculture after the revolution may not be attributable completely or entirely to increased out-migration of men from rural areas. Men's out-migration was much more characteristic of the rapid urbanization process preceding the revolution; in the first decade of the revolution there was an attempt to reverse that process. Later, owing to rising education among women, more educated women tended to migrate out of rural areas. Additionally, Iran has been rapidly turned into an urban society and many areas that were a village one or two decades ago are now small cities, earning the status of urban area.

The Islamization process that followed the revolution had a unique effect on employment patterns. The new constitution required the state to provide universal education and health care. However, the Islamic context entailed separate provision of such services for men and women. This made it easier for girls and women from conservative families, which comprised the majority of the population, to attend schools. It also meant that there was a substantial demand for female schoolteachers and health care professionals. Prior to the revolution, men could teach in primary and secondary schools, including sexually segregated schools, but after the revolution, school staff had to be exclusively female for female students. This stipulation created a shortage of math and physics teachers in high schools, a situation to which the state responded by encouraging women to enter university and study natural sciences. Nowadays women constitute more than half of the employees in education, health care, and social services (see the next chapter). The increase in the number of women employed in these professions is more pronounced in rural areas than in cities. This disparity corresponds to rising educational opportunities for rural women.

The expansion of female employment since the mid-1980s has been associated with greater numbers of women as employers, executives, and managers, increasingly in the private sector. This growth has been partly owing to women's rising educational levels (F. Moghadam 2004) and partly the consequence of relaxation of restrictions on women's economic activities and their growing work experiences.

While women's education and presence in high-skill jobs has increased, there has been a rise in the number of educated young women who have been unable to find any job. In fact, with the entry into the labor market of the large cohort of young people born in the 1980s, Iran is currently facing very high unemployment rates, well over 40 percent, among women in their twenties. Although the economy's structure has shifted toward the urban service sector, the supply of women who seek jobs in that part of the economy has grown much faster. The available jobs are captured by more mature and experienced employment seekers, leaving fewer positions for the younger cohorts, who are no longer willing to take manual low-pay jobs as in the prerevolution years. These trends and patterns along with other aspects of women's employment will be further examined in the next chapter. In the following section, we elaborate on some of the causes and consequences of women's rising employment.

Forces Behind and Consequences of Rising Female Employment

Iranian women's employment has changed qualitatively and quantitatively. In this section, we shall briefly discuss the causes and consequences of overall changes regarding education, marriage and family, health, women's volunteer works, art, and sports activities.

Education

As discussed in the previous chapter, women's role as volunteers in the literacy campaign was the driving force behind rising levels in basic literacy. More than two decades after the revolution, women constitute close to 60 percent of university students. This seems to be a complex consequence of educational and social policies under the Islamic Republic, which kept some opportunities closed for women but opened up others. In particular, segregation and affirmation of the family's (especially the male members') control over their daughters imposed restrictions on social and economic activities of women. However, the same policies reassured conservative families that education of women would not entail religious or cultural "decadence." Notably, education also became an accepted reason for postponing marriage and warding off pressure from elders on young women to get married. This acceptability rendered education as the main means for young women to gain control over their lives and shape brighter futures for themselves.

At the same time, education was made more accessible, and indeed mandatory, for Muslim women as a *jihad*. For example, many women from low-income households attended classes that were often held in mosques. In addition, the Reconstruction Jihad, an organization formed to help develop infrastructure and productive capacity in poor regions of the country, also became involved in the nationwide literacy campaign, making the struggle for women's literacy a double jihad in rural areas. These jihads mobilized rural women and inspired some urban women to go to rural areas as volunteers for basic literacy campaigns. In addition to prescribing the right for basic literacy for adults, the new constitution made it a state responsibility to provide for the education of the whole population. The government was now responsible for establishing public schools, which became a source of employment, and fulfilling this responsibility also paved the way for girls to have better access to education. Significant changes were the result of new sexual segregation policies. During the Shah's regime, many traditional families were reluctant to send their daughters to schools, especially to those where they came in contact with male teachers or male students. In fact, the Shah and his White Revolution provided literacy programs in both rural areas and urban areas, alongside vocational training schools for women. In fact, some of the postrevolutionary programs were exactly the same as what they had been before the revolution, but in the case of low-income and rural women, postrevolutionary programs were more in line with people's cultural background and norms and earned more support. The rate of illiteracy declined among women more than men, dropping from almost 70 percent in 1976 to below 20 percent in 2006. Literacy among young females increased even more significantly, reaching nearly 100 percent, as indicated in table 3.2.

The level of primary education enrollment for girls increased from 40 percent in 1965 to 122 percent in 2005 (table 3.3). Female enrollment in secondary educational institutions steadily increased

Table 3.2 Literacy Rate

Census Year	1956	1966	1976	1986	1996	2006
LITERACY RATE OF POPULATION 10 YEARS AND OVER						
Female	7.3	16.5	30.5	47.6	71.7	79.5
Male	22.2	39.0	53.2	68.0	83.3	88.5
Total	14.9	28.1	42.1	39.0	77.6	84.1
YOUTH LITERACY RATE (AGE 15–24)						
Female	10.0	23.6	41.2	65.4	90.3	96.1
Male	28.5	52.4	67.3	84.4	95.4	97.1
Total	19.0	37.6	54.1	75.1	92.9	96.6

Source: Statistical Center of Iran, www.sci.org.ir.

from 18 percent in the 1970s, reaching 78 percent by 2005. Increase in enrollments among women in tertiary education led to the increase in the proportion of female educators not only in primary and secondary schools but also in tertiary education.[4] The percentage of women studying in major universities in Tehran increased slowly over the course of a decade from the mid-1990s to 2004. Departments of women's studies were created in major universities throughout the country. These departments are mainly, if not exclusively, made up of women. The result of our fieldwork indicates that there is a rising interest in women's studies programs among men as well as women.

In the aftermath of the revolution, certain university disciplines were closed to women, including agriculture and mechanical engineering. While authorities prevented women's ability to study certain subjects, they actively encouraged them to pursue certain others, among them gynecology and pediatrics. Thanks to the pressure exerted by women (of both secular and religious backgrounds), the authorities repealed its prohibitions later and today there are no barriers to entry

---

4. Interview with Professor Shamsosadat Zahedei in Tehran, 2005.

Table 3.3 Enrollment Rates

Year	1965	1970	1975	1980	1985	1990	1995	2000	2005
PRIMARY									
Female	40	52	71	79	87	106	98	91	122
Male	85	93	114	112	109	118	104	96	100
Total	63	73	93	87	98	112	101	94	111
SECONDARY									
Female	11	18	33	32	36	46	69	76	78
Male	24	36	57	52	54	64	81	80	83
Total	18	27	45	42	45	55	75	78	81
TERTIARY									
Female		2	3	3	3	6	13	18	25
Male		4	6	6	7	14	21	20	23
Total	2	3	5	5	5	10	17	19	24

Source: World Bank, World Development Indicators Database, http://data.worldbank.org/data-catalog/world-development-indicators.

into any subject. When the ban on the above-mentioned subjects was lifted, the promotion of female-friendly subjects backfired. Since 2007 the Ministry of Science and Technology has instituted measures that favor male applicants in medical schools and other faculties where the percentage of female students has far surpassed that of males. It is argued that if the quota against female students is not imposed, Iran may soon be facing a shortage of male doctors, certainly a problem in a country defined by sex segregation. The topic was debated in Parliament in 2005 but it created a major uproar and fierce resistance in the country and was abandoned at that time; however, the practice of sex segregation in accepting students in different university disciplines was performed by the new government and the policy was finally approved by Parliament in 2008.

The Open University has played a crucial role in women's presence in higher education since its establishment in the 1980s. The Open University, or *Daneshgah-e Azad Eslami,* has expanded enormously and now has branches throughout the country, particularly in smaller cities. This is a private university with a lesser status, yet it is more accessible because its admission requirements are not as competitive as those of public universities.

Not only do women attend universities in higher numbers than men, they have a much higher propensity to finish their university studies (United Nations 2003). Many women attend universities because they have limited options to be active in society elsewhere. With soaring unemployment rates, staying at university seems a safe option. Another reason for the growing number of women in universities is the realization of many Iranian men that pursuing higher education will not necessarily lead to high-income jobs. For this reason, it is possible that some of the increase in female involvement in higher education is the result of men's not wishing to continue their education. Moreover, attending university provides an opportunity for single women to carve out a level of independent life. Women who leave home to continue their education and live in university dormitories for several years do not return home the same. They are resistant toward family authority. This quest for independence leads to an increased desire to seek sources of income and employment.

The expansion of tertiary education has also provided an opportunity for many young women to come to large cities and attend universities there. But there was a reverse trend that saw many women from larger cities go to smaller cities, where attitudes toward the role of women in public are more conservative. This large-scale temporary migration of young women had a huge impact on women's public role and their employment prospects. The women who came from smaller cities to big, urban centers became exposed to the more perceptible public role women played in large cities. By the same token, women from big cities who moved to smaller cities changed the face of smaller cities by being more active in public life. During the late 1970s and the early 1980s, when Bahramitash lived in Ardebil for several months, the city remained unaffected by the revolution and its Islamization process. Women wore chador and did not drive cars, both before and after the revolution. When she returned to the city in 2007 to conduct fieldwork, she was confronted with immense changes. The city was transformed. It had many young female students, especially visible in the city center. These young women were wearing headscarves instead of traditional chador. Women's public visibility was exemplified by the number of young women employed in ministries and state offices, some of them driving to work.

Family and Marriage

The decline of family authority, especially the decline in fathers' role in decision-making, has been documented in a longitudinal survey that examines the fathers' role in decision-making over a five-year span (comparing 1995 data with that of 2000) (Mohseni 2000). The research also shows a correlation between levels of education and changes in attitude (Mohseni 2000, 232).

Some of the decline in family authority correlates with the rising age of marriage for women. Women, on average, marry at least four years later today than they did a few decades ago and before the revolution. It is interesting to note that this rising age is contrary to commonly held views about the impact of Islamization. Table 3.4 shows that the average age of marriage for women in urban areas was 23.2 years in 2006 compared to 19 in the mid-1960s. In rural areas the corresponding figures are 17 years and 23.4 years respectively. The data indicate that the average age of marriage for rural women increased much faster than for urban women. During 1966–2006, the average age for first marriages increased by 1.3 years for men, while the increase was 5.3 years for women. These data suggest that in the aftermath of the revolution, women's average age of marriage rose more than that of men did (Moslem 2002). The rise in the age of marriage is closely related to the growing number of women in the labor force (See chapter 4.)

Furthermore, there has been an increase in the percentage of single women ages fifteen to nineteen, rising from 66.1 percent to 82.6 percent between 1976 and 2006 (table 3.5). For women in the twenty- to twenty-four-year age bracket, the increase was from 22.5

Table 3.4 Average Age at First Marriage

Census Year	1956	1966	1976	1986	1996	2006
WHOLE COUNTRY						
Male	24.9	25.0	24.1	23.6	25.6	26.6
Female	19.0	18.4	19.7	19.8	22.4	23.2
URBAN AREAS						
Male	25.7	25.6	25.1	24.2	26.2	26.5
Female	18.5	19.0	20.2	20.0	22.5	23.2
RURAL AREAS						
Male	24.3	24.4	22.7	22.6	24.5	25.5
Female	19.3	17.9	19.1	19.6	22.3	23.4

Source: Statistical Center of Iran, www.sci.org.ir.

percent to 49.9 percent during the same period. If we also take into account that women in rural areas tend to get married at an earlier age, then the figures become more significant. These young single women, who tend to have more university education, are predisposed to seek employment, further increasing the female labor supply.

Although there are still more men than women in the total population (fig. 3.3), the percentage of single women surpasses that of single men. Possibly some single women, if not the majority of them, have to rely on their own resources. In the event of a divorce, especially in cases where judges are not sympathetic toward the fate of women, divorced women can end up becoming financially self-supporting. According to recent statistics, female-headed households are on the rise (see chapter 6). This rise is coupled with a rising divorce rate, currently at 11.5 percent. The divorce rate has increased from 9.1 percent in 2001 to 11.5 percent in 2006 (Kazemipour 2007). Many widowed women may be self-supporting. Self-support is more critical in places like in Tehran, which has a population of 14 million. The divorce rate in the urban areas of Tehran province is 21.4 percent (Kazemipour 2007).

Table 3.5 Percentage of Single Women Age 15–24

Year	1956	1966	1976	1986	1996	2006
AGE GROUP 15–19 YEARS:						
Never Married	59.0	52.8	65.7	64.1	82.6	82.3
Divorced	0.8	0.5	0.2	0.1	0.1	0.2
Widowed	0.2	0.2	0.2	0.1	0.1	0.1
Total	60.0	53.5	66.1	64.3	82.8	82.6
AGE GROUP 20–24 YEARS:						
Never Married	15.7	13.4	21.4	25.6	41.3	49.2
Divorced	1.6	0.9	0.6	0.4	0.4	0.5
Widowed	0.7	0.6	0.5	0.2	0.2	0.2
Total	17.9	14.8	22.5	26.2	41.9	49.9

Source: Statistical Center of Iran, www.sci.org.ir.

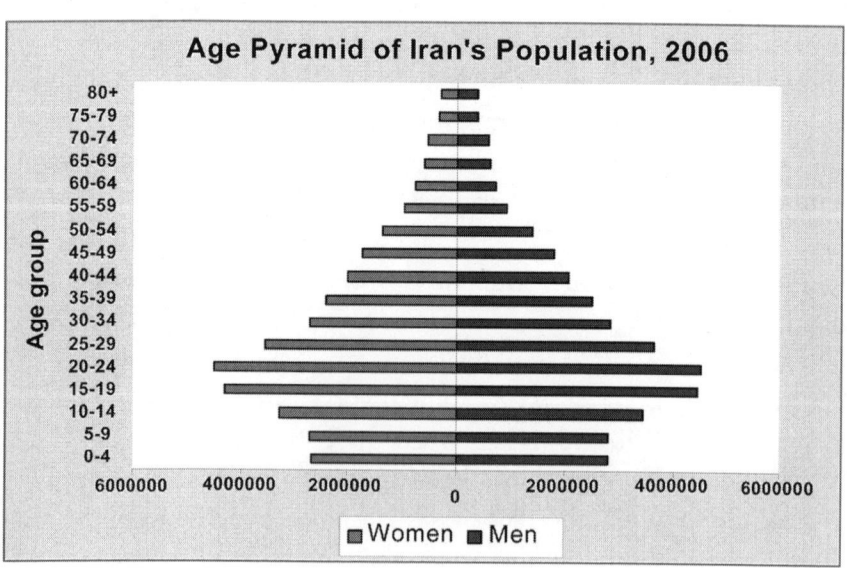

3.3. Age Pyramid of Iran's Population, 2006. *Source:* Statistical Center of Iran.

Health

Table 3.6 shows that life expectancy for women increased at a higher rate than that of men. Today women outlive men more than they did in the 1960s and 1970s. A woman who is born today is expected to live longer than a man, a fact that conditions many women to seek an independent source of income for their elderly years. Traditionally, women have relied on their children to provide for them in their old age. Because of the decline, particularly in major cities, in traditional family preferences, on the one hand, and the dramatic decline of the number of children in families and of fertility rates, on the other hand, women are left with fewer children to rely on.

The fertility rate in Iran declined from 7.0 births per woman in 1960 to 2.1 in 2005 (table 3.7). This dramatic decline means that women today have more free time than in the past few decades. With declining fertility rates, not only do women spend less time being pregnant and nursing, but they also have to devote less time to household chores. This change, along with the greater availability of machinery that facilitates household work (such as washing machines), has added to women's disposable time, which they can devote to improving the quality of life for themselves and their children, including greater participation in the labor market. Decline in fertility rates can, of course, be both the result and the cause of increase in female labor supply. Steady increase in female employment, in both formal and informal sectors, and in volunteer work

Table 3.6 Life Expectancy at Birth (Years)

Year	1960	1970	1980	1990	2000	2005
Female	48.5	54.0	59.7	66.2	70.9	72.8
Male	48.5	54.2	58.3	63.9	68.2	69.6
Total	48.5	54.1	58.9	65.0	69.5	71.1

Source: World Bank, World Development Indicators Database. http://data.worldbank.org/data-catalog/world-development-indicators.

Table 3.7 Fertility Rate

Year	1960	1970	1980	1990	2000	2005
Births per Woman	7.0	6.6	6.6	4.8	2.3	2.1

Source: World Bank, World Development Indicators database, http://data.worldbank.org/data-catalog/world-development-indicators.

has limited women's time to have more children; having fewer children and having better knowledge of economic activities have given them greater opportunities to seek paid employment.

*Women's Volunteer Work
(the Family Planning Campaign)*

Women's role as volunteers has been documented (Poya 1999; Rostami-Povey 2001). Here, we only focus on one type of volunteer work, one that had a major impact on national policy and simultaneously gave women an opportunity to realize their power through collective action. Following the revolution and during the war with Iraq there was a major increase in fertility rates. The rates reached such alarming levels that the Office of Budget and Planning, along with the academic community and the Ministry of Health, launched into action. The problem mobilized the Muslim doctors association. They lobbied the religious community, especially Ayatollah Khomeini, who finally endorsed a family planning program (Bahramitash 2007b).

As we have seen in chapter 2, during the 1980s Iran experienced a major economic stagnation. The dire straits of the economy, exacerbated by the war and by plummeting world oil prices, forced the government to rely increasingly on volunteer work. A major campaign was launched by religious authorities in order to mobilize women from low-income groups to perform work as health care workers for the national family program. In the rural sector, young women were employed as health care workers *(behvarz)* by the Ministry of Health, while in urban centers women, primarily from low-income neighborhoods, were mobilized to implement the nationwide program (Hoodfar and Assadpour 2000; Bahramitash 2007b). Encouraged by religious authorities, thousands of women joined the program as activists, going door-to-door, distributing birth control pills and other means of birth control. This was a highly successful program that stood in contrast to a similar program launched during the reign of the Shah in the 1970s. The Shah's campaign was characterized by its secular orientation and mainly implemented by the participation of middle-class women through state-funded venues. The Shah's program, which did not enjoy the support of religious authorities, failed to reach people in rural areas and low-income people in cities.

Just as the literacy program, endorsed by religious authorities, enjoyed considerable success, the family planning program in Iran turned out to be the most successful program in the world, according to the United Nations (Bahramitash 2007a). The credit for the success of the program should be attributed to the thousands of women who came from low-income households to their volunteer work. They were the ones who performed the bulk of the work necessary for a campaign that has become world-renowned. The campaign provided an opportunity for many of the women to be mobilized in a nationwide development project while its success brought them self-confidence. Volunteer organizations remained active and continued their work even after the national crisis. Today, Family Planning Association (FPA) is the largest NGO in the country. It has recently joined the International Planned Parenthood Federation (IPPF), the largest NGO global network on reproductive health, an organization that considers women's reproductive health as their basic right. It should be noted, however, that recently the fertility rate has increased; this news may be alarming for policy makers who have worked hard to bring down the fertility rate.

Sports, Arts, Cinema, and Literature

Following the revolution, women's presence in public life experienced a crisis, one that was nowhere as grave as in the domain of sports. For the urban middle and upper classes and those who came from the elite families, prerevolutionary Iran provided ample opportunities for women to pursue many different sports, which included ice-skating and bowling. Women of middle- and high-income backgrounds enjoyed both outdoor and indoor sports. After the revolution, however, all sports facilities were closed to women. This move created uproar among the secular middle and upper classes in urban areas, yet they were powerless and marginalized by the new regime. However, a new type of woman started to be vocal about the lack of sports facilities for women. The persistence of Faezeh Hashemi, daughter of Rafsanjani, and that of others such as Rafat Bayat eventually materialized in the launch of what later became known as the Muslim Women's Olympics. The first female Olympics were held in Tehran in 1993, an event that was the fruit of the advocacy of Faezeh Rafsanjani. Since then, several other all-female Olympics have taken place, in 1997 and in 2005. The event led to the formation of the Muslim Women Sports Council *(Shoray-e Hambastegy-e Varzesh Banovan)* and was supported by Rafsanjani during his presidency. The last Muslim Women's Olympics, in 2005, was supported by the mayor of the time, Mahmood Ahmadinejad, who later became president. Iranian women have also taken part in international Olympics and they enjoyed some success in sports such as shooting. The ramifications of these developments in female sports were that significant employment opportunities were created for women coaches and trainers. The Olympics not only mobilized women internationally but they provided an opportunity for women to demand access to separate sports facilities and all-female spaces for different sports activities. As a result, there have been a rising number of government-funded, all-female sports facilities throughout the country. Although sports started by being exclusive to the middle and upper classes, in the past few decades they have been extended to lower-class women as well.

Today women are taking part in competitive horseback riding, martial arts, and basketball, and have won medals in world Olympics in sports such as shooting, fencing, basketball, horseback riding, and canoeing. For the first time in history, a group of Iranian women in 2005 conquered Mount Everest.[5] However, quite ironically, conquering Mount Everest has been easier than attending a local soccer match. Women continue to be banned from entering a soccer stadium during men's games, a restriction that has become an extremely sore point for young women, many of whom continue to play soccer fully dressed and take part in international competition. Interestingly, Ahmadinejad made an effort to remove the ban in 2006, only to be vetoed by the conservative religious establishment in Qom.

Contrary to common held views, postrevolutionary Iranian women continued to be active, and in some areas such as cinema and literature more so than before the revolution. Female artists became leading figures in fund-raising and organizing events.

Women, particularly from the middle and upper classes, have taken a prominent role in the arts and in literature. In spite of restrictions imposed by the *Ershad-e Eslami* (Ministry of Culture and Islamic Guidance) on publication, there have been an increasing number of female novelists, playwrights, and translators. A few women have been working as owners of publishing companies. There are also a few successful women's magazines. The number of female journalists has been rising at a phenomenal rate, and they are part of a union. The trend toward increases in women's press has been curtailed in the aftermath of the one-million-signature campaign (this campaign aimed to collect one million signatures to change laws that discriminate against women). One of the prominent women's

---

5. The issue of gender politics continues around the issue of women's sports; there are some gains and some losses, Bayat, current member of Parliament, criticized the dismissal of the deputy for female sports. She argued that leaving the issue of advancing women's sports to sports clubs is insufficient and "we need to continue women's achievement in world Olympics." http://www.shirzanan.com/spip.php?article1083, accessed January 2008. This year the government was forced to increase its budget for women's sports from 9 percent to 30 percent.

presses, *Zanan*, has been shut down. (However, while carrying out fieldwork, Bahramitash learned from a member of the staff that the magazine will be published under a different name.)

After the revolution one expected the disappearance of women from cinema and television. Although there was a palpable decline in their presence following the first few years of the revolution, by the end of the 1980s female actresses and new faces started to enter cinema, theater, and television. This was an important development because it helped to normalize women's presence in the public sphere in postrevolutionary Iran. With the success of Iranian cinema in international film festivals, many women have entered the movie industry, not just as actresses but also as filmmakers. Currently there are several prominent female directors such as Rakhshan bani Etemad, Samira Makhmalbaf, Pouran Drekhshandeh, and Tahmineh Milani, outnumbering female directors in Hollywood, where there is only one female director. As for television, there is a family channel that focuses primarily on women and children. Many women continue to work as camerawomen, editors, and play and film scriptwriters.

Women's growing presence in these activities is significant. Their growing number illustrates that unlike what one may have expected from the Islamization process, women have become prominent even in professions related to arts and artistic expressions. Some of the changes that have occurred in women's employment, such as their increasing role in the professional categories (this includes different types including the cinema industry), will be documented statistically in the next chapter.

Some have argued that women are not able to appear in public in movies, in sports, and in other social activities without the veil, and this has put a damper on women's social presence. This prohibition applies more to the middle class and the elite and does not necessarily apply to women of low-income backgrounds who were never unveiled and who continued to wear the veil before and after the revolution. Generally, in spite of certain restrictions women continue to fight for public presence and at times have won the battle.

Women in the Office

Before the revolution, there was one female minister, but after the revolution women did not rise to that level, though they have been able to become elected both at the municipal and the parliamentary level. In the aftermath of the revolution, there was only one member of Parliament. However, during the reform a rise occurred in the number of women who held political office. Although no woman has become cabinet minister to date, something that was a sore spot for Khatami, the reform era saw a boost in women's political presence. The increase in the number of women in political office in Khatami's government earned him the massive support of women. For instance, the Bureau of Women's Affairs (BWA) (whose name was subsequently changed to Centre for Women's Participation) expanded its operations during the reform movement thanks to the government's allocating funds for its various activities. BWA, which was founded under Rafsanjani, was headed by Shahla Habibi, but the main driving force behind the BWA was the bureau's deputy, Massoumeh Ebtekar, whom Khatami later appointed to become Iran's first female vice president. Ebtekar was later assigned to head the Organization for the Protection of the Environment *(Sazman-e mohit-e-zist)* as well. The Centre for Women's Participation (CWP) under Khatami was headed by Zahra Shojai, who was made one of President Khatami's new deputies concurrently with Ebtekar. Behind the change of name, from Bureau of Women's Affairs to Centre for Women's Participation, was the transformation from focusing on women's issues to enhancing their role in society. Shojai, a vocal woman, was highly concerned with changing the public status of women. During an interview she pointed out that she did not lose any time or opportunity to remind members of the government about the important roles women play and why there is a pressing need to enhance their public role.[6] In an interview with a leading newspaper, Shojai demanded

---

6. Fieldwork interview, Tehran, 2004.

that housework and women's role as unpaid family workers (in rural areas) be considered as work and receive pay.[7]

Perhaps one of the most significant aspects of women's electoral performance was the 1999 elections, when many women became elected to be leading members of local councils. In fact, women were elected in more than a hundred cities in Iran.[8] Because of the high participation of women as voters, the Sixth Majlis (2000–2004) was dominated by the Reformists. The women who became new members of Parliament took a firm stand on women's issues and came to be called "the women's faction." Their group was led by Elaheh Kolaee, herself the first woman who entered Parliament without head-to-toe veiling, only wearing a headscarf to Parliament. The women's faction acted in unison as a voting bloc, not limited to the thirteen female members of Parliament but counting several male MPs among its members. They exerted considerable effort to push through legislation in favor of women, including those laws that directly affected women's access to resources. Mosa Gornabi demanded, in an interview, that women's inheritance should be equal to that of men. As a member of Parliament he represented Gaenat, a rural district in the province of Khorasan.[9] He was the driving force behind a bill that pushed for equality in inheriting agricultural land. The passing of the bill was blocked, however, by the Council of Guardians.

The Sixth Majlis was in many ways unlike its predecessor. The new female deputies entered office boldly declaring their intention to change the laws in favor of women. In collaboration with the Centre for Women's Participation, the women's faction in Parliament lobbied officials and high-ranking clerics to support their goals, among which was included the ratification of the UN Convention on the Elimination of Discrimination against Women (CEDAW). Their effort, again, was rejected by the Guardian Council. Nonetheless,

7. Pay for Housework, *Hamshahri*, April 24, 2005.
8. BBC World Persian-language service, July 31, 1999.
9. "Gavanin e ersieh," *Iran*, May 26, 2005.

the issue created a great deal of public debate and was widely covered in the media.

End of the Reform

Overall, the reform movement brought some changes regarding freedom of expression, reduction in the number of arbitrary arrests, and improvements in the rule of law. However, these achievements did not impress the opposition. Khatami's balancing act of arbitrating between religious conservatives from different factions on the one hand and secularists on the other hand frustrated Iran's political elites. Khatami's belief in gradual and slow transitions rather than dramatic change alienated his supporters, ultimately causing the movement to lose popular support. Some became skeptical about Khatami's intentions, and, although they never questioned his ability to bring about change, his willingness to do so became suspect. There were many factors leading to the decline of the reform, namely those related to economic policies.

Khatami's presidency had to contend with unfavorable economic conditions from the very beginning, partly because of low oil prices at the end of the 1990s, and partly because of outstanding obligations related to the debt crisis that erupted during Rafsanjani's term. Khatami pursued a fiscal policy that curbed subsidies and some social services. However, as the economy began a recovery, boosted by the rise of oil prices after 2001, the focus of economic policy became market reform, with less emphasis on redistribution. This focus meant that the true beneficiaries of rising oil revenues were more among higher income groups and people who were in better positions to take advantage of the new economic opportunities. Social services did not improve, partly because the Reformists wanted to restructure them to take power away from conservative groups and partly because the Reformists wanted to create opportunities for NGOs, many of which were managed by their own constituencies. NGOs mushroomed throughout the country and there was little coordination between them. They often used funds in a way that did not correspond to their mandates. At the same time, inflation and a rise in the real estate market and rental properties caused a significant burden to low- and middle-income families. The Reformists initially enjoyed the enthusiastic support of women. Their reliance on dynamic jurisprudence provided room for women to press for improved gender rights (Halper 2005). However, many of women's efforts did not bear fruit because of the rigid opposition of the entrenched conservative faction and the Reformists' own limitations, particularly their deficient and poorly formulated strategies for bringing about change under the Islamic Republic.

Interestingly, the power struggles among factions over the past two decades have weakened some of the conservative elite groups as well. They have lost any popularity that they might have enjoyed because of their strong opposition to changes broadly desired by the public. As a result, new elite groups have found opportunities to gain control over the government machinery. In particular, the way has been paved for younger conservatives who have revolutionary credentials because of fighting in the Iran-Iraq war and who maintain ties with the revolutionary armed forces and militia.

In the 2005 presidential elections, the two main Reformist candidates had two very different policy agendas, neither meeting the expectations of the people. The first focused on economic redistribution but it was not clear whether he could deliver on growth. The other candidate downplayed economic issues and tried to bank on the failed political reform agenda. In that election, Rafsanjani entered as a centrist candidate and tried to champion economic growth and less strict cultural policies, but lacked credibility that he would ensure broad benefits from oil rents and growth. Ahmadinejad, on the other hand, was the candidate of the new conservative groups. He promised reduction in corruption and attention to broad distribution of economic benefits, and projected an image of being able to deliver, especially regarding the redistribution of oil wealth, a combination that won him the office.

Ultimately, the slowness of improvements in the economic conditions of the lower and middle classes, while the country was enjoying the benefits of increased oil revenues, along with the perceived prosperity of the upper classes, eroded the political support of the Reformists. It was a widespread impression that Reformists were preoccupied with salvaging a faltering political reform agenda while they seemed more focused on their own factional politics than on serving the larger interest of the country. With growing apathy among the ranks of Reformist supporters, the conservatives won the parliamentary elections of 2004. Ahmadinejad won the presidency in a race against Rafsanjani, campaigning on the issues of government transparency, fighting corruption, and spending oil revenues on improving the basic life conditions of the population. His famous campaign slogan was "I will bring oil revenue to the people's dinner table."

The current Parliament is dominated by conservatives of different shades. The Speaker of Parliament and the president are both from the conservative camp, though from very different sides of the faction. While the president is associated with the new group of politicians connected with the revolutionary armed forces, Parliament is dominated by individuals more in line with the bazaar. Other conservative and reformist groups also maintain footholds in Parliament and other state institutions, keeping Iran's factional politics highly animated.

Ayatollah Khamne'i announced 2006–7 to be the year of national unity, inviting different factions to arrive at a consensus. Consensus is not an easy task, however, because Iran's political elite remains divided. For instance, even though there was agreement, at least in principle, on the debate over privatization, a debate that started under Rafsanjani, there is constant battle over how it is to be implemented. There is rising tension between the Rafsanjani-led faction and Ahmadinejad. Rafsanjani wants to see the privatization of state-owned industries, while his counterpart has been campaigning for what he calls "Justice Fund" *(Saham-e Edalat)*, Ahmadinejad's plan to privatize and sell state-owned factories to workers and other "deserving" groups, making them shareholders of their factories.

It has been argued that such attempts along with Ahmadinejad's support for left-wing Latin American leaders are part of the populist policies that mainly help him maintain office rather than bringing about real improvement in people's lives. Critics of the current administration argue that Sepah Pasdaran, or Revolutionary Guard, has grown its share of ownership of private and public enterprises. Some have argued that the president is using the military influence of Sepah Pasdaran to bolster support for his own government. It appears that since Ahmadinejad's rise to power, and in spite of his electoral campaign to redistribute wealth, the share of the state and of the revolutionary institutions in the economy has grown. Moreover, high inflation, unemployment, and slowing growth have been hurting the poor, Ahmadinejad's main constituency. Ahmadinejad's fiscal and monetary policy, for instance, has sharply increased the expenditure of oil revenues and expanded credit for the housing sector. This has boosted demand for all non-tradables, especially real estate, the cost of which has skyrocketed (an apartment in Tehran can cost the same as a similar one in New York, while it was a third of that a decade ago), with direct impact on the access of the poor and lower-middle class to affordable housing.

Moreover, Ahmadinejad's posturing toward the United States, although highly popular among the people in the Arab world, is not necessarily impressive at home, where many are critical of his mishandling of the economy. To many ordinary Iranians who are suffering the impact of economic sanctions, opposition to the United States is not a priority. Declining support has been evident in a recent electoral defeat of his supporters in the last municipal election. His faction, *Abadgran* (Reconstructivists), lost dismally during the municipal election of 2007. Moreover, in order to bring the budget deficit under control, the government reduced gas subsidies, an extremely unpopular policy. From the beginning, Ahmadinejad faced stiff opposition in Parliament. It took him several attempts before his cabinet was finally approved; the Parliament kept refusing his ministers. In December 2007, his minister of education resigned for fear of impeachment. Later, the economy minister, who had support in Parliament, resigned over substantial policy disagreements with the president. The political scene therefore continues to be plagued by factional politics. This is a very interesting time in Iran's politics, and it illustrates the country's complexities. During a time when both Parliament and the Office of the President are occupied by conservatives, reaching consensus is a real challenge to the ruling political elite.

Since Ahmadinejad came into power, the Centre for Women's Participation has changed its name once again to Centre for Women and the Family, a name change that signals a new era. Under its new mandate, the expansion of women's public role is no longer a priority and women are once again reduced to their roles as mothers and wives. Many members of the Centre have been replaced. The Centre stopped funding research groups, NGOs, and other activities related to enhancing the role of women in Iranian society. The library is missing books and documents.[10] There has been a stricter policy regarding the dress code, particularly in wealthy districts of Tehran where the *hejab* had been pushed to its limit with heavy makeup and narrowing scarfs.

Ahmadinejad during his term as the mayor of Tehran supported women's Olympics, and this support led to mobilization of religiously conservative women to advance his political career. Shortly after he was elected president, he announced that women should be allowed to attend football matches and could enter the Tehran Olympic Stadium. He was, however, attacked immediately and had to backtrack on his public announcement. The current political atmosphere is extremely different from that of the reform era, and there have been an increasing number of arrests of women's rights activists and academics.

Ahmadinejad seems to have lost his popularity because of his handling of the economy, his policies having alienated his constituency, that is, the poor and the underclass. He never had much support among middle- and upper-class women, many of whom campaigned for Rafsanjani. Many women's rights activists who come from middle-class urban backgrounds continue to campaign on issues related

---

10. Fieldwork 2007.

to legal rights. The campaign to collect one million signatures was led by women from academia. It is unclear whether a preoccupation with legal rights is a priority of women in all classes throughout the country. It appears that with the onslaught of economic hardship, women's economic rights may have a higher priority for the majority of women of low-income backgrounds.

Women's Employment: Policy Makers Facing Major Challenges

Many female government officials during the reform, including Elaheh Alaifar, head of the Office for Female Employment at the Ministry of Work and Social Affairs, helped to raise the issue of female employment to the level of public consciousness. By the end of the reform period, the government's economic policy gave female employment a top priority, along with universal health coverage for housewives and decent work conditions to ensure the safety of female workers. As a sign of the fall of the reform, these priorities do not seem to be important. The Ministry of Work and Social Affairs embarked on microcredit programs and self-employment as a means of income generation for women, and it also established a Credit Support Fund that allocates 60 percent of its resources to women. These developments will be discussed in chapter 6. In the rural sector, the Jihad for Reconstruction and the Agricultural Bank were responsible for providing microcredit to women. The new Parliament elected in 2005 has reversed some of the priorities of the reform era, the most important of which is facilitating female employment on the level of national policy.

Regarding employment and women's economic status, there has been a great deal of pressure on the legal system. For instance, in 1993 a law was passed by the name of *ojratol mesle*. This law gives women the right to ask for compensation of their housework in the event of a divorce. It was won on the basis of a particular Shari'a law that entitles women to ask to be paid for housework and for feeding their babies. However, given that judges are men and tend to be conservative, the law's implementation remains a challenge. What is interesting is that because there is an emphasis on women's role as homemakers by the current administration, the debate over wages for housework has gained a new momentum. Another example is laws passed to make the price of the bride compatible with the rate of inflation. These examples indicate that women continue to press for change and refuse to concede. Incidentally, resistance toward the regime over matters pertaining to gender rights is not limited to secular and middle-class women, but it includes many women who are Islamist. The latter have been more successful in their efforts because of their use of religious arguments to deal with discriminatory laws. As far as elected bodies are concerned, women's issues will remain highly critical. This will not be the case for unelected bodies such as the Guardian Council, which continues to block legal changes regarding women's rights.

Today Iranian women live longer, marry later, and are more educated than ever before in the history of the country. They bear fewer children, and are more likely to enjoy an independent lifestyle. All of these factors increase female labor force participation both in rural areas and in urban areas. Moreover, women's role as volunteers has given them self-confidence and has increased their public role, making them more assertive in demanding what they need. Many women have been involved in NGOs, and others have been engaged in other public activities. Iran's female labor force is becoming more and more skilled, although a great many of these skills would not be put into use in a country with high unemployment rates. As we shall see in chapter 7, many women have turned to the informal economy where employment opportunities are more elastic. The informal economy, however, remains in the shadow in spite of its huge size. With the expansion of the informal economy, which is a fairly typical phenomenon in the south (Benería and Roldan 1987; Castells and Portes 1989; Benería 1992; Benería 2003), it is likely that it will turn into an important source of employment for an increasing number of women who struggle with poverty, many of whom are heads of households. This is in addition to the underground economy, which includes an increasing number of part-time and or full-time sex workers as well as those who are engaged in drug distribution. Although there are no official data available, and the state ignores the existence of sex work, a member of the Welfare Office (Behzisti) indicated in an interview that rising prostitution, often caused by lack of shelter for those who leave their homes, is a major problem (interview by Bahramitash, Tehran, 2008). To tackle this problem the Welfare Office has recently opened shelters for women on an experimental basis.

To get a better picture of female employment, we will turn to a statistical analysis in the next chapter.

4

The Transformation of the Female Labor Market

ROKSANA BAHRAMITASH *and* HADI SALEHI ESFAHANI

IN PREVIOUS CHAPTERS, we covered the social, political, and economic context of prerevolutionary and postrevolutionary Iran. In this chapter we will focus on census data and quantitative analysis of this transformation. Much of the previously published work on female employment argues that because of the process of Islamization, women's employment declined in the aftermath of the 1979 Revolution (V. Moghadam 1988, 1995a; F. Moghadam 1994; Moghissi 1996; Afshar 1997; Alizadeh and Harper 2003; Behdad and Nomani 2006). Some academics have argued that Islamization may have in fact facilitated education, mobilization, and participation in public life for women who came from low-income families or religious backgrounds (Paidar 1995; Kian 1997; Hoodfar 1999; Poya 1999; Mehran 2003). Meanwhile, many factors other than Islamization—for example, demographic change, formation of new institutions, and internal and external shocks—have also been at work in complex and dynamic ways, influencing labor market conditions and interacting with the Islamization process. We make an effort in this chapter to sort out these issues to the extent that the census data permit.

The census data are available from the Statistical Center of Iran (SCI), www.sci.org.ir, in tabulated form on a decennial basis from 1956 to 2006. We will pay particular attention to the 2006 census data, which have become available recently and have not been used in past studies of the female labor market in Iran (e.g., Mehryar, Farjadi, and Tabibian 2004; Behdad and Nomani 2006). Some studies have gone beyond the 1996 census, using Household Expenditure and Income Surveys (HEIS) and Socio-economic Characteristics of Households (SECH) datasets produced by SCI (e.g., Salehi-Isfahani 2005b; Salehi-Isfahani and Marku 2006). However, those surveys are more recent and do not allow comparisons with prerevolution times. Also, the surveys are based on somewhat dated samples that do not match the recent census results. Of course, using census data has its own limitations. In particular, some of women's labor market activities may have gone unnoted in the process of data collection, especially in the earlier censuses. Also, in the 1976 and 1986 censuses, the seasonally unemployed were categorized as unemployed, whereas they were treated as employed in other censuses. We will try to take account of these shortcomings in our analysis of the census data.

The rest of this chapter is organized as follows. We first examine the broad trends and sectoral shifts in the economy and in the female labor market. Then we highlight the role of demographic factors, especially age structure of the population, in the observed pattern of change in the female labor force. In the next section we discuss the educational developments that seem to have played key roles in women's labor force participation (LFP). This discussion is followed by a focus on the structure of female employment in terms of occupations and positions. The last section is devoted to the unemployment problem, which is a major concern, particularly for young women in Iran.

Women's LFP and Employment in Iran: Trends and Complexities

The Overall Picture

During the past five decades, Iran's ten-years-and-older female labor force has grown more than sixfold, from 0.57 million to 3.62

million (see table 4.1). This growth was much faster than the 3.6-fold increase in the male labor force. There is a huge literature on underreporting of women's participation in the labor force, especially in rural areas (Benaría 1999b), and the problem is likely to have been more serious in earlier decades. However, focusing on urban areas, where undercounting may have been less serious, reveals an even more dramatic picture. The female labor force in urban areas was 0.19 million in 1956 and 2.5 million in 2006, an increase of 13.5 times, compared to the 7.9-fold increase for men. As a result, the share of women in the urban labor force rose from about 10 percent in 1956 to almost 16 percent in 2006 (fig. 4.1). This trend has persisted in recent decades, with a major exception during the 1976–86 period, when the urban labor force increased by 1.5 times for women and 1.6 times for men, lowering the share of women from 11.3 percent in 1976 to 10.6 percent in 1986 (table 4.1 and fig. 4.1). This decrease may be explained to some extent by the fact that many women worked as volunteers (Poya 1999). The 1976–86 decade also saw a striking decline in the rural female labor force of 41.5 percent (this decline is particularly noticeable when compared to that of men in rural areas, whose participation increased 14.8 percent [table 4.1]). As a result, the share of women in the rural labor force dropped from 17.6 percent in 1976 to 9.8 percent in 1986 (fig. 4.1). This sharp decline in the 1980s is what is often attributed in many academic writings to the rise of Islamism after the 1979 Revolution. But, as we have argued in chapter 2 and will show further below in light of census data, the phenomenon is complex and seems to have been caused by a host of factors besides Islamism.

A very puzzling aspect of the female labor market in Iran is the low participation rate of women (see table 4.1). In fact, for urban women, the LFP rate declined steadily between the mid-1960s and mid-1980 from 9.9 percent to 8.1 percent. In rural areas, the LFP rate continued to rise in the 1960s and most of the 1970s, reaching 16.7 percent in 1976. But then it dropped sharply after the revolution, reaching 7.9 percent in 1986, before it started to recover steadily during the past two decades. To develop a better sense of how low these rates are,

Table 4.1 Female Labor Force, 1956–2006

Year	1956	1966	1976	1986	1996	2006
Female Labor Force (10 years and over, in millions)	0.6	1.0	1.4	1.3	2.0	3.6
Growth Rate of Female Labor Force in Prior Decade	n.a.	*5.8%*	*3.4%*	*1.0%*	*4.4%*	*5.8%*
Female LFP Rate—Urban Areas	9.3	9.9	9.0	8.4	8.1	12.6
Ratio of Female to Male LFP Rates—Urban	*0.12*	*0.14*	*0.14*	*0.13*	*0.14*	*0.19*
Female LFP Rate—Rural Areas	9.2	14.3	16.6	7.9	10.7	12.3
Ratio of Female to Male LFP Rates—Rural	*0.11*	*0.17*	*0.21*	*0.11*	*0.17*	*0.18*

Source: Statistical Center of Iran, www.sci.org.ir.

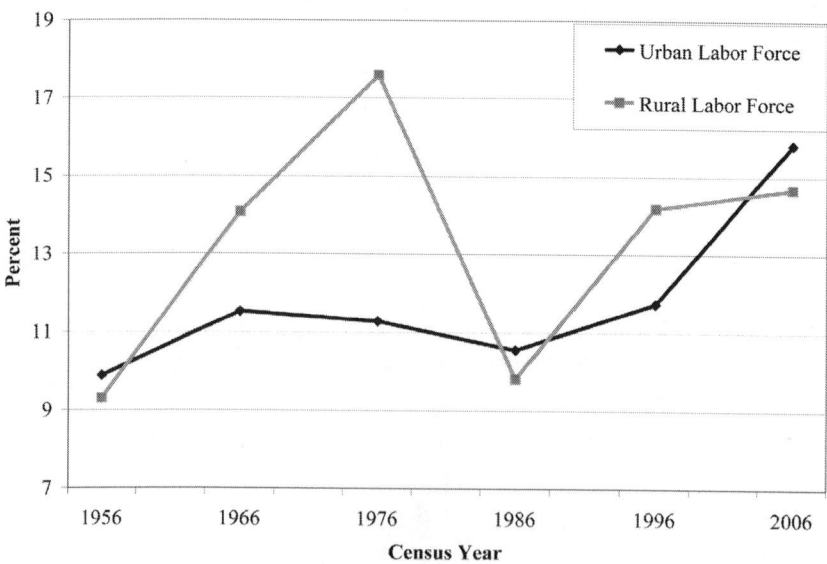

4.1. Share of Women in Labor Force. *Source:* Statistical Center of Iran.

one can compare them with the LFP rates of developed countries, which are on the order of 60 percent. Another comparison to make is with the male LFP rates. The middle row of table 4.1 shows that the ratio of female to male urban LFP rates was about 0.14 during most of the past four decades. This ratio means that the probability that a randomly selected woman in Iran would be participating in the labor force was only 14 percent the probability of a randomly selected man. This relative probability declined somewhat to 13 percent in the 1980s and has jumped up recently to 19 percent. For rural women, the relative probability had risen to 21 percent in the 1970s, dropped sharply to 11 percent in the 1980s, and has recovered to 17–18 percent in the 1990s and 2000s (see the bottom row of table 4.1).

The generally low LFP rate has been partly attributed to possible undercounting, something well established in gender and development literature, particularly by the pioneering work of Marilyn Waring (1990), and partly to cultural factors that have discouraged women's economic activity outside the home for centuries (Salehi-Isfahani 2005a). Furthermore, gender and development literature has documented that the impact of development has been inverse; this inversion did in fact happen in Iran between the 1960s and 1990s. Some of this decline in Iran may well be related to the decline of the urban women's LFP rate between the 1960s and the 1970s, probably owing to an additional combination of interrelated factors: the rise of oil revenues and urban family incomes and the increases in schooling opportunities and in the number of children per adult woman. These factors seem to have jointly reduced the value of participation in the labor market relative to schooling, child rearing, and homemaking (Karshenas 2001). This pattern is in fact not unusual; men's LFP can increase during a period of intense modernization while that of women does not and even declines. During this period, the share of women in the labor force declined despite the fact that at the time the economy was booming and there was a significant shortage of labor. It should also be noted that the high demand for labor before the revolution meant that for those who wanted to work, finding jobs was relatively easy. As a result, the decline in the female LFP rate at the time cannot be explained by difficulties in finding jobs. It is possible that structural changes were unfavorable toward women's employment. However, after the revolution, women, especially those of the urban middle and upper classes, were initially discouraged (in some cases forced) from participating in the labor market. As we will see below in table 4.12, urban unemployment rates were low in the 1960s and 1970s and the share of women in employment closely tracked their share in the labor force (compare the urban employment share graph in figure 4.2 with its counterpart in figure 4.1).

The situation in rural areas was different. There incomes were not rising as fast, and the growing carpet and weaving industry (see fig. 4.3) could compete more easily with other alternatives for girls and young women. Migration of rural men in search of better paid urban jobs also vacated positions in agriculture that were filled by women. As a result, the share of women in the rural labor force rapidly rose from 9.3 percent in 1956 to 17.6 percent in 1976 (fig. 4.1). The share

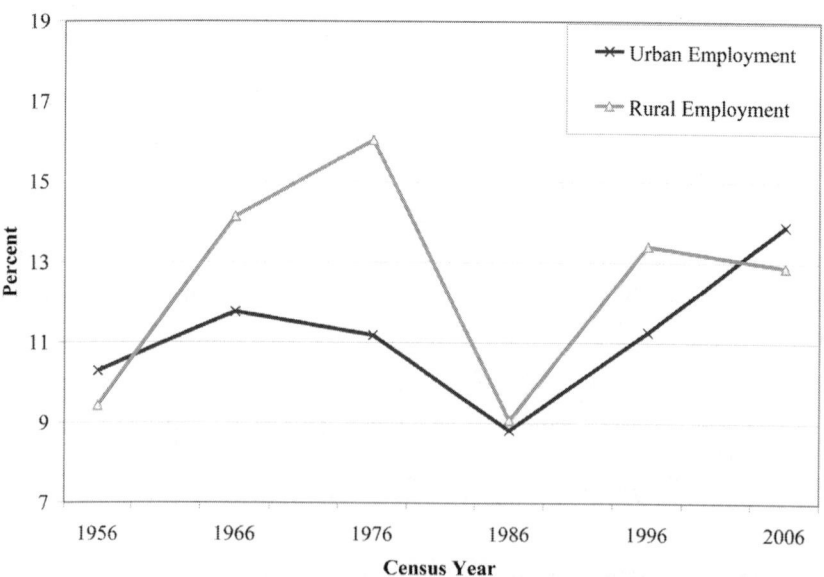

4.2. Share of Women in Employment. *Source:* Statistical Center of Iran.

of women in rural employment did not rise as fast and their unemployment is recorded as high in 1976 (see table 4.12 below). But the high unemployment rate is likely to be owing to the fact that the census data were collected during the fall and many seasonally unemployed women were recorded as unemployed, whereas in prior years they had been categorized as employed. In any event, the expansion of the female labor force in rural Iran during the 1960s and 1970s was similar to the experience of developing countries where many men migrate out and growth occurs largely through mass employment of women in labor-intensive, export-oriented activities.

The more controversial part of the decline in Iran's female LFP rate is the developments during the 1980s. The rise of Islamism after the revolution has been widely cited as a major factor in that decline. But a closer look at the data reveals a more complicated picture. The first issue to note in this regard is that the recorded drop in the female LFP rate between 1976 and 1986 census data is largely a rural rather than an urban phenomenon (see table 4.1). In urban areas the

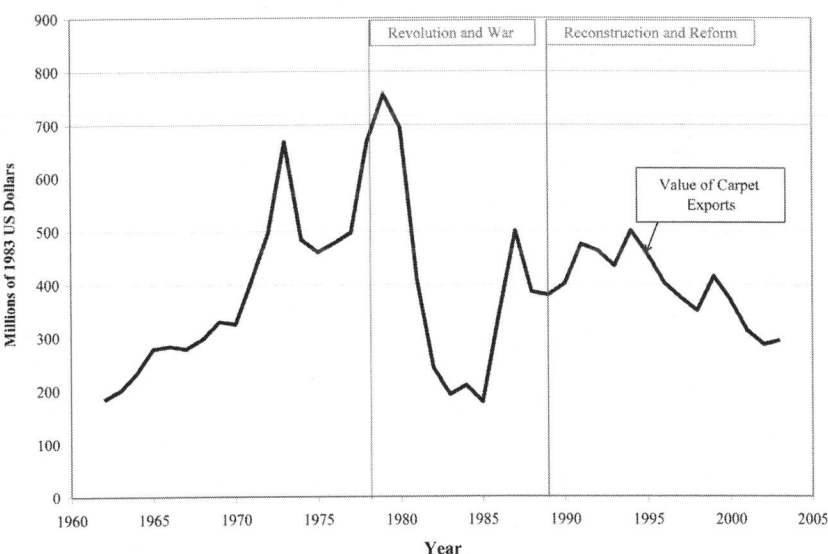

4.3. Value of Iran's Carpet Exports in Constant 1983 US Dollars. *Source:* NBER-United Nations Trade Data, Customs Administration, Islamic Republic of Iran.

decline appears to be a continuation of the prerevolution trend. In fact, increased demands of child rearing on the time of adult women may have played a role in the decline because fertility rose in the first decade after the revolution. In addition, the economic hardship and the severe shortages during the Iran-Iraq war forced women to spend a great deal of their time obtaining rationed goods in markets and taking care of many household needs that were not adequately met by markets.

However, two other factors worked in the opposite direction (i.e., encouraged female LFP). First, the new cohorts of women entering the urban job market were far more educated than those who retired. Because, as we show below, women with higher education have a greater propensity to participate in the labor market, this factor must have pushed up LFP rates. Second, because universities were closed in the early 1980s and operated with limited capacity in the rest of the decade, schooling in urban areas had diminished and there were fewer alternatives to participation in the labor market (see below for more detailed discussion of education trends). In other words, because most young women could not attend universities, they had more time that they could allocate to the labor force if they did not face other obstacles to participation.

Yet other factors had mixed effects of their own. During most of the 1980s, the war with Iraq was waging, Iran faced economic sanctions that affected its trade, and its oil revenues were dwindling. These factors caused significant deterioration in the economy. GDP per capita declined by one-third between 1978 and 1988 (Esfahani and Pesaran 2009), and Iran's carpet exports, the most important source of employment for female labor in the country, fell by more than 70 percent. These developments limited job opportunities for women and discouraged them from seeking jobs. On the other hand, declining family incomes are likely to have increased women's need to hold jobs. In addition, the fact that many men had been drafted by the armed forces to fight the war must have had a positive effect on the demand for women's labor. In the context of all these differing forces, the Islamization process discouraged secular urban middle-class women from participating in the labor force, but at the same time attracted others to fill the vacated positions as well as the newly created jobs in segregated services for female clients. The data presented in table 4.1 and figure 4.1 indicate that the net effect of all these factors was not very large in urban areas. Overall, between 1976 and 1986 the share of women in urban labor and their LFP rate dropped by 0.6 and 0.7 percentage points, respectively.

The combined impact of the above factors on women's share in total urban *employment* was larger. It dropped from 11.2 percent in 1976 to 8.8 percent in 1986 (fig. 4.2), implying that unemployment became a much more important problem for women than for men (see table 4.12 and section 5, "The Unemployment Problem," below). However, these figures may not portray an adequate picture because in the mid-1980s many young men had been drafted into military service and were, therefore, counted as employed, while there was no such mandatory employment position for women. To conclude, the role of Islamization in the decline of the female LFP rate is unlikely to have been large, especially when considering that in rural areas people were not secularized under the Shah and had remained Islamic, so that the revolution did not make a major change in their way of life. It did drive some women out of the urban labor force, but it also created opportunities for others to enter. The net effect may have indeed been negative. However, it seems to have been relatively small compared to the effects of other factors, which shaped the overall picture mostly through shifts in rural employment.

The prevalence of economic forces over the ideological and political factors during the 1980s becomes particularly clear when one examines the rural segment of the women's labor market. In rural areas, as mentioned above, the population was already quite compliant with the relevant norms. Yet the female LFP rate dropped very sharply. Some undercounting may have been a problem. Some of these factors have been discussed in chapter 1. Added to these factors there are other problems such as what occurred during the 1986 census, in which seasonally unemployed workers were recorded as unemployed or nonparticipant in the labor market. But this method of recording was similar to the pattern of the census in 1976. If anything, the departure of many young men who were drafted by the military forces during the war should have brought more women into positions that were recognized as participation by the collectors of labor statistics. As we will see below, this recognition was in fact the case in agricultural activities, where many women replaced men who had left their villages during the war and, as a result, female employment increased sharply. So undercounting cannot sufficiently account for the sharp drop in the female LFP rate in the 1980s. More plausible explanations are increased schooling of rural girls (see below for a discussion of the evidence) and, more important, the disruption of economic activities that typically employed women in rural areas, particularly carpet weaving (see fig. 4.3). The decline of unpaid family jobs, which was the bulk of rural female employment in 1976, further confirms these points.

Interestingly, the recovery of carpet production and similar economic activities during the 1990s (fig. 4.3) indeed helped revive the female LFP rate in rural areas, but not so much in urban areas, where those industries played a small role. The participation rate of women in the urban labor market remained low in the 1990s because of the continued high demands on parents' time and the increased schooling for the young population born in the 1970s and 1980s. These factors, reversed in the later 1990s as the consequences of reduced fertility, manifested themselves when the graduates came of working age and, unlike their less educated predecessors, started to demand jobs.

Sectoral Shifts

In the previous section we saw that economic changes had important impacts on the female labor market. To explore this issue further, we start with an overview of sectoral shifts over the past half-century. In the 1960s and 1970s, as oil revenues and family incomes increased, it became more difficult to attract most urban dwellers in Iran to the labor market for producing tradable goods at wage rates that would keep the products competitive with those from the rest of the world. As a result, the urban labor force shifted toward activities that did not face much competition from abroad, particularly services, and moved away from agriculture and manufacturing, except in the case of products that received subsidies and special attention from the government. Note that the shift from agriculture and manufacturing normally takes place in higher stages of economic development. But in Iran this shift happened early on and was driven by inflow of oil revenues, as opposed to economic development and increased productivity that would enable the smaller shares of the labor force to meet the demands of the population as a whole for agricultural and manufacturing products. In any event, the shift in the structure of the urban labor market in Iran can be seen clearly in figure 4.4. The trend accelerated after the revolution because of the disruption in foreign trade and imposition of an economic embargo that badly affected intermediate and capital goods flows and hampered manufacturing production in particular. There was a reversal of the latter effect in the 1990s, but the overall trend of the shift from agriculture and manufacturing to services in the urban sector seems to have continued into the 2000s.

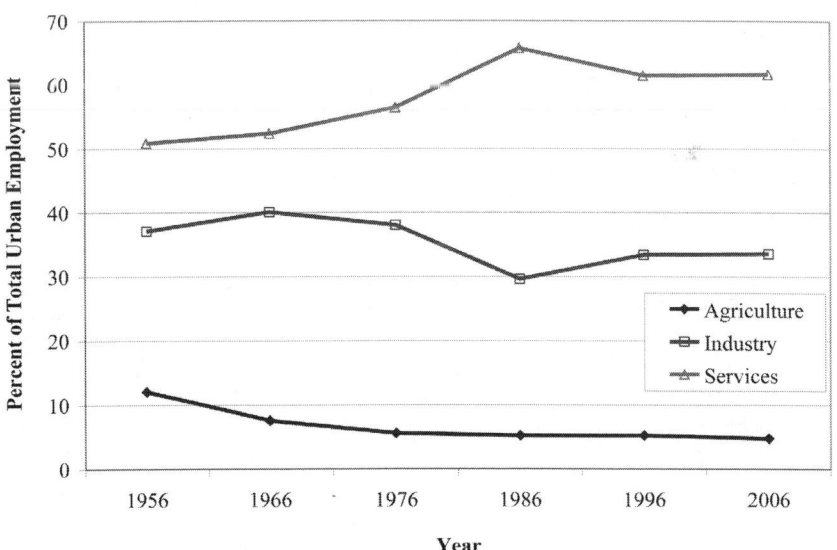

4.4. Employment Shares of the Main Economic Sectors in Urban Areas. *Source:* Statistical Center of Iran.

The picture of structural change in the rural sector was somewhat different before the revolution (see fig. 4.5). Manufacturing employment in rural areas in fact grew rapidly until the mid-1970s, essentially because of the expansion of the market for Persian carpets around the world. However, as we show below, the workers employed in that activity were mostly teenage girls, often working as unpaid family workers. The disruption of trade in the 1980s because of the revolution, war, and economic embargo sharply reversed that process. Since then, rural manufacturing employment has recovered somewhat, but like urban areas, overall employment has shifted away from agricultural employment and toward the service sector.

The sectoral composition of women's employment more or less followed the pattern for the labor force as a whole during the 1960s and 1970s. However, in rural areas, manufacturing remained by

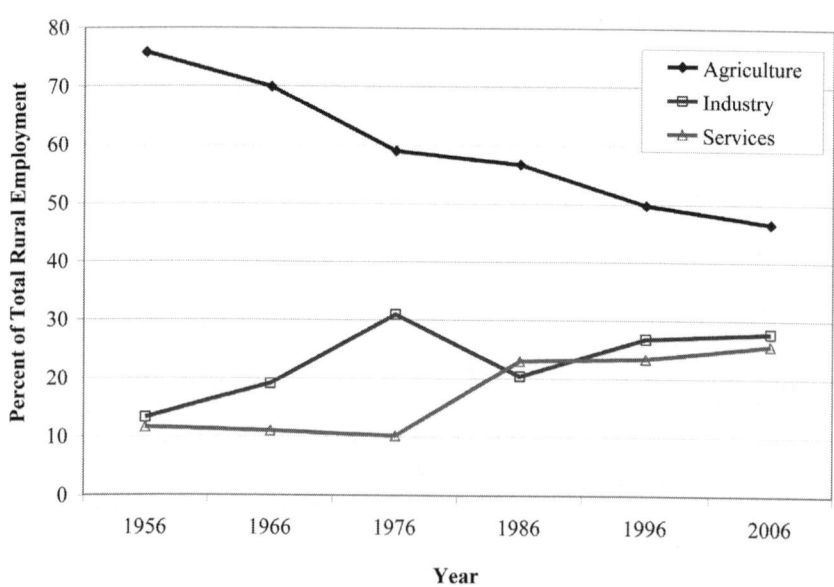

4.5. Employment Shares of the Main Economic Sectors in Rural Areas. *Source:* Statistical Center of Iran.

far the largest employer of women, mostly in carpet weaving and handicraft production. As table 4.2 shows, this concentration was on the rise over time and by 1976 reached almost two-thirds of the female employment in rural areas. Similar activities were also dominant in urban areas in the 1960s, but then rapidly diminished in the 1970s. Cottage industries that were the largest employers of women in urban areas moved to the rural areas and were replaced by the service sector. After the revolution, the decline of women's manufacturing jobs accelerated, in both urban and rural areas, as the impediments to its production proliferated. In the urban labor market, service sector jobs came to comprise about three-quarters of women's employment. The role of the service sector also grew in the rural job market for women. But the main shift in that market was a substantial increase in women's employment in agriculture, from about 29 percent of female employment in 1976 to more than 54 percent in 1986. As argued before, this shift must have been owing to the departure of many men from rural areas as a result of the draft or migration in search of better incomes, leaving women to tend the land. The end of the war and economic recovery in the early 1990s seems to have returned the rural economy to its prerevolution pattern for a while. As the military recruits were demobilized, the men who returned to rural areas took back many of their agricultural jobs and women again focused on cottage industry. However, that situation did not last long. Between 1996 and 2006, the role of manufacturing in the rural female labor market declined and agriculture and services gained substantially.

A final observation regarding the structure of the female labor market in Iran over the past few decades is the steady increase in women's presence in sectors that did not used to offer many jobs to women, such as sales, finance, transportation, communication, tourism, and utilities. The aggregated share of these sectors in female employment is shown in the "Other Sectors" row in table 4.2. Between 1976 and 2006, this share rose from 8.1 to 15.3 percent in urban areas and from 1.8 to 7.7 percent in rural areas.

Table 4.2 Sectoral Composition of Female Employment (Percentage of Total Female Employment)

Census Year	1956	1966	1976	1986	1996	2006
URBAN						
Agriculture	4.1	3.1	2.3	2.4	2.1	2.0
Manufacturing	39.6	45.7	31.2	11.8	19.2	18.3
Social, Personal, and Financial Services	52.5	45.6	58.4	73.6	68.7	64.5
Education, Health care, and Social Services	n.a.	33.4	37.8	52.7	53.0	43.1
Other Sectors	3.8	5.6	8.1	12.1	10.0	15.3
RURAL						
Agriculture	35.0	32.1	28.9	54.2	35.0	43.5
Manufacturing	52.7	61.1	65.9	33.6	51.0	35.7
Social, Personal, and Financial Services	11.1	4.9	3.7	8.2	9.3	13.1
Education, Health care, and Social Services	n.a.	1.9	2.5	5.6	7.1	8.7
Other Sectors	1.2	1.8	1.6	4.1	4.7	7.7

Source: Statistical Center of Iran, www.sci.org.ir.

Female LFP and Employment: The Role of Age Structure

Age structure of the population is a key determinant of the pattern of female LFP and employment, both at the aggregate and the sectoral levels. In this section we first focus on the role of teenagers in LFP and employment and then examine the overall picture for the entire age spectrum.

Teenage LFP and Employment

In the 1950s when access to schooling was limited and poverty was high, teenagers' participation in the labor force was similar to that of adults. In urban areas, the shares of women 10–19 years of age in the female labor force and female population were practically the same (see fig. 4.6), but in rural areas, teenagers were overrepresented in the labor force. Because of the post–World War II baby boom, the share of young women in the total population increased substantially between the mid-1950s and the mid-1970s. Meanwhile, in urban areas, this group started to attend school more often. As a result, its share in the labor force did not rise as fast as its population share. In fact, the share of youngsters in the female labor force dropped during 1966–76 (fig. 4.6). In rural areas, on the other hand, the presence of teenagers in the labor force increased sharply, well beyond the increase in their population share. Between the mid-1960s and mid-1980, women in the 10- to 19-year-old age group comprised more than 40 percent of the female labor force in rural areas, far above their corresponding population share. This trend was reversed after 1986, and the share of youth in the labor force dropped sharply in both rural and urban areas. Their population share also declined, following the drop in fertility rates in the 1990s.

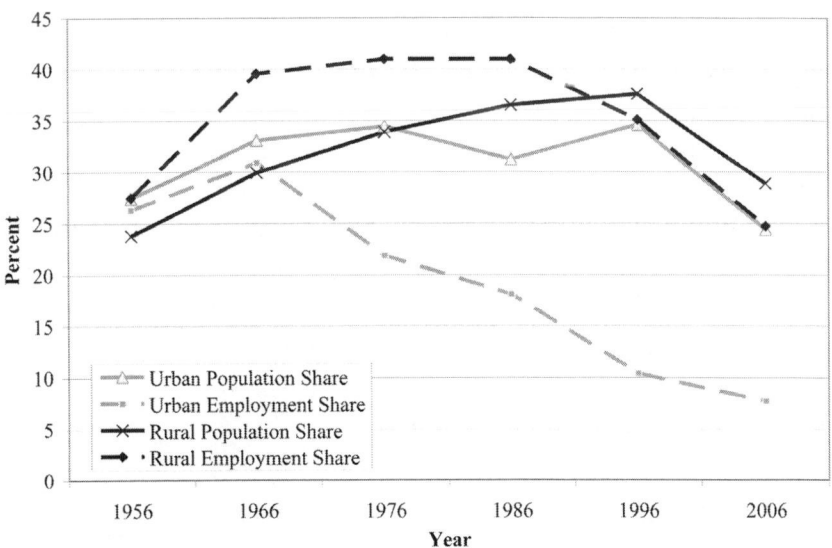

4.6. Share of Women Age 10–19 in Female Employment and Population. *Source:* Statistical Center of Iran.

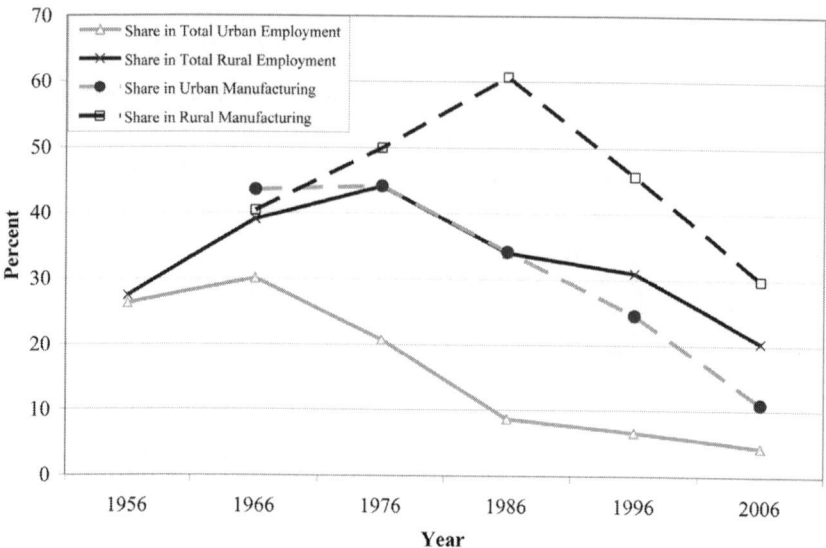

4.7. Share of Women Age 10–19 in Economy-Wide and Manufacturing Female Employment. *Source:* Statistical Center of Iran.

Figure 4.7 shows that shares of young women in rural and urban female employment followed similar patterns. However, the sectoral pattern of teenage employment was highly concentrated in manufacturing. Indeed, in 1966, women age 10–19 years comprised well over 40 percent of manufacturing employment in both rural and urban areas (fig. 4.7). This share declined after the revolution in urban areas, but rose sharply to 50 percent in 1976 and 60 percent by 1986 in rural areas. The type of manufacturing that young women were employed in was largely carpet weaving and cottage industry. As we will see below, most of these positions were unpaid family labor. These types of jobs and teenage employment in general have been quickly declining since the 1980s (fig. 4.7).

Age Structure of Female LFP

Beyond the 10–19 age group, the role of age in LFP has changed a great deal among Iranian women. In the 1950s, the LFP rate of urban

4.8. Age Pattern of Female Labor Force Participation in Urban Areas During Census Years 1956–2006. *Source:* Statistical Center of Iran.

women across different age groups was relatively flat, with women in the child-bearing ages of 20–35 years old participating at somewhat lower rates than those in other age groups. This rate can be seen in figure 4.8, which graphs the female LFP rates of different age groups in urban areas in selected census years. The graph for 1956 shows that the LFP rate of urban women in the 20–34 age group was about 8.2 percent, while those 35–59 years old participated at rates of 11.5–12.0 percent and younger women had participation rates of about 10 percent. It is notable that the LFP rate remained in the same range for women above 60 as well, largely because of the lack of any retirement or social security system for the kinds of low-skill jobs that most women held at the time. A similar age profile of the LFP rate existed in rural areas in 1956, but its peak belonged to the 15- to 19-year-old age group (see fig. 4.9).

Two decades later, the age pattern of the LFP rate had dramatically changed. As the graph for 1976 in figure 4.8 shows, LFP rates of urban women in the 20–34 age groups had doubled, while the rates

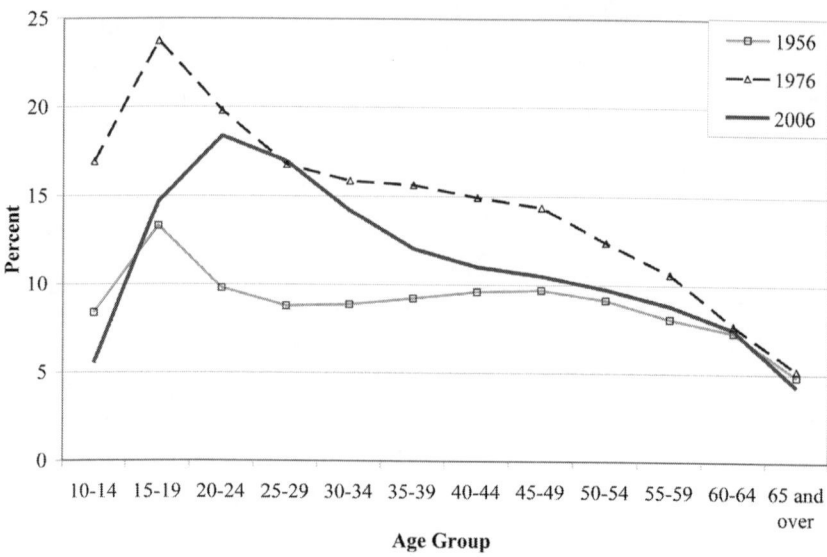

4.9. Age Pattern of Female Labor Force Participation in Rural Areas During Census Years 1956–2006. *Source:* Statistical Center of Iran.

for teenage women and those above 35 had fallen by half. This shift was largely a consequence of increased female education and expansion of skilled formal-sector jobs in urban areas. The 2006 data further show that these effects have clearly strengthened in recent decades. Compared to 1976, now LFP rates are much higher for the 20–49 age groups and lower for both younger and older generations.

In rural areas between 1956 and 1976, LFP rates had risen sharply for all age groups below 60, especially for the younger women (fig. 4.9). It seems that working opportunities in rural manufacturing, mostly carpet weaving, had brought more women of all ages to the market, prevailing over schooling as an alternative for girls. By 2006, this is no longer the case given that LFP rates have fallen sharply for women below 20 years of age. Participation rates are also visibly lower for women in the 35–59 age group. One explanation for the latter trend is that improvement in incomes and education may have reduced the incentive to work in menial jobs, which are the main opportunities in rural areas. This factor has been elaborated in chapter 5. Also, the wage rates in such jobs have been kept low by the rise of competition in international markets and by the presence of Afghan women who have much lower reservation wages.

The progression of LFP rates from 1976 to 2006 was by no means linear. The social and economic disruptions in the first decade of the revolution had major adverse effects on the labor market. We have seen that female LFP rates declined sharply between 1976 and 1986. Here we examine the age pattern of that decline to shed more light on what happened to the female labor market in the aftermath of the revolution. In particular, we make an attempt to estimate the extent to which the LFP rate had declined as a result of the political change and the war with Iraq.

Figure 4.10 compares female employment and LFP rates in urban areas in 1976 and 1986 across age groups. The first notable fact in this figure is that the LFP rate of the 20- to 24-year-old age cohort in 1986 was 13.5 percent, which was 2.5 percentage points lower than its 16 percent counterpart in 1976. If the trends before the revolution had continued, the LFP rate for this cohort would have probably remained around 16, as was the case in 2006 when participation rates for most other cohorts had increased compared to those of 1976. The reason is that while the 20–24 age group in 1986 might have had a greater disposition to participate in the labor market compared to its counterpart in 1976, it is likely to have had higher enrollments in higher education as well. Next, note that the 20- to 24-year-old cohort in 1976 had the highest LFP rate at the time (16 percent) and, based on the trends before the revolution, it would likely have increased its participation when it reached 30–34 years of age in 1986. However, the actual LFP rate for this group in 1986 was 14 percent. The comparison between the two figures in 1976 and 1986 suggests that the LFP rate of that cohort of women could have been at least 2 percentage points higher if the prerevolution trends had continued and if the disturbances caused by the revolution and its concomitant events had been absent. A similar argument applies to older cohorts as well and suggests for most cohorts of Iranian women that the urban LFP rate

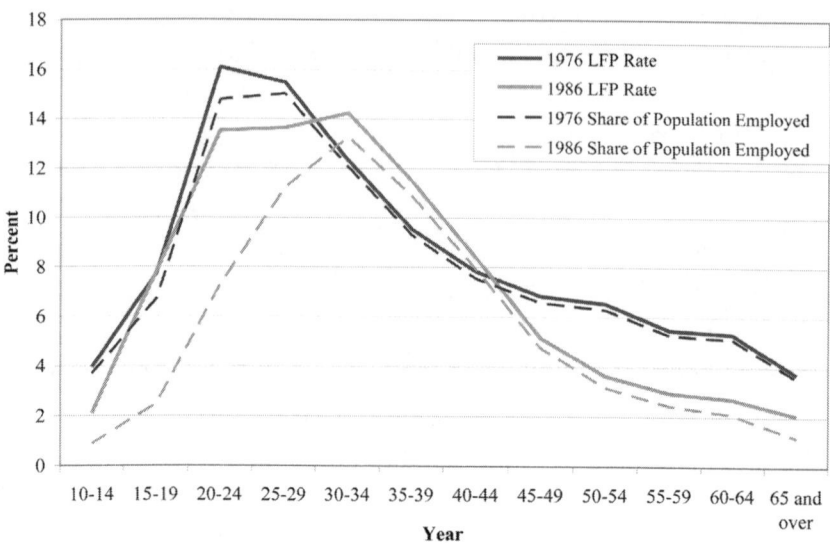

4.10. Age Pattern of Female Employment and Labor Force Participation Rate in Urban Areas, 1976–1986. *Source:* Statistical Center of Iran.

may have been curtailed by about 2.5 percentage points, possibly higher for some groups, especially those in the 45–60 age group. This curtailment is a substantial effect. It means that the female LFP rate in urban areas could have reached 11 percent in 1986, compared to the 8.4 percent rate actually observed. Despite the large drop for individual cohorts, the overall LFP rate of urban women dropped by only 0.7 percentage points between 1976 and 1986 (see table 4.1). This was because the new cohorts that entered the labor market in the 1960s and 1970s had higher participation rates than the older generations at the time and formed a significant proportion of the female labor force. The large negative effect on individual cohorts may be partly attributed to the rise of Islamism. But, as we have argued before, the economic disruptions caused by the revolution and the war are likely to have been far more important. This pattern is further confirmed by the pattern of broad and sharp decline in women's LFP in rural areas (fig. 4.11), where Islamism did not bring about much change but economic disruptions had visible adverse effects. In rural areas,

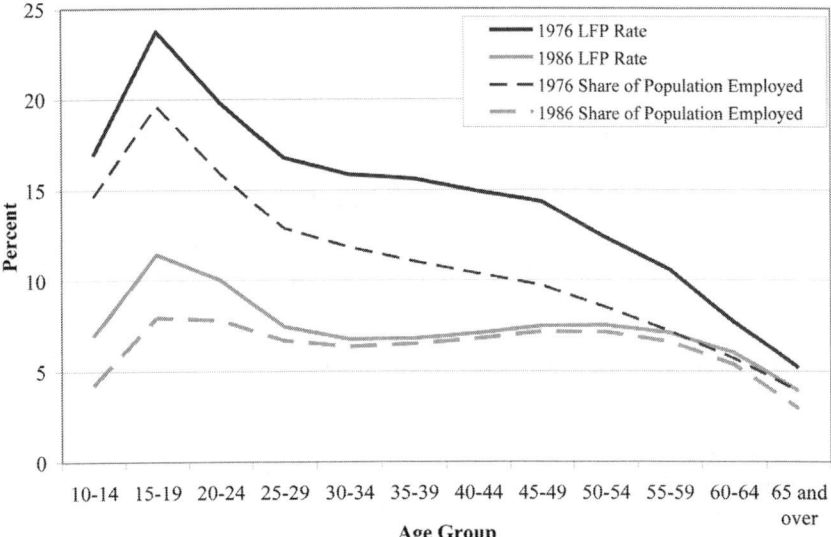

4.11. Age Pattern of Female Employment and Labor Force Participation Rate in Rural Areas, 1976–1986. *Source:* Statistical Center of Iran.

the prerevolution trends are unlikely to have increased female LFP rates beyond those achieved in 1976 because rising incomes and the expansion of schooling are likely to have eventually constrained the carpet industry and limited the jobs that it could offer. However, the drops of about 8–12 percentage points for younger rural women could have been avoided.

Education and Women's Labor Force Participation

A major force behind the transformation of the female labor market in Iran is education. The female literacy rate in urban areas was growing rapidly before the revolution and maintained its pace afterward, ranging around 51 percent in 1976 and reaching 85 percent in 2006 (table 4.3). By comparison, urban male literacy rose from 72 percent to 92 percent during the same period. Rural areas had also seen growth in female literacy rates before the revolution, but the level remained very low: As of 1976, only about 12 percent of women in rural areas were literate. This situation changed significantly after the revolution and the literacy rate quickly climbed to more than 30 percent in 1986 and more than 67 percent by 2006. The pace was much faster than the trend in rural male literacy, which climbed from about 37 percent to 80 percent between 1976 and 2006. Another indication of the proliferation of female education in rural areas after the revolution is the literacy rates among rural youth. As of 1976, only 13.4 percent of women age 15–24 years were literate, while the rate was 45.7 percent in 1986 and almost 92 percent in 2006 (table 4.3). Female youth literacy in urban areas has long become almost universal.

Female education at secondary and tertiary levels has similarly progressed and has served as a foundation for improved employment opportunities for women. Table 4.4 shows that between 1986 and 2006 the share of women with secondary education in the female population age 10 years and older has increased from about 3 percent to 17 percent. Meanwhile, the share of higher education degree holders in the female population 20 years and older has jumped from 1 percent to 8.3 percent. Women now comprise well over 50 percent of university students, and have been quickly catching up with men in terms of educational attainment.

Table 4.3 Literacy Rate (Percent)

Census Year	1956	1966	1976	1986	1996	2006
FEMALE POPULATION (AGE 10+ YEARS)						
Urban	20.6	36.0	51.1	61.4	79.9	85.0
Rural	1.0	3.4	12.2	30.5	58.2	67.2
FEMALE YOUTH POPULATION (AGE 15–24 YEARS)						
Urban	26.3	50.3	68.5	80.9	95.6	98.1
Rural	1.4	4.1	13.4	45.7	82.4	91.9

Source: Statistical Center of Iran, www.sci.org.ir.

These achievements have had important consequences for the female labor market in Iran. As Djavad Salehi-Isfahani has shown based on survey data (2005b), increased education leads to higher LFP rates and better employment opportunities. This improvement can also be seen in the census data. In table 4.5, we summarize the association between education levels and LFP rates in 1976 and 2006. Among women in 2006, higher levels of education are clearly associated with higher LFP rates and the differences are quite notable. While the rate is 6.3 percent for illiterate women and 8.8 percent for women with elementary schooling, it is 13.4 percent for those with high school education and 39.2 percent for those with tertiary education. This relationship does not hold for men, who have higher

Table 4.4 Iranian Women's Educational Attainment and Employment (Percent)

Census Year	1956	1966	1976	1986	1996	2006
LITERACY RATE						
Female population 10 years and over	7.3	16.1	30.9	47.6	71.7	80.3
Employed female population 10 years and over	n.a.	11.5	31.2	63.9	79.9	87.7
SHARE OF WOMEN WITH SECONDARY DEGREE IN						
Female population 10 years and over	0.2	1.1	2.9	7.0	12.1	16.8
Employed female population 10 years and over	n.a.	3.6	17.5	40.8	43.2	60.4
SHARE OF WOMEN WITH HIGHER EDUCATION DEGREE IN						
Female population 20 years and over	0.04	0.3	1.0	1.5	3.4	8.3
Employed female population 20 years and over	n.a.	1.5	8.0	14.6	26.6	40.4

Source: Statistical Center of Iran, www.sci.org.ir.

Table 4.5 Education and Labor Force Participation, 1976 and 2006

	1976			2006		
	Female %	Male %	Ratio of Female to Male LFP Rate	Female %	Male %	Ratio of Female to Male LFP Rate
ALL COUNTRY	12.9	70.7	0.18	12.4	65.6	0.19
Illiterate	13.3	90.8	0.15	6.3	67.3	0.09
Literate	12.1	53.9	0.22	14.0	65.4	0.21
Elementary	7.5	59.6	0.13	8.8	71.3	0.12
High school	22.7	57.0	0.40	13.4	64.4	0.21
Tertiary education	52.5	69.3	0.76	39.2	65.3	0.60

Source: Statistical Center of Iran, www.sci.org.ir.

participation rates when they have only elementary education. The relationship is also much weaker in rural areas.[1] It held quite strongly in 1976 among literate women, though the LFP rate for illiterate women was higher than for those with elementary education in that year, largely because the rural female labor force that lacked education significantly outweighed the urban one.

More insights regarding the role of education can be gained by examining the ratio of the LFP rates for women and men reported in table 4.5. This ratio compares the probability of participation for women relative to the probability for men at each educational level. The figures in table 4.5 show that this relative probability has a even clearer positive association with the level of education both in 1976 and in 2006. While the probability of participation for women with elementary education was only 12–13 percent of that for men in the

---

1. To save space, separate data for rural and urban areas for 2006 is not shown. Disaggregate rural-urban data for 1976 is not available.

same category, for those with tertiary education the relative probability was 60 percent in 2006 and 76 percent in 1976. A similar association also holds in both urban and rural areas separately (data not reported here). Note that for the more educated population, the LFP rates of women were closer to those of men in 1976 compared to 2006. The reason for the increase in the difference in 2006 is not clear. However, it may be the result of the limited supply of educated women in earlier decades, which made it easier for them to find jobs and encouraged more of them to participate in the labor market. We will explore this issue further below when we examine the unemployment problem.

An additional piece of evidence concerning the role of education in the female labor market is the educational attainments of employed women. As can be seen in table 4.4, in 2006 women with secondary education comprised over 60 percent of total female employment, much higher than their population share. It was also much higher than the corresponding employment share (3.5 percent) in 1976. Women with higher education had a share of more than 40 percent in female employment (for the population of 20 years and older), five times their share in the population and also five times the corresponding employment share in 1976. Below, in the section "Occupational Characteristics of Female Employment," we will present further evidence of the favorable impact of education on women's occupations and positions in the labor market.

Although the LFP rate tends to rise with the level of education, it declines when a large part of the population is attending school. Indeed, the latter effect was an important factor in the decline and slow recovery of women's LFP in the last three decades of the twentieth century. To demonstrate the significance of this factor, in figure 4.12 we present the share of students in the female population age 10 years and over. This share had been on the rise since the 1930s, but made a major jump and passed 10 percent in the 1970s, largely because of the expansion of education in urban areas. After the revolution, the rate of female school attendance experienced a decline in urban areas, but rose strongly in rural areas such that the overall share of students in

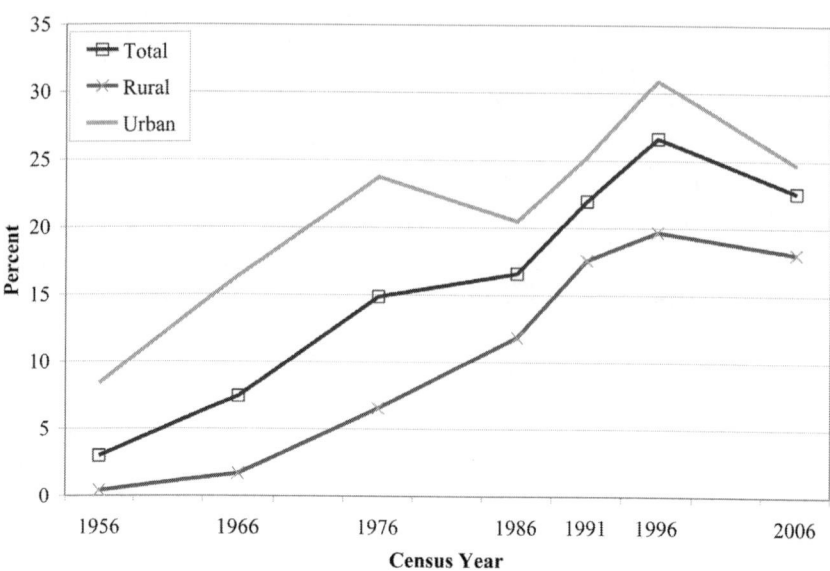

4.12. Share of Students in Female Population, Ten Years and Older. *Source:* Statistical Center of Iran.

the population increased. This increase is notable because, contrary to the observation made by Sohrab Behdad and Farhad Nomani (2006, 130), it suggests that female schooling may have had an important impact on the LFP rate in the 1980s, as schooling increased sharply in rural areas where the drop in LFP was particularly large.

The decline in urban schooling of women may be related to the Iran-Iraq war during 1980–88, when there were disruptions in the economy and many young women volunteered to support the effort.[2] However, a more important factor seems to have been the closure of universities in the early 1980s because of the Cultural Revolution. Although the universities were reopened after a few years, their capacities remained limited for some more years. Many women did not

---

2. Though this was an important contribution to the country, it was not recorded as LFP because volunteer work is not included in the formal definition of employment.

return or did not seek to enter universities at the time because by then they had children or were committed to other activities. Also, quite a few young people had left the country. In fact, the census data show that the decline in the share of students in the population was entirely owing to the decline in enrollment of young people 20–24 years of age. In fact, the share of female students in that age group in the total population fell by more than 25 percent. (The drop was much sharper for men in that age group because many of them were either drafted to go to war or left the country.) These observations also explain why the drop in schooling had an urban focus because universities are located in urban areas and rural women's education was more concentrated in primary and secondary levels rather than tertiary. It is interesting to note that after the reopening of the universities and the end of the war, the share of women attending school rapidly increased again in both rural and urban areas. Of course, there was also a huge cohort of baby boomers born after the revolution that entered school age at that time. As a result of these factors, the share of students in the female population age 10 years and over jumped from 16.6 percent in 1986 to 22.6 percent in 1996, partly accounting for the slow rise of the female LFP rate. This trend, however, has reversed in a major way since 1996, as those students have graduated and many of them are now seeking jobs, as we have seen in table 4.1 and figure 4.1.

The increased education of women and their increased entry into the labor force have also had a favorable interaction with a visible decline in their fertility rates since the late 1980s. As education and social services expanded, women lowered their fertility rates and found more time to attend school and join the labor force. Moreover, they have managed to help their children acquire better education, hence setting in motion a virtuous circle of increased human capital, low fertility, and high economic growth (Salehi-Isfahani 2005a).

Occupational Characteristics of Female Employment

We have seen that women in Iran are enjoying higher levels of education and have increased their participation in the labor market, especially in the service sector. This pattern is not too different from those observed in many other developing countries, especially in the Middle East and North Africa regions. But in many of those cases, the government employs the majority of educated women in a limited range of occupations with relatively low salaries. Therefore, a key question is to what extent Iranian women's employment relies on government positions? What are the types of occupations and positions that employed women hold? Has the range of occupations and positions held by women expanded or shrunk under the Islamic Republic? What role has increased education played in past changes? What are the likely future trends in the quality of the female job market in Iran? How do government policies influence the outcomes?

To address these questions, we start by examining the role of the public sector in the women's labor market in Iran. As can be seen in table 4.6, the share of the public sector in total female employment used to be small in the 1950s, but grew rapidly in urban areas to the point where in 1976 it accounted for almost half of urban women's employment. However, it is remarkable that government employment of women in rural areas remained quite limited. After the revolution public employment of women jumped sharply as many firms were nationalized and the revolutionary regime recruited many women to manage segregation and to help with new functions initiated by the government, particularly sexually segregated schooling. The share of the public sector in total female employment rose to 70 percent in urban areas and 8.5 percent in rural areas in 1986. Since then, the share has slowly risen in rural areas, reaching almost 11 percent in 2006, but it has quickly declined in urban areas, returning to its 1976 level (48.6 percent) by 2006. On the whole, the public sector does not seem to be the main source of new employment for women. The government has been creating about one-third of the new jobs occupied by women over the past two decades in both rural and urban areas. If this trend continues, the share of the public sector in female employment will continue to drop rapidly in the coming couple of decades.

Table 4.6 Share of Public Sector in Total Female Employment (Percent)

Census Year	1956	1966	1976	1986	1996	2006
Urban areas	13.5	17.6	48.6	70.0	63.2	48.6
Rural areas	1.4	0.5	3.0	8.5	9.3	10.9

Source: Statistical Center of Iran, www.sci.org.ir.

According to a general pattern of female employment throughout the world, the public sector has a greater propensity than the private sector to employ women. In the case of Iran, this tendency is especially true in the high-education categories, as shown in table 4.7, where we present the share of women in public and private sectors, disaggregated by the educational levels. However, a more important observation in this respect is that the private sector has been catching up fast with the public sector, particularly in absorbing women with higher education. Between 1996 and 2006, the number of women with higher education employed in the private sector rose by almost 8.5 times, while the same indicator in the public sector was 2.2 times and for men in the private sector it was 4 times. This rise had led to an almost doubling of the share of educated women in the private sector workforce. Interestingly, this growth has been even stronger in rural areas (table 4.7).

Along with the change in the educational pattern of private employment, the positions held by women in the sector have also changed dramatically. In the 1950s, over 72 percent of urban women with jobs were private sector employees and another 11 percent were self-employed. There were very few female employers. As a result of public sector expansion, by 1976 private employees were only 30 percent of total female employment in urban areas. Self-employment also fell below 9 percent. On the other hand, the rise of the carpet industry had added quite a few unpaid family workers to the female urban workforce (11 percent of the total). After the revolution, female employment in the urban private sector shrank to very low levels.

Table 4.7 Education and the Share of Women in Private and Public Employment, 1996 and 2006 (Share of Women as Percentage of Total Employment in Each Group)

	Private		Public	
	1996	2006	1996	2006
URBAN	6.1	9.9	18.7	22.5
Illiterate	6.2	8.6	7.0	7.8
Literate	6.0	10.1	19.2	22.8
Elementary	4.9	5.4	3.7	5.0
High school	6.7	11.2	22.4	15.4
Higher education	13.8	25.1	31.3	35.0
RURAL	14.4	8.6	7.9	7.8
Illiterate	14.2	16.7	9.6	12.4
Literate	14.5	11.5	7.7	11.0
Elementary	15.1	13.6	4.0	5.8
High school	6.4	8.8	9.5	9.0
Higher education	5.9	14.9	16.9	21.8

Source: Statistical Center of Iran, www.sci.org.ir.

By 1986, only the self-employed seemed to have maintained their share. However, since then, women's positions as private employees, self-employed, and employers in urban areas have expanded significantly, with unpaid family workers' positions remaining quite low. The increase in the share of female employers (almost eightfold) and the doubling of the share of self-employed women are particularly notable (table 4.8). In rural areas, the prevalent positions for women have been self-employment and unpaid family work. But even there the role of women as employers has been rising rapidly and is no longer negligible. The share of private employees in total female employment in rural areas was relatively high in the 1950s, but started to decline in the 1960s and has not recovered much since reaching a low point in the 1980s.

Education seems to be a major vehicle for women to reach entrepreneurial positions in the private sector. As table 4.9 shows, in 2006

Table 4.8 Distribution of Female Employment Across Private Sector Positions (Percentage of Total Female Employment in Each Area)

Census Year	1956	1966	1976	1986	1996	2006
SHARE OF PRIVATE SECTOR IN FEMALE EMPLOYMENT— URBAN AREAS	86.3	78.9	50.0	20.4	31.2	48.8
As employers	0.8	1.01	0.59	1.04	0.92	4.61
As self-employed	10.9	12.8	8.7	9.2	12.7	16.6
As private employees	72.5	59.5	29.8	7.8	13.1	25.3
As unpaid family workers	2.1	5.6	11.0	2.4	4.4	2.3
SHARE OF PRIVATE SECTOR IN FEMALE EMPLOYMENT— RURAL AREAS	98.5	98.6	96.2	87.1	86.5	85.2
As employers	0.5	0.44	0.35	1.79	0.92	2.82
As self-employed	28.5	26.5	12.1	28.8	28.6	34.6
As private employees	44.1	41.3	24.6	12.8	15.6	15.9
As unpaid family workers	25.4	30.3	59.2	43.8	41.5	31.9

Source: Statistical Center of Iran, www.sci.org.ir.

the share of women among employers with higher education was 15.7 percent, while it was 8.5 and less among employers with lower education. Some of these women may well be those employed in the informal sector. In chapter 8 we get a picture of the extent to which middle-class educated women are engaged in the labor market in well-paid professions and as entrepreneurs. The pattern among the self-employed is similar, though less pronounced. Women with higher education are also overrepresented among private sector employees. As we will see, these tend to be more professional and technical occupations. This representation is in sharp contrast with unpaid family labor, a category that largely consists of uneducated workers, predominantly women—82 percent of illiterate unpaid family workers are women.

We now turn to the trends in occupational structure of the women's jobs, summarized in table 4.10. In the 1960s, well over 60 percent of employed women could be categorized as production workers,

Table 4.9 Education and the Share of Women in Private Sector Positions, 2006 (Share of Women as Percentage of Total Employment in Each Group)

	Employers	Self-Employed	Private Employees	Unpaid Family Workers
ALL EDUCATIONAL LEVELS	7.4	8.3	11.4	45.8
Illiterate	6.5	9.7	10.0	82.4
Literate	7.5	7.9	11.6	37.2
Elementary	3.6	7.5	6.4	50.2
High school	8.5	8.5	12.9	21.0
Higher education	15.7	13.7	31.6	26.8

Source: Statistical Center of Iran, www.sci.org.ir.

who, as we have seen, were mainly engaged in carpet weaving and similar handicrafts. In the 1970s this share dropped in urban areas as the role of professional, technical, and service occupations in female employment expanded rapidly. The table shows that this trend continued strongly after the revolution, suggesting that during the crisis years of the 1980s, women in professional and technical occupations maintained their jobs much better than production workers. This is an important observation because it happened despite the fact that many women who were forced to leave their jobs because of compulsory dress codes after the revolution were among the professional and technical workers. It suggests that loss of female jobs in manufacturing because of economic decline may have been a much bigger force in shaping the fate of working women than the codes of conduct under the new regime. In any event, since the 1980s clerical and production jobs have grown, but professional occupations still engage almost half of the female workforce in urban areas. At the same time, the share of women working in executive, administrative, and managerial occupations has tangibly increased from 0.3 percent to 4.5 percent of all urban occupations pursued by women.

In rural areas, handicraft and agricultural occupations have remained dominant until recent years. However, there was a major

Table 4.10 Distribution of Female Employment by Occupational Categories (Percentage of Total Female Employment in Each Area)

Census Year	1966	1976	1986	1996	2006
URBAN AREAS					
Executive, Administrative, and Managerial	0.1	0.3	0.3	3.9	4.5
Professional and Technical	13.2	36.9	59.9	52.8	49.3
Administrative Support, Clerical, Services, and Sales	4.7	14.7	15.8	15.9	21.8
Farming, Forestry, and Fishing	2.3	2.2	2.4	1.7	1.2
Industrial Production, Transportation, and Simple Labor	60.7	30.6	13.5	21.7	19.3
RURAL AREAS					
Executive, Administrative, and Managerial	0.0	0.01	0.02	0.4	0.6
Professional and Technical	0.6	2.4	6.1	5.6	9.0
Administrative Support, Clerical, Services, and Sales	0.3	0.4	1.5	3.1	5.7
Farming, Forestry, and Fishing	31.7	28.8	54.3	30.7	35.8
Industrial Production, Transportation, and Simple Labor	65.4	66.5	34.8	57.0	45.1

Source: Statistical Center of Iran, www.sci.org.ir.

shift from manufacturing production to agriculture jobs in the 1980s, which was later largely reversed. At the same time, there has been a robust rise in the share of professional, technical, and service occupations among employed rural women.

Education, again, had been instrumental in the transformation of the occupational structure of female employment, far more than its role in male employment. This transformation can be seen in table 4.11, where we present the share of women in employment by occupation and educational attainment. The figures suggest that women's share in more skilled occupations generally rises with the level of education. For example, among rural professional and technical personnel in 2006, women's share was only about 12 percent in the subgroup with elementary education, compared to almost 40 percent in the subgroup with higher education. Similar patterns can be observed in executive, administrative, and managerial as well as clerical occupations.

To conclude, since the 1980s the composition of female employment in Iran has shifted strongly toward private sector jobs that require greater education, entrepreneurship, and professional skills. Furthermore, census data clearly suggest that education has been an important vehicle for Iranian women to move to such positions and overcome the higher barriers that they have faced in the labor market compared to men.

Table 4.11 Education and Occupational Structure of Female Employment, 1976 and 2006

Sector	Share of Women in Employment by Educational Level				
	Illiterate	Total Literate	Elementary	High School	Higher Education
1976					
All Occupations	16.0	10.6	6.2	18.9	23.3
Executive, Administrative, and Managerial	1.2	3.5	0.6	2.9	5.5
Professional and Technical	13.7	34.6	17.5	42.2	29.7
Administrative Support, Clerical, Services, Sales	10.9	8.6	3.3	15.6	16.9
Farming, Forestry, and Fishing	8.6	3.1	4.3	1.1	0.9
Industrial Production, Transportation, Laborer	26.5	7.0	8.3	3.0	5.4
2006					
All Occupations	13.7	13.6	9.0	11.9	30.8
Executive, Administrative, and Managerial	3.1	15.5	2.3	10.2	21.0
Professional and Technical	3.8	34.5	11.7	27.1	39.6
Administrative Support, Clerical, Services, Sales	9.6	13.7	6.9	14.9	23.7
Farming, Forestry, and Fishing	14.1	7.7	8.7	4.8	4.3
Industrial Production, Transportation, Laborer	13.3	7.6	9.4	7.0	7.6

Source: Statistical Center of Iran, www.sci.org.ir.

The Unemployment Problem

Our analysis so far highlights the important role of education in expanding the employment opportunities and the quality of jobs held by women. However, this process has been associated with higher rates of unemployment among women. As a result, many observers have wondered whether increased education has contributed to increased unemployment, or whether the association has been coincidental. Many other questions have also emerged. What are the factors that account for the rise of female unemployment? Has unemployment grown more for women than for men? Have education and government policies affected the likelihood of female and male unemployment differently? In this section, we make an effort to address these questions to the extent that the available census data permit.

Table 4.12 shows the history of unemployment rates in urban and rural areas based on census data since 1956. Note that as in most countries with very low income, unemployment was not a major issue in Iran during the 1950s. In those conditions, most people could not afford to remain unemployed and often took whatever job was offered to them. In the case of women, in particular, homemaking was viewed as the default option when jobs cannot be found, hence the negligible rates of female unemployment in the 1950s in both rural and urban areas. As incomes increased in Iran in the 1960s and 1970s, the unemployment rate among most groups except urban men grew. Part of the increase between 1966 and 1976 may be owing to the differences in the tallying of the seasonally unemployed workers between the two censuses. However, some increase in the unemployment rate of women can be observed even after accounting for this factor and treating all seasonal workers as employed.

After the revolution, female unemployment jumped by a significant margin in urban areas. The ratio of female to male unemployment rates presented in the third row of table 4.12 highlights the difference between women and men in this respect. In 1986, this ratio was 2.1, which means that at the time the probability that a female participating in the labor force remained unemployed was 2.1 times the probability

Table 4.12 Unemployment Rates in Urban and Rural Areas, 1956–2006 (Percent)

Census Year	1956	1966	1976	1986	1996	2006
URBAN AREAS						
Female	0.5	3.8	5.9	29.1	12.5	22.5
Male	4.9	6.0	5.0	13.6	8.4	9.8
Ratio of female to male Unemployment Rates	*0.1*	*0.6*	*1.2*	*2.1*	*1.5*	*2.3*
RURAL AREAS						
Female	0.3	10.9	21.7	20.6	14.3	25.5
Male	1.9	11.2	12.6	12.1	8.6	12.9
Ratio of female to male Unemployment Rates	*0.1*	*1.0*	*1.7*	*1.7*	*1.7*	*2.0*

Source: Statistical Center of Iran, www.sci.org.ir.

for a male participant in the labor force. This ratio dropped in the 1990s after the economy had recovered from the war and unemployment rates had declined. However, the female unemployment rate and its ratio to the male unemployment rate have risen sharply in recent years. In 2006, the probability of unemployment for women in urban areas stood at 2.3 times that of men. In rural areas, the relative probability remained constant at 1.7 between the 1970s and the 1990s, but has increased to 2 in 2006 (see table 4.12).

To examine the possible role of education in relatively high unemployment rates for women, in table 4.13 we summarize the pattern of unemployment by education level for women and men in 1976 and 2006. The first notable fact in this table is that in both years and for both sexes, the unemployment rates for those with tertiary education are lower than the rates for labor force participants with less education. However, the unemployment rate for those with high school degrees tends to be higher than those with lower levels of education. This suggests that the supply and demand imbalance at the secondary level of education may be significant, but education does not in general lead to increased unemployment. In addition, education does not seem to affect women's unemployment any more than it affects that of men. This can be seen in the third and last columns of table 4.13, which show the relative probability of unemployment for women across education levels. Note that in 2006 this variable was practically the same (about 2.45) for all literate groups, implying that education did not have any differential impact on women at the time. Interestingly, in 1976 that relative probability was declining with education and was in fact less than one for those with secondary and tertiary education. This suggests that in the 1970s, education may have worked in favor of women who sought jobs and lowered their unemployment rates below those of men with similar degrees. The reason for this pattern may be the relative scarcity and novelty of women with higher education in the 1970s. In contrast, in 2006 women were graduating from high schools and universities at the same rates as men, hence the uniformity of their unemployment experiences across educational levels. However, this uniformity does not by any means explain the substantially higher unemployment rate of women compared to men (2.5 times). That phenomenon is likely to reflect unfavorable labor market conditions for women and significant biases against them. It may also reflect other factors, such as the role of age structure and differences in educational fields among women and men. We explore these two factors in the rest of this section.

Table 4.13 Education and Unemployment, 1976 and 2006

	1976			2006		
	Female	Male	Ratio of Female to Male Unemployment Rate	Female	Male	Ratio of Female to Male Unemployment Rate
ALL COUNTRY	16.4	9.1	1.80	23.3	10.8	2.16
Illiterate	19.2	10.0	1.92	10.3	8.2	1.26
Literate	9.4	7.9	1.19	24.9	11.2	2.23
Elementary	14.4	6.9	2.09	21.3	8.5	2.51
High school	7.7	10.6	0.73	34.9	14.1	2.47
Tertiary education	3.0	4.4	0.70	16.7	6.8	2.44

Source: Statistical Center of Iran, www.sci.org.ir.

Table 4.14 shows unemployment rates of women in 1976 and 2006 across age groups. It is clear from the figures in this table that female unemployment was not a problem in urban areas. The youth (age 15–24) did experience unemployment rates of about 10 percent. But this rate is still quite low for this age group, which includes many low-skilled new entrants to the job market. Indeed, women in this age group faced a lower unemployment rate than men, as can be seen from the ratio of female to male unemployment rates in the second row of table 4.14. This ratio was rather high for women age 35 years and over because the rate of unemployment for men was extremely low at the time. The 2006 situation was dramatically different. The female youth unemployment rate was almost 50 percent and twice as high as the rate for males in that age group. Furthermore, the female unemployment rate was substantially lower for those beyond their twenties and its ratio to male unemployment rate was closer to one. It seems that the new cohorts of women that arrived in the urban labor market in the 2000s faced much higher risks of unemployment and were at a greater disadvantage compared to men. In the higher age groups, women either had found jobs already or were discouraged or retired and left the labor market, hence the relatively lower unemployment rates. The latter factor was partly caused by a government policy to facilitate retirement for women and expand the pension program. It was also partly the result of active discouragement or dismissal of women who were viewed as reluctant to accept the new rules under the Islamic Republic. In addition, the phenomenon commonly known as the "glass ceiling," which prevents women from progressing in their careers toward well-paid and highly professional jobs, exacerbated the situation after the revolution. From our fieldwork we have observed that many women in Iran complain about the fact that they are excluded from managerial positions. This exclusion is critical in the public sector, which is the part of the economy where normally women find it easier to march to the top. Islamism and patriarchal values may add to the general and global discrimination that exists against having women in managerial positions.

Table 4.14 Age and Female Unemployment Rate, 1976 and 2006 (Percent)

Age	15–24	25–29	30–34	35–39	40+
URBAN					
1976 Unemployment Rate	10.0	2.9	2.2	2.5	3.8
1976 Ratio*	0.9	1.0	1.5	2.2	1.7
2006 Unemployment Rate	49.0	25.4	11.2	5.5	2.9
2006 Ratio*	2.0	2.2	1.9	1.4	0.9
RURAL					
1976 Unemployment Rate	18.3	23.2	25.3	29.2	30.5
1976 Ratio*	1.4	2.5	2.7	2.9	2.5
2006 Unemployment Rate	40.1	28.2	15.9	8.0	2.5
2006 Ratio*	1.6	2.0	1.9	1.3	0.6

Source: Statistical Center of Iran, www.sci.org.ir.
* Ratio of unemployment rate of women to men.

The pattern of female unemployment in rural areas in 1976 was quite different from the urban one. Incorrect treatment of seasonal workers contributed to the high unemployment figures in rural areas, as shown in table 4.14. But, after controlling for the data problem, the female unemployment rate still turns out to be high, both in absolute value and relative to men, across all age groups in 1976. The situation in 2006 was different. The unemployment rate was relatively high, especially for the youth, very similar to the urban pattern of unemployment. It seems that compared to 1976, there has been notable convergence between rural and urban areas in recent years.

A final consideration regarding the pattern of unemployment is its connection with the field of study among those with higher education. It is often asserted that graduates of "softer" subjects such as social sciences and especially arts and humanities are not prepared to meet the requirements of employers and therefore tend to swell the ranks of educated unemployed. However, the unemployment data by field of higher education compiled in table 4.15 contradict this view. We find in fact that in 2006 it was the graduates of agriculture, engineering, and production fields that suffered the highest unemployment rates, among both men and women and in rural as well as urban areas, a phenomenon that may be related to glass ceiling. The lowest unemployment rates were experienced by the graduates of education, health, and welfare fields, followed by art, humanities, and services fields. The reason may be the relatively low expectations of the people in these fields that induces them to take jobs with lower pay more readily. It should be noted that women are well represented in these fields. As a result, their relative position compared to men in terms of the ratio of unemployment rates (the relative probability of unemployment for a woman in the labor force compared to a man) is the weakest among fields. Women's relative unemployment measure is lowest in agriculture, engineering, and production fields, where they are an absolute minority.

To conclude, female unemployment has risen sharply in recent years, but this is an economy-wide problem that has been exacerbated

Table 4.15 Field of Study and Unemployment among Population with Higher Education, 2006 (Percent)

Field of Study	Unemployment Rate		Ratio of Female to Male Unemployment Rate
	Female	Male	
URBAN	15.9	6.3	2.5
Education, Health and Welfare	8.2	2.1	3.8
Art, Humanities and Services	15.8	4.2	3.8
Sciences, Social Sciences, Law, and Business	19.9	5.4	3.7
Engineering and Production	24.5	9.1	2.7
Agriculture	37.3	11.2	3.3
RURAL	29.4	11.9	2.5
Education, Health and Welfare	15.9	4.6	3.4
Art, Humanities and Services	32.5	9.3	3.5
Sciences, Social Sciences, Law, and Business	37.7	14.2	2.6
Engineering and Production	41.4	14.5	2.9
Agriculture	40.7	20.7	2.0

Source: Statistical Center of Iran, www.sci.org.ir.

by the massive entry of young cohorts into the labor markets. Increased education does not seem to be a cause of higher unemployment nor to have a clear relation to the gender bias in unemployment risk. Finally, women's preferences for some fields of study more than others do not seem to contribute to their higher unemployment rates. Rather, cultural and policy biases may have driven up the female unemployment rate to over twice that of the male labor force.

Conclusion: Complexities and Nuances

New cohorts of Iranian women have started entering the labor market at unprecedented rates. They are seeking more professional, managerial, and entrepreneurial jobs and capturing such positions at faster rates than their male counterparts. Over the coming decades, these trends are bound to spin profound forces in Iranian society and bring about major economic, social, and cultural changes to the country. The surge in women's participation in the labor force has been delayed over the past three decades owing to a variety of factors. Although most of those factors were somehow associated with the 1979 Revolution, they are not necessarily rooted in the Islamic ideology of the new regime, as is often asserted in the journalistic and even academic literature. While Islamism may have played a role, particularly with regard to economic activity among secular middle- and upper-class women, for the majority of Iranian women a much wider range of adversities undermined LFP. The major change in Iran's politics and institutions after the revolution, the internal and external political tensions, and the war with Iraq in the 1980s all caused major disruptions in economic activity and trade. These in turn had significant negative consequences for job opportunities of Iranian women. At the same time, the economic and sociopolitical conditions in the early years of the revolution entailed a decline in higher education and a rise in fertility for a while, which further hampered women's ability to enter the job market. As the turmoil in political and economic conditions subsided later in the 1980s, fertility declined and schooling increased dramatically. A decade later, the large cohort of young women raised and educated after the revolution began to make its presence felt in the job market.

Our analysis of census data in this chapter shows that besides demographic change, sectoral shifts from agricultural and manufacturing to services have played crucial roles in women's LFP and employment. A significant part of the rise in female employment before the revolution was owing to the expansion of the carpet industry, which relied largely on uneducated female labor, especially girls in rural areas. But that type of manufacturing has become less viable owing to a combination of factors. As a result, women's employment has shifted toward service sector jobs, especially professional, technical, and clerical positions that require more education. This shift is very promising for women's enhanced role in the economy because many of them have heavily invested in education, positioning themselves to take advantage of the expanding demand for professional services. Indeed, we find that education has not only enabled women to move into better jobs, it has served as an important vehicle for women to overcome social and cultural biases against them and to outcompete men in the markets for many high-quality jobs. Of course, women continue to face major challenges in breaking into the old-boys club, and the restrictions on their social and economic activities, such as the renewed emphasis on dress codes in recent years, cannot be overlooked. Nevertheless, education has been an important means for women to diminish the impact of prejudices against them. Also, education at higher levels seems to lower the unemployment rate, which has become a major concern with the relatively weak performance of the economy and the entry of the postrevolution baby boomers into the labor market. Unemployment is a much more serious problem for women than for men because of the existing obstacles and social biases against women's participation in the economy.

To improve the labor market conditions for women, some have argued in favor of encouraging export-oriented manufacturing—a strategy that has worked well in some East Asian countries and in some MENA countries, especially Tunisia (V. Moghadam 1995b).

Such types of employment have been heavily criticized by gender and development literature because of its potentially exploitative impact. These types of export-oriented industries are unlikely to thrive in Iran because the substantial oil income has raised the wages of Iranian workers, rendering them uncompetitive with their counterparts in other low-income countries in the tradable sectors. This is an important reason why Iran's labor force has shifted toward services and other nontradable sectors, where remunerations could rise. However, as globalization brings more competition to all corners of each economy, focusing on nontradables increasingly restricts the options of the workforce. A good way to escape this fate is to invest the oil revenues in improved quality of human capital, and thereby to match the higher wages with greater productivity. This investment means shifting the economy toward the production of high-quality products with high-quality labor, along the lines of the shift toward high-end products in the Italian clothes industry. The educational successes of Iranian women in recent decades seem to point in that general direction and can serve as a pivotal means of achieving economic development with greater gender equity. However, to ensure that the path is indeed followed effectively, there is a need for significant enhancement of the educational system and the labor market institutions.

5

The Effects of International Trade on Gender Inequality in Iran

The Case of Women Carpet Weavers

ZAHRA KARIMI

ECONOMIC GLOBALIZATION is a historical process, the result of human innovation and technological advancements. It involves the increasing integration of economies around the world, particularly through trade and financial flows. Yet globalization has created inequality within and between nations, threatens employment and living standards, and thwarts social advancements by accelerating *"the race to the bottom."*

Globalization offers extensive opportunities for worldwide development, but it is not progressing evenly. Countries that have been able to integrate are seeing faster growth and reduced poverty. By contrast, many developing countries have not been able to gain from open and liberalized international trade, and face economic stagnation and declining standard of living for the vast majority of the workforce.

This chapter investigates the effects of surging international trade on gender inequality in Iran by examining the situation of carpet weavers. To provide a relatively clear picture of the handwoven carpet industry in Iran, in addition to the use of all available statistics and information, I have conducted interviews with ninety-six carpet weavers in Kashan (which is famous for its handwoven carpets worldwide).

This chapter starts with a review of the literature on globalization and gender inequality, especially in labor-intensive export sectors, where women are mainly concentrated; it shows how international competitions have led to a *"race to the bottom,"* especially in developing countries. Then the chapter focuses on Iran's export trends in order to show the effects of globalization on Iran's labor-intensive exports. It examines Iran's share in international carpet markets to analyze the effects of declining exports on changes of labor force structure in the handwoven carpet industry. In this regard the age, gender, education, and income of weavers and the position of carpet weavers in households are extracted from the results of our survey.

The Impact of Globalization on Gender Inequalities

Globalization has intensified in the past decade, leading to a new global outreach through an unprecedented surge in international trade flows and cross-border capital movements. The increased capital mobility combined with an accelerated pace of technological change pose serious opportunities and challenges for the development of the human resources and labor market policies in many developing countries. Not every developing country is going to be a winner in the new global contest. Adverse effects and asymmetrical impacts across various sectors and countries are widely expected. In fact, the distribution of benefits from trade liberalization is likely to be highly skewed between countries and within countries.

Competition between nations or states over investment and export-markets leads to the progressive dismantling of regulatory standards that is known as the "race to the bottom." This process implies that the states compete with each other as each tries to underbid the others in lowering production costs, real wages, and taxes to make itself more attractive to outside financial interests. This action would hurt all nations except the one that undercut the others (Tonelson 2002).

Some may believe, however, that the "race to the bottom" can help ameliorate poverty, for if businesses can operate for less money, they can cut prices while maintaining their profit margins. In other words, it can be possible to trade off employment and growth with labor standards. Yet, in general, the benefits of globalization in accordance with this competitive logic have not trickled down to those who make the products. The race to the bottom works to undermine the ability of governments to enforce labor standards such as workers' compensation and working conditions (Rodrik 1999). But the winner is the country that defines the bottom. Therefore, globalization has been associated with declining labor standards in most countries, especially in developing countries. Many governments ignore the violation of labor laws in order to encourage investment and to promote exports (Stiglitz 2002; Standing 1999).

Because of declining oil prices since the early 1980s, the appearance of economic stagnation on the one hand, and recommendations by international financial institutions such as the World Bank and IMF on the other, oil-exporting countries have started reform programs for privatization to increase the efficiency of economic sectors (Bell 1995). The main objectives of the reform policies were to accelerate growth, to diversify exports, and to create sufficient job opportunities in order to address a rise in unemployment. Economic reforms were not successful enough in many oil-exporting countries, as labor costs in these countries were generally higher than in many newly industrializing countries, especially India and China. Intensified competition among developing countries for capturing the markets of labor-intensive exports leads to an increase in employment but also to low-paid jobs for women during times of economic boom and layoffs and unemployment when there is a contraction of demand or because goods and services are produced at a lower rate elsewhere. Loss of employment as a result of import competition is concentrated among small-scale farmers and low-skilled workers, so women living in poverty are likely to suffer disproportionately, just as other women make inroads into paid work. The impact can be even greater as safety nets grow thinner and remain gender biased (Winters 1999).

The increase in women's share of paid employment has taken place at a time when the power of workers generally has eroded, owing to increased capital mobility, greater flexibility because of technological innovation, and labor market deregulation caused by the need to stay competitive. Although trade expansion may give women more advantages in terms of employment, their "comparative advantage" as workers lies in their lower wages and inferior working conditions. Women are crowded into a narrow range of sectors that produce standardized commodities such as textiles, garments, and electronics that compete on the basis of price alone, and in the informal sector, where work is characterized by long hours, insecure employment, unhealthful conditions, low wages, and often sexual harassment (Benería and Lind 1995; Williams 1999). The search for greater flexibility and lower costs has led to the exploitation of cheap female labor in many developing countries, with no increase in their welfare.

Poorest women workers in developing countries, in general, tolerate the heavy burden of harsh international competition by accepting low wages. They bear a double workload of productive and reproductive activities, and do not experience a change in the sexual division of labor in household tasks, especially in home-based paid work. In such cases women's employment is compatible with traditional female roles and is socially acceptable as women's work in terms of limited physical mobility outside the home (Berik 1987).

International Trade, Its Effects and Consequences

Since the late 1980s, the Iranian governments have tried to expand and diversify non-oil exports by facilitating export procedures and awarding prizes to exporters. Because of Iran's rich oil and gas reserves, chemical and petrochemical industries have a comparative advantage. Trade liberalization has expanded the international markets for resource and energy-based products. However, Iran could not increase the export of labor-intensive goods. Iran's non-oil exports face increasing competition in the international markets. During 1994–2005 the share of carpets in non-oil exports has declined from 44.2 to 4.4 percent (table 5.1). Hence, export of clothing has increased from USD 5.4 million in 1988 to 170.8 million in

Table 5.1 Persian Carpet Exports

Year	Value (USD Million)	Weight (Tons)	Total Non-oil Exports (USD Million)	Share of Carpet in Non-Oil Exports
1977	114.5	6000	523.2	21.9
1982	67	1000	283.7	23.6
1989	344.7	5220	1043.9	33.0
1994	2132.9	32816	4824.5	44.2
2000	619.5	2557	3762.7	16.5
2002	514.3	2092	4608.7	11.2
2004	490.1	1563	6847.1	7.2
2005	460.2	1362	10494.6	4.4

Source: Extracted from Iran Custom Administration Statistics, different years.

2005; its share in total non-oil exports remained low. With regard to the carpet industry, Iran has a much higher production cost compared to India, Pakistan, and China, and cannot keep its share in the export market.

Share of Iran in the International Carpet Markets

Persian carpets are treasured as magnificent works of art. There is widespread practice of the craft in almost all parts of the country. Carpet weaving is easy to learn; it provides employment for about one million people, mainly women, as a cottage industry.

However, for the past few decades Persian carpets have lost a significant degree of importance as commercial goods because of severe competition from other countries and from machine-made carpets. Political problems also take a toll on the Iranian exports. Before the 1979 Islamic Revolution in Iran, joint Iranian/American firms produced rugs specifically targeted at the American markets. After the crisis of the American hostages in 1980, the United States imposed sanctions against Iran and has prevented Persian carpets from being imported into the country, but some rug dealers continue to export Iranian carpets to the United States from Canada. Most American dealers, unwilling to risk their businesses, rely upon Chinese or

Turkish handmade carpets. As a response to the American demand for Persian carpets, carpets with Iranian designs from China, India, and Pakistan are flooding the market. For example, India offers 65 percent of its carpets with Persian designs (Eilland 1998). Increasing supply and more or less stable demand has pushed down the international price for carpets. The average price for one square meter of woolen handwoven carpet decreased from USD 300 in 1981 to about USD 90 in 2005 (Arman and Mohammadi 2005).

In 2005, China, India, Turkey, and Pakistan collectively held 60 percent of the global carpet market, two times the Iranian share. Within the last three decades, the international carpet trade grew from USD 350 million to about USD 2 billion; nevertheless Iran's market share has dropped from 60 percent to 30 percent. Iran still has the highest share in the international carpet markets, but because of falling Iranian production, the slack is taken up by other nations, particularly China, India, and Pakistan (table 5.2).

China's share in the international carpet market is rising. China's competitiveness stems from a huge supply of low-paid labor. The legal minimum wage in China is much lower than it is in Iran. For example, in 2003 the legal minimum wage in Shenzhen, the Chinese city with the highest monthly minimum wage, was equivalent to only

Table 5.2 Production, Employment, and Exports in Handwoven Carpet Industry in Major Exporting Countries, 2000–2005

	Iran	India	China	Pakistan	Turkey
Exports (USD Million)	550	370	400	250	90
Production (Million Sq. Meters)	6	NA	NA	4	5.2
Weavers (Million Persons)	1.5	1.5	NA	NA	NA
Avg. Price of Carpets (Per Sq. Meters, USD)	96	NA	NA	67	72
Market Share (Percent)	30	20	20	15	5

Source: World Trade Organization (2005).

USD 42 (the formal monthly minimum wage in Iran was about USD 150). Moreover, the average workday in labor-intensive industries amounts to about eleven hours each day, often with no days off—that is, about a seventy-hour workweek. When the long working hours are taken into account, a sizeable proportion of the workers are making considerably less than the minimum legal wage (Chan 2003). In 2003 the average monthly salary of carpet weavers in Iran and India was USD 61 and 23 respectively (National Iranian Carpet Center 2005). Labor cost of carpet production in India, China, and Pakistan is less than half of the labor cost of Persian carpets. Declining carpet prices owing to competition among rival countries for gaining a higher share in the international carpet markets is the most important reason for decreasing production and export of Persian carpets.

During 2000–2005, production of Persian carpets decreased from 7.5 to 5 million square meters.[1] Some of the major Iranian carpet exporters are no longer interested in investing in carpet production, as the profit margin in the handwoven carpet industry is very low. They believe that Persian carpets cannot compete with Chinese and Indian carpets and that the share of Persian carpets in the international market will shrink further in the future (National Iranian Carpet Center 2005).

Carpet weavers in Iran, India, Pakistan, Turkey, and Nepal face unfavorable work conditions. Countries with lower production costs are the winners in the global competition, and low real wages are essential causes of success in the export of handwoven carpets. Thus carpet weavers in developing countries must compete ruthlessly with each other, suppressing real wages and working conditions, to be able to preserve their jobs.

Low wages have changed the structure of the workforce in the Persian carpet industry. Most middle-income weavers have left the industry as they can find other jobs with higher wages. In some

---

1. About 70 percent of Persian rugs and carpets produced are exported.

middle-class families, weaving carpets is an activity that generates supplementary income and can be undertaken along with household chores or as a hobby. However, many poor families still rely on weaving and suffer when their incomes decline as a result of international competition. Afghan women and children are increasingly entering the industry as they cannot find alternatives to carpet weaving.

Employment in the Handwoven Carpet Industry

There are no precise data regarding home-based carpet weaving. The 1966 and 1976 censuses calculated home-based production, but in succeeding censuses in 1986 and 1996 there are no data regarding household production units. During 1976–86 the number and proportion of carpet-weaving households increased considerably. The total number of households that were engaged in carpet weaving increased from 248,178 in 1966 to 633,072 in 1976. During this period more than 80 percent of carpet-weaving households were in rural areas. The substantial increase in the carpet-weaving households indicates higher income for carpet weaving compared to other home-based industries such as spinning and cotton cleaning. Furthermore, carpet weaving is easy to learn and even children less than seven years old can learn to weave.

After the 1979 Islamic Revolution, production and exports of Persian carpets declined significantly because of the US sanctions against Iran. For example, during 1978–82 exports of carpets declined from 1.84 to 0.71 million square meters and carpet production decreased from 5 to 1.4 million square meters. Given that more than 90 percent of women workers in Iran's textile sector in rural areas are carpet weavers (Nomani and Behdad 2006), we can use the data regarding changes in textile employment as a good proxy of employment in handwoven carpets, especially for women in rural areas. Table 5.3 indicates that from 1976 to 1986 the number of workers in Iran's textile industry decreased from about 1,010,000 to 830,000. Women in rural areas lost about 340,000 jobs, mainly as carpet weavers.

Table 5.3 Employment in Iran's Textile Industry

	1966		1976		1986		1996	
	Number	%	Number	%	Number	%	Number	%
THE WHOLE COUNTRY								
Women	440,346	72	606,646	60	337,436	41	500,198	59
Men	171,270	28	403,600	40	492,850	59	348,006	41
Total	611,616	100	1,010,246	100	830,286	100	848,204	100
URBAN AREAS								
Women	108,767	49	124,898	32	192,995	33	131,028	36
Men	114,759	51	268,353	68	389,503	67	237,911	64
Total	223,526	100	393,251	100	582,498	100	368,939	100
RURAL AREAS								
Women	331,579	85	481,748	78	144,441	58	366,592	77
Men	56,511	15	135,247	22	103,347	42	110,050	23
Total	388,090	100	616,995	100	247,788	100	476,642	100

Source: Statistical Center of Iran, extracted from different censuses.

As mentioned earlier, in the 1980s rival countries increased their share in the international carpet markets. The excess supply of handwoven carpets reduced international carpet prices. Profit margins of investments on Persian carpets shrank; many carpet exporters gave up the trade; and volume of production and export of Persian carpets declined sharply.

The number of carpet-weaving workshops decreased significantly; the share of female wage earners in the textile sector decreased from 25 to 18 percent during 1976–96. In addition to the decline in export of handwoven carpets, an increase in the education level of girls reduced the number and proportion of women carpet weavers, especially among unpaid family workers in the textile sector (table 5.4). While the total number of women workers in the textile sector declined in this period, many women continued to weave carpets in the urban and rural areas as independent producers. Declining real wages of carpet weaving was another reason for encouraging weavers to produce carpets independently.

Table 5.4 Employment in Iran's Textile Industry by Working Position

	1976				1996			
	Women		Men		Women		Men	
	Number	%	Number	%	Number	%	Number	%
THE WHOLE COUNTRY								
Independent workers	95,126	16	105,882	26	181,303	36	107,215	31
Wage earners	150,209	25	221,598	55	92,247	18	120,160	35
Unpaid family workers	354,417	58	46,360	11	193,807	39	26,951	8
URBAN AREAS								
Independent workers	26,406	21	73,226	27	57,339	44	67,069	28
Wage earners	49,568	40	161,097	60	28,399	22	93,845	39
Unpaid family workers	46,318	37	10,081	4	34,545	26	6,163	3
RURAL AREAS								
Independent workers	68,720	14	32,656	24	122,935	34	40,127	36
Wage earners	100,641	21	60,501	45	63,578	17	26,311	24
Unpaid family workers	308,099	64	36,279	27	159,262	43	20,769	19

Source: Statistical Center of Iran, extracted from different censuses.

Weaving wages were generally lower than industrial wages. For example, in 1983 the average daily wage of weavers in Torkman Sahra was about half of the legal minimum wage (Jahad 1362). Our survey in Kashan shows a similar result for 2006. Therefore, weavers prefer to work independently if they can afford living expenses until the carpet is finished and sold.

Handwoven Carpet Industry in Kashan

Carpet weaving has been widespread in many Iranian cities and villages since the late seventeenth century. In the 1970s more than 58 percent of home-based production units and 33 percent of Iran's rural areas were engaged in carpet weaving. About 55 percent of carpet weavers lived in villages and 45 percent in towns and cities; among them 80 percent were women (Statistical Center of Iran 1977). There are different informal statistics regarding carpet weavers. According to the estimate of Iran Carpet Company, in 2005 about 1.3 million persons wove carpets on 900,000 looms in different parts of Iran (Iran Carpet Company 2006).

There were many carpet-weaving workshops in Kashan in the past, but at present carpets are woven at home. Supervising carpet weaving in workshops is easier, yet for escaping formal minimum wages, overtime payments, taxes, rent, and utilities expenditures, carpet dealers prefer to put the looms in the houses of weavers. Matching home-based production with the fluctuation of market demands is much easier and cheaper. The dealers can put more or fewer looms in the houses whenever they expect boom or bust in the market.

To give a picture of current employment patterns in the handwoven carpet industry, I conducted a survey in Kashan. I chose Kashan as representative of carpet-producing regions in Iran. Kashan is a city situated between Tehran and Isfahan, known for the quality of its handwoven carpets. Kashan's design is rated high in both domestic and international markets. This design needs a high-knot density, which requires great skill, much practice, and immense concentration. I had prior knowledge about the concentration of carpet weavers in Kashan city and its villages. The principal research tool I used was an extensive structured questionnaire comprising an introductory sequence of closed questions eliciting demographic data on age, education, marital status, occupation, and household structure, followed by several sequences of open-ended questions on the subject of wages, working hours, and job preferences. In addition to interviews with carpet weavers, the study heavily relies upon information generated through direct talks with carpet merchants and exporters, as well as with government officials.

The survey method used is snowball sampling. Because of the lack of formal data about carpet weavers, I contacted my relatives in

Kashan to assist me in finding a carpet weaver for setting up interviews. I also contacted Iran Carpet Company in Kashan to get the addresses of their carpet weavers, but my addresses were few. In all sites many weavers were introduced to me by the women I had already interviewed. I carried out the survey during October and December 2006. The sample consisted of sixty-eight carpet-weaving households, amounting to ninety-six weavers (eighty women and sixteen men) from Kashan and its five villages: Fin, Khozagh, Aran, Aliabad, and Ravand (table 5.5). Sixty percent of the sample weavers lived in Kashan and Ravand, because I had better connections in these sites. I visited many Afghan carpet weavers in these two sites, but I did not find Afghan weavers in other selected locations. It does not mean that Afghan weavers do not live in Fin; I simply did not come across them. Afghan weavers constitute 39 percent of our sample. The handwoven carpet industry is the most important accessible job for Afghan women and children in Kashan and its villages.

I selected different sites to cover the diverse economic structure of the region. Close to Fin and Ravand, there are job opportunities in industrial complexes and factories, while Khozagh and Aliabad do not have any industries. Nevertheless, the data set has been analyzed as a random sample, and the derived feature can be generalized

Table 5.5 Distribution of Carpet Weavers by Location and Nationality (Percent)

County	Iranian		Afghan		Total	
	Men	Women	Men	Women	Men	Women
Kashan	0	9	2	17	2	26
Fin	2	12	0	0	2	12
Ravand	2	9	8	13	10	22
Khozagh	0	4	0	0	0	4
Aran	2	10	0	0	2	10
Aliabad	0	6	0	0	0	6
Total	6	50	10	30	16	80

Source: Extracted from completed questionnaire.

cautiously. In addition to the regular questionnaire, I had informal talks with sample carpet weavers, and direct quotations in this chapter are from my recollections.

Employment Structure of Kashan's Handwoven Carpet Industry

About forty years ago, Kashan's economy was mainly dependent on handwoven carpets, and women had no other job opportunity but carpet weaving. Kashan is an industrial district now. Many women work in different industries such as blanket, china, and glassware factories. An increasing number of educated women work in education, health, and other services. So carpet weaving has declined considerably in Kashan city, but in rural areas where access to outside-the-home jobs is limited, women are engaged in weaving. The lower percentage of Iranian weavers in Kashan's urban areas, only 10 percent in our sample, suggests that Iranian women who live in these areas have better access to well-paid jobs. This access, however, is not true of Afghan immigrants in Kashan, many of whom are engaged in carpet weaving. Most of the Afghan immigrants live illegally in Iran and do not posses work permits.[2] Afghan men, generally, work in the construction sector and on dairy farms, and Afghan women and children weave carpets in Kashan and its surrounding villages. Carpet-weaving earning is vital to poor Afghan families, who have tended to have many children. Afghans learn the special Iranian weaving style and are among the best weavers of silky and high-density-knot carpets.[3]

---

2. A small number of Afghans were issued "white cards" stipulating their status as *panahandegan* (refugees), entitling them to the right to work.

3. An Iran Carpet Company official in Kashan said that about 50 percent of carpet weavers in Natanz and Delijan (Kashan's neighboring cities) are Afghans. Many Iranian women in these cities work in factories and are not interested in carpet weaving.

Age and Sex Structure of Carpet Weavers

Carpet weaving is generally women's work in most parts of Iran. In 1996 more than 91 percent of women industrial workers were in the textile and clothing sector, mainly in carpet weaving. Decreasing international carpet prices led to a decline in real wages of carpet weavers. Furthermore, Iran's declining share of the global market has exacerbated job losses among weavers' families (Iran Chamber of Commerce 2006). When discussing real wages, it is important to note that most carpet weavers are unpaid family workers. Home weaving is compatible with childcare and the performance of domestic tasks, though often stretching the length of the working day.

As mentioned earlier, about 80 percent of our sample weavers are women. The age and sex structure and education and income levels of Iranian and Afghan households in our sample, however, did not produce quite the same result. Our sample showed that a higher percentage, 87.9 percent, of Iranian weavers were women, and that the share for Afghans was 73.3 percent. As table 5.6 shows, Afghan men were more active in carpet weaving compared to Iranian men. At present Afghan weavers are among the best weavers of delicate designs of high-density-knot, silky carpets.

Male carpet weavers are divided in two different age groups. Among Iranians, a few men weave carpets with their wives after retirement. They knew carpet weaving from childhood, but they stopped weaving when they went to school. Afghan men tend to be

Table 5.6 Distribution of Sample Carpet Weavers by Sex and Nationality

County	Iranian		Afghan		Total	
	Number	%	Number	%	Number	%
Women	58	87.9	22	73.3	80	83.3
Men	8	12.1	8	26.7	16	16.7
Total	66	100	30	100	96	100

Source: Extracted from completed questionnaire.

Table 5.7 Distribution of Sample Carpet Weavers by Age, Sex, and Nationality (Percent)

	Iranian		Afghan		Total	
Age Group	Men	Women	Men	Women	Men	Women
7–10	0	0	28.6	15	20	5.0
11–15	0	5	57.1	25	40	11.7
16–20	0	12.5	14.3	15	10	13.3
21–30	0	17.5	0	20	0	18.3
31–40	0	27.5	0	15	0	23.3
41–50	66.7	22.5	0	10	20	18.3
51+	33.3	15	0	0	10	10.0
Total	100.0	100.0	100.0	100.0	100.0	100.0

Source: Extracted from completed questionnaire.

employed as weavers until they can find jobs outside the home. In our sample, there are not any male weavers in Afghan households more than 15 years of age, while there are not any male carpet weavers in Iranian households less than 48 years of age (table 5.7).

Sixty-five percent of Iranian women carpet weavers in the sample were housewives more than 30 years old; this rate for Afghan women is 20 percent, whereas 40 percent of Afghan women and 2.5 percent of Iranian women were less than 16 years old. All male Afghan weavers in our sample are single and were less than 21 years old, while their Iranian counterparts are married and were more than 40 years old. Distribution of education level demonstrates the dissimilarity between Afghan and Iranian carpet weavers more clearly.

Education Level

In the past three decades the education of Iranian women has increased substantially. Girls from traditional families did not have the right to study beyond five years before the 1979 Islamic Revolution, but after the revolution the attitude toward women's education changed. Girls from low-income families in most rural areas now have secondary and even higher education.

Table 5.8 Distribution of Sample Carpet Weavers by Education Level (Percent)

Years of Schooling	Iranian		Afghan		Total	
	Men	Women	Men	Women	Women	Men
Illiterate	0	20	14.3	50	10	30
1–5	100	60	71.4	40	80	53.4
6–8	0	20	14.3	10	10	16.6
Total	3	40	7	20	100	100

Source: Extracted from completed questionnaire.

In spite of widespread education even in rural areas, most weavers are illiterate or have about five years of schooling (84 percent of sample weavers). This illiteracy indicates that weavers are from the poorest households, as an increasing proportion of Iranian middle-income families support the education of their children, both boys and girls, and do not oblige them to work. So, we could not find many Iranians of school age in our sample. The illiteracy rate among Afghans in our sample is more than 53 percent; this rate for Iranian weavers in the sample is 20 percent. About 10 percent of Afghan weavers have more than five years of schooling; this rate for Iranians is 20 percent. This difference is to a large extent because of limitations imposed by the government on public schooling for Afghan immigrants in Iran. By and large Iranian girls attend school and generally do not weave carpets, while their Afghan counterparts not only weave carpets during summer vacations, but also during the school year (table 5.8).

Child Labor

In cases where adult members do not earn enough in low-income families, child labor existed in Kashan. Until the 1990s, children's work was one of the important features of Iran's handwoven carpet industry. In Kerman Province 5- to 7-year-old children were rented for one year to carpet production workshops (Social Research

Institute 1967). In the 1960s about 60 percent of carpet weavers were 5 to 19 years old, worked fourteen to fifteen hours per day, and got less than half of the adult wages. A survey in Yazd Province in 1982 showed that 50 percent of carpet weavers were less than 20 years old. Even in urban areas, more than 30 percent of women carpet weavers were less than 15 years old (Rashidian 1988). Earning changed in the 1990s because of a decline in fertility and a rise in education, especially for girls and even for low-income Iranian families.

In our sample Afghan families were more dependent on the earning of their children, both boys and girls. In the sample 85.7 percent of male and 40 percent of female Afghan weavers were less than 16 years old; these rates for Iranian weavers were 0 and 5 percent respectively. While in our sample there was no one below the age of 10 years, 28 percent of Afghan weavers were less than 11 years old. In the case of 11- to 15-year-old weavers, only 3 percent were Iranians, while 11- to 15-year-old Afghans constituted 48 percent of our sample. Young Iranians who worked as weavers lived in Aliabad village, about twenty kilometers from Kashan, whereas young Afghan weavers lived both in urban and in rural areas.

The average size of Iranian and Afghan households in our sample was 6.1 and 4.1 respectively. Many Afghans live in extended families; typically a husband, his two wives, and many children who had been carpet weavers since a young age. The houses of many Afghan families in Kashan's villages have become carpet-weaving workshops. In some houses, there were two or three carpet looms and up to ten persons wove simultaneously (table 5.9). While 12 percent of Iranian households in our sample had three weavers, 46.7 percent of Afghan families had three weavers. There were no Iranian households with more than three weavers in our sample, while 30 percent of Afghan families had more than three weavers, most of them children.[4]

---

4. Beside carpet weaving, Afghan children, especially boys, are active in different kinds of relatively difficult and low-paid jobs in agriculture, construction, and services sectors in Kashan urban and rural areas.

Table 5.9 Number of Carpet Weavers in Households by Nationality

No. Weavers	Iranian		Afghan		Total	
	Number	%	Number	%	Number	%
1	22	45.8	1	5	23	33.8
2	20	41.7	3	15	23	33.8
3	6	12.5	9	45	15	22.1
4	0	0	3	15	3	4.4
5+	0	0	4	20	4	5.9
Total	48	100	20	100	68	100

Source: Extracted from completed questionnaire.

About 50 percent of illiterate Afghans in our sample were less than 16 years old, while the ages of all illiterate Iranians were more than 35 years. Afghan girls are disproportionately affected by the poverty of their household. Gender disaggregate data in our sample indicated that about 17 percent of males and 56 percent of females who were less than 16 years of age in Afghan households were illiterate. The data show that for Afghan low-income carpet-weaver families, boys' education is more important than girls'.

I visited the father of a 14-year-old illiterate Afghan carpet weaver in Kashan's Bazaar. He received USD 800 (about IRR 8,000,000 [rials]) from the carpet dealer. This amount included the wages of his daughter for weaving carpets fourteen hours per day for eight months as well as for her mother's work. The money was spent for household expenses; both the mother and daughter worked as unpaid family workers. In a typical Afghan family in Ravand, a 15-year-old boy who was a student gave me his daily schedule. He told me that he wakes up at 5:30 a.m. and weaves carpet for about an hour before going to school. Coming back in the afternoon, he weaves until 10 p.m., and does his homework at carpet-weaving break time. He was lucky because he could continue his study in high school. His sister had to leave school to weave carpets with her mother for whole days, despite her eagerness to continue her studies. Their father had left Iran, and the family was entirely dependent on the children's earnings.

Earnings of Carpet Weavers

Carpet weaving is a highly laborious home-based job and it is often interrupted by different events that affect the family, such as illness of a family member, or wedding or mourning ceremonies. As a result, it is not easy to calculate the real daily or monthly earnings of women carpet weavers. A survey in 1986 showed that the average monthly wage of carpet weavers was more or less equal to the legal minimum wage (Zonooz 1988). In the past two decades the nominal wages have increased but the weavers cannot live on weaving income alone anymore. While the legal minimum wage is about USD 200 (approximately IRR 2,000,000 [rials]) in 2007, the average wage of carpet weavers was about USD 60 per month. Weaving is a very low-paying job. Therefore most other work can pay better than weaving.

Our sample weavers suffered from declining real wages. Their average income was much less than the formal minimum wage, and like other home-based and informal work does not have pensions and social insurance. An Iranian woman in our sample told me that she weaves carpet to help her family, but that her earnings were progressively declining. In 1991 she wove a carpet for USD 400 (IRR 4,000,000). She could invest her wages in building their house. Yet in 2006 she wove a similar carpet and received close to USD 700 (approximately IRR 7,000,000), yet because of the rising prices of the construction materials, she could not buy half of what she could buy with USD 400 in 1991; this shows the real wage decline of carpet weavers in comparison to the housing market.[5]

Carpet weavers do not typically have a written contract; their contracts are verbal agreements according to which advancement is paid, and when the job is done the middleman evaluates the weaver's wage in accordance with the quality and quantity of weaving, duration of weaving, and amount of advance payment. If weaving is longer than the expected time, the weaver receives a lower wage, as the

---

5. Only in the year 1995, the inflation rate was about 50 percent.

capital of the merchant was dormant. In most cases, the final payment is not in cash. The weavers have to accept a check to be cashed after one to three months.

It is often more profitable for the weaver's family not to receive any advance payment and to weave carpets independently.[6] However, this independence is not easy because of the high cost of materials. In 2007 the cost of material for a twelve-square-meter carpet was about USD 650. It took a year (on average eight hours per day) for two weavers to finish the carpet. They sold the carpet for USD 2,600. Their earnings were about USD 2,000 (USD 1,000 each). If they wove for a trader, their income would be half that. As most weavers are from low-income families and cannot afford to wait a long time for the weaving earnings, they prefer to get advance payment and weave for the carpet traders.

About 70 percent of our sample weavers (96 percent of Afghan and 49 percent of Iranian weavers) were wage earners. All Iranian men in our sample were independent carpet weavers. They were retired from their previous jobs and could finance household expenditures during the time they were weaving carpets. All the Afghan males were wage earners, because they were children of low-income families; they could not afford to continue without pay for a long time and had to receive money before finishing the carpets. Only one Afghan woman in our sample was an independent weaver (table 5.10).

The hourly wage of a carpet weaver in our sample was about USD 0.2. A 20-year-old Afghan man in Ravand told me that he wove carpets whenever he was unemployed. The daily wage of construction work is about USD 9, while if one weaves carpets ten hours per day, the wage is barely USD 3. As most Afghan women in Kashan urban and rural areas do not have alternative job opportunities other than carpet weaving, they have to accept low wages. In Aliabad, the monthly wage of two young girls and their mother was about

---

6. Most weavers in Kashan can get the raw material and then pay for it after finishing the carpet.

Table 5.10 Distribution of Sample Carpet Weavers by Kind of Production (Percent)

Type	Iranian		Afghan		Total	
	Men	Women	Men	Women	Men	Women
Wage earner	0	52.5	100	95	70	66.7
Independent	100	47.5	0	5	30	33.3
Total	100.0	100.0	100.0	100.0	100.0	100.0

Source: Extracted from completed questionnaire.

USD 200, while the wage of the head of household who worked as an unskilled construction worker was the same. In other words, the wage of construction work was three times that of the carpet weavers.

The carpet-weaving wage is not sufficient to provide for the minimum basic needs of a weaver's household, yet it helps them to accumulate money for building a house or buying means of production. In 50 percent of our sample households, the share of weaving earnings in the total income is less than 30 percent. As table 5.11 indicates, weaving wages are too low to cover the whole cost of living of most Iranian carpet-weavers' households, yet they can be an important part of total income revenue if the head of household is unemployed or has left the family. In 63.7 percent of Iranian families in our sample, carpet-weaving income was less than 31 percent of the household income. In such cases women are usually not obliged to finish the carpet quickly. They wove carpets whenever they were released from their reproductive work; weaving became a means to increase the family's assets rather than an absolute necessity. In contrast, 54.6 of Afghan and 12.2 percent of Iranian households gained more than 40 percent of their total earnings by carpet weaving. These families are thus highly dependent on carpet weaving, illustrating the degree to which Afghan families depend on the revenue generate by the industry.

Average per capita monthly income of the sample households was USD 62 during the time of the research. This average means that 50 percent of the sample household had per capita income of more

Table 5.11 Share of Carpet Weaving in Household Income (Percent)

Share of Income	Iranian	Afghan	Total
10–20 Percent	36.4	9.1	26.5
21–30 Percent	27.3	18.2	23.5
31–40 Percent	24.2	18.2	29.4
41–50 Percent	6.1	27.3	11.8
50+ Percent	6.1	27.3	8.8
Total	100	100	100

Source: Extracted from completed questionnaire.

than USD 2 per day. While per capita monthly income for 14.3 of the sample households (90 percent of them Iranians) was more than USD 100, for 22.9 percent of these households (88 percent of them Afghans) per capita income was less than USD 30 per month and less than USD 1 per day.

The results of our survey show that a transformation of the workforce has taken place in Iran's handwoven carpet industry. Three decades ago most families in Kashan were engaged in carpet weaving; yet because of the decline in carpet-weaving real wages, most middle-income households stopped weaving and Afghan immigrant weavers increasingly entered the industry.

Position of Carpet Weavers in Households

It is often argued that paid work can improve women's socioeconomic position, as women's participation in paid work can improve the standard of living of women and their families. However, our survey contests this position by showing that participation in paid work does not necessarily bring about an improvement in the status and roles of women. Carpet weaving is an activity based at home and tends to exacerbate rather than transform gender subordination, keeping women dependent on their husbands given that they often work as unpaid family workers. Home-based weaving is compatible with childcare and the performance of domestic tasks, though often stretching the length of the working day. While development of the carpet industry does promote employment among women, it does not increase the income of women carpet weavers to the point of fundamental change of their traditional status.

Women carpet weavers, generally, bear a double workload, and do not experience a change in the sexual division of labor in households, as carpet weaving does not challenge existing gender relations and the ideology embedded in daily social practices. The majority of women who were interviewed said that housework is endless and boring, and they preferred to weave carpets instead of doing housework. However, they did not regard weaving as formal employment. It is widely believed that weaving is not a serious job but that it is rather a hobby for women, whereas our data suggest that the family relies on this income either as the primary or secondary source of household revenue.

Carpet-weaving's earnings are generally invisible and unrecognized. Male members of the family sell produced carpets or receive the weaving wage from the carpet traders. A 53-year-old Iranian woman in Khozagh village said that she started carpet weaving at the age of 6. She continued weaving during her pregnancy and seven to ten days after delivering the baby. Although she had worked from early morning until sunset for the past forty-five years, she did not have any belongings; their house was in the possession of her husband. She tolerated the hard life without protest, as she had five daughters. She had to work to manage their life and to prepare her daughters' dowries.

Some of the women weavers had control of part of their earnings. One of the Iranian unmarried weavers told me, "When my father was alive, I had to weave from six a.m. until eight p.m. without any pay and I had to help in the housework too. Two years ago my father died. Now I pay half of my wage to my mother, and I buy golden necklaces and rings for myself with the rest of my earnings."

The situation of women carpet weavers in the Afghan households of our sample was worse than that of their Iranian counterparts. Some of them told me that they were even beaten by their husbands and had no right to participate in decision-making about the most important family affairs, despite their high contribution to the total household income.

Concluding Remarks

Economic globalization has increased Iran's exports significantly, yet this surge has been mainly owing to export of resource- and energy-based and capital-intensive commodities, while the share of Iran's main labor-intensive exports, especially handwoven carpets, has declined during the past two decades. Excess supply of handwoven carpets has reduced international carpet prices. The profit margin of investment in Persian carpets has shrunk; many carpet exporters have given up the trade; and the volume of production and export of Persian carpets has declined sharply. Harsh competition among developing countries for conquering the international carpet markets has suppressed the real wages of those countries with higher labor costs.

The findings of our survey in Kashan show that in the past women from middle-income families wove carpets. But increased oil revenues and economic growth have lifted the incomes of many families, while real wages in carpet weaving have been under pressure from international competition. As a result, carpet weaving has become a sign of poverty. The average earnings of carpet weavers are much lower than the formal minimum wage, and most women are not interested in carpet weaving anymore. However, women's carpet weaving remains a crucial source of income for many poor families. Some middle-class households also pursue the activity as a means of supplementary income and sometimes as a hobby. Meanwhile, a large number of women and children from low-income Afghan immigrant households have replaced Iranian weavers. The Afghan weavers work hard and accept low wages. It seems that without low-paid Afghan weavers, Persian carpets could not preserve their high position in the international markets.

As the economy grows and family incomes rise, carpet weaving in mass production form and as a major source of income for part of the population is likely to decline in Iran. However, this trend does not imply that the industry will necessarily be obliterated. Carpet weaving, especially as an economic activity dominated by women, can survive and maybe even thrive if it is turned into a high-quality art form that retains its leading position in world markets and entails high value added for workmanship.

In spite of the fact that women's earnings from carpet weaving are critical, particularly in low-income families, and given that the work is home-based, carpet weaving does not necessarily transform the subordination of women. Women's mass employment in the carpet industry in past decades gave them job opportunities without providing them with noticeable equality. For this reason, many women prefer not to work in this sector and with their rise in education move into other types of occupations.

6

Female-Headed Households in Iran
Microcredit versus Charity

ROKSANA BAHRAMITASH

THERE HAS BEEN INCREASING CONCERN about the issue of growing poverty among women in general, but among female-headed households in particular. The problem was emphasized during the Beijing+10 meeting in New York during March 2005. Throughout the world, women as heads of households fare worse than men, even in the rich Western countries. According to a UN report, for instance, women headed 62 percent of poor households in the Netherlands. Academics in the field of gender and development have argued that female-headed households are overrepresented among the poor. A recent UN report stated that the cycle of poverty "has continued to widen in the past decade, a phenomenon commonly referred to as 'the feminization of poverty.' Worldwide, women, on average, earn slightly more than 50% of what men earn. The feminization of poverty deprives women of access to resources, such as credit and land."[1] The poverty of female-headed households is a major problem, particularly in many parts of the world (Bullock 1994, 17–18; Buvinic 1990; Buvinic and Gupta 1997; Kennedy 1994; Tinker 1990, 5). A recent human development report on the Arab world indicates that

---

1. From http://www.un.org/womenwatch/daw/followup/session/presskit/fs1.htm, accessed November 2007.

female-headed households are on the rise, even in the Middle East and North Africa (UNDP 2005).

While concerns over poverty and the feminization of poverty are pertinent, stereotypes about female-headed households as being the "poorest of the poor" may not always be accurate, as Sylvia Chant points out (1997; 2003; this issue has also been raised by Valentine Moghadam). Moreover, the assumptions about women from low-income households being powerless victims rather than agents may be simplistic and erroneous. This error is illustrated by women squatters of Zahedan shantytowns who demonstrated their persistence in making demands of the mayor to recognize their ownership of houses built without legal means of occupying the land, as described at the end of this chapter.

In Iran, the issue of female-headed households started to become a public issue in 1979, when the 1979 Revolution and then the war with Iraq led to an increase in the number of female-headed households over the following decade. During the late 1990s and 2000s, there has been an increase in de facto female-headed households owing to increases in the number of drug addicts. This situation has become critical, and it may continue or worsen. Afghanistan is now number one in opium production, and stopping the flow of drugs across borders is notoriously difficult. Official figures indicate that there has been a 1 percent increase in female-headed household since the last census in 1996. The most recent census reveals that the number of female-headed households has reached 9.5 percent of all households. This information is particularly important because official data tend to underestimate real figures as many women are not willing to report themselves for a variety of reasons, one of them being that announcing oneself as the breadwinner of the family could bring shame to their husbands and create tension between spouses.

This chapter will focus on female-headed households and microcredit programs, because the latter have been celebrated as a magic bullet for poverty alleviation. The chapter will discuss female-headed households in relation to microcredit programs initiated by national and international organizations in Iran.

Female-Headed Households and the Muslim Tradition

Typically there are more female-headed households in the Caribbean and Latin American countries, where some men leave their families for another woman, often without paying child support. In Muslim traditions this pattern has not been socially acceptable.[2] Strong emphasis on the family throughout many parts of the Muslim world has traditionally provided women with extended family support. As Suad Josef points out, the Middle Eastern/Arab family has enjoyed strong family ties where women are taken care of by the community (Josef 1996, 196). Communal protection is also associated with patriarchy, where men are in charge of social and economic resources and dominate the public sphere. With transition from *Gemeinschaft,* or traditional society, to *Gesselshaft,* or urban society, which is correlated with decline of community care for its members and the weakening of social ties, more vulnerable members of the society are left without community protection. In this situation, women from low-income households can lose their traditional social safety nets.

According to Shari'a law, Muslim women in need of assistance have to be looked after by the *umma* (the Nation of Islam/the Muslim Community). This type of welfare assistance is technically funded through the resources of the *beyto'l mal* (Islamic treasury financed by Islamic taxes). It should be remembered that behind Shari'a law's prescription to provide for low-income female-headed households is a patriarchal model that defines a family as composed of a male breadwinner and a female homemaker. In the absence of the male breadwinner, the woman becomes the responsibility of the entire Muslim community.

---

2. In the Middle Eastern and North African (MENA) countries, polygamy is accepted and a man who wishes to enter into another marriage does not have to leave his first wife to marry another woman.

The Iranian Context

The interplay of community care and male honor in low-income households is particularly important within the Muslim cultural context. Fariba Adelkhah elaborates the significance of the Persian concept of *javanmardy,* which refers to a man of courage, modesty, humility, and rectitude. This is a national value in Iran (Adelkhah 2000, 31). Javanmardy requires that male members of the community take care of a woman left without a breadwinner. It is this aspect of Iranian culture that has traditionally helped to keep the number of female-headed households low. It is common for a brother-in-law, or other members of the family, to marry a relative's widow for the purpose of taking care of her, both emotionally and economically. These marriages in the Muslim tradition—which place emphasis on the widow's and orphan's welfare—are regarded as a sign of being a good Muslim and a *Javanmard*. While this tradition can be positive, it has also left many widows in the guardianship of male members of the family who are more interested in pursuing their own interests rather than those of the widow and her children.

Iran's postrevolutionary constitution emphasizes the role of the state in taking care of the poor. According to clause 4 of Article 21 of the Constitution of the Islamic Republic of Iran, there is to be "provision of especial insurance for the widows, the elderly women and the women heading the household." While Iran's constitution stipulates that widowed women and orphans must receive a pension from the state, state support has not been effectively delivered and various nonstate organizations such as charitable organizations have stepped in to provide for low-income, female-headed households.

The issue of the economic vulnerability of women who are heads of households was raised almost immediately after the revolution and during the war with Iraq. Although the revolution was relatively peaceful, there were still casualties, many of them from low-income households. The war with Iraq left more than a million casualties, either dead or wounded. In the case of war veterans, men became dependent on their wives and sons depended on their mothers. The feature film *Gilaneh*, made by Rakhshan Bani Etemad, offers an illustrative example. The movie follows a typical single woman in the rural north of the country. She struggles to take care of her son, a victim of chemical bombing. She is quite poor and assistance provided by the state is insufficient.

As was mentioned earlier, with the fall of the Taliban and Afghanistan's becoming the world's largest opium producer, the number of drug addicts in the region, and in Iran, has increased at an unprecedented rate. Fieldwork in Zahedan showed that male breadwinners' drug addiction has become a major drain on many families' resources and has left many wives as the de facto heads of households. Incidentally, drug addiction could potentially explain why Khorasan, a province neighboring Afghanistan with a huge refugee population, has the highest rate of female-headed households in the country.[3] This rate is because male drug addicts tend to leave their families in order to spend all their income on their own drug consumption.

Based on the earlier discussion on Muslim culture, one would expect male clergy to initiate efforts to care for female-headed households. However, as Azadeh Kian has documented (1997), leading clerics believed that community ties were sufficiently strong to assure that widows and orphans would be taken care of. It was Islamist women with political power who pushed for the recognition of the problem. They were particularly concerned with widows of the revolution and the Iran-Iraq war, and with women who lived as refugees in cities during and after the war. 'Atiqih Rajayi and Gohar-al Shari'a Dastghiyb, two female members of Parliament, worked assiduously to prepare a motion to address the predicaments of women who had lost their husbands. "We asked our brothers [male members] what they wanted to do with these women. We argued that we could not abandon them, and that the government should provide them material and moral assistance. But our male colleagues responded to our

---

3. See http://www.unescap.org/esid/psis/population/popin/profiles/iran/Down Load/soc_eco.zip, accessed December 2007.

request by saying that each woman had a brother, a father or a son who should pay her alimony [this is an interesting point and it indicates resistance to accept that the community was failing to take care of its vulnerable members]. We negotiated with them for several months to no avail. Eventually the same motion was passed by the Fourth Majlis which was credited with its initiation."

The campaign was successful because many of the female politicians belonged to leading clerical families. Gohar-al Shari'a Dasteghayb and 'Atiqih Rajayi (members of the First to Third Majlis), Marziyyeh Dabbagh (member of the Second, Third, and Fifth Majlis), and Maryam Behruzi (member of the First to Fourth Majlis) were members of the Islamic Republic Party and of the Tehran Society of Combatant Clergy *(royaniat e mobarz)*. These women were instrumental in placing the issue of female-headed households on the state agenda. Their effort translated into increased activity by charitable foundations (Kian 1997, 75–96). This effort was an attempt to apply the concept of the responsibility of umma to take care of its members.

The Statistical Picture

The Statistical Center of Iran defines a female-headed household as one where a woman is in charge of providing and managing the household's means of subsistence. This definition includes households where the man of the house is present yet owing to disabilities is unable to provide for the household. According to a UN document on female-headed households, census data from 1996 showed that such households made up 8.4 percent of all households. According to the latest data (2006), the current rate is 9.5 percent, an increase of more than 1 percent. This increase is high considering the fact that there has been not been a war. Added to this figure are a large number of refugee Afghan women. As confirmed by fieldwork observations (2004 to 2008), many Afghan women do not wish to return to Afghanistan and would prefer to stay in Iran.

Census data from 1996 estimated that there were about one million female-headed households. This is likely an underestimation.

Even this low number means that, calculating with an average of four dependants per household, over five million women, children, and disabled men fall into this category. The same data showed that only 3.33 percent of female heads of households in Iran get either retirement insurance or a pension, and one-eighth of them rely on charitable donations. Women heads of households in rural areas have the lowest monthly income of all female-headed households. Many households are headed by women of sixty-five years and older whose husbands are deceased (Sekhavati 2004).

As was stated before, these figures are likely an underestimation. Many women from peasant and low-income households may not report themselves as heads of households because that would mean that extended family, in-laws, and their community lack javanmardy. During my fieldwork in Zahedan, a city that is the capital of one of the most economically depressed areas of the country, Sistan and Baluchistan women were reluctant to declare themselves the breadwinner of the family. It took me a long time to find out that they were de facto heads of households and in some cases financed their husbands' costly drug habits. To admit to society or to the officials that their husband is a drug addict not only brings shame but could have legal consequences for their husband.

Although there may well be some difficulties regarding underreporting, the latest census data are a useful point of entry into developing an understanding of the extent of the problem. The following tables, extracted from the 2006 national census, show that the share of women among heads of households (9.5 percent) is the same in both urban and rural settings, but that it declines to 5.7 percent in nomadic areas (table 6.1). In tribal societies, where communal ties are strong, such as in Kohkiluyeh and Boyr Ahmad Province, the rate of female-headed households is the lowest. The share of female-headed households who are employed is higher in urban areas than in rural ones because of better opportunities for women to find jobs in urban areas. Moreover, many female-headed households in rural areas are headed by older women who are unable to perform the jobs available to them in rural areas. The rate is higher among nomads,

Table 6.1 Share of Women among Heads of Households by Activity Status (Percent)

	Total	Urban	Rural	Nomads
Total	9.5	9.5	9.5	5.7
Employed	1.8	1.8	1.7	2.6
Unemployed	1.8	2.3	1.0	1.9
Attending school	21.6	21.7	21.0	9.5
Receiving pension	30.6	28.1	38.9	45.5
Homemaker	96.4	96.2	96.9	98.0
Other	13.6	12.9	14.8	11.5
Status not stated	11.4	12.3	9.9	16.4

Source: Statistical Center of Iran, www.sci.org.ir.

which means that those who are being reported as female-headed households have a much higher rate of unemployment. The data also suggest that there are more female-headed households where women attend schools in urban and rural areas than in nomadic areas (this could be because educated women may feel prohibited from declaring themselves as heads of households). By contrast, women who receive a pension are more numerous among nomads than among women in urban and rural areas. The data suggest that women with a homemaker status tend to be overrepresented among heads of households. This tendency is interesting because it suggests that there is a social safely net that takes care of their needs so that they can remain homemakers.

Data on the composition of female-headed households (table 6.2) indicate that 14.1 percent of female heads of households are employed in urban areas and 13.9 percent of them in rural areas, while among the nomads the rate of employment in this category is 41.9 percent. Women who receive a pension in this category constitute close to half of the households in urban and rural areas but only 22.5 percent among nomads. Close to one-third of female-headed households are homemakers in urban and rural areas and among nomads.

The next part of the chapter focuses on two different approaches adopted to deal with the problem of female-headed households and

Table 6.2 Composition of Women Heads of Households (Percent)

	Total	Urban	Rural	Nomads
Total	100.0	100.0	100.0	100.0
Employed	14.1	14.1	13.9	41.9
Unemployed	0.6	0.6	0.5	0.8
Attending school	1.1	1.4	0.4	0.2
Receiving pension	48.3	48.2	48.4	22.5
Homemaker	31.0	31.3	30.4	28.1
Other	4.6	4.0	6.0	5.8
Status not stated	0.4	0.4	0.4	0.8

Source: Statistical Center of Iran, www.sci.org.ir.

poverty. First, it will discuss the charity model, used by revolutionary and religious organizations such as the Imam Khomeini's Relief Foundation); and second, it will follow the microcredit model, used primarily by national and international organizations. The chapter is focused on two microcredit programs, one adopted by a national organization, the Welfare Organization *(behzisty)*, and the other by an international organization, the United Nations Development Program in Sistan and Baluchistan.

The Charity Model

There are a wide range of charity organizations with outreach programs for women heading low-income households. They range from extremely informal, community-based organizations to those affiliated with mosques to highly formal organizations with state funding such as the Imam Khomeini's Relief Foundation (IKRF), the Martyr's Foundation (Bonyad-e Shahid), the Foundation for the Disempowered (Mostazafan), the Veteran Foundation (Janbazan), and the Foundation of Panzdah Khordad.[4] While informal organizations are more removed

---

4. This foundation refers to an event in June 5, 1963, when Ayatollah Khomeini protested against the Shah and the army opened fire at a demonstration.

from the state, closer to their beneficiary, and often nonbureaucratic, formal and nationwide foundations tend to cover those associated with civil organizations in support of the state. An Iranian-based academic argued that the IKRF in rural areas has been turned into a welfare organization that serves to provide political support for the state.

The IKRF is the largest single charity organization in the country with 4–5 million beneficiaries, some of whom are not residing in Iran. The IKRF runs programs in places outside of Iran such as Tajikistan, where it supports six thousand female-headed households and a total of thirty thousand beneficiaries (De Cordier 2007, 10–11). The organization also has a major branch in South Lebanon named Emdad Committee. While within Iran its recipients are victims of poverty, outside of Iran the IKRF provides relief to women and families in war-torn areas and to victims of natural disasters, such as the 2007 earthquake in Pakistan. On the official website, the IKRF states that its mission is to "give effective aid to the needy and deprived classes of the Islamic Nation." Here the Islamic Nation refers to the Islamic tradition of social responsibility of the Muslim community toward the poor, women and orphans in particular, and the name of this particular program is *ekram* (generosity with benevolence and respect for others). The IKRF focuses primarily on rural areas and city slums and operates within a closely knit community with ties to other religious organizations and the mosque. The IKRF's primary source of funding comes from inside the country, where it receives donations and collects Islamic taxes (*zakat:* taxes on the rich; and *khoms:* one-fifth of the income of wealthy members of Muslim society). The aim is to eliminate poverty and to provide for basic material needs, although the IKRF has other programs such as legal aid and counseling as well. The IKRF mission statement, as displayed on its website, states that it aims to protect and support "the oppressed people" (mostazafin) and make them self-sufficient (http://www.emdad.ir/Homepage, accessed November 2007).[5]

5. See http://www.emdad.ir/Homepage, accessed November 2007.

The IKRF covers fifty-two thousand villages, many of them in remote areas. Its charitable activities include managing pension plans and providing food, clothing, household goods, scholarships, shelter, and health and disability insurance. It gives credits for income-generating activities and offers no-interest loans for emergency use *(garzol hasaneh)*. The IKRF also provides bride price and financial assistance for newly married couples, improves access to literacy programs, establishes educational camps, provides funds for pilgrimages, and provides scholarships for male and female students (who have to live in dormitories). Other services include aid for housing and medical care, aid for those with disabilities, and improving access to employment.

The foundation puts a great deal of emphasis on promoting marriage among young people. It offers funds for those who wish to get married, by allocating resources for bride price and marriage loans for newly married couples. There are currently more than sixty-seven thousand young women who are under coverage by the foundation for the purpose of providing them with resources for marriage.

Programs for Female Heads of Households

The IKRF indicates that among the more than 1.5 million households with over 4 million beneficiaries that are covered by the foundation, more than one-third of households have female heads of households.

In addition to their main program for female-headed households, there is a special program, named after one the early postrevolutionary prime ministers, Rejai, who was one of the seventy-two high-ranking officials who was blown up in the office of the Islamic Republic Party headquarters in the early 1980s. Rejai has been regarded as an important martyr, and as a result a major program designed to address poverty among women in rural areas has been named after him: *tarheh shahid rejai*.[6]

---

6. See http://www.emdad.ir/Homepage.

The IKRF also provides for female heads of households where a family member or the breadwinner is imprisoned. About 1.7 percent of those covered by the IKRF are families of prisoners. Although men whose wives are in prison also benefit from the program, the most important beneficiaries are women.

Employment and Self-Sufficiency

For the purpose of this chapter, one of the most important programs of the IKRF is its income-generating activity (IGA). The program has a series of focuses. For instance, it provides self-sufficiency loans (microcredit) for purchasing capital goods. Unlike the microcredit model, the program supervises how the loan is used, and it also takes care of marketing the final product. The program provides training and the facilities needed for women to be engaged in an IGA.

Toward the end of 2007, the IGA programs had 75,492 women from female-headed households engaged in income-generating activities. These activities involved carpet and Kulim weaving, sewing and embroidery, agricultural production, handicrafts, and other activities in which women have been traditionally engaged. One of the mandates of the foundation is to empower women economically to the level of self-sufficiency. However, when one becomes self-sufficient she can still have access to marketing schemes and shops where the IKRF sells goods. The profit is technically then redistributed among those involved in an IGA. This type of IGA has a guaranteed income and women who work in these programs are de facto employees of the foundation.

Other Services

The foundation provides for other services such as medical care. By the end of 2007–8, IKRF will employ 13,774 doctors to work in various hospitals, clinics, and Para clinics throughout the country, offering medical services to their beneficiaries. Moreover, rising rental costs, a major concern for low-income households in general but for female-headed households in particular, have led to provisions for loans for shelter. In addition, the foundation offers legal aid and social work. In 2007 alone the foundation had twenty-seven thousand women and girls in its counselling programs. Social workers work for the beneficiaries on a whole range of services, including assisting women to find employment.

However, my fieldwork in major cities, particularly Tehran, indicated that access to assistance is exceedingly difficult and is often tied to having contacts and networking. Although the IKRF provides for a vast number of women, what is provided is often insufficient. Moreover, the bureaucratic nature of the foundation makes it susceptible to corruption. Also, beneficiaries of these programs often have to prove that they are not from the opposition but rather that they support the state and are good Muslims in order to receive aid.

Microcredit and the Self-Help Model

Muhammad Yunus, an economist originally from Bangladesh, won the Nobel Peace Prize in 2007 for starting a microcredit program that led to the establishment of the Grameen Bank. This is a bank that lends only to women. The Noble Peace Prize indicates an official endorsement of the microcredit model as an effective means to address poverty. The principle behind the model is that a group becomes collectively responsible for repayment of the loans of its members. This model mobilizes the target group, in this case women, to depend on each other for help and for support. The group also exerts pressure on members to repay their loan because of its collective responsibility. This model usually brings together people who have some kind of collateral or start-up capital, and its objective is to enhance their ability to generate an income.

The general literature on the topic tends to favor the model. In fact, a leading scholar of female poverty, Naila Kabeer, has come to endorse the model, while also pointing out its weaknesses (2001). The first problem with the model is that it fails to reach the really poor, namely those with no capital. Second, as the model aims at turning women into entrepreneurs, it can create and/or exacerbate class distinctions by providing opportunities for those with existing resources and increasing their wealth at the expense of the very poor. Third, self-help groups are not always collegial. There can be conflict within groups, as we shall see later in this chapter about my fieldwork in Zahedan.

The microcredit program for women, established by Yunus and his Grameen Bank, has been successful, and some have argued that its success is not unrelated to the fact that it was established in a Muslim country. In fact, Muhammad Yunus, in an interview with CNN, mentioned that when faced with men who were criticizing him for giving loans only to women, he responded by pointing out that the first female convert, the wife of the Prophet, was a businesswoman herself.[7] The model has been supported for reasons that go beyond poverty alleviation. The model often offers a certain degree of empowerment, and it has been celebrated because of its impact on lowering fertility rates and on increasing the education level of women (Pitt and Khandker 1998; Hulme and Mosley 1996). However, as Rahman argues, because of the hegemonic nature of patriarchal ideology in Bangladesh and at the Grameen Bank, the bank permeates bank-client relations in such a way that interhousehold relations are not transformed (Rahman 1999). In fact, far from transforming gender inequality, it reproduces hierarchical social relations. Ultimately, the success of the project lies in utilizing patriarchal structures rather than in facilitating their transformation. Nonetheless, the evidence and results seem to vary from case to case; therefore, it is important to examine different cases for individual assessment. Two microcredit initiatives, one adopted as a national program and the other by UNDP, will be examined in this chapter.

A National Program: Welfare Organization

In the late 1990s, the government sought to cut back on state funding for public services and to channel funds through civil organizations.

---

7. See http://www.cnn.com/2007/WORLD/asiapcf/11/05/talkasia.yunus/, accessed January 2008.

The Welfare Organization (WO), an organization working under the auspices of the Ministry of Health and responsible for welfare issues, was forced to cut its budget. The WO took a series of measures to deal with its shrinking resources. One of these measures was to conduct research to determine the efficiency of these programs, and to find the best use of the funds allocated to "the vulnerable groups." The results showed that 60 to 70 percent of all those receiving welfare could be incorporated into the labor market. The study also indicated that those who enter social assistance programs tend to become dependent on them. The WO sought to address "the problem" of dependency by developing an alternative strategy. In 1999, high-profile officials from the WO participated in an international workshop in India, organized by the Economic and Social Commission for Asia and by the Pacific Poverty Reduction Method (ESCA and PPRM). The program was designed to introduce policy makers to use of state-supported participatory models that help empower vulnerable members of society. The project's target group included people with disabilities and women from low-income families. Setareh Forozanfar, one of the Iranian delegates to the conference, inspired by the workshop, prepared a project in Iran that focused on female-headed low-income households. The program drew upon the basic ideas of ESCA and PPRM in ways that were compatible with Iranian society.

The program was launched in 1999. Based on the idea of self-help groups, it sought to divide welfare recipients into groups of five to seventeen women. About five hundred groups were formed throughout the country. The program focused entirely on urban areas. Interviews with those in charge of the program revealed that their reason for not including rural areas was because the closely knit social systems in rural areas were suspicious of urban middle-class officials meddling in their affairs. Officials found it hard to penetrate the rural fabric of Iran.[8]

---

8. This orientation was in sharp contrast with the Jihad for reconstruction, a program that from its start focused entirely on rural areas, seeking to empower cooperatives (interview with -Mafi, the head of Jihad for reconstruction, Tehran 2007).

The women formed self-help groups facilitated by social workers who could train them to eventually transform themselves into economic NGOs with official status. The official backing was designed to empower these women to enter into negotiations with various governmental offices and to mobilize support for their economic activities. In some cases, their official status enabled these groups to take advantage of state subsidies and utilize official support for their marketing strategies. The Ministry of Health allocated to each group an initial fund equivalent to about USD 2,000, given as a start-up fund for microcredit.

The program's focus was not exclusively on addressing issues of female poverty; it also sought to empower female-headed families, providing them with support in order to facilitate their public engagements. However, one of the leading figures of the program stated in an interview that social attitudes toward single women and corresponding cultural barriers were a major problem, not just for female heads of households but also for officials and social workers (Parviz Zarei, assistant to the project manager, October 2004). He also added that it was much easier to work in larger cities. The smaller and more remote the area, the larger the problems faced by the WO (this assessment was confirmed by Setareh Forozanfar, the project manager, during an interview in Tehran, November 2004).

Several social workers faced major challenges in places with strong family control and where the community kept a close eye on its members. Social workers involved in the project stated that in closely knit societies, help from the state brought shame to the women and the community because it meant that the community was incapable of taking care of itself, something discussed earlier in the chapter. Much of the fieldwork indicated that welfare recipients felt shameful about being openly assisted by the state. There was generally a preference to keep the matter as discrete as possible, but the problem was worse in places with low economic opportunities and in more community-based cities. More affluent provinces showed more openness to microfinance and income-generating activities.

Because of the decentralized nature of the program, each province in charge of implementing has to do it in its own way. This feature proved problematic, as the task of empowering women in economically impoverished areas can be difficult, and sometimes interventions from provincial headquarters were required. This was made all the more difficult because the local staffs were part of the same community as those receiving the aid and they hesitated to break informal ties and create formal groups.

Although the project managed to form groups, the next stage, mobilization for creating an economic enterprise, proved to be a major challenge. Many participants had little experience and doubted their ability to initiate such enterprises. Therefore it was very important that the WO commit itself to an initial start-up fund. The project often could not provide sufficient resources and, according to Frozanfar, the project manager and the WO were forced to seek alternative sources of funding. Support came from various governmental and nongovernmental organizations. Even religious authorities were urged to provide support. The WO sought out local clerics who were in charge of leading Friday prayers to bring up the issue in the mosque, making it into a matter of public debate. When programs were endorsed by religious leaders they enjoyed considerable success. In one particular case, an ayatollah in the city of Hamadan supported the initiative and in his sermons gave full support to income-generating groups formed by women from single-headed households (which included women who had become sole breadwinners because of their husband's drug addiction), and he asked women to join in the war against drug abuse (interview with Forozanfar, Tehran, 2004).

The program started with single-headed households only but it quickly grew to include married women whose husbands were either drug addicts or disabled. The task of having married women join the program proved more difficult than getting single women involved. In families where the man of the house was disabled or a drug addict, the incapacity of the man to earn an income continued to be a source of intra-household tension. Sometimes the men felt threatened when they saw the state support their wives instead of helping them. In some cases, husbands were hostile toward the program. These difficulties were similar to some of the challenges that Yunus and the Grameen Bank faced.[9] It was the job of the social worker to organize family counseling for the couple and to provide reassurance to the husband. Nonetheless, it was often easier for single women to leave their home and work than it was for married women. Their husbands stayed at home, monitored their every activity, and interfered with decision-making. These observations from our fieldwork provide evidence for the finding that men felt ashamed when their wives receive financial assistance from the state.

Looking at the overall picture, rich provinces such as Tehran, Khorasan, Farse, Gilan, and Mazandaran significantly outperformed poorer provinces, mostly because of the greater access to resources and business opportunities. One year into the project, some provinces were already able to form groups. The most successful program was found in the city of Shiraz, where thirteen groups were formed. In Chahar Mahal Bakhtiari, Hormozgan, Ilam and Kohkiloyeh, and Boyr Ahmad, four of the poorest provinces with a high nomad population (with the exception of Hormozgan), very little was achieved. Hormozgan, in the south of the country, is similar to the Gulf countries; as it has a substantial Arab population and strong family ties, it is resistant to state initiatives.

The program started by recruiting women between the ages of eighteen and twenty-four. Later, in response to official statistics that indicated that many single heads of households were older women and that older, widowed women of female-headed households were more likely to be poor, it was extended to cover women over the age of fifty. Moreover, it was viewed as a discriminatory practice to include only young women while many women over fifty were

---

9. Interview with Yunus by CNN, in which he states that in some cases men felt threatened and resisted women's access to credit, http://www.cnn.com/2007/WORLD/asiapcf/11/05/talkasia.yunus, accessed January 2008.

still capable of maintaining an active economic role. Each group had to be set up to ensure that at least one-third of the members had either a primary or a secondary level of education. The same ratio was required for members with skilled labor. Once the group was formed, the next step was to make the group work as a team. The role of social workers was to form a group that would work on building consensus. One of the social workers, Bahare Rozkhah, pointed out that *"many hours of hard work had to go into explaining and mediating between members of the groups so that the group would come to recognize itself as a group and engage in a collective activity as an economic unit"* (interview, Tehran, October 2004). Once the group was formed and teamwork was established, the role of the social worker would gradually diminish and the group was allowed to work as an autonomous team.

The group had to decide on what type of economic activity they would pursue, a step necessary to access microfinance and gain official NGO status. Most groups engaged in a variety of income-generating activities, such as food processing, dressmaking, and other traditionally female occupations. Occasionally female groups were able to engage in male-dominated professions such as setting up a bakery or a pizzeria. One example is a group in Esphahan, where women started a bakery and became extremely successful. Their product was very popular and it ended up capturing a significant market share. Many customers preferred their bread to the bread produced by male-operated bakeries of the district. The situation became threatening to the male bakers, and the bakery union filed a complaint with the mayor. The mayor carefully looked into the matter and asked the group for a meeting. The group of women successfully argued their case to the mayor and demonstrated why they should be able to pursue their operations without union restrictions. As the group had official status, it asked the WO to step in and support them. Their case was further buttressed by the backing of the Ministry of Health. The fact that the group was supported by the WO gave them a great deal of confidence when they engaged in collective negotiations with the mayor, and they eventually won their case. Some compromises had to be made, but the mayor stood by the group and helped them get a contract with a steel factory just outside the city. This contract meant that the union managed to keep its share of the market and the women's group now had a steady customer, becoming the sole supplier for the factory.

Although there were success stories, the program ran into various problems. At times the group's status as an NGO became a handicap. In other circumstances, different dilemmas existed. In some cases groups ran into problems with the local security officials because the latter treated them as a political organization. When this happened and a particular group ran into problems with the police and security officials, the WO had to intervene and reassure security officials that these were not political groups but economic NGOs supported by the state.

The implementation of the program faced major problems in poor provinces. During the second year of the project there were very few, if any, success stories reported from poor provinces. In the more affluent provinces, cases were referred to provincial officials and reported to the headquarters to be brought to the attention of the other provinces. There they went through a review process and, if approved, were sent to program managers in other areas to be studied and used to generate new ideas. These ideas were then disseminated among staff members and project managers throughout the country. As the number of successful cases was increasing, these cases became a potential tool for the promotion of the project. For promotional purposes, inter- and intra-provincial workshops were organized, where successful groups presented their achievements and spoke about their successes. This practice encouraged many women who were contemplating joining the program and was inspiring to those who were already involved.

Project mangers reported that the impact of these workshops reached far beyond women's groups. Local officials and religious authorities were often invited to take part in these workshops. The workshops were initiatives organized at the local, provincial, and national levels and functioned as a means for raising support for the projects. The WO went beyond provincial programs and approached government officials, religious authorities, and the media, inviting them to their workshops. Interviews with successful groups and group leaders were arranged by the WO in major media. In fact, the leading women's magazine in Iran, *Zanan,* reported on the project on several occasions to raise public awareness and sensitivity about the importance of self-help for women.

It is worth noting that a project was not terminated when a group failed in its income-generating activities, as the purpose was not purely economic but also about building self-reliance and confidence. Ziai, a project assistant and coordinator, indicated that in cases when the groups' initiatives did not generate income, the spirit of teamwork brought other advantages (interview by Bahramitash, 2004). Many of these groups ended up creating a support network that could be mobilized during times of crisis and offering its members a source of emotional support. The impression of the project managers was that entering into collective economic activity created a network that broke women's isolation and gave them a support group where they could share their problems. Feedback from a WO official indicates that these programs created formal networks of support, but, as we will see in chapter 7, informal networks are just as common in low-income neighborhoods. The main difference between formal and informal groups is that when a state organization is backing a group, the members enjoy an extra source of support. Some social workers said that the real importance of women's being involved in collective income-generating activity was that they began to realize that their problems were not the result of their individual failure and they were able to break out of their isolation. This outcome was highly beneficial as they understood that their situation did not result from their lack of competence. Naila Kabeer's finding in Bangladesh confirms that the process of collective action through microcredit is empowering (Kabeer 2001).

In terms of helping women gain confidence and self-reliance, the program yielded mixed results. In one instance, for example, when a woman wanted to file for divorce and consulted with her group, her fellow members convinced her not to go through the divorce and warned her of the problems she would face as a single mother. The group's advice to her was to stay in her marriage and try to resolve the marital problems. In other cases, the group's awareness that single women were not confined to their homes and were able to engage in economic activities enabled women to lead an independent life. This awareness was enough to convince one unhappy woman to file for divorce. In an interview Mandana Karimi pointed out that

> [o]ne of the most important outcomes of the work of successful groups was to affect a change of attitude both within families and in their neighborhoods regarding these women, ultimately bringing about a change regarding perceptions about women's abilities in general. The more the groups were successful, the more respect their extended family and their immediate community had for them, helping them to regain their dignity damaged by their previous identity as welfare recipients. They were no longer poor women who needed help but rather women who asserted themselves. Now they were able to provide for themselves and for their children and they became a source of pride, rather than shame, for their family. Some of these women, now empowered, become resource persons for their immediate relatives and friends. (Mandana Karimi, senior social worker, interview, Tehran, 2004)

As we shall see in another chapter, women who became successful entrepreneurs often turned into community leaders, with or without the help of the state.

The WO project manager, Setareh Forozanfar, argued that this program was more advantageous than the work of charity organizations because it created self-reliance, and the women who succeeded took charge of their own businesses. The women who succeeded preferred the WO programs to IKRF assistance. The WO programs provided more infrastructural support, in terms of training and capital, and the programs provided help with marketing their product. It is possible that many women would ultimately prefer being self-employed and running small businesses. We will explore this idea further in chapter 7.

When groups expanded their business activities beyond their initial members, they often brought in men as helpers and employees. This inclusion confirms the importance of women's role in extended family networks, an issue that will be discussed in more detail in the next chapter on the informal sector. Women would bring in their sons or sons-in-law to perform "heavier" labor or activities that required more "skills" such as accounting. According to the WO's policy, men could be involved as employees only when the group became a profitable economic unit.

The final surveys showed that the achievements of the projects in rich provinces were far more significant than those from poor provinces. In Khorasan Province, for example, self-help groups managed to organize thirty thousand women (Zarei, Rozikhah, and Karimi 2002–3). Some of the project managers felt that three years was not sufficiently long enough to assess the success or failure of a program.

My fieldwork on the informal sector indicates that informal groups where women come together and raise rotating credits for emergency use exist, and they function in a way similar to the WO program although often with fewer resources (see chapter 7). It is true that these funds are not channeled to business activities, but nonetheless they exist. Moreover, our research on the informal sector shows that women use personal contacts and extended family networks to raise funds for their businesses in the informal sector.

International Program:
United Nations Development Program

Shirabad is a suburban city not far from Zahedan, the capital of Sistan and Baluchistan. The city is on the border of Pakistan and Afghanistan and is one of Iran's most impoverished provinces. A mountain range separates the district from one of the most troubled regions of Afghanistan, Nimrooz Province, where opium cultivation is the main source of people's income. Drug trafficking and arms smuggling remain a major obstacle to implementing social programs. With the recent fall of the Taliban the situation has worsened. Afghanistan has become the number one opium producer in the world, and international drug dealers have set up factories in Afghanistan to process heroin, morphine, and other narcotics, which they export to Iran at a low price. Some of these narcotics travel through Iran on their way to Europe. The border between Iran, Pakistan, and Afghanistan is very much open, and gun and drug trafficking makes it next to impossible for the Iranian authorities to control the region. There are four army garrisons along the border but the soldiers are locked up in their garrisons and are not always capable of enforcing immigration laws. I was told that at times food and supplies are delivered to the garrisons because of dangers posing border guards without substantial protection (similar to the US effort in controlling drugs trafficked from Latin America, Iran is not capable of controlling drug trafficking along its borders.) The drug dealers have tanks, machine guns, and heavy artillery, and they wield significant influence over local police and officials. Moreover, a massive drought has devastated the region shared by Iran, Pakistan and Afghanistan. The drought destroyed the rural economy and has forced more people to enter the drug trade. The area suffers from high unemployment and has many Afghan refugee settlements. This part of Iran is not only economically depressed, it is also politically unstable, suffers from ethnic tension, and lacks security.

The city and area around Zahedan remain a place without borders, a city of illicit crime. One needs only to take a walk to the central market, situated close to an infamous drug route, to understand the scale of the situation. Even I, a woman, although dressed in local attire, was approached and asked what type of drugs, alcohol, or adult movies I desired. In February 2005, two weeks prior to my visit to the district, a police car was driving inside the city when it was attacked by rocket-propelled grenades. The car belonged to an army general who wanted to regain control over the infamous crossroads and impose order. The general and four other officers died instantly in the ambush. Their death was nothing out of the ordinary. Thousands of Iranian soldiers and police have lost their lives trying to control the border.

The collapse of the rural economy, resulting from years of drought, has left many with no source of income other than drug trafficking. In terms of industry, the city only has a small cement factory. Despite massive unemployment, rising migration to urban areas, and general lawlessness, the inhabitants of the city aspire to build a better life. This aspiration became apparent to me during fieldwork in 2005, when the city of Zahedan organized a national book fair with hundreds of publishers flying in from different parts of Iran. The fair, organized by the Ministry of Culture, has always been a success. I interviewed some publishers and found that the fair resulted in the sale of a huge number of books in what is undoubtedly one of the poorest parts of the country.

Sistan and Baluchistan Province has never completely been under state control, a reality that dates back to the early days of nation-building by Reza Shah after the First World War. The lack of state control continued during the reign of the later Pahlavi dynasty and during the Shah's regime. The lack of centralized control over the province meant that it experienced only a minimal number of government economic initiatives and social welfare programs. The situation has not changed much in the postrevolutionary era. After the revolution, the province did not experience significant changes. Revolutionary institutions had few recruits in the area, and I did not come across high-profile activities by the Imam Khomeini Relief Foundation (IKRF). The only successful postrevolutionary program seemed to have been the literacy campaign. It appears that security issues have undermined state welfare programs.

Facing a proliferation of drug use in the country, the government has been trying to improve the economic conditions in the aftermath of the drought. Rising numbers of drug addicts, particularly among the young and the unemployed, have become a major social problem within the entire country. It is hard to imagine how the drug problem in Afghanistan and Iran will come under control. In addition to the problem of drug and arms trafficking, the region has also been affected by sectarian tensions. The increase in the number of rural migrants to cities has further exacerbated these tensions. The rural Sunni populations now often live on the outskirts of cities with Shiite-dominated governments. As indicated by recent clashes in Pakistan, where minority Shiites who live under a majority Sunni government have been attacked and their mosques burnt, tensions between the two sects in the region may grow rather than subside. Tensions have recently been exacerbated as problems between Shiites and Sunnis in Pakistan spill over into Iran. Sectarian divisions are already present in this area, as poor rural Sunnis are more likely to be recruited into the illegal drug trade, and Shiites are traditionally part of city bureaucracies. Currently the local police and the army do not recruit among Sunnis because of a general lack of trust. The impoverishment of the rural economy, which employed predominantly Sunnis, made them more susceptible to enter drug trafficking. Additionally, Sunni Afghans have forged alliances with local Barouche Sunnis and are now a political force counterbalancing the municipal government. The city of Zahedan is guarded by checkpoints, but there are areas around Zahedan where the police do not travel for fear of drug lords. The current situation resembles a ticking time bomb and will lead to further disasters if conditions do not improve.

The general anarchy means that poverty will persist and interventions will be difficult. As is often the case in poverty-stricken areas, women are most affected. They remain at the mercy of the local community, a community plagued by the breakdown of families, the disintegration of tribal solidarity, and growing poverty. The dissolution of the community has meant the disappearance of traditional sources of support, and alternatives have not been forthcoming.

There are many insurmountable problems for women in this region. For example, in rural areas marriages are usually not registered; therefore, when families leave their villages and settle in shantytowns, they have no official records of their marriages. In many cases they lack citizenship documents and therefore their children are not entitled to public services such as attending public schools or receiving health care. The situation has been further exacerbated because Afghan refugees have ethnic features similar to those of the rural population. For these reasons, the government is taking a huge precaution by issuing ID cards, and often the officials cannot distinguish between people of Afghan origin (who according to international agreements between Afghanistan, Iran, and the UN have to be repatriated) and the local population. A large number of women interviewed said that they suffered from the consequences of not having an ID card. They could not obtain professional licenses or permits for launching businesses. Moreover, they had no legal protection in cases of domestic violence, and their abusive husbands were not subject to any legal charges.

A development program based on the South Asian Poverty Alleviation Program (SAPAP) was brought to this part of the country in the late 1990s as an initiative centered on the creation of self-help groups, people's mobilization, and microcredit. The United Nations Development Program (UNDP) focused on two areas in Sistan and Baluchistan Province, one program in Shirabad and the other in Dehan. The SAPAP model is part of a grassroots poverty alleviation program designed to set up a large number of self-help groups and, in rural communities, to mobilize resources through people's own efforts while working in partnership with local organizations. SAPAP is part of a larger UN approach characterized by a bottom-up, participatory, and people-led sustainable development model. This model centers poverty alleviation on the community. The model was initially developed for Asian countries, and it has already been implemented in several communities across six different Asian countries: Bangladesh, Nepal, India, Sri Lanka, Maldives, and Pakistan. The program is designed to empower people (women included) and to increase their collective bargaining power. In this respect, SAPAP aims to improve human development.

The project was launched by the UNDP office in Tehran, in collaboration with the Office of Social Security of the Institute of Management and Planning, and administered by the Family of Sustainable Development Fund, a local NGO headed by Parvin Maroofi. The project also drew upon resources provided by the municipal government and by the Office of Women in the provincial governments of Sistan and Baluchistan. Interestingly, the project was not specifically about women, but was originally a poverty alleviation program designed to improve living in these two shantytowns as a development model. The initiative did not meet with success in Dehan, but it gathered momentum in Shirabad. This energy was largely owing to the fact that women became active. The women of Shirabad turned the project into a women's project. In a majority of the cases, these women became involved in the project because their husbands were either too old to work, unemployed, and/or drug addicts. In an interview, Ali Farzin, a UNDP officer from Tehran, pointed out that the project had to respond to local needs and this meant that women became the target group (interview, Tehran, 2005.) In each project, women were divided into groups of twenty-five to thirty. The project in Shirabad distributed USD 40,000 as microcredit to 135 borrowers who then used the loan for income-generating activities.

This research was intentionally focused on Shirabad and not on Dehan, because researchers in Dehan would have faced serious problems owing to lack of security, extended periods without male protection in remote areas, and increased health hazards such as lack of easy access to clean water and to medical facilities.

One of the advantages of the project in Shirabad was its easy accessibility. The project was also able to hire two excellent local facilitators who managed the project for the entire three-year period. The facilitators in this project had a role that was somewhat similar to that of the social workers of the WO. Facilitators, when compared to social workers, played a more passive role and allowed the women to take charge because the project was designed for public mobilization. The program was run by two women, themselves heads of single-headed households, who were in charge of the entire project involving hundreds of women. The project did not have a clear idea as to how long it would last and there was some expectation that it would be extended beyond its initial term. This expectation may have been counterproductive, both for the women who participated and for the facilitators.

The facilitators organized groups and helped them choose their leaders, who later mobilized the rest of the group in pursuing different ventures. These ventures were decided upon by the participating women, and the project established training programs based on what the women had decided they needed. Traditionally feminine skills, such as sewing and needlework, made up the bulk of the program's offerings; training in first aid, computer use, and Quran reading was also provided. Some of these programs were administrated through the local mosque. Microcredit was distributed through group leaders on the basis of the priorities that the groups had decided upon. Unlike the WO-run programs, in which microcredit was given unconditionally, in this project groups had to first be able to save and show their savings before they could receive microcredit. This requirement was a major hindrance for those without starting capital. Moreover, the allocated microcredit was hardly enough, and many women were critical of the amount they received, as it was not enough for them to start a successful business.

Mehry (names in this section have been changed to protect the identity of the interviewees), a member of the project for three years, stated, "I have been waiting for my credit for three years and all I am told is that I will have to wait more." In other cases, women expressed their lack of satisfaction with the amount of the credit. Esmat, who was given 60 thousand *tomans* (the equivalent of USD 80 in 2005) told me, "this is just not enough. I am not only supporting my family but also my father." Belgise expressed her frustration with the USD 300 that she had received: "I have turned part of my house into a shop but I need more money to buy goods that I can sell." Often these women were faced with the challenge of not just supporting their own household but also that of their extended one, taking care of elderly parents and in-laws.

These women, similar to those interviewed in the informal sector in Tehran (see chapter 7), had a great sense of solidarity. In some cases their solidarity was extended even to their co-wives, as some women talked about taking care of their co-wives or children of their co-wives as part of the family. It appeared that many households were income-pulling units. This is not to overlook the fact that extended families and polygamous marriages are a site of conflict. Nonetheless, not one of the women interviewed expressed resentment about having to provide for their co-wives and for their children. On the contrary, they were willing to pull their resources together in order to make ends meet. What they resented was the fact that making ends meet was a difficult if not impossible task.

Generally, there were a lot of complaints, yet the number of women who wanted to join the programs was growing. The facilitators informed me that they had a long waiting list of women who came from far away to join the program. When I asked several members of the project who had complained about not receiving their credit why they continued to be part of the project, many of them did not give me an answer. The reason for the rising number of women seeking to join the program could be owing to the lack of an alternative and sheer desperation.

A common problem was that many of the women were married to much older men, either as a result of a family favor or in return for a loan that could not be paid. Marrying an older man meant that these women would end up taking care of their husbands. This was a common situation in cases when they were the last wife in a polygamous household (a situation exacerbated by widespread drug abuse).

In spite of the huge challenges these women were facing, they showed a great deal of resistance. One example was a squatters' movement in Hemat Abad, a shantytown just outside of Shirabad. Women were leading the squatters' movement and were resisting the city's attempt to demolish their houses. They managed to place a great deal of pressure on the mayor not to demolish their "illegal" property. Backed by national and international organizations, they demanded that the mayor recognize the shantytown as a village and provide it with electricity and water. They succeeded in forcing the mayor to recognize the rights of the people to stay in their houses, but it was not possible to have water and electricity. In order to secure a clean water supply, the women approached the Red Crescent and succeeded in getting a tank of clean water delivered on a regular basis. However, neither electricity nor telephone lines will be available for a long time to come.[10]

Conclusion

As the evidence from Shirabad indicates, women from the lowest-income province, in one of the most dangerous parts of Iran, face major challenges. In the face of these challenges they also resist and use every opportunity to empower themselves. In addition, I wish to emphasize the importance of informal organizations and strong community networks, particularly in low-income households, as we shall see in the next chapter on the informal sector. There is very little information on the informal/invisible ways in which women of low-income neighborhoods empower themselves. I have witnessed a variety of self-help programs that take place independent of national and international organizations. There is indeed a great deal of solidarity among women, many of whom raise emergency and other types of funds for members of their extended family, kin,

---

10. Just before the fieldwork was completed I found out that the WO had approached the UNDP in order to establish links with the project as part of their larger battle against drug addiction. The WO recognized the importance of empowering the women of Shirabad in combating drug addiction. Because a high percentage of these women who were involved in the project have husbands, sons, or fathers who are drug addicts, they are closely affected by the problem and have a vested interest in fighting it. By coming together as a group, and being supported by national and international organizations, they can aspire to becoming self-reliant, a goal the WO found as a crucial dimension of its own mandate to help victims of drug addiction. By recruiting these women into their program, the WO hoped to enhance the efficiency of its rehabilitation programs. The best chance that men have of recovery is through their immediate loved ones. In closely knit communities, the family takes care of the community's problem. Men's addiction was considered a community problem, as I learned from many women who shared their experience with addiction during my fieldwork. Many of these women are mothers to children who could potentially become drug addicts, and empowering them is crucial to determining the fate of the next generation.

and neighborhood. The importance of the social safety net remains vital and undocumented. An array of different sources of funding are embedded in extended family, kin, friends, and neighborhood networks in the form of charity, personal loans, or concessional credit. These sources of funding are distributed in an extremely dignified way and remain distinct from formal charities, social assistance, and microcredit given by formal, national, or international organizations. While it is true that with the process of modernization, community-based social values have been in decline, my fieldwork—even in the heart of the city of Tehran—shows that there is a huge social safety net in operation by women for women. Female communal support is critical to many women who find themselves in financial difficulty, and this solidarity cuts across classes and has remained largely intact despite urbanization.

This chapter focused on two different models and three different projects. The first model was charity programs. A major critique of charity programs, particularly formal charity, is that they tend to create dependency. In the case of state charity, this dependency may be an even larger problem. Moreover, all foundations are highly bureaucratized and subject to corruption. Additionally, it has been argued that state charities often distribute funds on the basis of political allegiance, particularly at the local level. Receiving funds from a quasi-state institution can become an important part of political alliance building, particularly where there are political tensions between the local community and that of the central governing elite, and between the general public and the ruling elite.

Another criticism posed about the charity model is that it remains tied to a community where men are leaders and the existing patriarchal power structures can be reinforced. Communities that need to recreate social cohesion under male leadership could seriously undermine women's access to independence in societies where independence for women as part of the trend toward modernization is occurring. The irony here is that it may be more likely that some women can empower themselves by receiving funds through a bureaucratic process rather than relying on the extended family network, which can be more susceptible to male dominance.

As far as microcredit and self-help programs are concerned, a major criticism is that a minimum amount of capital is required to join these programs. This requirement immediately excludes those who do not have any initial capital and who therefore fall outside of these programs. Although such cases were not characteristic of the WO, because the WO gave everyone a fixed amount and did not require them to have start-up capital, the UNDP did ask women to bring their own capital. As mentioned before, microcredit programs give loans on the basis of groups having a minimum capital, which leaves out those with no capital and the very poor and reinforces the existing class hierarchy within communities, which can further harm the poor. Furthermore, the model makes it a group responsibility to repay loans, a favorable condition for the lending agency like the Grameen Bank, but one that can create a great deal of intergroup conflict and tension. This was the case with the Shirabad project, in which some women complained about being penalized for their group members' lack of ability to pay back their share of the loan. Another major problem with UNDP and WO's project was that it did not provide a marketing strategy. The IKRF guarantees sale of the products and a stable source of income in economically depressed areas. In areas that are highly economically depressed with few opportunities to raise an income, a lack of marketing strategies and support sets up women to fail.

One major problem with the UNDP project was that the program had a time limit and was left in limbo toward the end, and it suffered immensely when the head of the UNDP was changed. In fact, the program was suspended soon after I finished my fieldwork, when resources were shifted to Bam in the aftermath of the Bam earthquake. Nonetheless, witnessing the enthusiasm as well as the disappointments and complaints shed light into the fact that such initiatives can provide change and bring community empowerment. The mere fact that UNDP poured some cash into the local economy no doubt had benefits, at least for some women.

With microcredit becoming the buzzword for fighting female poverty, it is important to pay attention to the critiques of the model. According to Rankin, the microcredit approach, when advocated by an international organization, undermines the role of the state as a welfare provider. Microcredit can be aligned with neoliberal economic policies promoted by the World Bank, an institution whose prime objective is to turn low-income women into entrepreneurs. This objective means that when women fail to improve their economic conditions, it is their individual fault and not the fault of the economic system or state structure. The failure of many of these credit groups in Shirabad to achieve economic success may be regarded as an individual failure by the women involved instead of being viewed as the result of structural problems in an economically depressed area plagued by unemployment, drug abuse, and refugee crises.

Although the microcredit programs have been criticized, it appears that they created a certain degree of self-confidence and the ability for group and collective mobilization. In the case of the UNDP project, it was designed to lead to collective mobilization and to empower its participants vis-à-vis local government. Indeed, the result of microcredit differs from one case to another; it offers many potentials and, depending on a particular set of circumstances, it can be a useful model. In both the UNDP and the WO projects, the results showed that women gained confidence and became engaged in public life, even in cases where their economic enterprise was unsuccessful.

It seems that Iran's experience resonates with what has been the general impact of modernization. In general, modernization has undermined women's traditional access to resources without providing new ones, resulting in rising poverty among women who are heads of households. Different parts of the country have different dynamics, but all of the efforts discussed above represent important sources of support for women from low-income households. Women from urban areas use their family, kin, and community network for credit and emergency funds, while women in the suburb of Zahedan asserted their rights to own their homes. It should therefore always be kept in mind that women continue to have their own ways of dealing with problems that are often overlooked, underestimated, underresearched, and often ignored by academics, policy makers, and social advocates.

7

Veiled Economy

Gender and the Informal Sector

ROKSANA BAHRAMITASH *and* SHAHLA KAZEMIPOUR

THE INFORMAL SECTOR has been defined by the International Labour Office as a group of household enterprises or unincorporated enterprises owned by households that includes informal own-account enterprises that may employ contributing family workers and employees on an occasional basis, and enterprises of informal economy that employ one or more employees on a continuous basis. This sector includes the black market or underground economy, dominated by illegal activities (arms smuggling, prostitution, drug trade, and other illegal jobs). In this research we have not analyzed the underground economy.

Official data tend to overlook the informal sector, particularly street vendors and home-based enterprises. This neglect is partially owing to the fact that some home enterprises try to hide their economic activities in order to avoid paying taxes. The informal sector, which is a growing part of the economy throughout the world, remains far less researched than the formal sector. The lack of data is a problem throughout the world, and it is particularly a problem in the Middle East and North Africa region, including Iran. In the case of Iran, there are no publications on the topic in English. Literature on employment is generally on the formal sector only, and even that research is sparse.

In this chapter we will first discuss our survey of the informal sector in Tehran and then we will concentrate on street vending. This chapter focuses more on those who come from low-income households and complements chapter 8 by Fatemeh Moghadam, who has provided us with her research on women in upper- and middle-class households. In the early chapters of this book we argued that women's employment has increased over the past decade. We based this assertion mainly on official data and the formal sector over the past few decades. With modernization of the agricultural sector, informal rural employment has declined, as rural employment has typically experienced a decline while urban labor markets have expanded. It can be speculated that in the face of rising unemployment, many women will enter the informal sector because it is relatively easy to enter and provides more opportunities than the formal sector.

Gender and the Informal Economy in Iran

The United Nations Country Assessment in 2003 reported that the informal sector constitutes 65 percent of Iran's GNP (United Nations 2003, 40) (corresponding figures for Asia, 65 percent; Latin America, 65 percent; and Sub-Saharan Africa, 72 percent [ILO 2002]). As is often the case in many parts of the south, this sector of the economy is tolerated by the state and sometimes even encouraged in an effort to alleviate poverty and increase employment. At the same time, the informal economy and its expansion can be a source of problems as it generates no tax revenue for the state. This has been a critical issue in the face of Iran's desire to move away from an oil-based economy. After the war with Iraq ended in 1988, the government boosted investment in employment-generating industries, which had the effect of expanding the informal economy. This investment was viewed as an effective way of combating the unemployment that plagued Iran's economy during the war.

As mentioned earlier, this is a large sector that employs many people, yet there has been little research on it, and what has been written has not paid attention to the role of women. Jomeh Poour's excellent research on informal activity in Said Khadan (a busy area in a Tehran middle-income neighborhood), for example, provides a great deal of insight into the topic but does not address the issue of gender (Jomeh Poour 2003). One reason for this omission is because sexual segregation makes it difficult for male researchers to conduct research; therefore, it is imperative for female researchers to be involved. It is very easy for researchers to just ignore women and focus on the general state of the sector, and for this reason data gathering on women's role in this sector has been handicapped.

When discussing the role of women in the informal sector, the issue of sexual segregation is an important topic that merits some discussion. There is worldwide gender segregation in the area of employment. Throughout the world men are overrepresented in high-paid, "skilled," and full-time jobs with fringe benefits, while women are overrepresented in low-paid, seasonal, and part-time employment with few or no fringe benefits (Joekes 1987; Anker 1998; Loutfi 2001). This sexual segregation is extended to the informal sector, where women tend to occupy the lowest-ranking jobs, those of home worker and daily wage laborer. It is therefore critical to have data on Iran, where general labor market sexual segregation coexists alongside social gender segregation and where one may assume that there is double segregation.[1]

While labor market gender segregation is typically against women, in the case of Muslim countries in general and Iran in particular, the impact of double gender segregation can be more complicated than is often assumed. Typically, in Muslim societies, women tend to be more engaged in activities, production, and services of goods that are exclusively female. In some ways this exclusiveness may benefit them, as they are free from male competition and sexual harassment in sexually segregated spaces. Some argue that the success of the Grameen Bank in Bangladesh, which gives loans to women only, has benefited from this aspect of Muslim culture. During our fieldwork we came

---

1. Lack of documentation is a major problem, prevents viable policy formulations, and leaves the bulk of female workers in this sector on the margins of social protection laws and labor policies.

across a whole range of income-generating activities in the informal sector. These women-for-women activities can be extremely varied, from providing rentals for wedding celebrations to interior design; from art exhibitions among women of high-income households to dressmaking; from private tutoring among women in middle-income households to home-based daycare centers; from catering and food processing to working as a maid by women of low-income households. We will return to this issue later as we discuss our research findings.

Survey of the Informal Sector in Tehran (Home-Based)

It is important to emphasize that we use the term "home-based" in a slightly different way than is the case with the general literature on gender and the informal economy. Usually when "home-based in the informal sector" is used, it refers to manufacturing of consumer goods for the world market. But Iran has been increasingly isolated from the world market because of economic sanctions, with the exception of the carpet industry, which is covered in a separate chapter. In this chapter we use "home-based" to make a distinction from street vendors, and our definition includes those who work in their own home or work in other people's homes as maids or other service providers.

This chapter is based on three sets of data. The first set is a survey of 415 women in Tehran, where 68.9 percent were working in the formal and the informal sector, and the rest were housewives. For this research we used a questionnaire and its results were subject to qualitative analysis. The research became the basis for two other surveys. The second and third surveys, completed in Tehran and Mashhad, were more unstructured and included open-ended questions. We interviewed thirty women working in home-based production from low-income households and thirty street vendors from Tehran and Mashhad. In total, the second and third surveys included sixty all-female businesses.

Research on the informal sector is very delicate and people do not easily respond to questions about their working activity and real income. This reticence was generally our experience, but it was more the case for women of high- and middle-income households who were nervous about not paying taxes. While the research was easier in low-income households, there were other problems there. Some of the interviewees from low-income households expected our research to bring changes and they asked our research assistants for help and financial assistance to be offered by the authorities. Because of the nature of the topic, the research relied on snowball sampling and we needed to build trust in order to obtain accurate information. We hired research assistants from different socioeconomic backgrounds to be able to use their personal contacts in different part of Tehran, a megacity of close to 14 million inhabitants (including the suburbs). Research assistants were all graduate students of social science programs who had taken courses in research methodology. They attended training workshops before and after pilot surveys, which we organized for them.

We put a great deal of emphasis on household income and used Tehran's map division into five districts (with sub-districts) prepared by the city for taxing purpose, and we also used its classification that included property values. Housing is an important factor in determining household income, as rents are extremely high and property prices can now compete with those in North America (in some places an apartment can be as expensive as a similar one in New York). We organized the respondents into five different income groups; very low, low, middle, high, and very high. In actual research, however, we did not measure income but rather expenditure, as it proved to be a much easier way of finding out accurate answers. In order to get accurate information we added some indirect questions such as the price of the interviewee's property, the location of their property, and ownership. Questionnaires were drafted based on a pilot study of thirty. We first held one workshop for our assistants, and then used the results of the pilot for the second workshop, which doubled as training for research assistants. Final questionnaires were distributed among six research assistants who were closely monitored. The interviews were based on standard and open-ended questions.

The survey used questionnaires that were filled out by the research assistants. It had several aims. First, it sought to provide documentation on women's role in the informal sector. Second, it aimed to compare informal and formal work. Third, it aimed to develop some understanding of why women enter into the informal sector. Fourth, it attempted to discover if employment in this sector brought any personal satisfaction. Fifth, and finally, it explored if and to what extent this type of employment increased women's economic decision-making power.

The following hypotheses were formulated:

(a) Women's employment in the informal sector is absent from the national census;

(b) Women of different households with different incomes are involved in the informal sector;

(c) This sector draws more from women of low-income households;

(d) Women with less education enter into the informal sector;

(e) Women entering the informal sector do so because they do not have an option for formal employment;

(f) Married women are more involved in the informal economy than single women;

(g) Female-headed households are more engaged in the informal economy than those who come from dual-income households;

(h) The informal sector relies on personal resources and those of the extended family network for its capital;

(i) Increased participation in the informal economy leads to an increase in women's economic decision-making;

(j) Income generated through informal work is spent on basic goods rather than luxury items;

(k) Women work in this sector because of economic necessity.

Findings

Reporting the Informal Sector

We found that our respondents by and large had not provided a great deal of information about their activities during the national census. Women with high income did not wish to declare their income because they would have to pay taxes and get the state involved in their affairs, which they resented. We will return to this issue when we discuss sexual segregation. Women preferred to keep the state out of their business as much as possible for a variety of reasons. Those in the middle-income bracket were also reluctant to declare their work. On the part of low-income households, the issue was slightly different. Some of these women worked as seasonal workers and the flexibility as well as the informality of their workplace and conditions make them view what they did as not really "work." It was very easy for them and our research assistants to overlook their income-generating activities because the informal sector for women in many cases is highly embedded in women's role as homemakers. This downplaying of their work was one of the hardest parts of the survey and we had to provide our research assistants with training so that they would include all types of work, particularly when women worked as unpaid family workers.

Household Income and Employment Status

Table 7.1 indicates that those with very low and low incomes were overrepresented in the informal sector. This result of the study resonates with findings from other countries where the informal economy draws women from low-income households more than those from middle- and high-income groups. Interestingly, the percentage of housewives increases from 14.8 percent to 18.3 percent between women with high and very high incomes, suggesting that women from a very high income bracket tend to choose not to work and instead remain housewives. This finding has interesting implications when economic decision-making within the household is discussed.

To examine the issue of household income and employment status, we asked about their income and supplemented it with their housing value and ownership. Table 7.2 confirms the results from table 7.1. The two tables indicate that women from very-high- and high-income groups tend either to be housewives or to work in the formal sector.

Table 7.1 Household Income and Employment Status (Percent)

Household Income	Housewife	Formally Employed	Informally Employed	Total
Very low	12.2	8.2	27.7	15.9
Low	33.0	18.4	30.7	26.6
Middle	21.7	38.6	20.4	27.8
High	14.8	19.0	11.7	15.4
Very high	18.3	15.8	9.5	14.4
Total	100.0	100.0	100.0	100.0

Table 7.2 Housing and Employment Status (Percent)

Household Income	Housewife	Formally Employed	Informally Employed	Total
Very low	8.5	7.5	17.3	11.1
Low	31.6	25.2	27.3	27.7
Middle	28.2	38.4	33.8	34.0
High	17.1	18.2	12.2	15.9
Very high	14.5	10.7	9.4	11.3
Total	100.0	100.0	100.0	100.0

An interesting finding was that many middle-class and particularly high-income women had some kind of daily domestic help. In effect, low-income women were subsidizing high-income women's income by providing them with extra time at low cost. In the case of low-income women (from our later research on women from low-income households), we found that they generally rely on extended family networks and friends, and in some cases they leave older children to take care of their siblings.

Before we go any further into findings from the research, it is important to discuss the issue of gender segregation and class. The results from Iran confirm what is found in other countries of the south, which indicates that gender segregation works against women's access to well-paid and formal occupations. We mentioned the issues of gender segregation and labor markets as worldwide phenomena added to Muslim societies' sexual segregation. We also discussed that sexual segregation in our research findings did not always work against women, and that there were cases where women benefited. This finding is particularly true for middle- and high-income women. During the fieldwork we came across a whole array of activities by middle- and upper-class women who really preferred to work informally and in sexually segregated space. These activities ranged from fashion shows to running small home-based galleries. In an interview with a female entrepreneur, Mona,[2] a forty-year-old woman, she indicated that she preferred to have students come to her house. She had a fairly large house and was able to allocate a separate space for her mini art studio. For her, having her students in the privacy of her home where she did not have to wear the veil and could listen to music while working and earning a very good income was far preferable to working outside. In fact, she closed her official gallery and was able to earn more money because of savings on rent and taxes. She also preferred the freedom and privacy of her mini studio, which was congenial. Women of middle- and high-income households are increasingly likely to become entrepreneurs, as was indicated in previous chapters, and for many of them it is ideal to be in the informal sector. Mona also added that working with other women in her own house provided her with a space free from the hassle of traveling through highly congested traffic and free from male harassments. Mona's is not an isolated case; in fact, in the aftermath of the revolution many women were either forced or chose to leave their jobs and stay at home. Many of our interviewees from middle- and high-income households have been self-employed since the revolution. This finding is significant because many academics have argued that female employment declined after the revolution. While it is true that

---

2. All names in this chapter have been changed to protect the privacy of the interviewees.

many women from high- and middle-income households were either forced or chose to leave their jobs, many of these women did not just sit at home but continued working in the informal sector (this situation is further elaborated by Fatemeh Moghadam in chapter 8), sometimes in their regular profession, sometimes in new professions.

The results shown in table 7.3 reinforce that women of high- and very-high-income households (46.7 percent and 40 percent) were far more satisfied with their work compared to those from very-low-income households (only 10.5 percent). These results showed that there was a relationship between income background and work satisfaction. This relationship could partly be owing to the fact that when women enter into the informal economy from a high-income economic background, they are more likely to set their own terms of employment than are women from low-income backgrounds.

Sexual segregation has created not just sexually segregated labor markets but separate and parallel markets dominated by women. For instance, during a series of visits to the Mahtab hairdresser salon (this salon was not informal; it had a sign, was part of the hairdressers' guild, and paid taxes) in the middle-income neighborhood of Said Khandan, Roksana Bahramitash became a participant observer of the salon and paid weekly visits to keep records of informal activities related to the formal one. In the case of the Mahtab hair salon (the name has not been changed because the salon is now closed), in a total of eight visits, Bahramitash encountered a range of different

Table 7.3 Work Satisfaction and Income Background among Those in the Informal Sector (Percent)

Work Satisfaction	Household Income Category				
	Very low	Low	Middle	High	Very high
Highly satisfied	10.5	25	37	46.7	40
Satisfied	10.5	17.5	33.3	33.3	40
Somewhat satisfied	15.8	20	11.1	33.3	0
Not very satisfied	31.6	7.5	7.4	6.7	0
Unsatisfied	31.6	25	11.1	0	0

economic activities. These activities included selling ladies' underwear, fortune telling, advertising for dressmakers, buying or selling real estate, providing rental information, and passing on referrals for daily care providers and maids. This market operated on the basis of personal contacts, and extended family and neighborhood networks.

Fatemah Moghadam's chapter, chapter 8, is more focused on middle- and high-income households and will elaborate on the issue further. Many women work in this sector, and in some respects it is related to the issue of highly educated women who are unemployed.

Education

Table 7.4 shows that those with primary schooling are overrepresented among women who are housewives and who work in the informal sector. The result indicates that 49 percent of women in the informal sector have primary education, compared to 11.1 percent of those with Master's and PhD degrees. This result ties in well with the general literature on women in the informal economy. Women who are poor tend to have lower educations and be overrepresented in the informal sector. As mentioned earlier, one of the reasons for the high representation of low-income women in the informal sector is their level of skills, and in this case, their level of formal education. This finding confirms our hypotheses by showing that the sector is easier for women to enter, and in cases where they have a low level of education they can still enter into this sector.

Table 7.4 Education and Employment Status (Percent)

Employment Status	Level of Education			
	Primary School	*Secondary School*	*Bachelor's*	*Master's and PhD*
Housewife	40.0	27.4	17.0	5.6
Formal employment	10.8	38.4	72.3	83.3
Informal employment	49.2	34.1	10.6	11.1
Total	100.0	100.0	100.0	100.0

This situation may, however, be changing as the number of educated women is on the rise.

Choosing the Informal Sector

Table 7.5 shows that the dominant reason for entering the informal economy is economic. The table shows that 64.7 percent of women entered because of economic hardship, and 58.3 percent because of financing economic needs; 47.5 percent declared that they work in order to gain economic independence, and 33.1 percent thought that this was necessary for their general independence. Of those entering the informal sector, 27.3 percent entered because of their husband's insufficient income, 26.6 percent for improving their family welfare, and the same number thought that their work was also their hobby. Of our sample 22 percent were female-headed households. Only 12.2 percent declared that they entered into the informal sector because they had no access to formal employment.

What was particularly intriguing about the result was that even women from high-income households had declared economic hardship as a factor in entering into this sector in order to generate more cash. However, this response brought questions about social values and norms governing definitions of economic hardship and necessity.

Table 7.5 Reasons for Entering the Informal Economy

Reason	%	Number of Women
Economic hardship	64.7	90
Economic necessity	58.3	81
Economic independence	47.5	66
Personal interest	36	50
Independence (general)	33.1	46
Insufficient income from spouse	27.3	38
Improving family welfare	26.6	37
Hobby	26.6	37
Female-headed household	22.7	33
Lack of access to formal employment	12.2	17

In some households items such as clothes and pocket money for children were regarded as economic necessities, while others from high-income backgrounds had a very different definition of economic hardship, which was apparent from their existing material wealth. One could perhaps assume that basic needs such as food and shelter were met. Clearly, further research is required to determine what is defined as an economic necessity. Moreover, it would be interesting to investigate what forces are at work when women from different social classes/income groups define their own needs and necessities, and how they define their economic independence. It is clear that some of these definitions are highly complex and in need of clarification, but because the research aimed to focus on low-income households, we did not pursue the topic. Table 7.5 also indicates that economic factors play an important role in women's choice to work in the informal economy. This finding is in accordance with the general literature on women in the informal economy.

Intriguingly, only 12.2 percent of women responded that their main reason for working in the informal sector was because they could not find jobs in the formal sector. This result is interesting because the general literature on the topic seems to indicate that women should prefer to be in the formal sector because the informal sector tends to be exploitative. It is possible that some women prefer to stay in the informal sector because they wish to maintain their role within their extended family network and the community. This finding is reinforced by another research study we have carried out on low-income households, which indicated that women, particularly older women, can gain power from maintaining strong extended family ties and community networks. While this finding applied only to women from low-income households, it may also apply to women from middle- and high-income households who may gain power over allocation of financial resources of the family because they have more time to spend at home and closely supervise expenditures.

Moreover, there is a body of literature that argues that in some cases women prefer flexible hours and closeness to their reproductive work to work in the formal sector. Some scholars, such as L.

Dignard and J. Havet, have argued that women's increasing participation in the informal sector is owing to the fact that this sector allows women to combine reproductive and productive work. Working informally provides a better working arrangement and more flexible hours suited to women's work as mothers and wives (Losby et al. 2002, 15). We will explore the issue further on, when we focus on low-income households.

Reasons for choosing to work in the informal sector can be highly complex and multilayered. For instance, Elizabeth, an Armenian woman who worked as a hairdresser in a middle-income downtown neighborhood, stated that she prefers to work at home because when she was working for a salon, it was hard for her to attend to her housework. After she had resigned from her formal work at a salon, she found that she was able to set her own hours and working conditions, and even earn more, working from home. Elizabeth also enjoyed working at home because it provided her with more space to develop friendships with her clients. Working at home gave her some power over her husband, who from time to time was forced to take on household chores such as shopping, cleaning, and cooking. Elizabeth mentioned that this was one of the advantages of working at home. When she was working outside, she had to make sure all household chores were done during the time she was at home. Elizabeth also mentioned that she had been reported by the neighbors to have been working at home and authorities from Revenue Iran had come to collect taxes, but she refused to pay. She learned to fight with the authorities and argue her case because she could barely pay the bills. After learning the tax rules she kept a bed in the room where she received her customers and, when the authorities came to collect taxes, she had the bed to show that this was their extra bedroom where she received her friends and that most of her work was free or done as favors to her friends—as a result she paid no taxes.

Table 7.5 indicates that our hypothesis that women enter into the informal sector because they do not have access to formal employment is not supported by the data, because we found out there is an element of choice involved. Preference for the informal sector may also be owing to the fact that much formal work is in the public sector and, with rising inflation, this sector is not economically as attractive as working in the informal sector. This hypothesis is confirmed by findings in earlier chapters that indicate that women's employment is rising in the informal sector.

Most of the literature on gender and globalization argues that informal employment is inferior to formal employment (Gallaway and Bernasek 2002; Chen 2001). Martha Chen argues that there is a significant overlap between being a woman, working in the informal sector, and being poor (Chen 2001, 72). Moreover, women generally tend to be at a lower level of employment in the informal sector, and wage gaps and earnings between men and women are major (Chen, Vanek, and Carr 2004).

Marital Status

Table 7.6 shows that single women work more in the formal sector than women who are married. About one-third of married women worked in the informal sector in our sample. The results show that 68.9 percent of those in the formal sector were single, as compared to 35.5 percent who were married, 21.3 percent who were widowed, and 38.3 percent who were divorced. Corresponding figures for the informal sector show that 29.5 percent of those in the informal sector are single. The table indicates that 54.1 percent of widowed women and 33.5 percent of those divorced were in the informal sector. It is interesting to note that women who are widowed have a high presence in the informal sector. This finding is in accordance with findings

Table 7.6 Women's Marital and Employment Status (Percent)

	Single	Married	Widowed	Divorced
Housewives	1.6	34.5	24.6	28.2
Employed in the formal sector	68.9	35.5	21.3	38.3
Employed in the informal sector	29.5	30	54.1	33.5
Total	100.0	100.0	100.0	100.0

discussed in earlier chapters from our analysis of women's overall employment in relation to their marital status. These are women who have lost their husbands and have to care for their households. This finding may confirm that women in the informal sector wish to combine their productive work with that of reproductive work. We also saw in table 7.5 that 22.7 percent of our respondents entered this sector because they were the main breadwinner in the family (also known as a female-headed household).

Informal Sector and Family Resources

Table 7.7 shows interesting results because it agrees with the literature on gender, globalization, and the informal sector. It indicates that the sector continues to rely on women's own resources and that of their extended family and kin networks. More than one-fifth of women financed their own enterprises, with about one-third of the capital being provided by family and friends. Only 6.5 percent received assistance from their husbands. Formal assistance remains low: 6.5 percent from retirement funds, 3.6 percent from microcredits financed by banks, 2.9 percent from bank loans, 5 percent from charity, and less than 1 percent from cooperatives. These results could be put in conjunction with what was discussed in the previous chapter on female-headed households and poverty alleviation models

Table 7.7 Informal Jobs and Sources of Initial Necessary Capital

Sources of Capital	Number	%
Women's personal savings	28	20.1
Family savings	25	18.0
Borrowing from friends and relatives	15	10.8
Husband's financial assistance	9	6.5
Retirement fund	9	6.5
Microfinancing from banks	5	3.6
Bank loans	4	2.9
Charity help	7	5.0
Cooperatives	1	0.7

based on microcredit. It is indeed troubling to find out that little official help appears to filter through to those who need funds to start their businesses.

Women of low-income households rely on members of the extended family, friends, their community, and even children of the house to take care of housework and child care. These kinds of services, when provided by family members and friends, are on the basis of reciprocity and mutual help. We will elaborate on this theme when we focus on the low-income households, especially when we analyze the issue of informal credit.

Economic Decision-Making

The research was also aimed to find out the relationship between household income and women's decisions over expenditures. Table 7.8 indicates that housewives tend to have medium decision-making power over household expenditures. This finding is understandable because of their reproductive role and the fact that they have to do much of the expenditure related to the family. Based on the findings in this research, formal employment does not increase women's decision-making power, and those who work in the informal sector fare better than those formally employed. This discovery can be explained

Table 7.8 Women's Employment Status and Decision-Making Powers over Basic Household Expenditures (Percent)

Level of Decision-making	Employment Status			Total
	Housewives	Formally Employed	Informally Employed	
Very low	12.0	19.5	15.1	15.9
Low	19.7	24.5	20.1	21.7
Middle	35.0	28.3	21.6	28.0
High	26.5	17.0	20.1	20.7
Very high	6.8	10.7	23.0	13.7
Total	100.0	100.0	100.0	100.0

by the fact that those informally employed tend to work at home, and spend at home, and therefore they are much more involved with household affairs and are likely to have more power over household expenditures than women who work outside the home. Regardless of class background and gender segregation, access to paid employment undoubtedly has implications for home-based gender dynamics; it can increase women's bargaining power in the household.

Table 7.9 indicates that women in this sector continue to spend much of their income on basic necessities, such as household expenses. The results confirm cross-cultural studies that have found that women tend to spend their income on basic goods for family consumption, whereas men have a higher propensity to spend on luxury goods (Bahramitash 2005). In low-income families, women's income may make a vital contribution to spending on basic needs. In our findings, close to 70 percent of what is spent on the household is generated by working women. As for children's clothing and education, 37 percent is generated by women working in the informal sector. Items such as personal necessities and savings come next. While women spend their income on necessities, their ownership of important items such property or automobiles remains low. This lack of ownership can act as a disadvantage when important decisions are made, particularly in the absence of the support of an extended family network.

Table 7.9 Income Expenditure and Informal Employment

Expenditure	Number	%
Contributing to household expenses	96	69.1
Children's clothing and education	52	37.4
Food and other daily necessities	50	36.0
Buying necessities for myself	48	34.5
Savings for myself	40	28.8
Charity donations	22	15.8
Buying gold and jewellery for myself	15	10.8
Purchasing a house or land	12	8.6
Purchasing an automobile	10	7.2

Women of Low-Income Households

Self-Employed and Wage Workers

After the survey, we continued to research the topic of women's employment in the informal sector, focusing on women from low-income households. We held four focus groups of four to six women and used the results to prepare an open-ended questionnaire for interviewing thirty women (including those in the focus group). The results were similar to what we had found in our larger structured survey. Here we will provide a summary of the research, as it presents important finding about microfinance. The research showed that women from low-income households use their social ties within the extended family and community networks both to improve their income-generating activities and as a source of credit. We came to find out that there is wide and common use of rotating credit clubs. The concept is based on a religious concept of loan with no interest (without *riba*), because interest is prohibited in the Islamic religion. We found widespread use of credit clubs by the name of *garzol hassaneh,* in which a certain number of women gather together as close friends or family members and each puts a fixed (agreed-upon) amount of money into their common box; one woman becomes the treasurer in charge of the common box. Then, each week, month, or another time period, one person, decided upon by either taking turns or through mutual agreement, is able to use the entire fund and return it. Because this system works on the basis of trust, there is hardly any danger of defaults in repayment. Often women in low-income neighborhoods act as an income-pooling collective, and access to such funds is an important part of their social safety net.

One of the important outcomes of using extended family and community networks has been the opening of opportunities for some women to play the role of community leaders. We found a case in which a woman hairdresser had turned her business into a drop-in center, which, besides generating an income for her and her extended family, acted as a center for stress relief, a place to share community problems, and a safe atmosphere where women provided each other with support in cases of domestic violence.

Women's access to microcredit through their social network is an important issue. There is a vast and growing literature on microcredit, a topic that has enjoyed a major boost with the 2007 peace prize given to Muhammad Yunus, the founder of the Grameen Bank. The bank and its policy to give microcredit to women of low-income households have become a magic bullet for development and poverty alleviation. There are some critiques of the model (Rahman 1999), but Kabeer argues that the model can benefit women by giving them power over economic decision-making and empowering them to deal with issues such as domestic violence (2001). While there is a huge literature on formal microcredit, the literature on informal by-women-for-women microcredit, which is the form it takes in Iran, is thin. Homa Hoodfar and Diane Singerman have documented some of the ways women in low-income households in Cairo raise credit through their community networks (Singerman and Hoodfar 1996). Women can increase their access to economic resources as well as community resources through informal financing in the form of microcredit. There were incidents in which women raised funds through their social network for their businesses. This fund-raising enhanced their role within their immediate family and, in some of the instances, allowed them to act as community leaders. This is indeed the case with formal microcredit, and while that has been documented, informal finance dominated by women remains underresearched.

Most of those interviewed were married, and their husbands were either seasonal workers in the informal sector or were unemployed. Esmat, a young woman with a child, had to take care of her husband, who was a food deliveryman and suffered from respiratory problems so that he could only work intermittently. The family depended on her income and she wished her husband was healthy so that she would not have to work as a maid. Through her work she had managed to link with an NGO (which was how we located her), which provided her with contacts when she wanted to apply for a bank loan and found her monetary and nonmonetary assistance.

From our research, at the high end of employment, there were self-employed women such as those who had hairdressing, dressmaking, and other all-female-related businesses; at the low end, there were many domestic workers. Although there was a great deal of complaint about the nature of their job and its pay, we found that when women worked within their own community they fared better. Our finding is in agreement with literature on the field of women in the informal sector. Home-based businesses provided more room for women and the self-employed, and they tended to have better working terms, which was not the case with wage workers in street vending. (Street vending will be discussed in the next section.) While home-based self-owned businesses, in conjunction with rotating credit clubs, provided space for empowerment, working as a wage worker (such as a domestic worker) was extremely demeaning. It left the laborers without community protection when they went to work with well-to-do families. In some instances in which the family was generous, they received help and support, but there were other cases in which women were insulted and were forced to do hard work in humiliating situations by their employers. The result of this research agreed with what has been found in the general literature on gender and development, where the self-employed enjoy better pay and working conditions, while wage laborers tend to be overrepresented among the worst paid and are at the bottom of employment strata (ILO).[3] In the next section we focus on street vendors, who, although they are technically considered self-employed, are among the most vulnerable of those in the informal sector.

Street Vendors

It was close to midnight when I (Bahramitash) walked on one of the main boulevards leading to the most important and holiest Shi'a

---

3. See http://www.cinterfor.org.uy/public/english/region/ampro/cinterfor/temas/informal/estad/doc.htm, accessed May 2008.

shrine in Mashhad. Every year millions of pilgrims come to this city from different parts of the country and region. The city is awake all night, and pilgrims continue to go back and forth throughout the night. Streets surrounding the shrine are safe and are filled with women from all walks of life, often in groups of more than two. It was past eleven at night, when I started part of our fieldwork alone. The streets were full of vendors, some of whom were women. Street vendors in Mashhad were far more relaxed than they had been in Tehran. I sat by Zahra (all names have been changed to protect interviewees), a street vendor who was selling scarves. Unlike the atmosphere in Tehran, where vendors seemed uncomfortable giving information, vendors in Mashhad had a lot of time and welcomed interviews. She was the head of a single-headed household and she received a pension from the Martyr Foundation Bonyad-e Shahid as the widow of a veteran. In addition to her pension, she worked as a vendor and earned between five to ten dollars a night selling copies of Gucci head scarves. She preferred working at night, when the weather is cool and there is no city control.

"What do you spend your income on?" I asked.

"On necessities," she replied.

"What kind of necessities?"

She replied that she supports her daughters, who are university students. I assumed that she was paying tuition but I was proven wrong. They went to public universities but had a lifestyle that required items such as a cell phone for which Zahra had to work. It was a major revelation to hear that a cell phone was considered a necessity by a street vendor. While Zahra was working to pay for items such as a cell phone, many others who were interviewed worked for real necessities such as food and shelter.

Street vending and hawking is one of the fastest growing types of activities in the informal sector. The organization Self-Employed Women's Association (SEWA), which first brought global attention to the issue of workers in the informal sector, was formed by street vendors in Ahmad Abad, India, in 1972. It was initially an association that included street vendors, home-based workers, agricultural laborers, construction workers, head loaders, and rag-pickers. The association is now large and internationally recognized, and works with Women in Informal Employment Globalizing and Organizing (WIEGO). WIEGO acts as an international network and organization to lobby for the passage of labor laws to protect women who work in the informal sector. Currently the organization that specifically focuses on vendors is StreetNet. StreetNet was launched in 1995 as a network of individual vendors, activists, researchers, and supporters working to increase the visibility, voice, and bargaining power of street vendors throughout the world. It organized a conference in Durban, South Africa, which twenty thousand street traders, 60 percent of whom were women, attended in 1999. As part of their mission, StreetNet has been expanded to strengthen street-vendor networks, through collecting information on street vendors everywhere and disseminating information on strategies to promote and protect the rights of street vendors.[4] According to WIEGO, street venders face the following problems: they have no legal status or recognition, they are harassed by local authorities, they remain vulnerable to local authorities who can evict them and confiscate their goods, and they face unsanitary and hazardous workplaces that often lack basic services. WIEGO indicates that street vendors have a negative image, yet they are a part of urban life, provide useful goods and services at affordable prices, and generate employment.

Our research on street vendors was carried out in a middle- and low-income part of Tehran and in Mashhad around the Shrine of Imam Reza. We used open-ended interviews and codified the results after interviews were done. Our samples included twenty-four cases in Tehran and six cases in Mashhad. The samples were randomly chosen and the time was before the Iranian New Year when the city is

---

4. Information for WIEGO can be found on their website: www.wiego.org. They are located in the United States. StreetNet Association is located in South Africa; their website is streetnet.org.za. The Self-Employed Women's Association (SEWA) is located in Ahmad Abad, India, www.sewa.org.

more lax in allowing vendors to sell goods. We avoided taping interviews because it would attract the attention of passersby. Most interviewees were asked standard questions, but streets are not always a place conducive to in-depth interviews. In a few cases we asked for an in-depth interview. Long interviews were generally very disruptive to vendors. We employed two research assistants so that one could ask the questions while the other took notes. The two young women were trained for the job and were familiar with street language. In some cases getting information from street vendors was difficult. One example was the flower vendors (we shall not mention the name of the square to protect the interviewees). An entire day was spent trying to persuade one of the flower vendors for a short interview, with no results. We asked our research assistants to return to that square later, which they did and managed to interview one of the women.

The result of thirty interviews of street vendors was that nearly all interviewees were between the ages of forty to fifty and above, with two exceptions. One was a young woman of eighteen and one was an eighty-four-year-old woman. The range of activities was similar. Most of them sold items that were used by women, such as women's underwear, and also children's clothes. Some sold men's clothes, particularly men's underwear. At the low end of the trade, vendors sold matches and at the high end, they sold flowers and higher quality clothes. Our sample was mainly from the streets but we also chose a vendor who sold her goods in the Tehran Metro.

While their education varied, most had secondary education. All of them were literate and some had been through literacy classes. Most of them worked between twelve to eighteen hours a day, depending on the season. Working time for women in Tehran was different from that of Mashhad, where mostly women (like other vendors) worked mainly at night. In this case they started just before the sun set but the peak hours were well into the night when pilgrims, particularly in the summer, found it easier to walk around the boulevards surrounding the shrine.

As mentioned, the state has a complicated relationship with the informal sector. While it is clear that this sector is vital to those deprived of formal employment, from time to time the city tries to bring the sector under control in order to avoid problems such as traffic congestion caused by street vendors.

Typically, street vendors gather in close proximity to businesses. Sometimes they compete with shops, causing friction with local shopkeepers. Shadi, a woman in her mid-thirties, had mastered martial arts in order to protect herself when she worked as a street vendor. During her interview, she mentioned that when she first started she was harassed by pedestrians and shopkeepers. She had to prove that she could defend herself and that harassing her would have dangerous consequences. She worked in Haft-e tir Square, a main shopping area. There one faces a great deal of harassment, but it is also a busy shopping area and sales are high. She explained that she had to struggle when she started many years ago, but now that there are more female vendors in that square, it is easier and there are fewer cases of harassment.

Research on street vendors was both interesting and challenging. In the case of the flower vendors, further research and interviews with Welfare Organization officials revealed to us that some of these vendors work as an organized group under a main distributor who does not want researchers to meddle with their business because of fear of charges of tax evasion. We encountered similar problems with street beggars. Bahramitash spent an entire morning doing an in-depth interview with a female beggar in an upper-middle-income neighborhood, but when she went over her notes, the information was contradictory. This discovery led to further research and interviews with social workers who work on problems related to street beggars. It was discovered that in many cases street begging is part of "organized crime." This situation is typical of major cities where street beggars need protection. In an interview with a social worker with thirty years of experience working for Welfare Office (she asked us not to mention her name), she revealed that in Lorestan Province many beggars are seasonal construction workers, and those who are professional beggars are part of an organized group. She explained that many beggars on the streets of Tehran (including an older woman whom Bahramitash had interviewed) are picked up by cars from shantytowns and placed on particular streets early in the morning and then are picked up at night. They pay part of their income to the organizer of their activity (interview by Bahramitash with a retired Welfare Office social worker, Tehran, 2007).

Most of the interviewees complained about being harassed and stopped by city officials. Nearly all of the interviewees had experienced one or several occasions when they had been stopped and in some cases their goods had been confiscated. Shadi had fought with city officials physically when her goods were taken away, and through physical fighting she had gotten them back. Those at the lower ends of the trade and the peddlers were sometimes taken to the Welfare Office as street beggars.

The informal sector is a major headache for the authorities. There have been several efforts to provide free space for vendors in parks but these spaces are limited and are only useful for those who sell high-end goods. The city organizes fairs and women who produce handicrafts can rent space at them at a subsided rate from the city. We targeted those who appeared to be in the worst conditions. This targeting was on purpose, to find out if and to what extent these women had benefited from some of the social programs provided by the state and foundations. In several cases these women received pensions and had insurance, and one reported that she had received funds from the Imam Khomeini Relief Foundation (IKRF). But in the majority of cases they were not receiving any assistance. In one in-depth interview Shahin stated that she takes pride in not asking for money from IKRF or any other organization. "I am not like these people who receive from IKRF and Welfare Organization both and still declare themselves poor; I am proud to rely on myself." We did face the challenge of verifying our information, and we tried to turn interviews into a social occasion. We often bought from street vendors as a way of compensating them for using their time. We tried to become part of the scene and at the same time help them sell their goods.

Perhaps the most interesting issue was marital status and the informal sector. The majority of those interviewed were widowed and all of them except four had lost their husbands. Where women were married, only two of the husbands were working; the other two were unemployed and disabled. These findings should be considered in conjunction with what is discussed in chapter 6 on female-headed households. Clearly street vendors were mostly from female-headed households. Street vendors tend to fall outside of data gathering, and this is one of the reasons that the number of female-headed households is underestimated (as is argued in chapter 6). Moreover, as discussed in chapter 6, female-headed households tend to be overrepresented among those from low-income households. In our sample, the range of income fell between three to twenty dollars a day, which put most of them in lower-middle and low-income households. Most of them earned an average of five to ten dollars a day.

In terms of access to credit for their business, street vendors primarily relied on their own resources and those of their extended family network and friends. In fact, the issue of extended family and community support was extremely important. In one of the cases, one woman had received her goods without paying because of personal trust. Personal trust, mutual help, and charity were extremely important to the lives of these women. Our eighty-four-year-old vendor, who sold secondhand books, was given books by a bookstore for free and enjoyed the protection and facilities that the bookstore owner provided for her. One interviewee who was selling goods such as shower caps and body scrubs was thankful for working women who passed by her and bought her odds and ends to help her out.

We found community protection and social safety nets at work particularly in low-income neighborhoods. One of the interviewees in Shush Square, one of the poorest neighborhoods in Tehran, was a woman in her late fifties who sold matches and did palm reading. When Bahramitash sat next to her on the street, the vendor quietly told her that she does palm reading and writes charms. Fatima was an interesting case because she was highly respected by everyone in the neighborhood. When it was lunchtime, several shopkeepers asked her if she wanted lunch. She had been working on that corner for the past twenty years. She is a widow who is well respected and who lives in a house given to her for free by her son-in-law. On her five dollars a day she ran charity activities, organized religious feasts, and collected money for the poor and the needy in the neighborhood. As she was palm reading, a city official passed by and told her that she should not do this in public, as palm reading was not allowed and if the city came he would not protect her. Clearly she enjoyed a great deal of protection by the neighborhood. This case showed that even street vendors, who tend to be working in the worst conditions, enjoy some protection if they are close to their community. Moreover, although their conditions are the worst, they still may be able to benefit from their community network.

Conclusion

Our survey produced the following results:

(a) The informal sector of the economy draws women from different income-level households.

(b) Those from high- and middle-income households tend to benefit from this sector for various reasons, while the results from low-income households are more mixed (some are exploited; some are empowered).

(c) Generally, the self-employed fare much better than wage workers, although street vendors, who are technically self-employed, are an exception.

(d) Women with less education are more likely to enter into the informal sector.

(e) Women entering the informal sector do so because they can combine productive and reproductive work.

(f) Married women are more involved in the informal economy than single women.

(g) Female-headed households are more engaged in the informal economy than those who come from dual-income households.

(h) The informal sector relies on personal resources and those of the extended family network for its capital and its market.

(i) Increased participation in the informal economy leads to an increase in women's economic decision-making power.

(j) Income generated through informal work is spent on basic goods rather than luxury items (although this finding could well be true of employment in the formal sector).

(k) Women work in this sector because of economic necessity, although those with high, middle, and low incomes had very different conceptions of what economic necessity was, and the necessities of one group could be regarded as luxuries by others. Moreover, many women enter into this sector because of their desire to gain economic independence.

From our focus on the low-income households, we came to realize that the informal sector can be a source of economic empowerment as well as exploitation. For women of low-income households who are self-employed, the sector is not always exploitative, and it can be empowering. Those who work as wage workers, either as street vendors or as maids, can be in a highly vulnerable situation. In the case of maids, they are at the mercy of their employer and can be subject to hardship, and their income is low and seasonal. Those who work as street vendors are also extremely vulnerable because they can run into trouble with the city, shopkeepers, and pedestrians. In both of these occupations, wage workers away from their extended family and community support complained about their jobs. There were exceptions. Some women working as maids for caring families were pleased that these families provided them with financial and emotional support, and some street vendors enjoyed the support of women passersby and/or shopkeepers.

While the picture is extremely complex and varies from case to case, typically women from high- and middle-income households enjoy greater benefits. Those from low-income households find their work embedded within their extended family and community network. Their work can be a major building block toward a community social safety net to deal with poverty. Social safety nets play a vital role for women from low-income households who come together to help and empower themselves both economically and emotionally. This finding was most striking when focus groups were held in low-income neighborhoods where several hours of taped informal conversation took place (with their permission) and analyzed afterwards. Many of these women received and gave economic and emotional support either as charity or as an act of friendship and solidarity, and they helped each other in times of crisis. While making ends meet was a massive undertaking in the face of high inflation and housing shortages, women of low-income households seemed to give generously to each other, and when misery was shared their solidarity was a source of empowerment and gave them agency against economic hardship. Underneath the veil of the hidden world of the informal sector, there is a huge and vital economic and social world where Iranian women generate an income, raise credit, take care of each other, and make ends meet.

8

Iran's Missing Working Women

FATEMEH ETEMAD MOGHADAM

AVAILABLE STUDIES ON IRAN suggest the existence of a large, diverse, and growing informal economy. Estimates on the share of the informal economy vary from 6 to 33 percent of the total GDP, and 47 percent of the labor force (Khalatbari 1994; Renâni 2001; Taher-Far 1997). Nearly all studies point to a substantial presence of women in the informal economy. The evidence also suggests considerable undercounting of women's work in Iran (F. Moghadam 2007). Using a sample of 350 women from the affluent northern part of Tehran, this chapter tests the hypothesis of the existence of a significant informal economy with female labor participants who do not fit the stereotype of being poor, uneducated, and unable to join the formal economy. Nevertheless they are gainfully employed in the unregulated and informal market economy, and are unaccounted for in the official statistics.

The concept of informal economy refers to "unregulated" and "unorganized" economic activities that take place outside the framework of corporate public and private sector establishments and may be unaccounted for in the formal official statistics. The intellectual origin of the concept is found in the failure of the formal dualistic Lewis-type economic models to address the existence of masses of gainfully and positively employed people in urban areas that these models assumed to be subsistence and surplus (Hart 1998, 845–46; Lewis 1954, 139–91). A number of leading scholars in the field view the existence of this entrepreneurial and self-employed economy as a positive and vibrant contributor to the economies of developing countries (De Soto 1989; Hart 1990, 137–60). In most studies undertaken by the ILO, however, the underlying assumption is that such workers are unable to enter the formal economy (ILO 2002).

A number of studies carried out within the advanced industrial countries are based on structuralist and institutionalist schools of thought. These studies do not make an a priori negative assumption about income and skill, focus on competitive and cost-reducing aspects of microfirms, and define informal as income-generating activities that result in the production of legal goods and services but are not regulated by the formal institutional/legal rules and are denied formal protections (Portes 1994, 426–49; Feige 1990, 989–1002). A recent study on Latin America indicates that such activities are not limited to those unable to join the formal economy and that women may prefer informal self-employment over formal employment in order to balance family and work responsibilities (World Bank 2007; Williams 2006, 1).

Most empirical studies on the subject, however, have been undertaken in poor slum areas, on new rural-urban migrants and self-employed or family workers with little formal education. The underlying presumption is that such workers are unable to enter the "formal" labor market (Todaro 1989, 268). The present study, however, was undertaken within the affluent northern part of Tehran and tested the hypothesis of the presence of educated middle- and upper-class women within the informal economy.

Since the 1970s, another issue that gained recognition and growing popularity and support is the underestimation of women's work in labor statistics and national income accounts. Feminist economists have pointed out that official national statistics underestimate women's work in four major areas: agricultural and subsistence production, paid work in the informal economy with poor and recent urban migrant women, domestic production and related tasks, and volunteer work (Benería 1997, 112). None of these studies, however, points at the undercounting of labor market participation of educated middle- and upper-class women. A study by the World Bank on the MENA region can be interpreted as empirically supportive of the hypothesis of undercounting of educated and skilled women's labor market participation. But the study itself treats the findings as paradoxical. While MENA's achievements in education, fertility, and life expectancy compare favorably with those of other regions, the rate of female labor force participation is significantly lower than rates elsewhere in the world (World Bank 2004, 1). This paradox is generally explained by sociocultural factors. Here I suggest that another explanation may be the existence of a sizeable unmeasured and hidden informal female economy that is inclusive of not only poor and unskilled female workers but also middle- and upper-class educated and skilled women. Therefore this chapter examines the hypothesis of undercounting of labor force participation of educated and affluent women in Iran.

With some modifications, the definition of informality used in this study is in conformity with the structuralist and institutionalist schools of thought: no a priori negative assumption is made about income and skill, and the income-generating activities result in the production of legal goods and services but are not regulated by the formal institutional/legal rules (Portes 1994, 426–49; Feige 1990, 989–1002). I will, however, depart from a strictly institutionalist/legalist approach. Because gender studies on Iran often refer to specific sociocultural factors impacting labor participation, I will use Douglas North's broader concept of institutional constraints, which is inclusive of both formal legal and informal social constraints (North 1990, 36–39). Also note that the standard concept of informal economy was developed in contrast to Arthur Lewis's dualistic model of development with unlimited supplies of labor from subsistence traditional farmers. In this study, however, the perceived dualism and the "untapped supply of labor" come from housework. Thus the distinction to note in the official labor statistics is not "employed" versus "unemployed," but active labor versus full-time housewife/homemaker. While I recognize the positive and gainful contributions of homemakers, for the purpose of this study active informal labor is defined as those who report as full-time homemakers in the official statistics but are involved in gainful employment in the market and earn cash incomes.

Background

As indicated by table 8.1, three distinct periods can be found in the participation of women in the labor market in Iran. For the period 1956 (the first available population census) to 1976 (the last prerevolution population census), the share of women in active labor nearly doubled. For this period oil revenues were rising, the Iranian economy was experiencing rapid growth, the public sector was expanding, and the explicit policy of the state was utilization of female labor for economic growth. In official government documents there are frequent references to women as an "untapped supply of labor" that should be utilized for economic growth. This period was followed by the Islamic Revolution (1978–79) and the subsequent rise of the Islamic government.

In the first decade after the revolution a combination of factors—falling oil revenues, insecurity and uncertainty in property relations and their impact on investment, and a general state of inefficiency in the management of state and para-state (foundations) operations in Iran—generated a deep recession. This period was also marked by a strong attempt by the government to Islamize the society. Thus female employment policy was designed in this context, and as a reversal of what were perceived as the "immoral and Westernized"

Table 8.1 Composition of Economically Active Population (Ten Years and Older) (Percent)

Year	1956	1966	1976	1986	1996	2000*
Males	90	87	80	90	87	88
Females	10	13	20	10	13	12
Total	100	100	100	100	100	100

Source: ILO 1967, 20; 1971, 28; 1982, 23; 1992; 31; Statistical Center of Iran 1997, 109–11.
* Source for this year is Statistical Center of Iran 2000a, 18.

policies of the Shah. In this context, women's primary occupation was considered to be wifehood and motherhood, and in the labor market to be female occupations such as teaching and health-related services. As indicated in table 8.1, the share of women in active labor declined to about two-thirds of its prerevolutionary period.

In general, Iran has pursued a policy of normalization and reconstruction of the economy since the death of Ayatollah Khomeini in 1989. While the explicit ideology of the state continues to be that of Islamization of the society, there is an ongoing process of debate, reinterpretation, and adjustment of religious texts to what are perceived to be the requirements of a modern society. Thus the proper role and rights of women in an Islamic society have become subject to controversy and change. In comparison to the earlier years, the ideology and the policy approach are more open and flexible in relation to women and their role in society and in the labor market. As indicated by table 8.1, in comparison to 1986 the share of active female labor has risen in Iran. Nevertheless the 13 and 12 percent shares in total active labor (1996 and 2000, respectively) remained well below the nearly 15 percent share for 1976. According to the latest population census, however, this share was 15.5 percent, higher than the 1976 share.

Another way of explaining the decline in labor participation is the rising share of female students ten years and older in the population. As indicated by table 8.2, the combined share of active labor and students in the total female population ten years and older was about 27.7 percent in 1976. This combined share declined to 24.8 percent in 1986. But the share rose to 30.7, 35.7, and 34.8 percent for 1991, 1996, and 2006, respectively. It can be argued that many young girls go to school instead of taking low-wage factory and other jobs. Indeed the historical trends in many developed countries indicate that the rise in female education may initially cause a decline in blue-collar female labor until at some future date a large number of women join the market as white-collar workers (Blau and Freber 1986, 68–69).

Table 8.2 Labor Market Participation and Education of Female Population (Ten Years and Older) (Percent)

Year	1956	1966	1976	1986	1996	2006
Active	9.2	12.6	12.9	8.2	8.7	9.1
Homemaker*	79.5	73.3	68.8	68.7	63.7	58.4
Student	3.0	7.4	14.8	16.6	22.0	26.6
Other	8.3	6.7	3.5	5.5	5.6	5.9
Total	100	100	100	100	100	100

Source: Statistical Center of Iran, www.sci.org.ir.
* This category is not exclusive to housewives and includes family members whose primary occupation is housework.

While these general explanations appear realistic, there is consensus that the data substantially underestimate women's participation in agriculture.[1] It seems, however that the same survey methods were used for the entire period. Therefore the comparability of the data

---

1. In general there is consensus that the data grossly underestimate women's participation in agriculture. Measurement of women's work in agriculture in Third World countries is subject to debate. The consensus is that rural women perform many agricultural production and processing activities that are not accounted for in rural surveys. In the case of Iran, measurement problems are especially acute. This problem is owing to the design of the questions and the frequency of visits by data collectors. On each survey, the respondents are asked if they worked on farm during the last ten days, and only one annual visit is undertaken by the survey team. If for seasonal reasons, women did not perform agricultural tasks, their overall participation is not reported. By contrast, in Turkey, for each survey more than one visit during different seasons is carried out. The latter may reflect a more accurate picture of labor participation. Thus the actual participation rates in Iran are higher than the data suggest for the entire period of 1956–2000. Furthermore, rural development and education usually result in declining female participation in agriculture, as young girls attend school instead of working on farms. Thus a more accurate measurement of female labor in agriculture is likely to affect not only the absolute number, but also the shape of change over time in female labor participation.

is not affected by this underestimation. Some observers have noted yet another, and puzzling, problem of underestimation. They suggest that the postrevolutionary surveys underestimate the participation of urban white-collar and professional women (Khalatbari 1994). The proponents of this view argue that the first postrevolutionary decade was accompanied by the harassment of working women, particularly within the nontraditional middle and upper classes. While many such white-collar and professional women continued to participate in the labor market, they found it convenient to introduce themselves as full-time homemakers to the official census data collectors. This argument can be further strengthened by the fact that recession and a declining household income may have induced many women to find ways to be gainfully employed and reduce the burden of a declining family income. Over time these women are likely to have discovered other advantages to being evasive about their employment status, such as avoidance of taxes, licensing, and other regulations. These factors have thus generated an underground female labor market that performs legitimate and socially desirable tasks. While this logic sounds reasonable, I could not find any empirical studies to support the assertion. The present study, therefore, makes an exploratory attempt to examine the topic.

The Survey

The ultimate objective of this microsample survey was to examine the informal labor market participation of the middle-class educated and professional women in Tehran. Therefore, I selected populations that were biased in favor of overrepresentation of middle-class and working-age women. The geographic area in which the survey was conducted was the northern affluent parts of Tehran. Within that geographic area, locations were selected that were perceived to be frequented by the above-mentioned women. Because the intention was to compare and contrast the relative share and characteristics of the informal with the formal labor market participants, I aimed at selecting a sample that was inclusive of both categories and did not appear biased in favor of either. Thus I aimed at selecting a sample that appeared random and unbiased in its inclusion of women working in the public, the private formal, and the informal sectors.[2] The survey did not aim at examining the labor market participation of students, and locations in which there would have been a large representation of young female students were deliberately avoided, such as areas near the universities. Instead, locations were selected that were likely to be frequented by young as well as mature working-age women likely to be a part of the labor force. Within these conditions that tended to cluster the population as middle- and upper-middle class, and working age, the sample included any individual woman who volunteered to complete the questionnaire.[3] While any working-age woman who was willing to respond was not discriminated against, the questions were focused on labor market participation. Therefore, it is possible to assume that the type of questions may have generated more enthusiasm and attracted more volunteers among working women than full-time homemakers. Thus it is possible to assume that the sample may have been biased in favor of working and against full-time homemaking women. The survey was undertaken in 2001.

In conducting the survey, I had two major constraints: a very low budget and lack of a government permit to conduct the survey. Therefore, I undertook a low-budget and a low-profile survey and prepared a set of brief and user-friendly questionnaires. The questionnaires were also designed to protect the privacy and anonymity of the respondents; names and addresses were not asked. Through a network of friends and acquaintances the questionnaires were distributed to offices and institutions that had women customers, cli-

---

2. We did not use government offices or any private office that had a disproportionate number of government employees as customers or clients.

3. A significant number of surveyed women who did not possess a high school degree is likely to be related to women who worked as cleaners and other blue-collar positions in the surveyed businesses.

ents, and volunteer (charity) workers, and to those who volunteered to fill out the questionnaires.[4]

Description of the Data

The bulk of the sample women are of working age (minimum age of seventeen years, median and mean of mid-thirties, and only 8 percent older than fifty-five). About 60 percent were married and the rest single (table 8.3). In terms of education, about 72 percent ranged from at least a high school to at most a bachelor's (32 percent) degree. About 18 percent had master's and doctoral degrees, and 9 percent did not complete high school (table 8.4). About 94 percent of the women stated that they were participants in the labor market and had cash earnings; only 6 percent declared themselves full-time homemakers.[5] Of those who were employed, about 79 percent worked full time and the rest were largely working half time (table 8.5). Of those who worked, 68 percent were employed in the private sector, 17 percent in the public, and the rest in both sectors (table 8.6). The most important primary reason cited for working was contribution to family expenditures; combined primary and secondary breadwinners were 35 percent of the sample; 12 percent were primary breadwinners and 23 percent were secondary. Financial independence was the second most frequent reason for working cited by women, 29 percent, and personal fulfillment in pursuit of a career, 22 percent, was the third most important reason (table 8.7).

All women were asked about how they introduced themselves in the official population census and other surveys: full-time homemaker, employed, or student. More than 36 percent stated that they

---

4. The bulk of respondents were customers, clients, and volunteer workers of the following: a travel agency, the office of a newspaper and a magazine, a hairdresser, a dressmaker, a private language instruction class, a cancer-related charity organization, two photo studios, and an engineering consulting firm.

5. As stated earlier, the sample is likely to have been biased against full-time homemakers.

Table 8.3 Marital Status of Women in Survey Sample

	All Women		Employed Women	
Status	Frequency	%	Frequency	%
Single	137	40.3	125	40.8
Married	203	59.7	181	59.2
Total	340	100.0	306	100.0

Table 8.4 Education Attainments of Women in Survey Sample

Education Categories	All Women		Employed Women		Informal Sector		Formal Sector	
	Frequency	%	Frequency	%	Frequency	%	Frequency	%
Less than high school	31	9.2	23	7.5	18	18.4	3	1.5
High school diploma	71	21.1	62	20.3	27	27.6	34	17.4
Post–high school diploma	65	19.2	62	20.3	22	22.4	40	20.5
Bachelor's degree	109	32.2	102	33.3	27	27.6	69	35.4
Master's degree	48	14.2	44	14.4	4	4.1	37	19.0
Doctorate	14	4.1	13	4.2	0	0.0	12	6.2
Total	338	100	306	100	98	100	195	100

Table 8.5 Time Spent on Work by Women in Survey Sample

Employment Category	Working Women		Informal Sector		Formal Sector	
	Frequency	%	Frequency	%	Frequency	%
Full-time	233	78.7	53	57.6	173	90.6
Half-time	54	18.2	36	39.1	14	7.3
Less than half-time	9	3.0	3	3.3	4	2.1
Total	296	100.0	92	100.0	191	100.0

Table 8.6 Public versus Private Employment of Women in Survey Sample

Employment by Sector	Frequency	%
Private	203	68.1
Public	52	17.4
Both	43	14.4
Total	298	100.0

Table 8.7 Reasons for Working of Women in Survey Sample (Percent)

Reasons for Working	Primary Reason	Secondary Reason
Main Family Breadwinner	12	6
Secondary Family Breadwinner	23	15
Financial Independence	29	23
Personal Fulfillment in the Career	22	28
Performing a Non-Housework-Related Occupation	6	13
Interest in Working Outside the Home	8	8
Total	100	100

declare themselves full-time homemakers. Of those who had reported in our sample as gainfully employed, about 33 percent stated that they introduced themselves as full-time homemakers, or about 53 percent of all women who are employed in the private sector (table 8.8).[6] Thus about one-third of all working women in the sample were not counted in the official statistics and can be considered participants in the informal economy. We asked these women why they did not declare themselves to be employed. About 53 percent stated social and cultural factors, code for the government's religious ideology, as the primary reason, and more than 33 percent cited social and cultural factors as the secondary reason for not declaring. Other factors such as licensing and tax evasion were also significant primary and

6. Note that only about 2 percent of the sample are students. Therefore in some of the subsequent analysis we have omitted them.

Table 8.8 Responses in Official Surveys versus Informal Survey

	All Women		Employed Women	
Response in Official Surveys	*Frequency*	%	*Frequency*	%
Homemaker	120	36.5	98	32.8
Employed	203	61.7	195	65.2
Student	6	1.8	6	2.0
Total	329	100.0	299	100.0

Table 8.9 Reasons for Not Declaring Employment in Official Surveys

	Primary Reason		Secondary Reason	
Reasons for Not Declaring Employment*	*Frequency*	%	*Frequency*	%
Tax evasion	19	20.7	5	15.2
Licensing and permits	18	19.6	16	48.5
Social and cultural factors**	49	53.3	11	33.3
Other	6	6.5	1	3.0
Total	92	100.0	33	100.0

* Respondents could give one primary and one secondary reason. As indicated by the frequency of the responses, a larger portion responded to the primary than to the secondary reasons.

** These are code words for the problems and inconveniences associated with the ideological and theocratic aspects of the regime.

secondary reasons. The combined primary reason for tax evasion, licensing, and permits was 37 percent, and the combined secondary reason was 40 percent (table 8.9).

A comparison of the educational attainments of the women in the informal and formal sectors shows the following: about 18.5 percent of the women in the informal sector, and only 1.5 percent of those in the formal sector, did not complete high school. Furthermore, none of the women in the informal sector had doctoral degrees. Only 4.1 percent of the women in the informal sector had master's degrees, compared to 19 percent in the formal sector. These numbers somewhat conform to the general wisdom that the less educated women participate in the informal labor market. Comparisons of those with high school, post–high school, and bachelor's degrees (27.6, 22.4, and 27.6 percent for the informal sector, respectively) support the hypothesis of the existence of a significant educated white-collar participation by women in the informal labor market (table 8.4).

In terms of the time spent on work, about 58 percent of the informal participants worked full time, 39 percent half time, and only 3 percent less than half time. These numbers are lower than the 91 percent full-time participants of the formal sector, but nevertheless are indicative of the importance and significance of the contribution of the informal sector (table 8.5).

The average annual income of individual (not family) working women in the sample was estimated at IRR 19,510,000, which is higher than the average annual income of an urban family (not individual) in Iran, Rls.18,564,952 for 1999 (Statistical Center of Iran 2000b, 829). Assuming that on average in each family two people work, the average income of the surveyed women is more than twice the national average. This finding is consistent with the sampling approach of selecting a geographic area that is more affluent than the average in Iran. As indicated by table 8.10, a larger percentage of women in the informal sector (23 percent) fall in the lowest income category, as compared with about 10 percent in the formal sector, a factor that is consistent with the common belief about the informal sector. But beyond that the data does not conform to the expected norms. It indicates that a significant share, more than 43 percent, of the women in the informal sector fall into the upper-income categories, in comparison with nearly 48 percent in the formal sector. Thus at the upper end the income differential between formal and informal does not appear substantial.

Given that I expected a large percentage of women in the informal sector to work from their own homes, I included questions pertaining to work from home. About 44 percent of all working women work from their own homes. The share for the informal sector is much higher: 80 percent (table 8.11). More than 56 percent of the women in the informal sector were involved in activities ranging from sewing and knitting (15.5 percent), artistic (14.1 percent), teaching (8.5

Table 8.10 Income Levels of Employed Women in Survey Sample (IRR 10,000)

Income Groups	All Employed Women		Informal Sector		Formal Sector	
	Frequency	%	Frequency	%	Frequency	%
<=500	44	14.9	22	22.7	18	9.7
500–1500	118	39.9	33	34.0	79	42.5
1500–2500	62	20.9	18	18.6	43	23.1
2500–4500	49	16.6	15	15.5	34	18.3
4500+	23	7.8	9	9.3	12	6.5
Total	296	100.0	97	100.0	186	100.0

percent), food (7.0 percent), technical (5.6 percent), and hair and cosmetics (5.6 percent). This finding is in sharp contrast to the formal sector, in which only about 20 percent of the women were involved in similar activities, and with the exception of those involved in technical (10.1 percent) and to a lesser extent teaching (3.6 percent), participation in the other activities was minimal. While women active in the informal sector were involved in a wide range of activities, these were by and large different and distinct from the types of activities that women in the formal sector were involved in. For all women working from home, accounted for and unaccounted for, the most important marketing techniques appear to be word of mouth (70.5 percent primary method and 42.4 percent secondary), promotion in private gatherings (13.3 percent primary and 34.5 percent secondary), and advertisements in residential buildings, art galleries, and showrooms (6.7 percent primary, 15.4 percent secondary) (table 8.12). These findings point at the small scale of operations of these enterprises.

Finally, the most common responses to the question pertaining to obstacles to business and career advancement were childcare and housework, and social and cultural problems; 27.5 percent of all working women cited each of these two factors as the primary obstacle to their career and business advancements. This response share was higher in the informal sector: 29.4 percent cited childcare, and 29.7 percent social and cultural factors as the primary obstacles, and

Table 8.11 Share of Women Who Work from Home
(Percentage of the Total Sample Observations Within Each Sector)

Occupational Categories	All Employed Women	Informal Sector	Formal Sector
All categories	43.9	80.3	24.5
Teaching	6.3	8.5	3.6
Technical	8.1	5.6	10.1
Artistic	5.9	14.1	2.2
Sewing	4.5	11.3	1.4
Knitting	1.8	4.2	0.7
Food	2.7	7.0	0.7
Hair and Cosmetics	3.6	5.6	1.4
Other	10.9	23.9	4.3

Table 8.12 Marketing Methods of Women Who Work from Home (Percentage of the Sector Total)

Method	All Employed Women		Informal Sector	
	Primary	Secondary	Primary	Secondary
Promotion through friends and acquaintances	70.5	42.3	68.8	40.0
Ad in residential buildings, art galleries, showrooms, etc.	6.7	15.4	7.8	20.0
Promotion in private gatherings	13.3	34.6	14.1	37.1
Ad in stores and business centers	2.9	5.8	4.7	2.9
Other	6.7	1.9	4.7	0.0
Total	100.0	100.0	100.0	100.0

7.1 percent and 25.0 percent as the secondary factor, respectively. Women in the informal sector also cited difficulty in finding skilled workers (14.7 percent), insufficient demand (13.2 percent), and lack of personal interest in advancement (10.3 percent) as the primary reasons (table 8.13). It seems that all working women in the sample view the social and ideological aspects of the society to be as much of an obstacle to professional advancement of women as child-bearing and child-raising.

Table 8.13 Obstacles to Advancement of Career/Business (Percentage of Sector Total)

Obstacle	All Employed Women		Informal Sector	
	Primary	*Secondary*	*Primary*	*Secondary*
Childcare and housework	27.5	18.3	29.4	7.1
Government regulations	8.7	9.7	0.0	7.1
High wages and employment insurance	3.4	8.6	2.9	14.3
Problems in finding skilled workers	10.1	9.7	14.7	3.6
Insufficient demand	9.4	17.2	13.2	17.9
Lack of personal interest in advancement/expansion	8.7	12.9	10.3	25.0
Social and cultural problems	27.5	21.5	27.9	25.0
Other	4.7	2.2	1.5	0.0
Total	100.0	100.0	100.0	100.0

Conclusions

In summary, the findings of this study support the hypothesis of the existence of a sizeable white-collar informal and unaccounted-for female labor market in Iran. Admittedly the extent of the representativeness of the sample, even within the context of the affluent northern Tehran, cannot be verified. Therefore the study is exploratory and one needs to be careful in making generalizations. Nevertheless the findings suggest that the informal female economy in Iran is not limited to poor and unskilled workers and is inclusive of workers with higher education and income. It also suggests that these workers are involved in diverse economic activities that are generally of a small scale and distinct from the types of activities performed by the formal sector.

The survey did not directly ask questions about discrimination in the labor market. The fact that the respondents view social and cultural problems as a major obstacle to their advancement, and perceive it as important as child-bearing and child-raising, can be interpreted to mean that they feel discriminated against. Furthermore, about one-third of the working women stated that they declare themselves as full-time homemakers in the official statistics and 53 percent of those cited social and cultural factors as the primary reasons for hiding their employments from the government. These statements are also indicative of suspicion about the government, its ideology, and the overall social and cultural factors. In conformity with findings elsewhere, the study also found tax evasion and avoidance of regulations as important factors. These and many other aspects and reasons for informality are worthy of further exploration and future studies.

9

Iranian Immigrant Women's Labor Market Strategies

A Complex and Entangled Process

ZOHREH MIRZADEGAN NIKNIA

> Americans' perception of us [Iranian women] oscillates between an "exotic belly dancer" to a "backward woman who is kept under chador (covering)." I am bothered by these Western stereotyped images of Middle Eastern women. It makes me self-conscious and at times defensive. Faced with such a distorted image, at the presence of my non-Iranian friends and coworkers, I am forced to defend views that I privately disagree with to prevent further stereotyping.
> —One of the participants

THIS CHAPTER, although it has a different geographical focus—the United States—similar to previous chapters is an examination of Iranian women's labor market strategies and outcomes within relevant contexts. Similar to their cohorts in Iran, labor force participation (LFP) of Iranian women in the United States is low in relation to the LFP of Iranian men, native-born women, and other immigrant women in the United States (Bozorgmehr 1996, 1998; Tohidi 1993; Waldinger and Gilbertson 1994). The level of Iranian women's LFP is partly informed by the realities of the US socioeconomic structures and institutions. Similar to other women, native or immigrant, they must contend with such constraints as the existing gender gaps in occupation and income (Massey 1999; Goldin 1990; Sassen 1991, 2004; Raijman and Tienda 1999). Moreover, similar to other immigrants, their labor market success may be hindered by the lack of (1) English language proficiency, (2) transferable skills and education, (3) work experiences in the United States, and (4) familiarity with the US job market (Chiswick 1978a, 1978b; Borjas 1988; Schoeni 1998). However, according to national and regional studies based on census and survey data, labor force participation among Iranian immigrant women is low despite their English language proficiency and relatively high level of education—often acquired in the United States (Bozorgmehr 1996, 1998; Tohidi 1993; Waldinger and Gilbertson 1994), an outcome that is presumed anomalous within the neoclassical human capital framework: the dominant theory of migration.

In this chapter, I reexamine the above-noted low LFP of Iranian women in the United States within a critical feminist framework by contextualizing the migration, settlement decisions, and outcomes within the unique sociohistorical contexts of the Iranian women's exit and reception, and the consequent constraints and capabilities. The goal of this chapter, similar to the previous ones, is to present a more nuanced understanding of Iranian women's labor market outcomes. The data and analysis not only consider individual characteristics, but also emphasize the significance and interdependence of economic, political, historical, social, cultural, and familial contexts, and their combined influence on Iranian employment options and exercises. The chapter is based primarily on a larger interdisciplinary qualitative case study. It relies mostly on primary data that I have collected during a two-year fieldwork. However, in order to provide an empirical context for the case study, I conducted two preliminary quantitative studies prior to the start of the interviews. This mixed-method approach provides an appropriate framework for examining Iranian immigrant women's labor market outcomes. The rich data collected through face-to-face in-depth interviews complement the quantitative data, and together they present a more historical, contextualized, complicated, and realistic picture of Iranian women's work experiences and their perception of those experiences. Thus the study provides not only new data but also new insight.

Gender and Migration

Migration is a global phenomenon that is not limited to a particular region, and the numbers are growing. According to the International Organization for Migration (2005), in 2000 there were 175 million international migrants; more than half were female, prompting the term "feminization of migration." The increase in the number of migrants, both internal and international, is owing to globalization and the consequent social transformation. Globalization affects economic, political, and cultural processes, thus "transform[s] social relationships in both rich and poor countries, creating the conditions for much greater human mobility" (Castles and Miller 2009, 301; Trager 2005). The growing global inequality, it is believed, combined with "improved transport and communication technologies, and rising transnational consciousness all lead to more movement and to greater diversity in patterns and outcomes" (Castles and Miller 2009, 301; Barker and Feiner 2004; Sassen 2004; Trager 2005).

Given that migration "disrupts and realigns" one's everyday life, and, although women constitute more than half of the international migrants, the literature often discounts the significance of gender-specific variations (Hondagneu-Sotelo 1994). Factors that affect the decision to emigrate as well as the integration processes and outcomes vary significantly for men and women. It is noted that the structural changes in the economies of sending and receiving countries create different sets of incentives and constraints for men and women (Sassen 1991, 2004). For example, women have been affected differently by various changes in US immigration policies (Gabaccia 1994; T. A. Sullivan 1994; Schoeni 1998).

In general, globalization has impacted women differently and has not only increased the overall global inequities; the same processes that have enabled and empowered some groups of women have had negative consequences for other groups of women. Lourdes Benería notes,

> Globalization and the increasing mobility of women have facilitated the employment of migrant women from South in specific

areas of services in high-income countries, such as in care work. We are only beginning to evaluate the impacts of such phenomenon on individuals and families, both in South and the North. . . . Professional women have moved into privileged male jobs, contributing to decreasing gender gaps in some countries. On the other hand, most women remain at the bottom of labor market hierarchies, hence there is some evidence showing that these trends are generating increasing inequality among women. (Benería 2003, 163)

Saskia Sassen articulates similar concerns:

Globalization allows links to be forged between countries that send migrants and countries that receive them; it also enables local and regional practices to go global. The dynamics that come together in the global city produce a strong demand for migrant workers, while the dynamics that mobilize women into survival circuits produce an expanding supply of workers who can be pushed or sold into those types of jobs. The technical infrastructure and transnationalism that underlie the key globalized industries also allow other types of activities, including money-laundering and trafficking, to assume a global scale. (Sassen 2004, 274)

Susie Jolly and Hazel Reeves emphasize the link between migration, development, and gender. Migration, they argue, can contribute to the receiving countries' development, and remittances and diaspora investment can support the sending countries' development; however, these processes and their outcome are gendered (2005, 1). The question as to who benefits "depend[s] on sex-segregated labour markets and gendered migration policies which provide differential opportunities for women and men. Sometimes immigration policies push 'unskilled' women workers into irregular and more risky migration channels. Migration may also hinder development through the social disruption of displacement due to conflict, or through 'brain drain' and possible increases in HIV/AIDS rates, to which women and men are at different risks" (2005, 2).

Although the gender dynamic is unexplored, some scholars contend that globalization, corresponding social transformation, and the consequent global inequalities have contributed to the "brain-drain" from developing regions to the developed. For example, Castles and Miller contend, "Differentiated migration regimes have been set up, to encourage the highly skilled to be mobile, while low-skilled workers . . . are excluded. . . . in a globalized world, 'mobility has become the most powerful and most coveted stratifying factor'. . . . Control of migration and differential treatment of various categories of migrants have become the basis for a new type of transnational class structure" (2009, 57). Moreover, the "brain-drain," although benefiting the receiving country, often bears negative consequences for the sending country, blunting its development. The UK International Development Committee (IDC) 2004 report states, "It is unfair, inefficient and incoherent for developed countries to provide aid to help developing countries to make progress towards the Millennium Development Goals (MDGs) on health and education, whilst helping themselves to the nurses, doctors and teachers who have been trained in, and at the expense of, developing countries" (quoted in Jolly and Reeves 2005, 26).

Noting similar concerns, Hatton and Williamson state that although the full negative impact of "brain drain" is yet unknown, the possibility that "migration to the OECD robs less-developed countries of their best and brightest" has created concern and prompted the recent debate about emigration of "qualified doctors, engineers, and information technology specialists from Third World" (2005, 327). Summarizing the emigration to Organisation for Economic Co-operation and Development (OECD) countries from sixty-one low- and middle-income countries' data, Hatton and Williamson conclude that for "most source countries, the proportion of adults (aged 25 and over) who have emigrated is small (5 percent or less)"; however all of the countries have "higher emigration rates for those with tertiary education than for all citizens" (2005, 328, table 15.4, 329). The data indicate that fifteen of these countries, including Iran, have "lost more than 20 percent of their highly educated manpower through emigration but far smaller proportion of their total workforce" (328). More specifically, although only 1.5 percent of the total adult population of Iran has immigrated to OECD countries, the migrants constitute 25.6 percent of the country's adult population with tertiary education (Hatton and Williamson 2005, 329). The socioeconomic consequences of emigration of the highly educated and skilled Iranians, also noted by Bahramitash, Esfahani, and Olmsted (this volume), could have negatively affected the economic development of Iran. Moreover, the absence of a political and economic relationship between Iran and the United States, which has limited the possibility of diaspora investment as well as transfer of skill and knowledge, also could have contributed negatively to the economic development of Iran. These phenomena and their gender implications require further research.

Research Method and Strategy

The chapter is based primarily on an interdisciplinary case study. However, prior to the start of the fieldwork I conducted two quantitative comparative studies. The first quantitative study was based on data from the March supplement to *Current Population Survey* (CPS) for 1990–95, comparing all immigrant women in the United States to the native-born (US Bureau of the Census 1990–95). The result pointed to significant bifurcation among various immigrant groups. It showed that immigrant women as a whole have lower rates of labor force participation, are less likely to be employed, have lower family and individual incomes, are more likely to be married and less likely to be divorced or separated, have higher fertility rates, and are likely to be either more or less educated than native-born women. Human capital theory, which is the dominant framework within migration literature for the evaluation of the immigrant's economic integration, was used for a multivariate analysis of the data. However, the results did not completely fall within the predicted theoretical outcomes; thus they were rendered inconclusive, suggesting the necessity for further probing.

The second quantitative study was based on data from the 1990 Census *1 percent Public Use Micro Sample* (PUMS) (US Bureau of the Census 1990). It compared the socioeconomic status of Iranian women to that of native-born women. The data indicated that Iranian women have higher levels of education than the native-born, and similar to other women immigrants are more likely to be married and less likely to be divorced or separated. Moreover, the data showed that Iranian women have lower labor force participation than both the native-born and other immigrant women, despite their relatively high levels of education and English language proficiency, a phenomenon noted by other researchers. Although these quantitative studies provide an overall comparative picture of Iranian women immigrants' socioeconomic status and an empirical context for the case study, they cannot portray a realistic picture of Iranian women immigrants' migration experience nor explain the process through which those labor market outcomes emerge. Even though "there is certainly merit to analyzing the economic activities of individuals using census-type data," the result "provides a limited vision of immigrants' economic integration process" (Raijman and Tienda 1999, 253; Waldinger and Bozorgmehr 1996).

To probe further, I did a follow-up qualitative case study, using the Kansas City metropolitan area as the geographical focus. I chose this community because I was living in Kansas City and had established the goodwill and trust that proved critical in securing access and facilitating the process. The two-year period of fieldwork (1999–2001) consisted of direct and participant-observations of the Iranian immigrant community, as well as in-depth face-to-face interviews with sixty Iranian women. The interview subjects were first-generation legal immigrants, selected through multilevel snowball sampling. I contacted more than 120 women; 60 agreed to participate. I did a follow-up face-to-face and a phone interview during 2005–6.

I met the women where they felt most comfortable; the majority preferred their home, a few came to my house, and several interviews took place in coffee shops. The sessions lasted between three to seven hours. Iranian etiquette required at least thirty minutes of socializing over a cup of tea before the start of the interviews, which provided a chance to establish a social relation and assured greater collaboration. Presented with a choice, most of the participants preferred to be interviewed in Persian, a few insisted on English, and several interviews were in both languages. In the subsequent translation, every effort was made to maintain the intended meaning and convey the embodied emotions; however, unavoidably, some nuances are lost in the process.

To assure the participants their due voice and visibility, throughout the chapter I have incorporated key passages from the interviews that emphasize certain shared experiences, views, and perceptions. One "aspect of postcolonial, as well as feminist, studies," Olmsted contends, is to provide the space for groups who have been invisible or misrepresented "to speak and represent themselves" (2004, 171). Furthermore, although the focus of the chapter is economic status, the research and analysis are grounded in historical, political, cultural, and social aspects of migration and settlement processes. As Olmsted argues, "economics cannot be studied outside the context of cultural, social, political, and historical processes and economics can no longer maintain imperialistic stand that it has much to offer non-economists, but the opposite is not the case. Ahistorical, decontextualized economic analysis" is incapable of exposing the oppressive and unjust structures that we help create and maintain (2004, 179).

Immigrant Women

Historically, the United States has been one of the major immigrant receiving countries and presently it is experiencing another episode of "mass migration," which is partly prompted by the liberalization of migration policies (Immigration Act of 1965). Alejandro Portes and Reuben G. Rumbaut state that "America, that 'permanently unfinished' society, has become anew a nation of immigrants. Not since the peak years of immigration before World War I have so many newcomers sought to make their way in the United States.... Unlike the older flows, however, today's immigrants are drawn not from

Europe but overwhelmingly from the developing nations of the Third World, especially from Asia and Latin America" (2006, xxiii). The "new wave" or "contemporary" immigrants in the United States, because of their Third World origin, are often characterized as poor and uneducated. However, there is great diversity among these immigrants. They "come in luxurious jetliners and in the trunks of cars, by boat, and on foot." They are "manual laborers and polished professionals, entrepreneurs and refugees, preliterate peasants and some of the most talented cosmopolitans on the planet" (Portes and Rumbaut 2006, xxiii). They make up "the most educated and the least educated groups in the United States" and are the "groups with the lowest and the highest rates of poverty, welfare dependency, and fertility" (Rumbaut 1997a, 23).

Since the early 1930s, more than half of all immigrants to the United States are women. Concerned about separation of family, the 1921, 1923, and 1924 US immigration policies gave preference to wives of US citizens and thus facilitated their inflow. Furthermore, the Immigration Act of 1965 eliminated country quotas and gave priority to family reunification. Even though the policy makes no gender distinction, women are more likely to take advantage of the family reunification provision, resulting in a greater number of "green card marriages" and women immigrants (Gabaccia 1994, 39; T. A. Sullivan 1994; Enchautegui and Malone 1997; Schoeni 1998). Moreover, mirroring the overall pattern and composition of the contemporary immigrants, there is an increase in the number of women from non-European nations including Iran and other Middle Eastern countries (T. A. Sullivan 1994; Enchautegui and Malone 1997; Schoeni 1998).

While immigrant women have slightly lower levels of education than their male counterparts, there is a great diversity among various groups, mirroring the overall patterns of contemporary immigrants. Women originating from the Philippines and the Middle East, including Iran, have higher average years of education than both the native-born and other immigrant groups, whereas those originating from Mexico have the lowest (Schoeni 1998). Women immigrants have lower rates of labor force participation and higher rates of unemployment than native-born women. However, there is variation between immigrant groups (T. A. Sullivan 1994, 35; Schoeni 1998).

Overall the contemporary women immigrants have a wider range of skills and work experiences. This occupational bifurcation continues and may even increase as they integrate into the US labor market (Gabaccia 1994; Enchautegui and Malone 1997; Schoeni 1998). In general, the "distinct sets of resources and vulnerabilities" and the "distinct context of exit and reception" of different immigrant groups affect their adaptation process. The variations in political, social, financial, and human capital "combine in ways that produce cumulative social advantages or disadvantages," generating different processes and outcomes (Rumbaut 1997a, 12).

The Iranian Immigrants

According to the 2000 census, 283,225 of the US population were born in Iran; however, the Iranian Studies Group, an independent research organization at MIT, offers a higher estimate (691,000) for 2004. Iranian immigration to the United States is relatively recent. They are mostly from the upper and middle class and come from urban areas. The Immigration and Naturalization Service has recorded two waves of immigration: before and after the 1978–79 Iranian Revolution. The majority have come during and immediately after the revolution; according to the 2000 census, the number of Iranian immigrants in the United States rose by 74 percent between 1980 and 1990.

The contemporary patterns of global migration are rooted in historical relationships and shaped by a multitude of political, demographic, socioeconomic, geographical and cultural factors (Castles and Miller 2009, 299; Portes 1996; Sassen 2004). Similarly, the migration of Iranians in the United States is rooted within the broader social, political, economic, military, and cultural relationships forged between the two societies of Iran and the United States during the past several decades. The discovery of oil in Iran created a major link between Iran and the West/United States. This connection gained significance as oil became a strategic commodity and a global "prize." Similarly, the oil linkage and revenue were influential in the Shah's westernization and modernization policies. The modernization projects created a demand for technocrats. Furthermore, the oil revenue facilitated the emigration of young Iranians, mostly male, who came to the United States to acquire the education and skills necessary to implement the Shah's westernization and modernization projects. This initial wave of Iranian immigrants was facilitated by the liberalization of immigration policy in the United States (Immigration Act of 1965). On the eve of the revolution, Iranians in US universities were the largest student group from any country.

The Iranian revolution, postrevolutionary Islamist policies, the Iran-Iraq war, and the existing network of family ties in the United States created the material and ideational conditions for the second wave of Iranian immigrants. The second group consists of the family members of the first group, as well as exiles and refugees. However, the hostage crisis and the break in diplomatic relations between Iran and the United States, as well as the US-imposed economic sanctions, have negatively impacted the migrant flow. Presently it is mostly limited to and sustained through family reunifications, many initiated through cross-national marriages of naturalized US-citizen Iranian immigrants with Iranian nationals (2000 census).

According to 2000 census data, Iranian immigrants in the United States are among the highly educated immigrants. More than 70 percent have tertiary levels of education and more than half have bachelor's degrees or higher, which points to the phenomenon of "brain drain." According to Akbar Torbat, in 2001 there were eight thousand Iranian medical doctors and four thousand Iranian professors in the United States (2002). Based on the 2000 census data, the median income of Iranians in the United States is higher than both native-born median income and that of other immigrant groups, mostly attributable to high levels of education and entrepreneurial skills.

Almost 60 percent of Iranians are in managerial, professional, and related occupations. Labor force participation of Iranian men is 63.8 percent, which is the same as the native-born LFP and higher than the LFP of all foreign-born men. However, the LFP of Iranian women, 49 percent, is lower than the LFP of the native-born (59.9 percent) and the LFP of all immigrant women. Iranians have higher rates of self-employment (11.6 percent) than both the native-born and all foreign-born (6.5 percent). According to 2000 census data, the median annual household income of Iranians is $59,773 and the median income of Iranian men is $52,333, which is higher than that of native-born men ($49,298), all immigrant men ($44,999), and Iranian immigrant women ($36,422). Iranian immigrants have lower poverty rates compared to the native-born and all immigrants: 13.9 percent, 15.1 percent, and 20.1 percent, respectively.

The Participants' Profile

The Kansas City metropolitan area, the geographic focus of the case study for this research, is home to about 1.5 percent of the Iranians in the United States (Modarres 1998). It has a representative and diverse Iranian population, with variation in age, age at arrival, date of arrival, duration of residency in the United States, English language proficiency, socioeconomic background, education, marital status, labor market status, occupation, and religion and other intraethnicity (Ansari 1992; Bozorgmehr and Sabagh 1988; Modarres 1998). The community, similar to others in the United States, can be categorized into the pre– and post–Iranian revolution emigrants. The presence of several universities within or near Kansas City explains the initial migration of Iranians to the area. Either the women whom I interviewed or their husbands, siblings, or children had attended these universities. The Iranian revolution and Iran-Iraq war brought the second wave. These were family members of the first group, as well as political or religious refugees and exiles, benefiting from family reunification and refugee visa provisions of the US immigration policy.

The sample included nine prerevolution and fifty-one postrevolution migrants. For most of the participants, the decision to settle in the United States was gradual and gendered. Almost all emphasized that they had had no intention of settlement upon arrival, and decided to stay primarily because of the postrevolutionary political, social, and economic uncertainties in Iran; some noted the gender inequities of the Islamist policies. Upon arrival, only seventeen had permanent residency status, the rest were students, visitors, or refugees. However, at the time of the interview, forty-two were US citizens and eighteen were permanent residents in the process of securing citizenship. Most had acquired their legal status through family reunification, eleven through "green-card marriages."

At the time of migration, most of the participants were between the ages of nineteen and forty, whereas, at the time of the interview, most were between the ages of twenty-six and fifty-five. The majority of the women were Muslim, one was Christian, three were Zoroastrian, and two were Bahai. Moreover, at the time of the interview, forty-nine of the women were married, five were divorced, two were widowed, one was separated, and three were single. Thirty-two of the participants had married prior to migration and twenty-four had married since. Most had married Iranians; seven had married non-Iranians, and one had married an Iranian of a different religion. The majority of the women interviewed had baccalaureate or higher levels of education, reflecting the high levels of education among Iranian immigrants in the United States. A few had some college education, and one-third had a high school diploma or less. Except for a few, all participants, similar to other Iranians in the United States, were from urban areas and upper-middle socioeconomic backgrounds, characteristics noted by Bahramitash and Esfahani as well as Olmsted in previous chapters.

Summaries of the labor market status and occupation of the participants are presented in tables 9.1 through 9.4. The data show that twenty-six (43 percent) had full-time jobs, nineteen (32 percent) had part-time jobs, five (8 percent) were self-employed, and ten (17 percent) were not in the labor force. Half of the women were working in professional, managerial, and entrepreneurial occupations; they were US-educated, fluent in English, and had work experiences in the United States. Thirty-five percent of the women were working in the secondary or informal sector, and 17 percent were housewives.

However, as shown in table 9.3, a great proportion of the husbands (84 percent) were in professional, managerial, and entrepreneurial occupations; 12 percent were in sales and services; 4 percent were retired; and only 4 percent were employed in the secondary sector.

Similar to other Iranian immigrant communities, self-employment is high among Iranian immigrants in Kansas City. The sample included twenty-seven family businesses owned and operated by the women, their husbands, or both, six of which were home-based daycare businesses operated by the women. Few indicated that they have opted for self-employment to escape anti-Iranian, anti-Muslim sentiments of employers and or coworkers. The assets of these family businesses were from several thousands to one million dollars. Eight of the women were unpaid employees and three were paid employees in family businesses. However, some of the women, to assure themselves of income and financial independence, had decided against working as unpaid employees in family businesses and had opted for paid employment elsewhere.

Table 9.4 presents income levels of the participants and their husbands. The data do not include everyone, because four of the participants did not share information about their own income and thirteen declined information about their husband's income. The average yearly income of the participants was $30,000. Fifteen of the women had zero earnings; five were unpaid employees in their family businesses. The majority of the women earned $35,000 or less, whereas two had income of over $100,000. The lowest income was zero (the unpaid employees in family businesses) and the highest was $140,000. The result reveals a gender gap in income; on average, the husbands earned $108,000, and the majority earned more than $50,000; eleven had income above $100,000. The overall economic success of Iranians is rooted in the high levels of education, often acquired in the United States. The human capital was energized with financial capital, as well as the family and ethnic community's social capital. Many of the family businesses were financed by the imported wealth brought over by the postrevolutionary immigrants and aided by their labor.

Table 9.1 Labor Market Status of Participants, January 2001

Labor Market Status	Numbers	%
Not in the Labor Force	10	17
Full-time	26	43
Part-time	19	32
Self-employed	5	8
Total	60	100

Source: Compiled from data collected through face-to-face interviews with sixty first-generation Iranian immigrant women residing in Kansas City.

Table 9.2 Occupation of Participants, by Type

Occupation	Numbers	%
Professional, Managerial, and Entrepreneurial	29	48
Sales and Service	21	35
Housewife	10	17
Total	60	100

Source: Compiled from data collected through face-to-face interviews with sixty first-generation Iranian immigrant women residing in Kansas City.

Table 9.3 Occupation of Spouses, by Type

Occupation	Numbers	%
Professional, Managerial, and Entrepreneurial	42	84
Sales and Service	6	12
Housewife	2	4
Total	50	100

Source: Compiled from data collected through face-to-face interviews with sixty first-generation Iranian immigrant women residing in Kansas City.

Table 9.4 Dollar Income of Participants and Spouses

Income	Participant		Spouse	
Amount (in dollars)	Numbers	%	Numbers	%
0	15	25	0	0
Less than 16,000	10	17	0	0
16,000–35,000	11	18	2	4
36,000–50,000	8	13	4	8
51,000–75,000	7	12	10	20
76,000–100,000	3	5	10	20
More than 100,000	2	3	11	22
Unknown (not given)	4	7	13	26
Total	60	100	50	100

Source: Compiled from data collected through face-to-face interviews with sixty first-generation Iranian immigrant women residing in Kansas City.

However, several participants complained about lack of economic security in the United States, which points not only to the reality of the inherent uncertainties of the global capitalist economies, but also to migration-imposed loss of familial and social support. In general, the participants believed that as immigrants they had to be better qualified, more accommodating, working harder, and able to learn and adopt the culture of self-promotion and assertiveness in order to succeed in the US job market.

The Trajectory of Labor Market Outcomes

In general, the gender and migration literature is inconclusive on the net effect of migration on women's well being. Jolly and Reeves summarize the contradictory nature of interconnected factors that influence the outcome in the following statement:

> Individuals may migrate out of desire for a better life, or to escape poverty, political persecution, or social or family pressures. There are often a combination of factors, which may play out differently for women and men. Gender roles, relations and inequalities affect

who migrates and why, how the decision is made, the impacts on migrants themselves, on sending areas and on receiving areas. Experience shows that migration can provide new opportunities to improve women's lives and change oppressive gender relations—even displacement as a result of conflict can lead to shifts in gendered roles and responsibilities to women's benefit. However, migration can also entrench traditional roles and inequalities and expose women to new vulnerabilities as the result of precarious legal status, exclusion and isolation. (Jolly and Reeves 2005, 1)

Similarly, the Iranian women's migration and integration process has resulted in a trajectory of outcomes and levels of well-being. For example, as was outlined in the previous section, the participants' labor market strategies range from those who readily accepted traditional gender roles and are housewives to those whose objection to traditional gender roles combined with their husband's rejection of any change have led to marital conflicts. These conflicts have either forced the women into a reluctant acceptance, an assumption of the double burden of home and work responsibilities, or have concluded in family breakups. However, the presence of compromise and consensus has produced other outcomes.

Consensus and Compromise

Some participants have forged labor market strategies that have been colored by consensus and compromise, and have assured family stability. The choices include: (1) the decision to stay home and willingly assume a traditional gender role; (2) work for pay and take on the "second shift"; (3) equally share the household and childcare responsibilities with the husband; (4) work in the family business as a paid or unpaid employee, and have flexible work schedules that accommodate the domestic responsibilities; and (5) establish home-based businesses that allow reconciliation of the public and private roles.

Several participants had opted to stay home and were happy with their choice. They believed that it contributed to the overall economic success of the family and promoted a sense of stability and peace within the family. The following comment from one such woman represents the shared sentiment of these housewives:

> American women put themselves under a lot of pressure in their quest of gender equality and independence. I do not mind letting someone else take care of me.

However, although some of the participants had decided against paid employment in favor of being a housewife and a homemaker, there were others who had willingly assumed the double burden of outside employment as well as the house and childcare responsibilities. These women believed their income was necessary and contributed to the family's higher standard of living, and they equally believed in maintaining the traditional gender roles. A professional woman, speaking with a sense of pride, explained,

> Whatever I have done for my family and children has been by choice. I have most of the household responsibilities and let my husband make most of the decisions, especially financial ones. The American culture promotes individualism even within the family; thus, each family member continuously asks, "what is in it for me?" I believe this self-centered individualistic attitude is the main reason for the high incidence of family breakups.

There were also a few participants with both spouses working and sharing the domestic responsibilities, and some working women who benefited from hired help or extended family.

Several participants with variation in age, duration of residency, education, English language ability, family structure, socioeconomic background, and family income, to avoid some of the problems associated with paid employment, had opted for home-based businesses such as daycare and food catering. These women indicated satisfaction with their choice and the ability to reconcile their public and private lives. Throughout our discussion, they all emphasized that their job preference accommodated their family responsibilities. One explained,

> I decided to have a home-based daycare at home when my children were little and continued even after they were grown. It is a good compromise. When the children are picked [up] in the afternoon, I am also done with my housework and ready to play.

Another, who had an elderly husband, commented,

> I chose to have a daycare in my home because it allows me to take care of my husband and tend to my housework while earning an income.

Although a few complained about the isolation and lack of opportunity for development of skills, all indicated that the income has given them a greater role in household decision-making and a sense of freedom, security, and control. One who had never worked for pay in Iran boasted,

> For the first time in my life I have financial control; I can help my children and grandchildren even when my husband declines to do so.

Similarly, a young educated woman explained her choice:

> My income has contributed to the family finances, but more importantly it has given me a greater role in household decision-making and a sense of security and control. I have been able to purchase expensive personal items and take trips without feeling guilty.

Contested Gender Boundary

Although family considerations loom high in Iranian women's economic role and strategies, for some the new cultural context and the migration-imposed socioeconomic hardships have created gender role ambivalence and discontent, and at times have produced marital conflicts and even breakups. Conflicts surface either because the women have reluctantly given in to the traditional gender roles and are resentful, or, despite the women's labor market engagement, gender boundaries are continuously contested by both spouses. Several participants, although they were enjoying comfortable lifestyles, expressed dissatisfaction with their traditional role as housewives, and especially their lack of financial independence and control. An educated woman complained about the decline in her post-migration status. Resentful of the sacrifices she has made, with great frustration she confessed,

> I have been reduced from a professional woman to a housewife. What bothers me is that I know I have more potential and feel unfulfilled. Life in the US has given my husband more control and created more frustration for me.

Another educated woman, despite a very comfortable lifestyle, also expressed dissatisfaction:

> My qualification does not afford me a good job. However, I have contemplated starting a business, but my husband is not supportive, leaving me dependant and unhappy.

However, the result of this investigation reveals that the expressions of the conflict, possible resolution, or unhappy dissolution are still rooted in the home cultural categories. The Iranian women, although they aspire to greater power and control within their households, are still committed to cultural categories such as *modar va hamsare fadakar* (selfless mother and wife) and *hambasegiye khanevadeh* (family unity). When children are involved, marital conflicts and breakups present greater challenges and more taxing dimensions. A grandmother shared her perceptions of the dilemma faced by Iranian women:

> *Hambastegiye khanevadeh* (family unity) still is accorded a high priority by the Iranian women. Thus they bear the consequences

of divorce differently than their American counterparts. It is disingenuous to encourage them to emulate the host society's individualistic attitudes, when they suffer even more when marital conflicts end in family breakups.

Moreover, the women were also concerned about their coethnic reaction during the conflict, separation, or divorce. (Interestingly, these negative sentiments are fast changing in the urban area of Iran as documented in previous chapters, which points to the existing disjunction between the immigrants' perceptions and memories and the existing cultural norms in Iran). A young divorcee described her frustrating experience:

> The pursuit of a career and financial independence created tension in my marriage. I had to choose between marriage and work; I chose the latter. But the Iranian community treats women divorcees less favorably than men.

Considerations and Constraints

The Context of Reception: Unwelcome Immigrants

Although the United States is a nation of immigrants, the context of reception has varied for various ethnic groups. Some immigrant groups including Cubans have encountered a supportive context of reception that has aided the process and outcome of their socioeconomic integration. However, the hostage crisis and the negative portrayal of Iran and Iranians in the media have created an inhospitable context of reception. The projected stereotyped images have forced many to deemphasize their Iranian and Muslim identities. The process of labor market segmentation "means that people's chances of getting jobs depend not only on their human capital but also on gender, race, ethnicity and legal status. . . . migrant workers may belong to racial or ethnic minorities, stigmatized through ideologies of racism and experiences of colonialism. Such factors may be reinforced by resentment of foreign workers for social and cultural reasons (for instance, hostility to Islam)" (Castles and Miller 2009, 239).

A young woman recounted her adjustment experience during the hostage crisis: "In high school, to escape anti-Iranian sentiments and abuse, I was hesitant to reveal my Iranian identity. When I entered the university, I changed my name." A hairstylist, with sadness in her voice, remembered the prejudiced attitude of one of her clients, who asked her where she was from, a question often asked of immigrants. When she responds, he quickly jumps up from his chair and angrily utters, "I will not allow an Iranian to touch my hair." Another woman who had emigrated at a young age complained, "even though I speak non-accented English, my last name and phenotype provoke curiosity; however, once people realize I am an Iranian, they view me differently and negatively." Some confessed that the negative perceptions have intensified after the tragic events of 9/11 and the anti-Muslim/anti–Middle Eastern sentiments. One complained,

> My daughter was in New York when the terrorists jammed the planes into the World Trade Center. Knowing that she worked close by, and unable to reach her by phone, I was in total shock and despair. More devastating was the collective disregard of my coworkers for what I was going through. Because I was an Iranian and a Muslim, I was made to feel responsible and unworthy of any sympathy.

Other participants also recalled incidents of mistreatment and believed they were denied educational and job opportunities because of their nationality; they felt that these experiences have made them defensive and insecure, and have negatively affected their choices. To escape the real and perceived discrimination in hiring and promotion, many Iranians, both men and women, have pursued alternative labor market strategies such as self-employment. These perceptions are partly reflective of the existing gender, class, religion, race, and ethnicity-based labor market discriminations, intensified for groups burdened by a combining set of these categories. To hold multiple identities of "woman," "Muslim," "Middle-Eastern," "immigrant," and "Iranian," some believed, triggers prejudicial encounters.

A "Family-Centered" Worldview

The Iranian women's gender role perceptions and thus the mode of their economic integration, similar to other immigrant groups (Zhou and Bankston 1998), are influenced by postmigration opportunities as well as by the migration-imposed economic necessities. The differential in gender opportunities in the home and the host countries, combined with the family's socioeconomic status, has produced various possibilities. However, Iranian women's labor market choices are partly rooted in their "family-centered" worldview, a characteristic that some scholars argue differentiates the American and immigrant life experiences (Jones-Correa 1998; Gabaccia 1994; Zlotnik 2000; Der-Martirosian 1996; Foner 1997; Kibria 1994; Rumbaut 1997b). Similarly, Bahramitash and Esfahani (this volume) contend that the family consideration has contributed to the low level of LFP of Iranian women in Iran as well as of women in other MENA countries.

The postmigration choices are tempered with the priority that Iranian women accord to the concept of family and the significance attached to its unity (*habastegiye khanevadeh*). Several participants of different ages, economic status, educational background, and labor force status expressed a sense of nostalgia for traditional gender roles, the consequent certainty of a division of labor, and perceived harmony and stability within the family. As we were having tea in her home, an educated housewife shared her resolve and commitment:

> Men are providers and women are managers of the household. This is the essence of a marriage partnership. This is how my parents conducted their lives. Each had an established and respected role, which resulted in peace and stability within the family.

Similarly, a professional woman declared,

In our culture, after a woman marries, her first and foremost priority becomes the family unit—keeping the marriage strong, and raising successful children—thus, any self-sacrifice toward this goal is expected and respected by the society. However, in Western culture, the emphasis is on individualism; thus, self-sacrifice, even by a wife and a mother, is viewed negatively and a sign of weakness; the women are viewed as naïve and even stupid.

A grandmother and a recent immigrant insisted,

> It is the woman's responsibility to create a peaceful home for her family. In the long run, she will be rewarded tremendously if she decides to stay home and take care of her family—to dress her children in the morning and send them to school with care and affection. The husband will be more encouraged and will be inclined to work even harder to support the family.

A professional woman who had invited me for our interview to her home on her day off summed up the family-centered worldview by stating,

> I believe women need to work for pay, even if it creates a double shift. It gives women a sense of worth, satisfaction, higher standard of living for the family, and most importantly a sense of freedom and security. Knowing that you can end a marriage and still feel financially secure can produce healthier spousal relations. But I strongly believe in a balanced approach; family unity must be at the center of all decisions.

Thus labor force participation, so heavily relied upon in migration literature as a yardstick of the immigrant women's socioeconomic success, may be a simplistic and even misleading indicator. Within a family-centered communal cultural framework, Iranian women immigrants themselves may *perceive* and *define* success differently.

Double Burden: Absence of Kinship Support

In one case study of Latin American immigrants, Michael Jones-Correa concludes,

> Within the context of the Latin American family, women's work is meant to be temporary, not an end in itself . . . Women generally work fewer hours, work less regularly, and get paid less for the work they do than men . . . In part, this is because women participation in the labor force does not relieve them of their traditional family responsibilities. (1998, 337)

Similarly, almost all the Iranian women who participated in this study, regardless of their labor force status, stated that they have most of the housework and childcare responsibilities. However, women with work experiences in both Iran and the United States noted that the postmigration loss of kinship relations and hired help had made their domestic roles more burdensome, lessened their educational and employment options, and further complicated their labor force participation. A professional woman commented,

> In Iran the women functioned within an existing familial and other social support; they shouldered the home responsibility with no worry about the rest. Sometimes I feel sorry for myself, I have to juggle everything and have nobody to help me.

The participants who benefited from the presence of an extended family commented that their pursuit of higher education or a career would have been all but impossible without the help of their kin.

Class Considerations

Because of the distance, lack of diplomatic relations between the United States and Iran, and the consequent expense, the selection bias has favored emigration of Iranians who are from upper- and middle-class backgrounds (noted in previous chapters by Bahramitash, Esfahani, and Olmsted). Although some families and individuals have recovered, maintained, or surpassed their premigration socioeconomic status through education, imported wealth, or entrepreneurship, many have not. These immigrant households have been forced to pull resources together and strategize for economic survival. One of the research questions that prompted this study was how class consideration has affected Iranian women immigrants' labor market outcomes. The result of this investigation—both the observation and the interviews—indicates that class considerations were often overlooked, especially during the initial years of settlement and adjustment.

After sharing interesting tales of a privileged lifestyle during the Shah's regime, a participant recounted the difficulties that her family had experienced in postrevolutionary Iran, the difficult journey out of the country, and the hardship that she and her family had endured during the first several years of their stay in the United States. She further confessed that the family's postmigration financial distress has pushed her into accepting low-status jobs in the United States:

> For many years we had a great life in Iran and the whole family benefited from my husband's high sociopolitical standing. [She cursed the revolution for disrupting her established life, but soon recovered from her remorse, smiled, and indicated that she feels lucky that she and her husband are alive, safe, and secure, and concluded her long migration and settlement story—which had brought many tears to her eyes—by stating]: What amazes me is that in Iran husbands' work and the income supported a large and extended family. Here, everyone is working and pitching in, yet no one feels financially secure.

However, the present study reveals that once the Iranian immigrant family overcomes the initial economic distress, class considerations become important criteria for the women's labor market choices and strategies. They leave jobs that do not correspond to their recovered family social status. A participant, although enjoying a very comfortable lifestyle, was resentful at being a "stay-home wife." She expressed her frustration:

> Because of all the postrevolutionary uncertainties and lack of educational opportunities for the children, I left a good life and a good job to come to the US. I took a secretarial job in the family business but left after a few years when the company was sold. Being out of the labor market for a long period of time, I don't have the qualifications for the types of jobs I wish to have.

Her dilemma, echoed by other participants, describes how class consideration has constrained labor force participation of some of the Iranian women. The initial or even continuing downward socioeconomic status often has been justified and accepted by Iranian immigrant women because (1) of the perceived lack of freedom and limited opportunities in postrevolutionary Iran; (2) it was assumed a consequence of the revolution, thus believed beyond one's control and temporary; and (3) it has been redeemed partly through membership and participation in various ethnic group and organizations.

Immigrant Strategy: A Gendered Response

Migration literature points to "gender-differentiated immigrant strategies" (Jones-Correa 1998, 336; Ferber and Nelson 1993; Espin 1999; Gabaccia 1994; Pedraza 1991). Husbands, some scholars contend, may feel threatened and worried about the loss of their traditional dominant roles:

> While men were more eager to return [to their native country], . . . women tended to postpone or avoid return because they realized it would entail their retirement from work and the loss of the newfound freedom . . . As a result, a struggle developed over . . . return that revolved around traditional definition of gender and privileges

which the migration itself had challenged and which many men sought to regain by returning home. (Espin 1999, 24)

Similarly, this investigation reveals that the Iranian community also has manifested a gender-differentiated response in forging strategies to overcome postmigration economic hardship. Several of the women interviewed had been housewives in Iran; thus, their status—typical of their generation and class—was tied to their husband's socioeconomic standing. The women, in order to maintain or recover some elements of the family's premigration socioeconomic status, sought outside employment, worked as unpaid labor in family businesses, or worked in the informal sector. Their husbands, unhappy about the loss of their status and unable to secure jobs comparable to the ones left behind, often resisted settlement. Those who stayed were reluctant to accept entry-level jobs. A young woman noted differences in her parents' attitude as she recalled her family's experience, an observation confirmed by other participants:

> My father resisted migration and settlement. He had left behind a good job and was not willing to begin at ground zero. He felt worthless and miserable about his lost identity, thus was restless and eager to return. However, my mom, who had quit her good job in Iran in favor of a very low-level job in the US, worked very hard to make sure we secured legal documentation and got settled. It was incomprehensible for me to see my mother give up a very comfortable life in Iran in order to live under miserable conditions in the US. Later, I realized that not only was she trying to provide better educational opportunity for her children, but she also wanted to be free from certain familial and societal constraints.

Moreover, researchers have noted that when women immigrants assume the role of the provider within their family, "there emerges a relationship that is deviant, unrealistic, one which presents a potential threat to male authority" (Kudat 1982, 298, quoted in Brettel and Simon 1986, 15). The wife, in these instances, carries a great physical and emotional burden. She not only becomes the breadwinner of the family, but "has to see that her husband does not really feel that this is so. This unrealistic and unstable relation seems to be associated with high divorce rate" (Kudat 1982, 298, quoted in Brettel and Simon 1986, 15).

The present investigation points to similar findings. To keep peace within the family, some of the women who either earned more or were the sole income earners stated that they have taken measures to mend their husband's lost sense of authority and autonomy. An exiled woman who had never worked prior to migration and had left a very comfortable lifestyle in Iran believed that although her job and income were necessary for her family's economic survival, she had to downplay her financial contribution and the reversed gender role.

Concluding Remarks

> There was a Door to which I found no Key,
> There was a Veil past which I might not see . . .
> —Omar Khayam, twelfth-century
> Persian poet

This chapter has focused on the Iranian women who have migrated and settled in the United States. These women, as noted previously, are mostly from the upper middle class, urban, highly educated, secular, and mostly postrevolution migrants. Their decision to emigrate was a response to a combination of economic, social, cultural, and political pressures and incentives partly generated by forces such as the revolution, the Iran-Iraq war, and domestic policies in Iran, past and present. The unique sociohistorical context of Iranians' migration and the corresponding contexts of their exit and reception have affected the process and the outcome of their socioeconomic integration. Most Iranian immigrants in the United States for a long time believed themselves to be temporary residents, sojourners ready to return home once conditions in Iran permitted the move. This belief has influenced their settlement decisions and their mode of incorporations.

However, the life stories of the participants reveal gender differences in migration experiences and perceptions. Faced with postmigration economic hardships, many families forged strategies to assure success. Some of the women crossed the traditional gender boundaries in order to secure jobs and help the family through the initial years of migration and settlement. Patriarchal gender relations had to give in to more conjugal relations for the sake of economic survival of the family. For some, the children's education became a unifying goal and provided a sense of purpose and an impetus for spousal cooperation and partnership. Nonetheless, at times, the blissful gender relation was temporary and ended once the initial economic distress was over. In some situations, women were under pressure to leave the paid employment and resume traditional gender roles. Although some accepted, others resisted and resented the changed gender attitudes, which have created marital discontent, conflict, or even disintegration.

Some households have been forced to pull resources together and strategize for economic survival. However, the study reveals that the Iranian migrant women often displayed more flexibility and willingness than their husbands to work at jobs that were considered below their premigration socioeconomic status. Some secured employment in the informal and secondary sectors. They justified the downfall in status as a necessary migration adjustment and pressed hard to keep the family together and the children in school. Few viewed this as an opportunity for economic independence and empowerment. Nevertheless, once the economic distress was overcome, class considerations resurfaced and gained prominence in the Iranian migrant women's labor market strategies. The women whose skill and education did not allow access to "good jobs," jobs within their premigration class standing, sometimes left the job market. However, the consequent loss of financial independence, some claim, has produced inequitable gender relations within their households.

The findings also reveal that the persistent negative context of reception has limited the Iranian women's opportunity and desire for cultural, social, and economic incorporation, and thus has adversely impacted their migration experiences and perceptions. Unrolling of the unwelcome mat was prompted by the hostage crisis and the consequent break in diplomatic relations between Iran and the United States, and further intensified by the tragic events of 9/11, as well as by the labeling of Iran as part of an "axis of evil" by President George W. Bush. As one participant complained, "We are all forever perceived guilty by wrongful association." The high incidence of self-employment among Iranian migrants, as well as the presence of formal and informal employment in ethnic enclaves, may point to a lack of opportunity and/or desire, and a strategy to escape hostile workplace environments. The low level of intermarriages, high coethnic friendship circles, and low level of English language adoption (indicators of sociocultural incorporation) among first-generation Iranian immigrants may also be owing to the negative perceptions of Iran and Iranians in the United States.

Last, I would like to suggest the following as a topic for future research. One of the main reasons given by the participants, substantiated by observation of the Iranian immigrant community at large, for migration and settlement in the United States is the expanded educational opportunities and better and more secure future for their children. Thus it is important to investigate whether the tremendous emotional and financial sacrifices of the first-generation Iranian immigrants have produced or will produce the intended results. The second-generation Iranian immigrants are brought up to value education. Because of their parents' relatively high socioeconomic status, most live in middle- and upper-income neighborhoods, and thus they are very likely to attend good schools. Furthermore, they are encouraged to be competitive, assertive, and "American." They speak non-accented English; many have American first names, and some have anglicized their last names. They identify themselves as "Americans" even though it may be a hyphenated version. They do not engage in a continuous comparison between "us" and "them" as their parents did, and are more willing and able to accept and operate within the host country's cultural frames of reference. In choosing friends, dating, marriage, jobs, and careers, they do not feel confined to the

Iranian immigrant community, and thus go beyond the walls of ethnicity and the ethnic community. Consequently, the second-generation Iranian immigrants are expected to travel a smoother path in the process of their integration—cultural, social and economic—and to emerge less emotionally bruised than their coethnic predecessors if the host society affords them the opportunity to integrate into the mainstream of the American society.

References ❈ *Index*

References

Abrahamian, E. 1982. *Iran Between Two Revolutions*. Princeton, NJ: Princeton Univ. Press.

Abu-Lughod, L. 1998. "Introduction: Feminist Longings and Postcolonial Conditions." In *Remaking Women: Feminism and Modernity in the Middle East*, 3–31. Princeton, NJ: Princeton Univ. Press.

Acemoglu, D., and J. A. Robinson. 2005. *Economic Origins of Dictatorship and Democracy*. Cambridge, UK: Cambridge Univ. Press.

Acemoglu, D., M. Golosov, and A. Tsyvinski. 2008. "Markets versus Governments." *Journal of Monetary Economics* 55 (1): 159–89.

Acemoglu, D., J. Simon, and R. James. 2001. "The Colonial Origins of Comparative Development: An Empirical Investigation." *American Economic Review* 91 (5): 1369–1401.

Adelkhah, F. 2000. *Being Modern in Iran*. New York: Columbia Univ. Press.

Adelkhah, F. 2004. *Being Modern in Iran*. Translated by Jonathan Derrick. Vancouver: British Columbia Univ. Press.

Afshar, H. 1996a. "Islam and Feminism: An Analysis of Political Strategies." In *Feminism and Islam*, edited by M. Yamani, 197–216. New York: New York Univ. Press.

———. 1996b. "Women and the Politics of Fundamentalism in Iran." In *Women and Politics in the Third World*, edited by H. Afshar, 121–41. London: Routledge.

———. 1997. "Women and Work in Iran." *Political Studies* 45 (4): 755–67.

Alizadeh, P. 2001. "The State and the Social Position of Women—Female Employment in Postrevolutionary Iran." In *The Economy of Iran: The Dilemmas of an Islamic State*, edited by P. Alizadeh, 261–87. London: I. B. Tauris.

Alizadeh, P., and B. Harper. 2003. "The Feminisation of the Labour Force in Iran." In *Iran Encountering Globalization: Problems and Prospects*, edited by A. Mohammadi, 180–96. New York: Routledge.

Amsden, A. 1985. "The State and Taiwan's Economic Development." In *Bringing the State Back*, edited by P. B. Evan, D. Rueschemeyer, and T. Skocpol. Cambridge, UK: Cambridge Univ. Press.

Amin, S. 1989. *Eurocentrism*. New York: Monthly Review Press.

Amine, C. M. 2002. *The Making of Iranian Women: Gender, State and Popular Culture, 1965–1945*. Gainesville: Univ. Press of Florida.

Amy, L. 1997. "Gender, Development and Urban Social Change: Women's Community Action in Global Cities." *World Development* 25 (8): 1205–23.

Anker, R. 1998. *Gender and Jobs: Sex Segregation of Occupations in the World*. Geneva: International Labour Office.

Anker, R., and M. Anker. 1995. "Measuring Female Labour Force with Emphasis on Egypt." In *Gender and Development in the Arab World: Women's Economic Participation: Patterns and Policies*, edited by N. Khoury and V. Moghadam, 148–76. London: Zed Books.

Anker, R., H. Melkas, and A. Korten. 2003. „Gender-Based Occupational Segregation in the 1990's." ILO Working Paper, Declaration/WP/16/2003. Geneva: International Labour Office.

Ansari, M. 1992. *The Making of the Iranian Community in America*. New York: Pardis Press.

Arman, A., and M. Mohammadi. 2005. "The Study of Factors that Effect on [sic] Iranian Hand-Woven Carpet Exports." *Economic Studies Quarterly* 6 (3): 38–52, Ahvaz, Iran: Chamran Univ.

Assaad, R. 2005. "Informalization and Defeminization: Explaining the Unusual Pattern in Egypt." In *Rethinking Informalization: Precarious Jobs, Poverty and Social Protection*, edited by N. Kudva and L. Benería. Ithaca, NY: Internet–First Univ. Press. Available at D-Space Repository at Cornell University. http://hdl.handle.net/1813/3716.

Assaad, R., and M. Arntz. 2005. "Constrained Geographical Mobility and Gendered Labor Market Outcomes under Structural Adjustment: Evidence from Egypt." *World Development* 33 (3): 431–54.

Assaad, R., and F. El-Hamidi. 2001. "Is All Work the Same? A Comparison of the Determinants of Female Participation and Hours of Work in Various Employment States in Egypt." In *The Economics of Women and Work in the Middle East and North Africa*, edited by E. M. Cinar, 117–50. Amsterdam: JAI.

Bahar, B. 1983. "A Historical Background to the Women's Movement in Iran." In *Women of Iran: The Conflict with Fundamentalism*, edited by F. Azari, 170–89. London: Ithaca Press.

Bahramitash, R. 2004. "Market Fundamentalism versus Religious Fundamentalism." *Critique: Journal of Middle Eastern Studies* 13 (1): 33–46.

———. 2005. *Liberation from Liberalization: Gender and Globalization in Southeast Asia*. London: Zed Books.

———. 2007a. "Female Employment and Globalization During Iran's Reform Era (1997–2005)." *Journal of Middle East Women's Studies* 3 (2): 56–86.

———. 2007b. "Family Planning, Islam and Women's Human Rights in Iran." *International Development Studies Journal* 4 (1): 33–50.

Bahramitash, R., and H. S. Esfahani. 2009. "Nimble Fingers No Longer! Women's Employment in Iran." In *Contemporary Iran*, edited by A. Gheissari. Oxford, UK: Oxford Univ. Press.

Barker K., and S. E. Feiner. 2004. *Liberating Economics: Feminist Perspectives on Families, Work, and Globalization*. Ann Arbor: Univ. of Michigan Press.

Beck, L., and N. Keddi. 1978. Women in the Muslim World. London: Harvard Univ. Press.

Behdad, S., and F. Nomani. 2006. *Class and Labor in Iran: Did the Revolution Matter?* Syracuse, NY: Syracuse Univ. Press.

Bell, S. 1995. "Privatization Through Broad-Based Ownership Strategies: A More Popular Option?" Working Paper No. 33. Washington, DC: World Bank.

Bellah, R. N. 1957. *Tokugawa Religion: The Values of Pre-Industrial Japan*. Glencoe, IL: Free Press.

Benería, L. 1992. "Accounting for Women's Work: The Progress of Two Decades." *World Development* 20:1547–60.

———. 1997. "Accounting for Women's Work: The Progress of Two Decades." In *Women, Gender, and Development Reader*, edited by N. Visvanathan, L. Duggan, L. Nisonoff, and N. Wiegersma, 112–18. London: Zed Books.

———. 1999a. "Globalization, Gender and the Davos Man." *Taylor and Francis Journals* 5 (3): 61–83.

---. 1999b. "The Enduring Debate over Unpaid Labour." *International Labour Review* 138 (3): 287–309.

---. 2003. *Gender, Development and Globalization: Economics as if All People Mattered*. New York: Routledge.

Benería, L., and A. Lind. 1995. "Engendering International Trade." In *A Commitment to the World's Women: Perspectives on Development for Beijing and Beyond*, edited by N. Heyzer. New York: UNIFEM.

Benería, L., and M. Roldan. 1987. *The Crossroads of Class and Gender: Homework, Subcontracting and Household Dynamics in Mexico City*. Chicago: Univ. of Chicago Press.

Benería, L., and G. Sen. 1981. "Accumulation, Reproduction and Women's Role in Economic Development: Boserup Revisited." *Journal of Women in Culture and Society* 7:279–96.

Benería, L., M. Floro, C. Grown, and M. MacDonald. 2000. "Globalization and Gender." *Feminist Economics* 6 (3): vii–xviii

Bennholdt-Thomsen, V., and M. Mies. 1988. *The Subsistence Perspective*. London: Zed Books.

Berik, G. 1987. *Women Carpet Weavers in Rural Turkey: Pattern of Employment, Earning and Status*. Geneva: International Labour Office.

---. 1999. "Globalization." In *The Elgar Companion to Feminist Economics*, edited by J. Peterson and M. Lewis, 402–10. Cheltenham, UK: Edward Elgar.

Bhagwati, J. N., and P. Desai. 1970. *India: Planning for Industrialization*. London: Oxford Univ. Press, for the OECD.

Blau, F. D., and Marianne Ferber. 1986. *The Economics of Women, Men, and Work*. Englewood Cliffs, NJ: Prentice-Hall.

Borjas, G. J. 1988. *International Differences in the Labor Market Performances of Immigrants*. Kalamazoo, MI: W. E. Upjohn Institute for Employment Research.

Boserup, E. 1970. *Women's Role in Economic Development*. New York: St. Martin's Press.

Bozorgmehr, M. 1996. "Iranians." In *Refugees in America in the 1990s*, edited by D. W. Haines, 213–31. Westport, CT: Greenwood Press.

---. 1998. "From Iranian Studies to Iranians in the United States." *Iranian Studies*, no. 31:3–30.

Bozorgmehr, M., and G. Sabagh. 1988. "High Status Immigrants: A Statistical Profile of Iranians in the United States." *Iranian Studies* 21 (3–4): 4–34.

Brettel, C., and R. J. Simon. 1986. "Immigrant Women: An Introduction." In *International Migration*, edited by R. Simon and C. Brettel, 3–20. Totowa, NJ: Rowman and Allanheld.

Browning, M. 1992. "Children and Household Economic Behavior." *Journal of Economic Literature* 30 (3): 1434–75.

Buckman, G. 2004. *Globalization: Tame It or Scrap It?* London: Zed Books.

Bullock, S. 1994. *Women and Work*. London: Zed Books.

Burnell, B. 1999. "Occupational Segregation." In *The Elgar Companion to Feminist Economics*, edited by J. Peterson and M. Lewis, 578–83. Northampton, MA: Edward Elgar.

Buvinic, M. 1990. "The Vulnerability of Women-Headed Households: Policy Questions and Options for Latin America and the Caribbean." Paper presented at the Economic Commission for Latin America and the Caribbean Meeting on "Vulnerable Women," Nov. 26–30, Vienna.

Buvinic, M., and G. R. Gupta. 1997. "Female-Headed Households and Female-Maintained Families: Are They Worth Targeting to Reduce Poverty in Developing Countries?" *Economic Development and Cultural Change* 45 (2): 259–80.

Çagatay, N., D. Elson, and C. Grown. 1995. "Introduction. Special Issue on Gender, Adjustment and Macroeconomics." *World Development* 23 (11): 1827–26.

Carrington, W., and E. Detragiache. 1998. "How Big Is the Brain Drain?" IMF Working Paper 98/102 (Washington). http://www.imf.org/external/pubs/ft/wp/wp98102.pdf.

Castells, M., and A. Portes. 1989. "World Underneath: The Origins, Dynamics, and Effects of the Informal Economy." In *The Informal Economy: Studies in Advanced and Less Advanced Developed Countries*, edited by A. Portes, M. Castells, and L. A. Benton, 11–40. Baltimore: Johns Hopkins Univ. Press.

Castles, S., and M. J. Miller. 2009. *The Age of Migration: International Population Movements in the Modern World*. New York: Guilford Press.

Chan, A. 2003. "A Race to the Bottom: Globalization and China's Labour Standards." *China Perspectives* 46:41–49.

Chant, S. 1997. *Women-Headed Households: Diversity and Dynamics in the Developing World*. London: MacMillan Press.

———. 2003. "Female Household Headship and the Feminization of Poverty: Facts, Fictions and Forwarded Strategies." Working Paper Series,

Issue 9. London: London School of Economics, Gender Institute. http://personal.lse.ac.uk/chant/default.htm, accessed Sept. 2008.

Chen, M. 2001. "Women in the Informal Sector: A Global Picture, the Global Movement." *SAIS Review* 21:71–82.

Chen, M., J. Vanek, and M. Carr. 2004. *Mainstreaming Informal Employment and Gender in Poverty Reduction: A Handbook for Policy-Makers and Other Stakeholders.* London: Commonwealth Secretariat/IDRC 2004.

Chiswick, B. R. 1978a. "The Effect of Americanization on the Earnings of Foreign-Born Men." *Journal of Political Economy* 86 (5): 897–921.

———. 1978b. "The Earnings of Immigrants and Their Sons." *Challenge,* May–June, 55–60.

Cuno, K. M. 1999. "A Tale of Two Villages: Family, Property, and Economic Activity in Rural Egypt in the 1840s." In *Agriculture in Egypt from Pharaonic to Modern Times,* edited by A. K. Bowman and E. Rogan, 301–29. Oxford, UK: Oxford Univ. Press.

De Cordier, B. 2007. "Shiite Aid Organizations in Tajikistan." *ISIM Review* 19 (Spring): 10–11.

De Soto, H. 1989. *The Other Path.* Translated by June Abbott. New York: Harper and Row.

Deeb, L. 2006. *An Enchanted Modern: Gender and Public Piety in Shi'i Lebanon.* Princeton, NJ: Princeton Univ. Press.

Der-Martirosian, C. 1996. "Economic Embeddedness and Social Capital of Immigrants: Iranians in Los Angeles." PhD diss., Univ. of California, Los Angeles.

Dignard, L., and J. Havet, eds. 1995. *Women in Micro- and Small-Scale Enterprise Development.* Boulder, CO: Westview Press.

Easterly, W. 2001. *The Elusive Quest for Growth: Economists' Adventures and Misadventures in the Tropics.* Cambridge, MA: MIT Press.

———. 2006. *The White Man's Burden: Why the West's Efforts to Aid the Rest Have Done So Much Ill and So Little Good.* New York: Penguin Press.

Eilland, M. 1998. *New Directions for Iranian Carpets.* London: Calmann and King.

Elson, D. 1993. "Gender Aware Analysis and Development Economics." *Journal of International Development* 5 (2): 176–90.

———. 1995. "Gender Awareness in Modeling Structural Adjustment." *World Development* 23 (11): 1851–68.

Enchautegui, M. E., and J. M. Nolan. 1997. "Female Immigrants: A Socioeconomic Portrait." *Migration World Magazine* 25 (4): 18–23.

Escobar, A. 1995. *Encountering Development: The Making and Unmaking of the Third World.* Princeton, NJ: Princeton Univ. Press.

Esfahani, H. S. 2006. "Alternative Public Service Delivery Mechanisms in Iran." *Quarterly Review of Economics and Finance* 45 (2–3): 479–525.

Esfahani, H. S., and M. H. Pesaran. 2009. "The Iranian Economy in the Twentieth Century: A Global Perspective." *Iranian Studies* 42 (2): 177–211.

Espin, O. M. 1999. *Women Crossing Boundaries: A Psychology of Immigration and Transformations of Sexuality.* New York: Routledge.

Fallaci, O. 1976. *Interview with History.* New York: Liveright.

Fazel, G. R. 1977. "Social and Political Status of Women among Pastoral Nomads: The Boyr Ahmad of Southwest Iran." *Anthropological Quarterly* 50 (2): 77–89.

Feige, E. L. 1990. "Defining and Estimating Underground and Informal Economies: The New Institutional Economics Approach." *World Development* 8 (7): 989–1002.

Ferber, M. A., and J. Nelson. 1993. *Beyond Economic Man: Feminist Theory and Economics.* Chicago: Univ. of Chicago Press.

Foner, N. 1997. "The Immigrant Family: Cultural Legacies and Cultural Changes." *International Migration Review* 32 (1): 961-75.

Foran, J. 1989. "The Concept of Dependent Development as a Key to the Political Economy of Qajar Iran (1800–1925)." *Iranian Studies* 22 (2): 5–56.

Frank, A. G. 1967. *Capitalism and Underdevelopment in Latin America.* New York: Monthly Review Press.

Friedl, E. 1997. *Children of Deh Koh: Young Life in an Iranian Village.* Syracuse, NY: Syracuse Univ. Press.

Gabaccia, D. 1994. *From the Other Side: Women, Gender, and Immigrant Life in the U.S., 1820–1990.* Indianapolis: Indiana Univ. Press.

Gallaway, J., and A. Bernasek. 2002. "Gender and Informal Sector Employment in Indonesia." *Journal of Economic Issues* 36 (2).

German, L. 1996. "Do Women Want to Stay at Home?" *Socialist Review,* no. 198 (June).

Goldin, C. 1990. *Understanding the Gender Gap: An Economic History of American Women.* New York: Oxford Univ. Press.

———. 1994. "The U-Shaped Female Labour Force Function in Economic Development and Economic History." Working Paper No. 4707, National Bureau of Economic Research. http://www.nber.org/papers/w4707.pdf, accessed June 2008.

Gran, J. 1977. "Impact of the World Market on Egyptian Women." *MERIP Reports* 58 (June): 3–4.

Hakim, C. 2000. *Research Design: Successful Designs for Social and Economic Research*. London: Routledge.

———. 2003. "Competing Family Models: Competing Social Policies." *Family Matters* 64 (Autumn): 52–61.

———. 2006. *Work-Lifestyle Choices in the 21st Century: Preference Theory*. Oxford, UK: Oxford Univ. Press.

Hakimian, H. 2006. "From Demographic Transition to Fertility Boom and Bust: Iran in the 1980s and 1990s." *Development and Change* 37 (3): 571–97.

Halliday, F. 1979. *Iran: Dictatorship and Development*. London: Penguin.

Halper, L. 2005. "Law and Women's Agency in Post-Revolutionary Iran." *Harvard Journal of Law and Gender* 28 (1): 85–141.

Hamshahri. 2005. 24 Apr., sec. 26.

Hart, K. 1998. "Informal Economy." In *The New Palgrave: A Dictionary of Economics*, edited by J. Eatwell et al., 2:845–46. Houndmills, UK: Palgrave Macmillan.

———. 1990. "The Idea of Economy: Six Modern Dissenters." In *Beyond the Marketplace: Rethinking Economy and Society*, edited by R. Friedland and A. F. Robertson, 137–60. New York: Aldine de Gruyter.

Hasso, F. S. 2005. "Problems and Promise in Middle East and North Africa Gender Research." *Feminist Studies* 31 (3): 653–79.

Hatem, M. 1994. "Privatization and the Demise of State Feminism in Egypt." In *Mortgaging Women's Lives: Feminist Critiques of Structural Adjustment*, edited by P. Sparr. London: Zed Books.

Hatton, T. J., and J. G. Williamson. 2005. *Global Migration and the World Economy*. Cambridge, MA: MIT Press.

Hondagneu-Sotelo, P. 1994. *Gendered Transitions: Mexican Experiences of Immigration*. Berkeley: Univ. of California Press.

Hoodfar, H. 1999. "The Women's Movement in Iran at the Crossroad of Seclusion and Islamisation." In *Women Living Under Muslim Law*.

The Women's Movement(s) Series, no. 1 (Winter): 112–24. Montpellier, France: Women Living Under Muslim Law.

Hoodfar H., and S. Assadpour. 2000. "Where Religion Is No Obstacle: The Politics of Making a Successful Population Policy in the Islamic Republic of Iran." *Studies in Family Planning* 31 (1): 1–17.

Hulme, D., and P. Mosley. 1996. *Finance Against Poverty*. London: Routledge.

ILO LABORSTA. *Database on Labour Statistics*. http://laborsta.ilo.org/.

ILO (International Labor Organization). *Key Indicators of the Labour Market Programme*. http://www.ilo.org/public/english/employment/strat/kilm/download.htm.

———. 1967, 1971, 1982, and 1992. *Yearbook of Labour Statistics*. Geneva: ILO.

———. 2002. *Decent Work and the Informal Economy*. Geneva: ILO.

Immigration Act of 1965. 1965. H.R. 2580; Pub.L. 89-236; 79 Stat. 911.

Inkeles, A. 1964. *What Is Sociology? An Introduction to the Discipline and Profession*. Englewood Cliffs, NJ: Prentice Hall.

International Organization for Migration, 2005. *World Migration 2005: Costs and Benefits of International Migration*. Geneva: International Organization for Migration.

Iran Carpet Company. 2006. "Iran's Carpets and Flooring." http://www.irancarpet.ir, accessed 2007.

Iran Central Bank (different years). *Economic Report*. Tehran: Iran Central Bank.

Iran Chamber of Commerce. 2006. "Demand Dips for the Fine Rugs." http://www.iccim.ir, accessed 2006.

Jahad. 1362. "Carpet Weavers in Turkman Sahra." Tehran, *Reports of Jahad-e Sazandegui*, no. 56:38–46. In Persian.

Joekes, S. 1987. *Women in the World Economy: An INSTRAW Study*. New York: Oxford Univ. Press.

Jolly, S., and H. Reeves. 2005. *Gender and Migration: Overview Report*. Cutting Edge Pack Series. London: Institute of Development Studies.

Jomeh Poour, M. 2003. *Mashaghe gere rasmi be onvaneh ney masaleh shahry va abad ejtemai va eghtesady an: baresi moredy dar poul sayyd khandan* (Looking at the Informal Sector as an Urban Socio-Economic Problem: The Case of Sayyd Khadan). Tehran: Fasnameh Olome Ejtemai (Allmeh Tabbatano Univ. Quarterly).

Jones-Correa, M. 1998. "Different Paths: Gender, Immigration and Political Participation." *International Migration Review* 32 (2): 326–39.

Josef, S. 1996. "Gender and Family in the Arab World." In *Arab Women: Between Defiance and Restraint*, edited by S. Sabbagh, 194–202. New York: Olive Branch Press.

Kabeer, N. 1991. "Gender Dimensions of Rural Poverty: Analysis from Bangladesh." *Journal of Peasant Studies* 18 (2): 241–62.

———. 1994. *Reversed Realities: Gender Hierarchies in Development Thought*. London: Verso.

———. 2001. *Bangladeshi Women Workers and Labour Market Decisions: The Power to Choose*. London: Verso.

Kabeer, N., and S. Mahmud. 2003. "Globalization, Gender and Poverty: Bangladeshi Women Workers in Export and Local Markets." *Journal of International Development* 16 (1): 92–109.

Karshenas, M. 2001. "Economic Liberalization, Competitiveness, and Women's Employment in the Middle East and North Africa." In *Labour and Human Capital in the Middle East*, edited by D. Salehi-Isfahani, 92–147. Reading, UK: Ithaca Press.

Karshenas, M., and V. Moghadam. 2001. "Female Labor Force Participation and Economic Adjustment in the MENA region." In *The Economics of Women and Work in the Middle East and North Africa*, edited by E. M. Cinar, 51–74. New York: JAI Press.

Kazemipour, S. 2007. *Ezdeag and Talagh Javanan Keshvar 1385*. Tehran: Regional Centre for Population Studies and Research on Asian and the Pacific. In Persian.

Kennedy, E. 1994. "Development Policy, Gender of Head of Household, and Nutrition." In *Poverty and Well-Being in the Household: Case Studies of the Developing World*, edited by E. Kennedy and M. González de la Rocha, 25–42. San Diego: Center for Iberian and Latin American Studies, Univ. of California.

Khalatbari, F. 1994. "Eqtesade zirzamini" (The Underground Economy). *Majalleh Ronaq* 1373, 1, no. 1:5–11 and no. 2:11–18.

Kian, A. 1995. "Gendered Occupation and Women's Status in Post-Revolutionary Iran." *Middle Eastern Studies* 31 (3): 407–21.

———. 1997. "Women and Politics in Post-Islamist Iran: The Gender Conscious Drive to Change." *British Journal of Middle Eastern Studies* 24 (1): 75–96.

Kian-Thiebaut, A. 2008. "From Motherhood to Equal Rights Advocate: The Weakening of Patriarchal Order." In *Iran in the 21st Century, Politics, Economics and Conflict,* edited by H. Katouzian and H. Shahidi, 86–106. London: Routledge.

Kibria, N. 1994. "Household Structure and Family Ideologies: The Dynamics of Immigrant Economic Adaptation among Vietnamese." *Social Problems* 41 (1): 81–96.

Lal, D. 1983. *The Poverty of "Development Economics."* London: Institute of Economic Affairs.

Lewis, A. 1954. "Economic Development with Unlimited Supplies Labour." *Manchester School of Economic and Social Studies* 22:139–91.

Lewis, R., and S. Mills, eds. 2003. *Feminist Postcolonial Theory: A Reader.* Edinburgh: Edinburgh Univ. Press.

Little, I. M. D. 1982. *Economic Development: Theory, Policy and International Relations.* New York: Basic Books.

———. 1988. "The Experience and Causes of Rapid Labour-Intensive Development in Korea, Taiwan Province, Hong Kong, and Singapore and the Possibilities of Emulation in Export-Led Industrialization." In *Export-Led Industrialization and Development,* edited by E. Lee. Singapore: Koon Wah.

Losby, J., J. F. Else, M. E. Kingslow, E. L. Edgcomb, E. T. Malm, and V. Kao. 2002. "Informal Economy Literature Review." Washington, DC: Aspen Institute. http://www.ised.us/doc/Informal%20Economy%20Lit%20Review.pdf, accessed Sept. 2008.

Loutfi, M. F. 2001. *Women, Gender and Work.* Geneva: International Labor Office.

Malek, M. 1991. "The Impact of Iran's Islamic Revolution on Health Personnel Policy." *World Development* 19 (8): 1045–54.

Marossi, A. 2006. "Iran Is Knocking at the World Trade Organization Door: Iran's Economy and the World Economy—Challenges and Opportunities." *Journal of World Trade* 40 (1): 167–85.

Massey, D. 1999. "Why Does Immigration Occur? A Theoretical Synthesis." In *The Handbook of International Migration,* edited by C. Hirschman, P. Kasinitz, and J. DeWind, 34–52. New York: Russell Sage Foundation.

McClelland, D. C. 1964. "Business Drive and National Achievement." In *Social Change: Sources, Patterns, and Consequences,* edited by A. Etzioni and E. Etzioni, 275–90. New York: Basic Books.

Mehran, G. 2003a. "The Paradox of Tradition and Modernity in Female Education in the Islamic Republic of Iran." *Comparative Education Review* 4 (3): 269–86.

———. 2003b. "Khatami, Political Reform and Education in Iran." *Comparative Education* 39 (3): 311–29.

Mehryar, A., G. Farjadi, and M. Tabibian. 2004. "Women in Iran from 1800 to the Islamic Republic." In *Women in Iran,* edited by L. Beck and G. Nashat, 182–203. Chicago: Univ. of Illinois Press.

Meriwether, M. E. 1994. "Women and Economic Change in Nineteenth-Century Syria: The Case of Aleppo." In *Arab Women: Old Boundaries, New Frontiers,* edited by J. E. Tucker, 65–83. Bloomington: Indiana Univ. Press.

Minh-Ha, T. 1989. *Women, Native, Other.* Indianapolis: Indiana Univ. Press.

Mir-Hosseini, Z. 1999. *Islam and Gender: The Religious Debate in Contemporary Iran.* Princeton, NJ: Princeton Univ. Press.

Moallem, M. 2005. *Between Warrior Brother and Veiled Sister: Islamic Fundamentalism and the Politics of Patriarchy in Iran.* Berkeley: Univ. of California Press.

Modarres, Ali. 1998. "Settlement Pattern of Iranians in the United States." *Iranian Studies* 31 (1): 31–50.

Moghadam, F. E. 1985. "An Evaluation of the Productive Performance of Agribusinesses: An Iranian Case Study." *Economic Development and Cultural Change* 33 (4): 755–76.

———. 1994. "Commoditization of Sexuality and Female Labor Participation in Islam: Implications for Iran, 1960–90." In *In the Eye of the Storm,* edited by M. Afkhami and E. Friedl. Syracuse, NY: Syracuse Univ. Press.

———. 2004. "Women and Labour in the Islamic Republic of Iran." In *Women in Iran,* edited by L. Beck and G. Nashat, 136–81. Chicago: Univ. of Illinois Press.

———. 2007. "Women, Gender and Informal Sector: Iran." In *Encyclopedia of Women and Islamic Cultures.* Leiden: Brill Academic Publishers.

Moghadam, V. 1988. "Women, Work, and Ideology in the Islamic Republic." *International Journal of Middle East Studies* 20 (2): 221–43.

———. 1995a. "Women's Employment Issues in Contemporary Iran: Problems and Prospects in the 1990s." *Iranian Studies* 28 (3–4): 175–202.

———. 1995b. "The Political Economy of Female Employment in the Arab World." In *Gender and Development in the Arab World: Women's Economic Participation: Patterns and Policies*, edited by N. Khoury and V. Moghadam, 6–34. London: Zed Books.

———. 2002. "The Two Faces of Iran: Women's Activism, the Reform Movement, and the Islamic Republic." In *Nothing Sacred: Women Respond to Religious Fundamentalism and Terror*, edited by B. Reed, 91–104. New York: Thunder Mouth Press/Nation Books.

———. 2003. *Modernizing Women: Gender and Social Change in the Middle East*. Boulder, CO: Lynne Rienner.

———. 2005. "Women's Livelihood and Entitlements in the Middle East: What Difference Has the Neoliberal Policy Turn Made?" *Journal of Middle East Women's Studies* 1 (1): A110–146.

Moghissi, H. 1996. "Populism and Feminism in Iran: Women Struggle in Male-Defined Revolution Movement." *Middle East Journal*. Bloomington: Indiana Univ. Press.

Mohanty, C. T. 2003. *Feminist Without Borders: Decolonizing Theory, Practicing Solidarity*. Durham, NC: Duke Univ. Press.

Mohseni, M. 2000. *Study of Awareness, Attitudes, and Socio-Cultural Behavior in Iran*. Tehran: Secretariat of Public Culture of Iran. In Persian.

Morgan, R. 1984. *Sisterhood Is Global: The International Women's Movement Anthology*. New York: Anchor Press.

Morgan, S. P. 2003. "Is Low Fertility a Twenty-First-Century Demographic Crisis?" *Demography* 40 (4): 589–603.

Moser, C. 1989. "The Impact of Recession and Adjustment at the Micro Level: Low Income Women and Their Households in Guayaguil, Ecuador." *The Invisible Adjustment: Poor Women and the Economic Crisis*. New York: UNICEF.

Moslem, M. 2002. *Factional Politics in Post-Khomeini Iran*. Syracuse, NY: Syracuse Univ. Press.

Najmabadi, A. 1987. *Land Reform and Social Change in Iran*. Salt Lake City: Univ. of Utah Press.

———. 1998. "Feminism in an Islamic Republic: Years of Hardship, Years of Growth." In *Islam, Gender, and Social Change*, edited by Y. Haddad and J. Esposito. New York: Oxford Univ. Press.

National Iranian Carpet Center. 2005. "Production and Employment in Hand Woven Carpet Industry in Iran." http://persiancarpetnc.ir/en/default.aspx.

Nomani, F., and S. Behdad. 2006. *Class and Labor in Iran: Did the Revolution Matter?* Syracuse, NY: Syracuse Univ. Press.

North, D. 1990. *Institutions, Institutional Change and Economic Performance.* Cambridge, UK: Cambridge Univ. Press.

Olmsted, J. C. 1996. "Women 'Manufacture' Economic Spaces in Bethlehem." *World Development* 24 (12): 1829–40.

———. 2001. "Men's Work/Women's Work: Employment, Wages and Occupational Segregation in Bethlehem." In *The Economics of Women and Work in the Middle East and North Africa*, edited by E. M. Cinar, 151–74. Vol. 4 of *Research in Middle East Economics*. Amsterdam: JAI/Elsevier.

———. 2003. "Reexamining the Fertility Puzzle in the Middle East and North Africa." In *Women and Globalization in the Arab Middle East: Gender, Economy and Society*, edited by E. Doumato and M. P. Posusney, 73–92. Boulder, CO: Lynne Rienner.

———. 2004. "Orientalism and Economic Methods: (R)reading Feminist Economic Discussions of Islam." In *Postcolonialism Meets Economics*, edited by E. O. Zein-Elabdin and S. Chrusheela, 165–82. London: Routledge Press.

———. 2007. "'Globalization' Denied: Gender and Poverty in Iraq and Palestine." In *The Wages of Empire: Neoliberal Policies, Armed Repression, and Women's Poverty*, edited by A. Cabezas, E. Reese, and M. Waller. Boulder, CO: Paradigm.

———. 2008. "Post-Oslo Palestinian (Un)Employment: A Gender, Class, and Age Cohort Analysis." *Economics of Peace and Security Journal* 3 (2).

Paidar, P. 1995. *Women and the Political Process in Twentieth Century Iran.* Cambridge, UK: Cambridge Univ. Press.

Palmer, I. 1991. *Gender and Population in the Adjustment of African Economies: Planning for Change.* Geneva: ILO.

———. 1992. "Gender, Equity and Economic Efficiency in Adjustment Models." In *Women and Adjustment Policies in the Third-World*, edited by H. Afshar and C. Dennis, 69–83. London: Macmillan.

Pedraza, S. 1991. "Women and Migration: The Social Consequences of Gender." *Annual Review of Sociology* 17:303–25.

Pesaran, M. H. 2001. "Economic Trends and Macroeconomic Policies in Post-Revolutionary Iran." In *The Economy of Iran: Dilemmas of an Islamic State*, edited by P. Alizadeh, 63–99. London: I. B. Tauris.

Pitt, M., and S. R. Khandker. 1998. "The Impact of Group Based Credit Programs on Poor Households in Bangladesh: Does the Gender of Participants Matter?" *Journal of Political Economy* 106 (5): 958–96.

Portes, A. 1994. "The Informal Economy and Its Paradoxes." In *The Handbook of Economic Sociology*, edited by N. J. Smelser and R. Swedberg, 426–49. Princeton, NJ: Princeton Univ. Press.

Portes, A., and R. G. Rumbaut. 1996. *Immigrant America: A Portrait*. Berkeley: Univ. of California Press.

Poya, M. 1999. *Women, Work and Islamism*. London: Zed Books.

Ragui. A., and F. El Hamidi. 2001. Is All Work the Same? A Comparison of the Determinants of Female Participation and Hours of Work in Various Employment States in Egypt. In *The Economics of Women and Work in the Middle East and North Africa*, 117–50. Amsterdam: JAI.

Rahman, A. 1999. *Women and Microcredit in Rural Bangladesh: An Anthropological Study of Grameen Bank Lending*. Boulder, CO: Westview Press.

Raijman, R., and M. Tienda. 1999. "Immigrants' Socioeconomic Progress Post-1965: Forging Mobility or Survival." In *The Handbook of International Migration*, edited by C. Hirschman, P. Kasinitz, and J. DeWind, 239–58. New York: Russell Sage Foundation.

Rashidian, K. 1988. *A Survey on Carpet-Weaving in Kashan's Rural Areas*. Tehran: Tehran Univ. Press.

Ravandi, M. 1978. "Tarikh Ejtema'i Iran." *Social History of Iran* 3. Tehran.

Renâni, M. G. 2001. "Sâkhtâre Eshteghâl dar Bakhshe ghire Rasmi va naqshe on dar jazbe Niruye Ensânye Motakhasses" (Structure of Employment in the Informal Sector and Its Impact on Attracting Skilled Labor Force). Unpublished report. Tehran: Moasseseh Pazhuhesh va Barnâmeh Rizye Amuzeshe Âli, Vezârate Olum, Tahqiqat va Fanâvari (Institute of Research and Planning for Higher Education, Ministry of Higher Education, Research and Training).

Rodrik, D. 1999. "Where Did All the Growth Go? External Shocks, Social Conflict, and Growth Collapses." *Journal of Economic Growth* 4 (4): 385–412.

———. *Has Globalization Gone Too Far?* Washington, DC: Institute for International Economics.

———. 2008. *One Economics, Many Recipes: Globalization, Institutions, and Economic Growth*. Princeton, NJ: Princeton Univ. Press.

———. "The New Development Economics: We Shall Experiment, But How Shall We Learn?" In *What Works in Development? Thinking Big vs. Thinking Small*, edited by J. Cohen and W. Easterly. Washington, DC: Brookings Institution Press.

Rostami-Povey, E. 2001. "Feminist Contestations of Institutional Domains in Iran." *Feminist Review* 69 (Winter): 44–72.

———. 2005. "Trade Unions and Women's NGOs, Diverse Civil Society Organisations in Iran." In *Development NGOs and Labour Unions, Terms of Engagement*, edited by D. Eade and A. Leather, 303–20. Sterling, VA: Kumarian Press.

Roudi-Fahimi, F. 1999. "Iran's Revolutionary Approach to Family Planning." *Population Today* 27 (7): 4–5. Population Reference Bureau. http://www.prb.org/Content/NavigationMenu/PRB/AboutPRB/Population_Today1/july_aug99_pt.pdf.

———. 2002. "Iran's Family Planning Program: Responding to a Nation's Needs." Population Reference Bureau. http://www.prb.org/pdf/IransFamPlanProg_Eng.pdf.

Rubin, M., and P. Clawson. 2005. *Eternal Iran: Continuity and Chaos*. Basingstoke, UK: Palgrave Macmillan.

Rumbaut, R. G. 1997a. "Ties That Bind: Immigration and Immigrant Families in the United States." In *Immigration and the Family: Research and Policy on U.S. Immigrants*, edited by A. Booth, A. C. Crouter, and N. Landale, 3–46. Mahwah, NJ: Lawrence Erlbaum Associates.

———. 1997b. "Assimilation and Its Discontent: Between Rhetoric and Reality." *International Migration Review* 31 (4): 923–60.

Salehi-Isfahani, D. 2001. "Fertility, Education, and Household Resources in Iran, 1987–1992." In *The Economics of Women and Work in the Middle East and North Africa*, edited by E. M. Cinar, 311–38. Vol. 4 of *Research in Middle East Economics*. Amsterdam: JAI Press.

———. 2005a. "Human Resources in Iran: Potentials and Challenges." *Iranian Studies* 38 (1): 117–47.

———. 2005b. "Labor Force Participation of Women in Iran: 1987–2001." Unpublished manuscript. Blacksburg: Department of Economics, Virginia Tech.

Salehi-Isfahani, D., and M. Marku. 2006. "Women and Market Work in Iran: A Cohort Approach." Unpublished manuscript. Blacksburg: Department of Economics, Virginia Tech.

Sanasarian, E. 1982. *The Women's Rights Movement in Iran: Mutiny, Appeasement, and Repression from 1900 to Khomeini*. New York: Praeger.

Sassen, S. 1991. *The Global City: New York, London, and Tokyo*. Princeton, NJ: Princeton Univ. Press.

———. 2004. "Global Cities and Survival Circuits." In *Global Women: Nannies, Maids, and Sex Workers in the New Economy*, edited by B. Ehrenreich and A. R. Hochschild, 254–74. New York: Owl Books.

Schoeni, R. F. 1998. "Labor Market Outcomes of Immigrant Women in the United States: 1970 to 1990." *International Migration Review* 1:57–77.

Sekhavati, M. 2004. "Women's Poverty in Iran." *Defenders' Newsletter*. http://www.wunrn.com.

Sen, G. 1987. *Development, Crises, and Alternative Vision: Third World Women's Perspectives*. New York: Monthly Review Press.

Seyf, A. 2001. "Iranian Textile Handicraft in the Nineteenth Century: A Note." *Middle Eastern Studies* 37 (3): 49–58.

Shakhatreh, H. 1995. "Determinants of Female Labour-Force Participation in Jordan." In *Gender and Development in the Arab World: Women's Economic Participation: Patterns and Policies*, edited by N. F. Khoury and V. M. Moghadam. New York: St. Martin's Press.

Shariati, A. *Fatima Is Fatima*. N.d. Tehran: The Shariati Foundation Tehran—The Islamic Republic of Iran. http://onlinebooks.library.upenn.edu/webbin/book//lookupname?key=Shariati%2C%20Ali, accessed 2010.

Shekarloo, M. 2005. "Iranian Women Take on the Constitution." In *Middle East Report*, July 21. http://merip.org/mero/mero072105.html.

Shiva, V. 1991. *Stolen Harvest: The Hijacking of the Global Food Supply*. Cambridge, MA: South End Press.

Singerman, D., and H. Hoodfar, eds. 1996. *Development, Change, and Gender in Cairo: A View from the Household*. Bloomington: Indiana Univ. Press.

Skocpol, T. 1985. "Bringing the State Back In: Strategies of Analysis in Current Research." In *Bringing the State Back*, edited by P. B. Evan,

D. Rueschmeyer, and T. Skocpol, 33–37. Cambridge, UK: Cambridge Univ. Press.

Social Research Institute. 1967. *Iran's Hand-Woven Carpet Industry in Kerman Province*. Tehran: Tehran Univ. Press.

Spivak, G. C. 1999. *A Critique of Postcolonial Reason: Toward a History of the Vanishing Present*. Cambridge, MA: Harvard Univ. Press.

Standing, G. 1989. "Gender Equity and Globalization: Macroeconomic Policy for Developing Countries." *World Development* 17 (7): 1077–95.

Standing, G. 1999. *Global Labor Market Flexibility: Seeking Redistribute Justice*. New York: St. Martin's Press.

Statistical Center of Iran (Markaz-e Amar-e Iran). 1977. *Detailed Report of 1976 Census*. Tehran: Iran Statistics Center.

———. 1990. "Salnameh Amary-e Keshvar" (Annual Statistical Yearbook). Tehran: Markaz- Amar-e.

———. 1992. *Preliminary Results of 1991 Population Survey*. Tehran: Markaz- Amar-e.

———. 1997. *Sarshomary-e Omoomy-e Nofus va Maskan 1375: Natiyej-e Tfssili* (Population Census, 1996: Detailed Results). Tehran: Markaz- Amar-e.

———. 2000a. *Amargyri az Vijegyhay-e Eshteqal va Bikary-e Khanevar* (Survey of Characteristics of Employment and Unemployment). Tehran: Markaz-e Amar-e.

———. 2000b. *Markaze Amare Iran Salnameh Amarye Keshvar: 1378–379* (Iran Statistical Yearbook: Mar. 1999–Mar. 2000). Tehran; Statistical Center of Iran.

Stiglitz, J. E. 2002. "Employment, Social Justice and Societal Well-Being." *International Labour Review* 141 (1–2): 9–29.

———. 2003. *Globalization and Its Discontents*. New York: Norton and Co.

Sullivan, T. A. 1994. "Women Immigrants, Work, and Families." *Phi Kappa Phi Journal* 74 (3): 34–36.

Sullivan, Z. 2000. "Eluding the Feminist, Overthrowing the Modern? Transformations in Twentieth-Century Iran." In *Global Feminisms Since 1945*, edited by B. G. Smith, 215–42. London: Rutledge.

Taher-Far, K. 1997. "Nqshe fa'aliathaye zirzamini dar Iran ba ta'kid bar angizeye farare maliati" (The Role of the Underground Economy in Iran with Emphasis on Escape from Taxation). Payan-nameh karshenasye arshad (Dissertation submitted for completion of the position of senior expert). Daneshgahe Tehran (Tehran Univ.), 1376 (1997).

Tansel, A. 1999. "Public-Private Employment Choice, Wage Differentials and Gender in Turkey." *Yale University Discussion Paper No. 797.* http://www.econ.yale.edu/growth_pdf/cdp797.pdf.

———. 2002. "Economic Development and Female Labor Force Participation in Turkey: Time-Series Evidence and Cross-Province Estimates." ERC Working Papers in Economics 01/05. http://ideas.repec.org/p/met/wpaper/0105.html.

Tinker, I. 1997. "The Making of the Field: Advocate, Practitioners and Scholars." In *The Women, Gender and Development Reader,* edited by L. Duggan, L. Nisonoff, and N. Wiegersma, 33–42. London: Zed Books.

———. 1990. "A Context for the Field and for the Book." In *Persistent Inequalities: Women and World Development,* edited by I. Tinker, 3–13. Oxford, UK: Oxford Univ. Press.

Todaro, M. P. 1989. *Economic Development in the Third World.* 4th ed. New York: Longman.

Tohidi, N. 1993. "Iranian Women and Gender Relations in Los Angeles." In *Irangeles: Iranians in Los Angeles,* edited by R. Kelly, J. Frielander, and A. Colby, 175–83. Los Angeles: Univ. of California Press.

———. 2007. "Muslim Feminism and Islamic Reformation." In *Feminist Theologies: Legacy and Prospect,* edited by R. R. Ruether, 93–164. Minneapolis: Fortress Press.

Tonelson, A. 2002. *The Race to the Bottom: Why a Worldwide Worker Surplus and Uncontrolled Free Trade Are Sinking American Living Standards.* New York: Westview Press.

Torbat, A. 2002. "The Brain Drain from Iran to the United States." *Middle East Journal* 56 (2): 272–95.

———. 2005. "Impacts of the US Trade and Financial Sanctions on Iran." *World Economy* 28 (3): 407–34.

Trager, Lillian. 2005. *Migration and Economy: Global and Local Dynamics.* Lanham, MD: AltaMira Press.

Tucker, J. E., ed. 1994. Introduction to *Arab Women: Old Boundaries, New Frontiers.* Bloomington: Indiana Univ. Press.

UN-Habitat. 2005. "Paper 5: Muslim Women and Property." www.unhabitat.org/downloads/docs/3546_30551_ILP%205.doc, accessed 2010.

UNDP (United Nations Development Program). 2005. *The Arab Human Development Report: Towards the Rise of Women in the Arab World.* New York: Regional Bureau for Arab States.

UNHCR (United Nations High Commissioner for Refugees). 2007. "Statistical Yearbook 2006: Trends." In *Displacement, Protection and Solutions.* http://www.unhcr.org/statistics/STATISTICS/478cda572.html.

United Nations. 2003. *Common Country Assessment for the Islamic Republic of Iran in 2003.* Tehran: United Nations Development Program.

US Bureau of the Census. 1990. *1 Percent Public Use Micro Sample.* Washington, DC: U.S. Department of Commerce, Bureau of the Census.

———. 1990–95. *Current Population Survey: March Supplement.* Washington, DC: U.S. Department of Commerce, Bureau of the Census.

Wade, R. 1992. *Governing the Market: Economic Theory and the Role of Government in East Asian Industrialization.* Princeton, NJ: Princeton Univ. Press.

Waldinger, R., and M. Bozorgmehr. 1996. "The Making of Multicultural Metropolis." In *Ethnic Los Angeles,* edited by R. Waldinger and M. Bozorgmehr, 3–38. New York: Russell Sage Foundation.

Waldinger, R., and G. Gilbertson. 1994. "Immigrant's Progress: Ethnic and Gender Differences among U.S. Immigrants in the 1980s." *Sociological Perspectives* 37 (3): 431–44.

Wallerstein, I. 1974. *The Modern World System: Capitalist Agriculture and the Origins of the European World Economy in the Sixteenth Century.* New York: Academic Press.

Waring, M. 1990. *If Women Counted.* San Francisco: Harper Collins.

Weber, M. 2001. *The Protestant Ethic and the Spirit of Capitalism.* London: Routledge.

Williams, C. C. 2006. *The Hidden Enterprise Culture: Entrepreneurship in the Underground Economy.* Northampton, MA: Edward Elgar.

Williamson, O. E. 1985. *The Economic Institutions of Capitalism: Firms, Markets, Relational Contracting.* New York: Free Press.

Winters, A. L. 1999. "Trade and Poverty: Is There a Connection?" In *Trade, Income Disparity and Poverty. No. 5.* Geneva: World Trade Organization Special Studies. http://www.wto.org/english/res_e/booksp_e/disparity_e.pdf, accessed 2005.

World Bank. 2004. *Gender and Development in the Middle East and North Africa. Women in the Public Sphere.* Washington, DC: World Bank.

———. 2007. *Informality in Latin America and the Caribbean.* Washington, DC: World Bank.

———. 2010. *World Development Indicators Database.* http://data.worldbank.org/data-catalog/world-development-indicators.

World Trade Organization. 2005. *WTO Statistics Database, Trade Profiles.* Geneva: WTO. http://stat.wto.org, accessed 2006.

Yegenoglu, M. 1998. *Colonial Fantasies: Towards a Feminist Reading of Orientalism.* Cambridge, UK: Cambridge Univ. Press.

Zarei, P., B. Rozikhah, and M. Karimi. 2002–3. "baresy rezayatmandi zanan sarparst khanvar az khadamat bakhshe dolai va gir dolati hozeh omor ejemai" (Examining Satisfaction among Female-Headed Households in Governmental and Non-Governmental Sectors). Project Report. Tehran: Behzity. In Persian.

Zarinebaf-Shahr, F. 1998. "Economic Activities of Safavid Women in the Shrine-City of Ardebil." *Iranian Studies* 31: 247–61.

Zein-Elabdine, E., and S. Charusheela, eds. 2004. *Postcolonialism Meets Economics.* London: Routledge.

Zhou, M., and C. Bankston III. 1998. *Growing up American: How Vietnamese Children Adapt to Life in the United States.* New York: Russell Sage Foundation.

Zlotnik, H. 2000. "Migration and the Family: The Female Perspective." In *Gender and Migration*, edited by K. Willis and B. Yeoh, 27–45. Cheltenham, UK: Elgar Reference Collection.

Zonooz, Behrouz. 1988. *A Survey about the Textile Industry in Yazd Province.* Tehran: Genu Research Institute.

Index

Page numbers in italics denote figures and tables.

Abu-Lughod, Lila, 21
Addiction. *See* Drugs
Adelkhah, Fariba, 194
Afghanistan, 30; carpet weavers from, 178n3, 179, 181–83, 189; literacy rate for carpet weavers from, 181, 183; opium production in, 192, 195, 213–14; refugees from, 25, 37, 46, 178, 178n2, 189, 214, 217; women in, 24, 141
Africa, 4, 8. *See also* MENA (Middle East and North Africa) countries
Age: carpet weavers by sex, nationality, and, *180;* carpet weavers with sex structure and, 179–80; first marriage and average, *105;* unemployment rates for 1976 and 2006 by, *161*
Age pattern: of employment and LFP rate in rural areas, *143;* of employment and LFP rate in urban areas, *142;* of LFP in rural areas, *140;* of LFP in urban areas, *139*
Age pyramid (Iran), *106*
Agricultural production: capital invested in, 29; as IGA, 202; shift to cash crops for export, 54; women's role in, 53–54, 56, 135, 261n1
Ahmadinejad, Mahmood: elections of 2005 and, 116; NGOs under, 91; political report card, 118–19
AIDS/HIV, 276
Akhundzadeh, Mirza Fath Ali, 58
Alaifar, Elaheh, 120
Algeria, manufacturing in, 43
Alizadeh, Parvin, 49
Alliance Society (Hey'at-e Mo'talefeh), 71n5
Amin, Samir, 9
Amsden, A., 5
Anker, Martha, 30
Anker, Richard, 30, 49
Annan, Kofi, 14
Anticolonialist movement, 7–8
Aram, Sam, 84n1
Arts, 111–12
Asadabadi, Sayyid Jamal al-Din (al-Afghani), 7, 58
Ashraf (princess), 64
Assaad, Ragui, 27, 28
Ataturk, Kemal, 59
Automotive industry, 81
Awqaf (trusts), 57
"Axis of evil," 303

Baby boomers, 164
Bahramitash, Roksana, 1, 11, 35n9, 84n1, 103; on decline of manufacturing in postrevolution period, 24; de-veiling and great-grandmother of, 59n1; on education's influence on women, 39, 278, 285; on service sector growth, 46–47; on sexual segregated labor markets, 235; on street vendors, 250, 252; on women's preference for informal sector, 18, 24
Bakhtiaris, 56
Baladi women, 21
Bangladesh, women in, 16–17
Banks: Grameen, 203, 204, 208, 223, 228; loans from foreign, 78; Shari'a law and interest charged by, 83–84. *See also* World Bank
Bayat, Rafat, 88, 110, 111n5
Bazargan, 67
Beggars, street, 250–51
Behdad, Sohrab, 33, 34, 148; on impact of revolution on class relations, 50; on issues with census data, 37; on state's preference for males in upper-level work groups, 47
Behruzi, Maryam, 196
Benería, Lourdes, 55, 275–76
Beyto'l mal (Islamic treasury financed by Islamic taxes), 193
"Big Push," 3
Birth, life expectancy at, *107*. *See also* Fertility rates
Black feminists, 19
Black market, 226
Bonyad-e Shahid (Martyr's Foundation), 199
Bonyads (foundations tied to Supreme Leader), 78, 81

Boserup, Ester, 11, *55*
Bourguiba, Habib, 61
Boycotts. *See* Economic sanctions
Boyr Ahmad: forced settlements of tribes in, 63; low rate of female-headed households in, 197; nomad populations in, 63, 208; pastoralists, 55–56
Boys, in child labor, 173, 182n4. *See also* Children
Brain drain, 29, 35–37, 35n9, 277
Brazil, economic growth in, 13
Bureau of Women's Affairs (BWA), 113
Bush, George W., 303
Business/career, obstacles to advancement of, 269, 271. *See also* Home-based businesses
BWA (Bureau of Women's Affairs), 113

Capital, 29, 133, 189, 231; foreign investments with, 26, 78; goods, 202; human, 149, 165, 274, 278, 282, 286, 293; informal jobs and sources of initial, *241;* invested in agricultural sector, 29; invested in automotive industry, 81; mobility, 167, 169; start-up, 203, 206, 207, 212, 219, 223, 241
Career/business, obstacles to advancement of, 269, 271. *See also* Home-based businesses
Carpet industry, 53, 128, 152; age/sex/nationality of weavers in, *180;* carpet weavers in handwoven, 173–89; children in, 173, 177–78, 181–83, 187, 189; in China, 46, 170, 171–72; economic sanctions influencing, 33; export value in

US dollars, *129;* growth of, 54; high cost of materials in, 185, 185n6; in India, 171–72; literacy rate in, 181; made up of cottage industries, 138, 170; in Pakistan, 171–72; Persian carpet exports, *170;* production, employment, and exports in handwoven, *171;* refugee labor in, 46; share of Iran in international carpet, 170–73; share of weaving in household income, *187;* weavers by kind of production in, *186.* See also Handwoven carpet industry

Carpet weavers: Afghan, 178n3, 179, 181–83, 189; age and sex structure of, 179–80; case of women, 166–90; childcare for home-based, 179, 187; conclusions, 189–90; education level of, *181;* explanation of, 166–67; globalization's impact on gender inequalities and, 167–69; in handwoven carpet industry, 173–89; high cost of materials for, 185, 185n6; household position of, 187–89; illiteracy in, 181, 183; international trade's effects and consequences, 169–70; location/ nationality of, *177;* male, 179–80; minimum wage for, 184; number in households by nationality of, *183;* receiving less than minimum wage, 175–76, 189; sex/nationality of, *179;* share of Iran in international carpet markets with, 170–73; wages, 184–87

Carpet weaving, as IGA, 202

Carrington, William, 35

Carter, Jimmy, 28

CEDAW (Convention on the Elimination of Discrimination Against Women), 114

Census Bureau, Iran, 30, 52

Census Bureau, US, 283

Centre for Women's Participation (CWP), 113, 114, 119

Chant, Sylvia, 192

Charitable foundations, 20; helping female-headed households, 194, 196, 197; IKRF activities as, 199–201; poverty and, 81

Charity models: employment and self-sufficiency, 202; explanation of, 199–201; female-headed households and, 199–203; microcredit v., 191–225; other services, 202–3; programs for female-headed households, 201–2

Charusheela, S., 10

Cheap labor, 12

Chen, Martha, 240

Childcare: as double burden for working women, 290–91, 297; for home-based carpet weavers, 179, 187; as obstacle to career and business advancements, 269, 271. *See also* Children

Child labor: boys in, 173, 182n4; girls in carpet industry and, 177–78, 181–83; in low-income Afghan households, 189

Children, 194, 212; in carpet industry, 173, 177–78, 179, 181–83, 187, 189; carpet weaving compatible with childcare and, 179, 187; childcare for, 179, 187, 269, 271, 290–91, 297; child support for, 193; clothing for, 238, 243, 249; custody rights for, 84–85;

Children (*cont.*)
education for, 181, 243, 299–300, 302, 303; education interrupted to care for, 149–50; in female-headed households, 197; health care and, 216; as potential drug addicts, 221; in poverty, 185; as priorities over career, 18; taking care of elderly parents, 107; taking care of siblings, 233, 242; television programming for, 112. *See also* Fertility rates
Child support, 193. *See also* Children
China, 13, 87, 168; carpet industry in, 46, 170, 171–72; economic growth in, 12, 13; minimum wage in, 171–72; "Persian" carpets made in, 46
Cinema, 112, 195
Class power, 56. *See also* Social class
Clinton, Bill, 28
Clothing, for children, 238, 243, 249
Cloth weaving, 53–54
Clubs, rotating credit, 213, 244, 246
Cold War, 2
Collectivity, 7
Colonization: anticolonialist movement against, 7–8; hurting women's work in Egypt, 20–21; Muslim women losing property ownership due to, 57; voting rights and, 15; "white man's burden" and, 7, 11. *See also* Modernization; Postcolonial feminist theory in Iran
Communist Party of Iran, 60
Community, 26; bonding among women with income-generating activities, 211; empowerment, 223; healing and preaching, 57; importance to women's sustenance, 54, 193–94, 195–96, 200, 206, 212, 216, 238, 246, 252–53; problems taken care of by families, 221–22; religious, 58, 108; role in nomadic life, 56; treatment of divorced women in Iranian, 293
Concessional credit, 222
Convention on the Elimination of Discrimination Against Women (CEDAW), 114
Conversion, between public and private sectors, 56
Cottage industries: carpet industry made up of, 138, 170; growth of, 20, 97; move to rural areas, 135; textile industry's link to, 54. *See also* Home-based businesses
Council of Guardians of the Constitution, 88, 89, 114, 121
Coups d'état: 1921, 59; 1953, 61–68, 70n4; engineered by United States, 4, 60, 61–68
CPS (*Current Population Survey*), 278
Credit: concessional, 222; informal, 242; males threatened by women's access to, 207–8, 208n9; rotating clubs for, 213, 244, 246; short-term, 178; street vendors and access to, 252. *See also* Loans; Microcredit
Credit Support Fund, 120
Cultural diversity, production processes influenced by, 53–58
Cultural values: characteristics of Middle Eastern, 7; characteristics of Western, 6–7; economic prosperity in exchange for adopting Western, 6–7, 9–10. *See also* Western culture

Current Population Survey (CPS), 278
Custody rights, 84–85
CWP (Centre for Women's Participation), 113, 114, 119

Dabbagh, Marziyyeh, 196
Dastghiyb, Gohar-al Shari'a, 195, 196
Data: accuracy question with, 37, 42n12; employment, 30–32; KILM, 31, 38–39; LABORSTA, 40, 42, 44, 49; missing working women and description of, 264–71
Decision-making: fathers and decline in, 102; informal sector and economic, 242–43; women and household expenditures, *242*
Deeb, Laura, 21
Detragiache, Enrica, 35
Development: liberation theology and, 8; local religion as impediment to, 7, 9, 19; modernization and, 2–10; as modern "white man's burden," 7, 11; of Sub-Saharan Africa, 4; theoretical framework for gender and, 11–14; women adversely influenced by, 11–12; worldwide, 4–6, 12–13
Diffuseness, functional, 7
Dignard, L., 238–39
Discrimination, 65, 272, 294; production disruption v., 95n3; wage, 50; women ending, 64, 114; against women in management, 161; against women in veils, 67, 75
Distribution: of carpet weavers by location/nationality, *177*; of female employment and occupational categories, *155*; income, *66*; of private sector positions, *153*; of sample carpet weavers by kind of production, *186*; by sector of female employment in MENA countries, *44–45*
Divorce: as means to independence, 211–12; *ojratol mesle* compensation law with, 120–21; rising rate of, 105; treatment of women in Iranian community, 293
Doctors: family planning programs supported by, 108–9; female, 65; numbers employed by IKRF, 203; percentage leaving after revolution, 35; recruited by developed countries, 277, 284; shortage of male, 102
Dovom-e Khordad (May 23), 90
Drekhshandeh, Pouran, 112
Drugs: addiction, 195, 207, 218, 221, 221n10; opium, 192, 195, 213–14; trafficking, 215
"Dual economy," 3

Early, Evelyn, 20–21
Earnings. *See* Wages
Ebtekar, Massoumeh, 113
Economic and Social Commission for Asia/Pacific Poverty Reduction Method (ESCAPPRM), 205
Economic growth, 11, 12–13, *94*
Economic justice agenda, 68–69, 74–75. *See also* Social justice
Economic sanctions, 22; GDP influenced by, 29, 35n8; against Iran, 29, 29n3, 33, 92, 170, 173; against Iraq, 34; isolation and, 211; against Palestine, 34

Index

Economic status of women, 54–55, 57
Economy: dual, 3; gender and globalized, 22, 25–52; influenced by migration, 278; informal, 226–55, 256; public role of women in postwar, 76–82; Tunisia's policy with, 12, 28; underground, 215, 226; women's key role in domestic, 55. *See also* Cottage industries; Home-based businesses; Informal sector; Political economy; Private sector; Public sector
Education: attainments of women in survey sample, *265;* carpet weavers by level of, *181;* for children, 181, 243, 299–300, 302, 303; employment and attainment in, *145;* employment's link to, 99–104; employment status and, *236;* of female population and labor market participation, *261;* field of study and unemployment among population with higher, *162;* handwoven carpet industry and, 180–81; higher, 35–36, 101, 102–3, 145, *162;* influence on women, 39, 278, 285; informal sector and, 236–37; interrupted to care for children, 149–50; LFP for 1976 and 2006, and, *146;* LFP influenced by, 130, 143–49; link to work in public sector, 47; as means to ward off marriage, 99–100; in Palestine, 47–48; Quranic, 59, 59n1; social class and, 59–60; structure of employment for 2006, *156;* unemployment from 1976 and 2006, with, *159;* women in health care and, 43, 64, 74–75, 80; women in private and public employment, 1996 and 2006, and, *152;* women in private sector, 2006, and, *154*
Egypt: modernization's influence on women in, 20–21; wages frozen in, 27; women in, 7, 8, 15, 20–21, 27, 28
Ekram (generosity with benevolence/ respect for others), 200
Elder, Sara, 31n5
Elections: of 1951, 60; of 1997, 22, 86, 89–90; of 1999, 114; of 2001, 91; of 2004, 117; of 2005, 89, 116; of 2007, 118; during absolute monarchy, 67; women running in presidential, 88–89
Elite class, 87
Embargo, 22. *See also* Economic sanctions
Embroidery, as IGA, 202
Emdad (Relief) Committee, 81
Employment, female: charity model of self-sufficiency and, 199–203; data on, 30–32; decline in, 65; education and occupational structure for 2006 with, *156;* education and share of women in private and public, *152;* education and status of, *236;* education attainment and, *145;* forces behind/consequences of rising, 99–115; gender politics and, 22, 83–122; household income and status of, *233;* LFP rate in rural areas and age pattern of, *143;* LFP rate in urban areas and age pattern of, *142;* MENA countries and distribution by sector of, *44–45;* occupational categories and distribution of, *155;* political economy in reform

era and, 86–99; political economy of, 22, 53–82; private sector positions and distribution of, *153*; sectoral composition of, *136*; share of public sector in total, *151*; shares of main economic sectors in rural areas, *134*; shares of main economic sectors in urban areas, *133*; teenage LFP and, 136–38; in textile industry, 173, *174*; in textile industry by working position, *175*; trends/complexities with women's LFP and, 124–36; women age 10–19 in, *138*; women age 10–19 in population and, *137*; women in, *128*; women's marital status with, *240*
Employment status, 232–36
Encountering Development (Escobar), 9
Entrepreneurial class, 76
Ershad-e Eslami (Ministry of Culture and Islamic Guidance), 111
ESCAPPRM (Economic and Social Commission for Asia/Pacific Poverty Reduction Method), 205
Escobar, Arturo, 8, 9
Esfahani, Hadi, 34n6, 285; on education's influence on women, 39; on manufacturing decline in post-revolution period, 3; on migration of skilled workers, 278; on service sector growth, 46–47
Etemad, Rakhshan bani, 112, 195
Executions, political, 70n4
Exiled class, 77
Expediency Council, 88
Exports: agricultural production's shift to cash crops for, 54; manufacturing for, 164–65; non-oil, 169; Persian carpet, *170*; value of carpet in US dollars, *129*

Fadaiayn-e Khalgh-Aksariyyat (People's Fadaian–Majority Faction), 70, 70n4
Fallaci, Oriana, 64
Families: children taking care of parents, 107; children taking care of siblings, 233, 242; community problems taken care of by, 221–22; informal sector and resources of, 241–42; marriage and, 104–7; Muslims and importance of, 18; of prisoners, 202; spouses and, 192, 237, *287*, 290, 292, *292*; start-up capital from friends and, 241; worldview centered around, 295–96
Family Planning Association (FPA), 109
Family Planning Campaign (FPC), 108–9
Family planning programs, 108–9
Fanon, Frantz, 66, 68
Farzin, Ali, 218
Fathers, 102. *See also* Males
Fatima Is Fatima (Shariati), 67
Fazel, G. Reza, 55–56
Female employment. *See* Employment, female
Female-headed households. *See* Heads of households, females
Female labor force. *See* Labor force, female
Female labor market. *See* Labor market
Feminists, 80, 257, 274, 280; black, 19; against illiteracy, 75; on impact of reducing government, 27; on

Feminists (*cont.*)
Islamism's nature, 21; postcolonial theory, 14–19; torture of activist, 67; Western, 17
Fertility rates, 38–39, 39n11; decline in, 107, 121, 127, 130; MENA countries' labor force, literacy rate, and, 40–41, 42n12; population and, 108
Feyerabend, 10
Foreign investments, 26, 78
Forozanfar, Setareh, 205, 206, 207, 212
Foucault, Michel, 9
Foundation for the Disempowered (Mostazafan), 199
Foundation of Panzdah Khordad, 199, 199n4
FPA (Family Planning Association), 109
FPC (Family Planning Campaign), 108–9
Frank, Andre Gunder, 4
Friedl, Erika, 56, 63
Functional diffuseness, 7
Functional specificity, 7

Gaza, 14, 22. *See also* Palestine
GDP. *See* Gross domestic product
Gemeinschaft (traditional society), 193
Gender: boundaries contested in labor market strategies, 291–93; globalization, Iranian experience and, 22; inequality, 85–86; informal economy and, 227–29; informal sector, veiled economy, and, 226–55; migration and, 275–78; rights and reform movement, 83–86; theoretical framework for development and, 11–14

Gender inequalities, carpet weavers impacted by, 167–69
Gender laws, 85
Gender politics, employment and, 22, 83–122
Gesselshaft (urban society), 193
Gilaneh (film), 195
Girls, in child labor, 173, 177, 181–83. *See also* Children
Globalization: comparing Iran to other MENA countries, 38–42, 51–52; defining, 27; economic, 26–30; gender, Iranian experience and, 22; IMF and World Bank as advocates for, 26; impact on gender inequalities and carpet weavers, 167–69; through process of migration, 29–30; shrinking world of, 26n1
GNP (Gross national production), 227
Goods, capital, 202
Gornabi, Mosa, 114
Government, reducing size of, 27
Grameen Bank, 203, 204, 208, 223, 228. *See also* Yunus, Muhammad
Great Depression, 2–3
Green-card marriages, 285
Gross domestic product (GDP): from 1935 to 2010, 92–93, 94; decline between 1978 and 1988, 130; economic sanctions influencing, 29, 35n8; informal economy's share of, 256
Gross national production (GNP), 227
Guardian Council. *See* Council of Guardians of the Constitution

Habibi, Shahla, 113
Hajar, 85

Hakim, Catharine, 18
Handicrafts, as IGA, 202
Handwoven carpet industry: age and sex structure of carpet weavers in, 179–80; child labor in, 181–83; education level in, 180–81; employment in, 173–89; employment structure of Kashan's, 178; explanation of, 173–75; in Kashan, 175–78; position of weavers in households with, 187–89; wages in, 184–87. *See also* Carpet industry
Hashemi, Faezeh, 110
Hasso, Frances, 19
Hatem, Mervat, 27
Hatton, T. J., 277
Havet, J., 239
HDI (Human Development Index), 92
Heads of households, females: by activity status, *198;* charitable foundations helping, 194, 196, 197; charity model, 199–203; children in, 197; composition of, *199;* conclusion, 221–25; explanation of, 191–92; IKRF programs for, 201–2; in Iranian context, 194–96; males and, 196; microcredit, self-help model, and, 203–21; Muslim tradition and, 193; in Netherlands, 191; among nomads, 197–98; poverty among, 191–92; statistical picture of, 196–99
Health, 107–8
Health care: as basic service, 72, 98; brain drain's influence on, 35, 35n9; children and, 216; family planning and, 108–9; shortage of male doctors in, 102; in urban and rural areas, *136;* women working in education and, 43, 64, 74–75, 80

HEIS (Household Expenditure and Income Survey), 49n14, 124
Hey'at-e Mo'talefeh (Alliance Society), 71n5
Higher education: brain drain and, 35–36; field of study and unemployment among population with, *162;* women in, 102–3, 145; women's studies in, 101. *See also* Education
HIV/AIDS, 276
Home-based businesses, 271; cottage industries as, 20, 54, 97, 135, 138, 170; marketing methods of women with, *270;* share of women with, *270*
Hoodfar, Homa, 245
Hooglund, Eric, 69n3
Household Expenditure and Income Survey (HEIS), 49n14, 124
Household income: employment status and, *233;* in informal sector with employment status, 232–36; share of carpet weaving in, *187*. *See also* Income
Households: carpet weavers' positions in, 187–89; expenditures and power of women's decision-making, *242;* informal sector and low-income, 244–53; males unable to serve as heads of, 196; number of carpet weavers by nationality in, *183*. *See also* Heads of households, females
Housework, divorce and compensation for, 120–21
Human capital, 282, 293; energized with financial capital, 286; framework of neoclassical, 274; increased cycle of, 149; oil

Human capital (*cont.*)
revenues improving quality of, 165; theory, 278
Human Development Index (HDI), 92
Hussein, Saddam, 14, 70n4

ID (Index of dissimilarity), 49
IDC (International Development Committee), 277
IGA (Income-generating activity), 202
IKRF. *See* Imam Khomeini's Relief Foundation
Illiteracy. *See* Literacy rate
ILO. *See* International Labor Organization
Imam Khomeini's Relief Foundation (IKRF), 215, 252; charitable scope of, 199–201; employment and self-sufficiency advocated by, 202; IGA of, 202; other services provided by, 202–3; programs for female-headed households, 201–2; WO programs compared to, 212–13, 223
IMF. *See* International Monetary Fund
Immigrants: Afghan, 25, 37, 46, 178, 178n2, 189, 214, 217; hindrances to labor market success, 274; labor market strategies and Iranian women, 273–304; strategies and gendered response, 299–301; unwelcome, 293–95; women, 280–82. *See also* Migration
Immigration Act of 1965, 281
Import substitution industrialization (ISI), 3, 5
Income: distribution, 66; expenditure and informal employment, 243; household, 187, 232–36, 233; Iranian immigrants' median annual household, 284, 286; Iran's 2000 annual per capita, 93; levels of employed women survey sample, 269; work satisfaction in informal sector with, 235
Income distribution, 66
Income-generating activity (IGA), 202
Index of dissimilarity (ID), 49
India, 168; carpet industry in, 171–72; economic growth in, 13
Individualism, 7, 290, 296
Informal credit, 242
Informal sector, 256; as percent of GNP, 227; choosing, 237–40; conclusion, 253–55; economic decision-making and, 242–43; education and, 236–37; explanation of, 226–27; family resources in, 241–42; findings, 231–42; household income and employment status in, 232–36; jobs and initial capital, 241; lack of documentation in, 228n1; low-income households and, 244–53; marital status in, 240–41; reasons for entering, 237; reporting on, 231–32; self-employed workers in, 244–46; sex segregation in, 228; street vendors in, 246–53; Tehran and survey of, 229–30; wage workers in, 244–46; women's preference for, 18, 24; work satisfaction/income background in, 235
Intelligentsia. *See Roshanfekr*
International Development Committee (IDC), 277

International Labor Organization (ILO), 1, 31n5; composition of economically active population, *259;* informal sector's GNP percent makeup from, 227; KILM data, 31, 38–39; LABORSTA data, *40, 42, 44,* 49; on wage disparity between women and men, 13

International Monetary Fund (IMF), 5; globalization favored by, 26; reductions in government size favored by, 27; reform programs for economic efficiency and, 168

International Organization for Migration, 275

International Planned Parenthood Federation (IPPF), 109

International Women's Conference, 64

Investments, foreign, 26, 78

IPPF (International Planned Parenthood Federation), 109

Iran, 34n7; annual per capita income for 2000, 93; anticolonial movement in, 7–8; as axis of evil, 303; as barbarous, 15; brain drain in, 35–37; carpet industry and international share of, 170–73; census bureau, 30, 52; compared to other MENA countries, 38–42, 51–52; development and modernization in, 2–10; economic sanctions against, 25, 29, 29n3, 33, 92, 170, 173; female-headed households in, 191–225; female unemployment in, 49; gender, globalization, and experience of, 22, 25–52; gender and informal economy in, 227–29; immigrants from, 282–84; labor force trends in, 32–38; as largest recipient of refugees, 36–37; manufacturing in, 43, 46; migration process and influence on, 29–30; missing working women of, 256–72; oil as link between US and, 282–83; political economy of prerevolutionary, 59–68; political parties in, 60, 66, 69–70, 70n4, 71, 89–90; postcolonial feminist theory in, 14–19; public role of women in postwar economy of, 76–82; structure of political configuration in, 88; theoretical framework in, 10–19; war with Iraq, 73, 92, 194, 284; Western portrayal of, 1–2; women's work and postrevolutionary, 73–76. *See also* Iran, postrevolutionary; Iran, prerevolutionary

Iran, postrevolutionary: background to, 53–58; modernization, Islamism and, 22, 53–82; public role of women in, 76–82; to reform movement, 22, 83–122; women's work and, 73–76

Iran, prerevolutionary: the Shah after 1953 coup, 61–68; the Shah and Reza Shah (1914–79) in, 59–61

Iran Carpet Company, 176, 177, 178n3

Iranian experience: conclusions, 50–52; data on female employment, 30–32; explanation of, 25–26; female labor force trends, 32–38; gender, globalization, and, 22; (economic) globalization of, 26–30; MENA countries compared to, 38–42, 51–52; sectoral analysis, 42–50

Iran-Iraq war, 73, 92, 194, 284
Iraq, 1, 34n7; economic sanctions against, 34; war with Iran, 73, 92, 194, 284
ISI (Import substitution industrialization), 3, 5
Islamic Human Rights Committee, 85
Islamic Republican Party, 70n4, 71
Islamism: feminists on nature of, 21; as impediment to development, 7, 9, 19; modernization, revolution, and, 22, 53–82; role in social justice, 66–67, 68–69; stereotypes, 14, 303
Isolation, breaking out of, 211
Israel, economic sanctions imposed by, 34

Janbazan (Veteran Foundation), 199
Javanmardy (man of courage, modesty, humility, rectitude), 194
Jihad, 100, 205n8
Jobs, 56–57, 241. *See also* Employment, female
Jolly, Susie, 276, 288–89
Jones-Correa, Michael, 297
Josef, Suad, 193
June 5, 1963, 199n4

Kabeer, Naila, 16, 203, 211
Kapsos, Steve, 31n5
Karimi, Mandana, 212
Karimi, Zahra, 23, 33, 37, 46
Kashan, handwoven carpet industry in, 175–78
Kazemipour, Shahla, 18, 24
Key Indicators of the Labor Market (KILM) data, 31, 38–39

Keynes, John Maynard, 3
Khamene'i, Ali (ayatollah), 76, 77n6, 117
Khatami, Mohammad, 22, 77; elections of 1997 and, 86, 89–90; elections of 2001, 91; NGOs under, 91; political support of women, 113; reform movement and, 89–91, 115
Khayam, Omar, 301
Khomeini, Ruhollah (ayatollah), 72, 81, 90, 199n4, 260; economic justice agenda of, 68–69, 74–75; family planning program endorsed by, 108–9; land reform under, 69–70; literacy campaign under, 75; on public role of women, 85; successor to, 76, 87; support of traditional merchant class, 71, 71n5
Kian, Azadeh, 195
Kilim weaving, as IGA, 202
KILM (Key Indicators of the Labor Market) data, 31, 38–39
Kolaee, Elaheh, 114
Korea, 6
Korten, Ailsa, 49

Labor force, female, *126;* 1956–2006, *126;* age pattern in rural areas of, *140;* age pattern in urban areas of, *139;* growth of male labor force v., 124–25; reasons for shift in, 96–97; refugee, 46; trends in, 32–38
Labor force participation (LFP): in 1976 and 2006, 30; in 2005, 52; age structure of female, 138–43; age structure's role in, 136–43;

decline in, 65, 125, *126*, 127, 130; education in 1976 and 2006, with, *146;* education influencing, 130, 143–49; overall picture of, 124–32; rate in rural areas and age pattern of female employment, *143;* rate in urban areas and age pattern of female employment, *142;* sectoral shifts in, 132–63; teenage, 136–38; trends/complexities with employment and women's, 124–36

Labor market: age structure and LFP in, 136–43; complexities and nuances in, 163–65; education and LFP in, 143–49; education of female population and participation in, *261;* employment and LFP in, 124–36; explanation of, 123–24; female employment characteristics in, 149–56; outcomes, 288–89; status of participants for January 2001, *287;* strategies for Iranian immigrant women, 273–304; transformation of female, 23, 123–65; unemployment problem in, 157–63

Labor market strategies: absence of kinship support with, 297; class considerations with, 297–99; conclusion, 301–4; consensus and compromise with, 289–91; considerations and constraints with, 293–301; contested gender boundary with, 291–93; explanation of, 273–74; family-centered worldview of, 295–96; gender and migration with, 275–78; gendered response with, 299–301; immigrants' hindrances to success with, 274; immigrants unwelcome in, 293–95; immigrant women and, 280–82; Iranian immigrants and, 282–84; for Iranian immigrant women, 273–304; participants' profile and, 284–88; research method and strategy with, 278–80; trajectory of outcomes for, 288–89

LABORSTA data, *40,* 42, *44,* 49. *See also* International Labor Organization

Land reform: under Khomeini, 69–70; progress made with, 65; during White Revolution, 61–62. *See also* Property

Laundry women, 57

Laws: divorce and *ojratol mesle* compensation, 120–21; gender, 85; Shari'a, 83–84, 193; veiling, 73–74, 112

Lebanon, women in public sector in, 47

Left, the, 8, 11, 60, 66, 70n4, 87, 89–90

Lewis, Arthur, 3, 258

LFP. *See* Labor force participation

Liberation theology, 8, 66

Life expectancy, at birth, *107*

Literacy rate, *101, 144;* from 1995 to 2005, 39; Afghan, 181, 183; campaign, 75; in men, 143, *146;* MENA countries' fertility rate and, *40–41,* 42n12; in women, 47, 100, *146*

Literature, 111

Loans: dissatisfaction with amount of, 219; from foreign banks, 78; no-interest, 201. *See also* Grameen Bank

Lower class, 56–57, 67
Lurs, 56

Macroeconomic theory, 3
Maids, 57, 64
Makhmalbaf, Samira, 112
Malek, M., 35
Males: carpet weavers, 179–80; decision-making in decline for, 102; dependent on public sector for work, 47; drug addiction in, 195, 207, 218, 221n10; growth of female labor force v., 124–25; *javanmardy* and, 194; literacy rate in, 143, *146;* migration of, 97, 128; military service for, 63; narrative and shift toward women's rights, 85–86; ratio of female unemployment to, 157; sex segregation and, 75–76; shortage of doctors, 102; threatened by credit extended to married women, 207–8, 208n9; unable to serve as head of household, 196; in upper-level work groups, 47; wage disparity between females and, 13, 13n1
Manufacturing: in Algeria and Morocco, 43; decline in post-revolution period, 3, 24; export-oriented, 164–65; women employed in, 43, 46
Marcos, Ferdinand, 4
Marketing methods of women working from home, *270*
Maroofi, Parvin, 217
Marriage: average age at first, *105;* education as means to ward off, 99–100; families and, 104–7; green-card, 285; in Muslim tradition, 194; polygamy and, 193n2, 220; status in informal sector, 240–41; status of women in survey sample, *265;* women's employment status with, *240*
Martyr's Foundation (Bonyad-e Shahid), 199
Massacres, 4
May 23 (*Dovom-e Khordad*), 90
MDGS (Millennium Development Goals), 277
Melkas, Helina, 49
MENA (Middle East and North Africa) countries, 16, 18, 22, 150; distribution of female employment by sector for, *44–45;* export-oriented manufacturing in, 164–65; female labor force, literacy, and fertility rates in, *40–41, 42n12;* globalization and comparing Iran to other countries in, 38–42, 51–52; poverty in, 17; World Bank study of, 257–58
Merchant class, Khomeini's support of traditional, 71, 71n5
Meriwether, Margaret, 20
Microcredit: charity v., 191–225; explanation of, 203–4; UNDP and, 213–21; WO and, 204–13
Middle class, 65, 130, 173
Midwifery, 59
Migration: gender and, 275–78; globalization through process of, 29–30; immigrants and, 25, 37, 46, 178, 178n2, 189, 214, 217; of men, 97, 128; women moving from rural areas with, 98
Milani, Tahmineh, 112

Military service: for males, 63; veterans of, 194, 247; for women, 63
Millennium Development Goals (MDGs), 277
Minimum wage: for carpet weavers, 184; in China, 171–72; weaving wages lower than, 175–76, 189
Ministry of Culture and Islamic Guidance (*Ershad-e Eslami*), 111
Moallem, Minoo, 15
Mobility, capital, 167, 169
Modernization: background to era of, 53–58; colonization, voting rights, and, 15; development and, 2–10; nomad's influenced by, 56; political economy of prerevolutionary Iran with, 59–68; postrevolutionary Iran, women's work, and, 73–76; public role of women with, 76–82; revolution, Islamism, and, 22, 53–82; Revolution of 1979 and, 19, 25–26, 65, 68–72, 163; in Soviet Union, 2–3
Moghadam, Fatemeh, 24, 50, 227, 236
Moghadam, Valentine, 48; in favor of Tunisia's economic policy, 12, 28; on Moroccan women in manufacturing, 43; on production disruption v. discrimination, 95n3
Mohanty, Chandra, 17
Money. *See* Capital
Morocco, 43, 47
Moslem, Mehdi, 87
Mossadegh, Mohammad, 60
Mossavi, 71
Mostakberin (those exploiting the masses), 68
Mostazafan (Foundation for the Disempowered), 199
Mostazafin (those exploited and marginalized), 68
Mo'talefeh, 81
Mujahedin-e-Khalgh (People's Mujahedin), 70n4
Muslim Brotherhood, 7
Muslims, 8, 58; backwardness of, 15; importance of family to, 18; marriage in tradition of, 194; racism in workplace against, 19; Shi'a, 67; tensions between, 216; tradition and female-headed households with, 193; treatment of women, 15–16; women losing property ownership with colonization, 57
Muslim Women's Olympics, 110, 111n5, 119
Muslim Women Sports Council (*Shoray-e Hambastegy-e Varzesh Banovan*), 110

Nannies, 57
Narcotics. *See* Drugs; Opium
Nasser, Gamal Abdul, 8
National Front, 60
Nationality: carpet weavers by location and, *177*; carpet weavers by sex, age, and, *180*; carpet weavers by sex and, *179*; number of carpet weavers in household by, *183*
Netherlands, female-headed households in, 191
New Institutional Economics (NIE), 5
Newly industrialized countries (NICs), 6
Newspapers, 85. *See also* Press, women's
NGOs. *See* Nongovernmental organizations

NICs (Newly industrialized countries), 6
NIE (New Institutional Economics), 5
Niknia, Zohreh, 18, 19, 24
9/11, 294, 303
No-interest loans, 201
Nomads: in Boyr Ahmad, 63, 208; female-headed households among, 197–98; modernization's influence on, 56
Nomani, Farhad, 33, 34, 37, 50, 148
Nongovernmental organizations (NGOs), 90, 109, 119, 217; growth of, 115; precarious existence of today's, 91; WO and, 207, 209, 210; women's involvement with, 121, 206, 245. *See also specific NGOs*
Nori, Nategh, 89
North, Douglas, 258

Occident, 10
Occupational categories, employment distribution by, *155*
Occupational segregation, ID with, 49
Occupational structure, for 2006 employment, *156*
OECD (Organisation for Economic Co-operation and Development), 277
Oil, 95; fluctuating revenue, 93–94; as link between Iran and US, 282–83; nationalized, 60; plunging prices, 77; price shocks of 1973–74 and 1979–80, 3, 5; revenues improving quality of human capital, 165; rising prices, 259
Ojratol mesle law, 120–21

Olmsted, Jennifer, 39n11, 285; on deglobalization's influence on women, 14, 22; on invisible/misrepresented groups, 280; on Iran's economy influenced by migration, 278; on postcolonial and feminist studies, 280
Olympics. *See* Muslim Women's Olympics
Open University (*Daneshgah-e Azad Eslami*), 102–3
Opium, 192, 195, 213–14. *See also* Drugs
Organisation for Economic Co-operation and Development (OECD), 277
Organizational interdependency, 7
Organization for the Protection of the Environment (*Sazman-e mohit-e-zist*), 113
Orient, 8–10
Ottoman period, women holding property in, 57

Pahlavi, Mohammad-Reza, 60
Paidar, Parvin, 18, 54
Pakistan, 36–37, 171–72
Palestine, 34n7; economic sanctions against, 34; education in, 47–48; Gaza and, 14, 22
Parents, 107. *See also* Males; Women
Parsons, Talcott, 2
Participants: income of spouses and, *288;* labor market status of, *287;* occupation by type, *287*
Particularism, 7
Pastoralists, 55–56
Pensions, for widows, 247

Persian carpets: decline in production and export of, 189; economic sanctions with, 170; produced in China, 46. *See also* Carpet industry; Carpet weavers

Pinochet, Augusto, 4

Planned Parenthood. *See* International Planned Parenthood Federation

Police, secret. *See* SAVAK

Political demonstrations, 70n4, 89, 199n4

Political economy: of prerevolutionary Iran, 59–68; reform era's female employment and, 86–99; of women's employment, 22, 53–82

Political executions, 70n4

Political office, women in, 113–15

Political parties: banning of, 70; executions of top officials, 70n4; in Iran, 60, 66, 69–70, 70n4, 71, 89–90. *See also* Elections; *specific political parties*

Polygamy, 193n2, 220

Poour, Jomeh, 227

Population: age pyramid of Iran's, *106;* Boyr Ahmad's nomad, 63, 208; composition of economically active, *259;* fertility rate and, *108;* with higher education, unemployment, and field of study, *162;* labor market participation and education of female, *261;* students in female, *148;* women, age 10–19, in female employment and, *137*

Portes, Alejandro, 280

Postcolonial feminist theory in Iran, 14–19

Post Colonialism Meets Economics (Zein-Elabdin and Charusheela), 10

Poverty: charitable foundations and, 81; cheap labor and, 12; children in, 185; among female-headed households, 191–92; feminization of, 24; in MENA countries, 17; rural, 14

Power: class, 56; household expenditures and women's decision-making, *242;* ruling elite vying for, 87; women's decline in production with authority and, 56

Presidency, women running for, 88–89

Press, women's, 85–86, 111–12, 211

Prisoners, families of, 202

Private sector: conversion between public and, 56; employment of females across, *153;* full-time homemakers in, 264, 266; survey sample and public sector v., *266;* women in education, 2006, and, *154;* women working in, *152*. *See also* Cottage industries; Home-based businesses

Production: activities, 53–54; cultural diversity influencing, 53–58; disruption v. discrimination, 95n3; distribution of sample carpet weavers by kind of, *186;* sectoral shares in non-oil value-added, *95;* textile industry dominated by home-based, 54

Property: bill to equalize inheritances and, 114; ownership by women, 20, 57; women in shantytowns with ownership of, 192; women's lost access to ownership of, 57

Public sector: conversion between private and, 56; feminization of, 47–49; males dependent on work in, 47; survey sample and private sector v., *266;* women working in, 47, 59–60, *151, 152*
Public Use Micro Sample (PUMS), 279

Quranic education, 59, 59n1

Ra, 195
Racism, against Muslims in workplace, 19
Rafsanjani, Ali Akbar Hashemi, 28, 87, 89, 110, 113; elections of 2005, 116; gender inequality and, 85–86; political support of women, 119; recovery and unification efforts, 76–78; rise in female employment under, 80
Rahman, A., 204
Rajayi, 'Atiqih, 195, 196
Rajol-e siasy (politically learned human), 88–89
Rationality, 7
Reconstruction, 205n8
Reeves, Hazel, 276, 288–89
Reform movement: end of, 115–20; forces behind/consequences of rising female employment in, 99–115; gender rights and, 83–86; Khatami and, 89–91, 115; policy makers facing major challenges with, 120–22; political economy and female employment in, 86–99; postrevolution to, 22, 83–122
Refugees: Afghan, 25, 178, 178n2, 189, 214, 217; in Iran, 36–37; in labor force, 46; in Pakistan, 36–37
Rejai, 201
Relative self-sufficiency, 7
Religion: community and, 58, 108; as impediment to development, 7, 9, 19. *See also specific religions*
Reversed Realities (Kabeer), 16
Revolution, 50; of 1979, 19, 25–26, 65, 68–72, 163; doctors leaving after, 35; *Dovom-e Khordad,* 90; Islamism, modernization, and, 22, 53–82; White, 61–63, 62n2, 69. *See also* Iran, postrevolutionary
Revolutionary Guards (Sepah Pasdaran), 70n4, 118
Reza Shah, 56; coup d'état in 1921, 59; de-veiling policy by, 59; women in public workforce under, 59–60
Rights: colonization and voting, 15; custody, 84–85; Muslim world and women's, 15–16; reform movement and gender, 83–86. *See also* Reform movement
Roman Catholics, 8
Rosentein-Rodan, Paul Narcyz, 3
Roshanfekr (enlightened), 58
Rostami-Povey, Elaheh, 80
Rostow, W. W., 3
Rotating clubs for credit, 213, 244, 246
Rozkhah, Bahare, 209
Rumbaut, Reuben G., 280
Rural areas: cottage industries moving to, 135; decline of LFP in, 125; deteriorating conditions for women in, 63; drug trafficking in, 215; employment shares of main economic sectors in, *134;* health care in, *136;* marriage in, *105;* poverty

in, 14; unemployment in, 129, 161; unemployment rates for 1956–2006, in, *158;* urbanization and share of women in urban and, *97;* women's migration away from, 98

Said, Edward, 8–9
Salehi-Isfahani, Djavad, 145
Sanctions. *See* Economic sanctions
SAPAP (South Asian Poverty Alleviation Program), 217
SAPs (structural adjustment programs), 5
Sassen, Saskia, 276
Saudi Arabia, 1
SAVAK (secret police), 67–68
SCI (Statistical Center of Iran), 123
Seamstresses, 57
SECH (Socio-economic Characteristics of Households), 124
Secret police. *See* SAVAK
Segregation: occupational, 49; sex, 50, 75–76, 102, 228, 235
Self-Employed Women's Association (SEWA), 247, 248n4
Self-employment: among Iranian immigrants, 286; wage workers and, 244–46. *See also* Cottage industries; Home-based businesses; Street vendors
Self-help models: explanation of, 203–4; microcredit and, 203–21; UNDP, 213–21; WO, 204–13
Self-sufficiency, charity model of employment and, 199–203
Sen, Gita, 55
Sepah Pasdaran (Revolutionary Guards), 70n4, 118
Service sector, growth, 46–47, 135

SEWA (Self-Employed Women's Association), 247, 248n4
Sewing, as IGA, 202
Sex: carpet weavers by age, nationality, and, *180;* carpet weavers by nationality and, *179. See also* Males
Sex segregation: increased female employment with, 50, 75–76, 235; in informal sector, 228; shortage of male doctors and, 102
Shah, the, 10, 22; after 1953 coup d'état, 61–68; data on female employment and, 32; elections under, 67; on role of women in public life, 64; White Revolution and, 61–63, 62n2, 69, 100; women tortured under, 67
Shantytowns, 192, 220
Shari'a law, 83–84, 193
Shariati, Ali, 66–67, 68, 72
Shi'a Muslims, 67
Shojai, Zahra, 113–14
Short-term credit, 178
Siblings, care of, 233, 242. *See also* Children
Singerman, Diane, 245
Single women, percentage of, *106*
Sixth Majlis, 114
Skocpol, T., 5
Social class: considerations with labor market strategies, 297–99; education and, 59–60; jobs related to, 56–57; *mostakberin*, 68; *mostazafin*, 68; power of, 56. *See also* Elite class; Entrepreneurial class; Exiled class; Lower class; Merchant class; Middle class; Upper class
Social justice, 66–67, 68–69
Socio-economic Characteristics of Households (SECH), 124

South Asian Poverty Alleviation Program (SAPAP), 217
Southeast Asia, economic growth in, 11–12
Soviet Union, 2–3, 57–58
Specialization, 7
Specificity, functional, 7
Spinners, 57
Sports, 109–11, 111n5
Spouses, 237; dollar income of participants and, *288;* gender boundaries contested by, 292; occupation by type, *287;* tension between, 192; working and sharing domestic duties, 290. *See also* Families
"Stages of economic growth," 3
Start-up capital: from friends and family, 241; microcredit as self-help model for, 203, 206, 207, 223; WO and, 212; women without, 203, 219
Statistical Center of Iran (SCI), 123
Stereotypes, Islamism, 14, 303
Stoevska, Valentina, 31n5
Street beggars, 250–51
StreetNet Association, 248, 248n4
Street vendors: access to credit for, 252; in informal sector, 246–53; interviews with, 247, 250–51, 252–53; organization for, 248
Structural adjustment programs (SAPs), 5
Students, in female population, ten years and older, *148*
Sub-Saharan Africa, 4
Suharto, 4
Sukarno, 8
Survey sample: education attainments of women in, *265;* income levels of employed women in, *269;* marital status of women in, *265;* public v. private employment of women in, *266;* time spent on work by women in, *265;* women's reasons for working in, *266*
Syria, women in, 20

Taiwan, 6
Taleghani (ayatollah), 88
Talgani, Azam, 88
Taliban, 84, 195, 214
Tansil, 34n7
Taxes: *Beyto'l mal* financed by Islamic, 193; evasion of, 231–32, 266; reasons for not declaring income, 231–32
Teenagers, employment and LFP with, 136–38
Tehran, informal sector survey of, 229–30
Tehran Society of Combatant Clergy, 196
Television programming, for women and children, 112
Textile industry: dominated by cottage industries, 54; employment by working position, *175;* employment in, 173, *174;* number of women working in, 33–34, 37. *See also* Carpet industry; Carpet weavers
Theology, liberation, 8, 66
Theoretical framework: gender and development's, 11–14; in Iran, 10–19; postcolonial feminist theory's, 14–19
Theories: development, 11–14; gender, 11–14; human capital, 278;

macroeconomic, 3; postcolonial feminist, 14–19
Time, in survey sample, *265*
Torbat, Akbar, 29, 34n6, 35n8, 283
Torture, of women and feminists, 67
Trade, 169–70. *See also* Exports
Trafficking, drugs, 215
Trends, in female labor force, 32–38
Tucker, Judith, 19–20
Tudeh Party, 60, 66, 69
Tunisia, 12, 164
Turkey, decline in female labor force, 34n7

UAE (United Arab Emirates), 39
Umma (Nation of Islam/the Muslim Community), 193
UN. *See* United Nations; *specific UN programs*
UN Convention on the Elimination of Discrimination against Women (CEDAW), 114
Underground economy, 215, 226. *See also* Street vendors
UNDP. *See* United Nations Development Program
Unemployment, 49, 99; from 1976 and 2006, with education, *159;* HEIS used to estimate, 49n14; among population with higher education and field of study, *162;* problem, 157–63; ratio of female to male, 157; in rural areas, 129, 161; in urban areas, 161
Unemployment rates: for 1976 and 2006, by age, *161;* in rural areas for 1956–2006, *158;* in urban areas for 1956–2006, *158*
UN-HABITAT (United Nations), 57

UNHCR (UN Refugee Agency), 36
United Arab Emirates (UAE), 39
United Nations (UN), 4, 13, 14, 57, 92
United Nations Country Assessment, 227
United Nations Development Program (UNDP), 199, 213–21
United States: census bureau, 283; coups d'état supported by, 4, 60, 61–68; economic sanctions imposed by, 25, 29, 29n3, 33, 92, 170, 173; green-card marriages in, 285; Immigration Act of 1965 in, 281; Iran viewed as "axis of evil" in, 303; labor market strategies of Iranian women immigrants in, 273–304; oil as link between Iran and, 282–83; White Revolution supported by, 62n2
Universalism, 7
UN Refugee Agency (UNHCR), 36
Upper class, 65
Urban areas: age pattern of LFP in, *139;* decline in LFP in, 65, 130; employment shares of main economic sectors in, *133;* health care in, *136;* increase of female labor force in, 125; marriage in, *105;* unemployment in, 161; unemployment rates for 1956–2006, in, *158;* urbanization and share of women in rural and, 97
USAID, 3
U-shaped transformation argument, 13–14

Veils: de-veiling and, 59, 59n1, 63, 65, 114, 234; discrimination against

Veils *(cont.)*
    women wearing, 67, 75; veiling laws and, 73–74, 112. *See also* Women
Veteran Foundation (Janbazan), 199
Veterans, military, 194, 247
Volunteer work, Family Planning Campaign and women's, 108–9
Voting rights, in colonial times, 15

Wade, R., 5
Wages: carpet weavers, 184–87; China's minimum, 171–72; discrimination with, 294; disparity between women and men, 13, 13n1; frozen in Egypt, 27
Wage workers, self-employed workers and, 244–46
Waldheim, Kurt, 13n1
Wallerstein, Immanuel, 4
Waqf (property endowed for religious/charitable use), 20, 57
Weber, Max, 6
Welfare assistance and Shari'a law, 193
Welfare Organization (WO), 199, 250, 251; fight against drug addiction, 221n10; IKRF's services compared to, 212–13, 223; microcredit and self-help model with, 204–13; start-up capital and, 212
West Bank, 14
Western culture: characteristics of, 6–7; economic prosperity in exchange for adopting, 6–7, 9–10; feminists in, 17; images of Middle Eastern women, 273; portrayal of Iran, 1–2; women as modern/secular/liberated in, 19–24

"White man's burden," 7, 11. *See also* Colonization
White Revolution, 63, 69, 100; land reform during, 61–62; supported by United States, 62n2
Widows, 105, 240, 247. *See also* Women
WIEGO (Women in Informal Employment Globalizing and Organizing), 248, 248n4
Williamson, J. G., 277
WO. *See* Welfare Organization
WOI (Women's Organization of Iran), 64, 65
Women: in Afghanistan, 24, 141; Baladi, 21; in Bangladesh, 16–17; as breadwinners, 192; community bonding among, 211; community's importance to sustenance of, 54, 193–94, 195–96, 200, 206, 212, 216, 238, 246, 252–53; development's adverse influence on, 11–12; doctors, 65; in Egypt, 7, 8, 15, 20–21, 27, 28; immigrants, 280–82; interpretation of *rajol-e siasy* and, 88–89; Iran's missing working, 256–72; laundry, 57; in Lebanon, 47; literacy rate in, 47, 100, *146;* in manufacturing, 43, 46; in military service, 63; in Morocco, 43, 47; Muslim world and rights of, 15–16; negatively influenced during transition to modernism, 54–55, 57; NGOs and, 121, 206, 245; Oriental/traditional/Islamic/enslaved, 19–24; ownership of property by, 20, 57; in Palestine, 47–48; percentage of single, *106;*

in political demonstrations, 70n4, 89; in political office, 88–89, 113–15; postcolonial feminist theory and, 14–19; running for president, 88–89; in Syria, 20; television programming for, 112; tortured during Shah's reign, 67; veils and, 59, 59n1, 63, 65, 67, 73–74, 75, 112, 114, 234; wage disparity between men and, 13, 13n1; Western images of Middle Eastern, 273; Western/modern/secular/liberated, 19–24; widows, 105, 240, 247; working in textile industry, 33–34, 37. *See also* Carpet weavers

Women in Informal Employment Globalizing and Organizing (WIEGO), 248, 248n4

Women's faction, 114

Women's Organization of Iran (WOI), 64, 65

Women's rights, shift from male narrative to, 85–86

Women's studies, in higher education, 101

Workplace, racism against Muslims in, 19

World Bank, 3, 5, 6, 30, 47; globalization favored by, 26; reductions in government size favored by, 27; study of MENA region, 257–58; unemployment estimates using HEIS, 49n14

Yunus, Muhammad, 203, 204, 208, 208n9, 245

Zanan, 85–86, 112, 211

Zarinebaf-Shahr, F., 57

Zein-Elabdin, E., 10

Ziai, 211